C0-AYI-748

THE CLIMATE OF REBELLION IN THE EARLY MODERN OTTOMAN EMPIRE

The Climate of Rebellion in the Early Modern Ottoman Empire explores the serious and far-reaching consequences of the Little Ice Age in Ottoman lands. This book demonstrates how imperial systems of provisioning and settlement that defined Ottoman power in the 1500s came unraveled in the face of ecological pressures and extreme cold and drought, leading to the outbreak of the destructive Celali Rebellion (1596–1610). This rebellion marked a turning point in Ottoman fortunes, as a combination of ongoing Little Ice Age climate fluctuations, nomad incursions, and rural disorder postponed Ottoman recovery over the following century, with enduring impacts on the region's population, land use, and economy.

Dr. Sam White is Assistant Professor of History at Oberlin College, where he teaches courses on global and environmental history. He has received grants and fellowships from Columbia University, the American Research Institute in Turkey, and the Delmas Foundation. His articles have appeared in the *International Journal of Middle East Studies* and *Environmental History*, among other publications. This is his first book.

Studies in Environment and History

Editors
Donald Worster, University of Kansas
J. R. McNeill, Georgetown University

Editor Emeritus
Alfred W. Crosby, University of Texas at Austin

Other Books in the Series

Donald Worster *Nature's Economy: A History of Ecological Ideas, second edition*
Kenneth F. Kiple *The Caribbean Slave: A Biological History*
Alfred W. Crosby *Ecological Imperialism: The Biological Expansion of Europe, 900–1900, Second Edition*
Arthur F. McEvoy *The Fisherman's Problem: Ecology and Law in the California Fisheries, 1850–1980*
Robert Harms *Games Against Nature: An Eco-Cultural History of the Nunu of Equatorial Africa*
Warren Dean *Brazil and the Struggle for Rubber: A Study in Environmental History*
Samuel P. Hays *Beauty, Health, and Permanence: Environmental Politics in the United States, 1955–1985*
Donald Worster *The Ends of the Earth: Perspectives on Modern Environmental History*
Michael Williams *Americans and Their Forests: A Historical Geography*
Timothy Silver *A New Face on the Countryside: Indians, Colonists, and Slaves in the South Atlantic Forests, 1500–1800*
Theodore Steinberg *Nature Incorporated: Industrialization and the Waters of New England*
J. R. McNeill *The Mountains of the Mediterranean World: An Environmental History*
Elinor G. K. Melville *A Plague of Sheep: Environmental Consequences of the Conquest of Mexico*
Richard H. Grove *Green Imperialism: Colonial Expansion, Tropical Island Edens and the Origins of Environmentalism, 1600–1860*
Mark Elvin and Tsui'jung Liu *Sediments of Time: Environment and Society in Chinese History*
Robert B. Marks *Tigers, Rice, Silk, and Silt: Environment and Economy in Late Imperial South China*
Thomas Dunlap *Nature and the English Diaspora*
Andrew C. Isenberg *The Destruction of the Bison: An Environmental History*
Edmund Russell *War and Nature: Fighting Humans and Insects with Chemicals from World War I to Silent Spring*
Judith Shapiro *Mao's War Against Nature: Politics and the Environment in Revolutionary China*

(*continued after Index*)

To Emily and Mocha.
And now Violette (maybe you can help with the next book).

THE CLIMATE OF REBELLION IN THE EARLY MODERN OTTOMAN EMPIRE

Sam White
Oberlin College

CAMBRIDGE UNIVERSITY PRESS
Cambridge, New York, Melbourne, Madrid, Cape Town,
Singapore, São Paulo, Delhi, Tokyo, Mexico City

Cambridge University Press
32 Avenue of the Americas, New York, NY 10013-2473, USA

www.cambridge.org
Information on this title: www.cambridge.org/9781107008311

First published 2011

Printed in the United States of America

A catalog record for this publication is available from the British Library.

Library of Congress Cataloging in Publication data

White, Sam, 1980–
The climate of rebellion in the early modern Ottoman Empire / Sam White.
p. cm. – (Studies in environment and history)
Includes bibliographical references and index.
ISBN 978-1-107-00831-1 (hardback)
1. Climatic changes – Social aspects – Turkey – History. 2. Social change – Turkey – History. 3. Social conflict – Turkey – History. 4. Turkey – History – Ottoman Empire, 1288–1918. 5. Turkey – Environmental conditions. 6. Turkey – Climate – History. 7. Turkey – Population – History. 8. Natural resources – Turkey – History. 9. Natural resources – Turkey – Management – History. I. Title. II. Series.
QC903.2.T87W44 2011
956′.015–dc22 2011002258

ISBN 978-1-107-00831-1 Hardback

CONTENTS

ACKNOWLEDGMENTS

Research for this project was made possible by fellowships and grants from Columbia University, the Delmas Foundation, and the American Research Institute in Turkey. I would like to thank Professors Adam McKeown, Richard Bulliet, and Christine Philliou for their comments on the original dissertation.

Along the way, through e-mails, conferences, and chance encounters, my research benefited from timely encouragement, advice, and correction from a number of scholars in America and Turkey: my thanks to Faruk Tabak, Tony Greenwood, Mikdat Kadioğlu, Meryem Beklioğlu, Linda Darling, Baki Tezcan, Günhan Börekçi, Haggay Etkes, Owen Miller, Tim Newfield, Mehmet Erler, Oktay Özel, Fariba Zarinebaf, Lajos Rácz, and any others I have neglected to mention. All errors, of course, are entirely my own. On my travels, Mustafa Geçim of Sille, Konya, introduced me to fat-tailed Karaman sheep. Back in Ohio, Geoffrey Parker kindly shared his latest manuscript on the Little Ice Age, and my colleagues at Oberlin, Zeinab Abul-Magd and Suzanne Miller, offered comments on the early manuscript that helped turn it into a real book.

This book owes a debt of gratitude to two colleagues in environmental history: to Alan Mikhail, for sharing panels at the ASEH and MESA and for his wonderful work advancing Ottoman and Middle East environmental history, and especially to John McNeill, for unfailing guidance and support.

Finally, a special thanks to my Ottoman instructors at Cunda, Wheeler Thackston and Selim Kuru, and especially to my Turkish instructor at Columbia University, Etem Erol, without whose patience, encouragement, and many cups of tea and coffee, this project would never have gotten off the ground. (*Gönül ne kahve ister ne kahvehane/Gönül sohbet ister kahve bahane.*)

PREFACE

This book began as an attempt to understand the impact of human land use on the environment of the Near East during early modern times. In the course of that research, I started to look at a number of climate studies, including new data from the analysis of tree rings. It was then I discovered that Ottoman lands had entered their longest drought in the past six centuries from 1591 to 1595. Recalling the outbreak of the devastating Celali Rebellion in Anatolia in 1596, I figured the timing had to be more than mere coincidence. However, as I worked at the problem, the path from climate to crisis proved more complicated than I had imagined, and the ramifications of these events proved much more far-reaching than I had anticipated. In the end, that question became the focus of a whole new study.

In the attempt to understand how the Little Ice Age triggered a general crisis in Ottoman lands, my research shot out in a number of directions. Ultimately, this work had to cover a wide range of topics from provisioning, settlement, agriculture, and land tenure, to demographics, climatology, and the course of famines and epidemics. In some cases, other historians had already cleared the way for me, but as often as not, I was forced to cut my own trails through the evidence, sometimes leading to unexpected conclusions.

Although the argument that follows may be complicated in parts, the overall structure of this work remains fairly straightfoward. Part I provides the context of the crisis: It investigates the imperial management of provisioning and land use, and how population pressure and inflation rendered this "imperial ecology" vulnerable to disruption from warfare and natural disasters. Part II provides the narrative of the crisis: It explains the climatology of the Little Ice Age in the Near East and demonstrates in detail how climate fluctuations led to waves of famine, flight, and rebellion starting in the 1590s. Finally, Part III analyzes the crisis as a shift in human ecology: It explores the long-term consequences of Little

Ice Age disasters, particularly the way that nomadic invasions and a flight to the cities prolonged the contraction of population and agriculture in the Near East, leaving the Ottoman Empire relatively thinly populated and underdeveloped by the late eighteenth century.

For the most part, this study has followed the usual conventions of Ottoman historical writing. To transliterate Ottoman phrases, I have employed standard Turkish orthography, particularly the conventions followed in recently published *mühimme defters*, using as few accents and diacritical marks as necessary. I have also used the plural "-s" with Ottoman words for the sake of simplicity. (The actual Turkish plural is "-lar" or "-ler" and many Ottoman words used irregular Persian and Arabic plurals.) All dates have been converted into the Gregorian calendar with the new year beginning in January, except where quoting directly. I have typically left Ottoman weights and measurements in the text with metric equivalents in parentheses where appropriate. For the most part, these conversions are based on Walther Hinz, *Islamische Masse und Gewichte* (1955), as well as the works of Suraiya Faroqhi and Halil İnalcık. In the use of technical terms from Ottoman history and from climatology, this study has tried to strike a reasonable balance between precision (for the specialists) and readability (for everyone else).

Finally, a note on sources: My principal fount of evidence for the critical developments of the late sixteenth century has come from the Ottoman Archives (Başbakanlık Arşivi) in Istanbul and particularly the series of documents known as *mühimme defters* (MD), which translates roughly as "registers of important matters." These are notebooks that include copies of orders from the imperial divan issued in the name of the sultan, prefaced by summaries of reports or petitions. (Because most researchers currently work with scans and not original notebooks, I have cited these orders by *defter* and document number only, leaving out the page numbers cited in older works.) Generally speaking, these are among our most important sources of information on the sixteenth- and early seventeenth-century Ottoman Empire. Their limits and their potential should become clear as more explanations and examples follow in the text. Elsewhere, this study has relied largely on narrative accounts, particularly seventeenth-century and early eighteenth-century Ottoman chronicles. In a work of this scope, and one intended to reach beyond a specialist audience, it would prove distracting (if not downright impossible) to offer the sort of exhaustive critical analysis of these sources advocated by some recent Ottomanists. Instead, I have opted to triangulate statements in these chroniclers' accounts with evidence from official documents, reports from foreign observers, and where climatic events are concerned, with data reconstructed from physical proxies. As the reader will see, the results demonstrate that their narratives of natural and human disasters at the heart of this study do not represent mere rhetorical flourishes, as sometimes supposed, but rather descriptions of real events.

GLOSSARY OF OTTOMAN TERMS

akçe	a small silver coin, the standard Ottoman monetary unit in the sixteenth century
ardab	a measure of grain equal to about 70 kilograms or 90 liters
askeri	belonging to the ruling military class in the Ottoman Empire
avarız	an extraordinary wartime cash tax, which came to be levied regularly in the seventeenth century
beylerbeyi	provincial governor
bölük-başı	commander of a mercenary army or a unit of *sekbans* (*q.v.*)
celali	term applied to some bandits and rebels in the sixteenth and seventeenth centuries
celep	a wealthy individual charged with supplying sheep
cizye	the imperial head tax levied on non-Muslims
çeki	about 250 kilograms
çeltükçi reaya	peasants growing rice in a special sharecropping arrangment on state lands
çift	a pair of oxen, or by extension, the amount of land a pair of oxen could plow
çift-bozan akçesi	the fine that the *reaya (q.v.)* had to pay in order to lawfully leave their land
çiftlik	a farm; in the seventeenth and eighteenth centuries this term was used to describe larger, often commercial, estates
çift resmi	the tax levied on *reaya* households according to the size of their land holdings
deşişe	the regular distribution of grain from Egypt to the Hijaz

dirhem	unit of weight equal to about 3 grams, or a silver coin of that weight
ferman	an imperial rescript
hane	a household
iltizam	a tax farm
imaret	a building complex established by a pious foundation, especially a soup kitchen
kadı	a judge and local administrator
kantar	a variable unit of weight, usually around 50 kilograms
kasap	a butcher; *kasaps* also had to put up capital to help guarantee the meat supply in Ottoman cities
kaza	a judgeship, the administrative district of a *kadı*
kile	about 1 bushel, or 36.4 liters, but even more than other measurements the *kile* could vary from region to region
kışla	winter pasture
korucu	guardian of a *miri koru* (*q.v.*)
kuruş	a larger silver coin, which became the standard monetary unit in the eighteenth century
levend	an irregular soldier
malikâne	a lifetime tax farm
malikâne-divani	a system by which tax revenues from the *reaya* were shared between the imperial government and owners of large estates or *vakıfs* (*q.v.*)
mezraa	fields or pasture outside the village lands, usually uninhabited and used only periodically
miri	belonging to the state, as in *miri koru*, or state forests
mücerred	unmarried man past the age of puberty
müd	a highly variable measure of grain, usually equal to about 500 liters in official Ottoman accounts of this period; the "Bursa *müd*" was perhaps 110 liters to 120 liters
mufassal	detailed, as in *mufassal tahrir defter*, or detailed cadastral survey
mühimme defter	a "register of important matters" consisting of imperial orders usually prefaced by summaries of petitions from the provinces
mülk	freehold
nahiye	the smallest administrative unit, consisting of part of a *kaza* (*q.v.*)

narh	the officially set price for commodities
nüzul	an imperial requisition in kind, usually of grain
okka	see *vukiye*
öşür	a tithe on the *reaya* (*q.v.*)
palanka	a fort
pekmez	grape molasses
reaya	Ottoman subjects, particularly tax-paying villagers
rencber gemi	a rented vessel
sancak	a district, a division of a *vilayet* (*q.v.*)
sancakbeyi	governor of a *sancak* (*q.v.*)
sekban	an irregular infantry soldier; or just a member of any irregular military unit, militia, or private army
sipahi	a cavalry soldier holding a *tımar* (*q.v.*)
sohta	a madrasah student; imperial orders commonly used the term to refer to unemployed students in violent gangs
suğla	irrigated land
sürgün	forced resettlement
sürsat	forced purchase
tahrir	cadastral survey
temlik	an imperial practice of granting land as *mülk* (*q.v.*)
tezek	dried animal manure used for fuel
tımar	assignment of land revenues in return for military service
vakıf	pious foundation
vilayet	a province, usually consisting of several *sancaks* (*q.v.*)
vukiye	a unit of weight, usually about 1.28 kilograms
yayla	summer pasture
zimmi	a non-Muslim subject

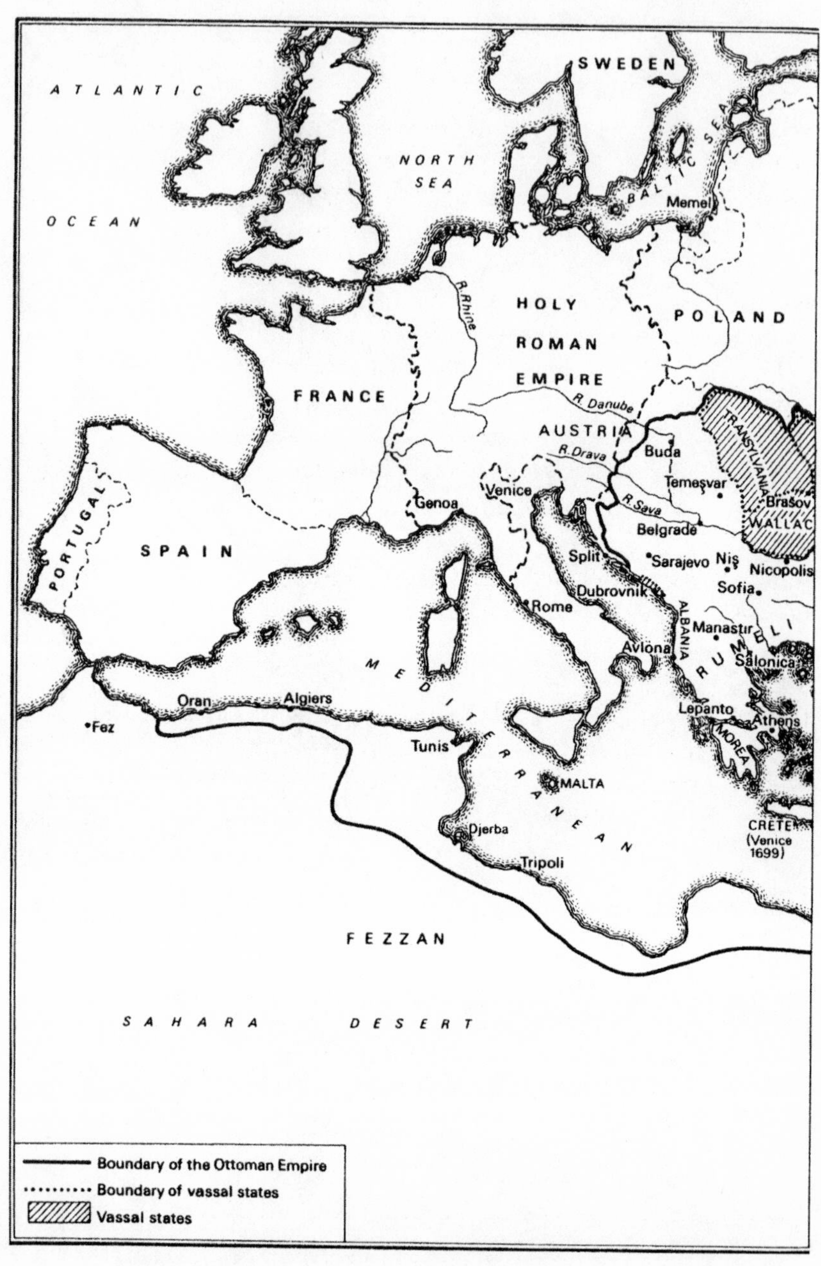

Ottoman Empire c. 1550. *Source:* Halil İnalcık and Donald Quataert, eds., *An Economic and Social History of the Ottoman Empire, 1300–1914* (New York: Cambridge University Press, 1994). Reprinted with permission.

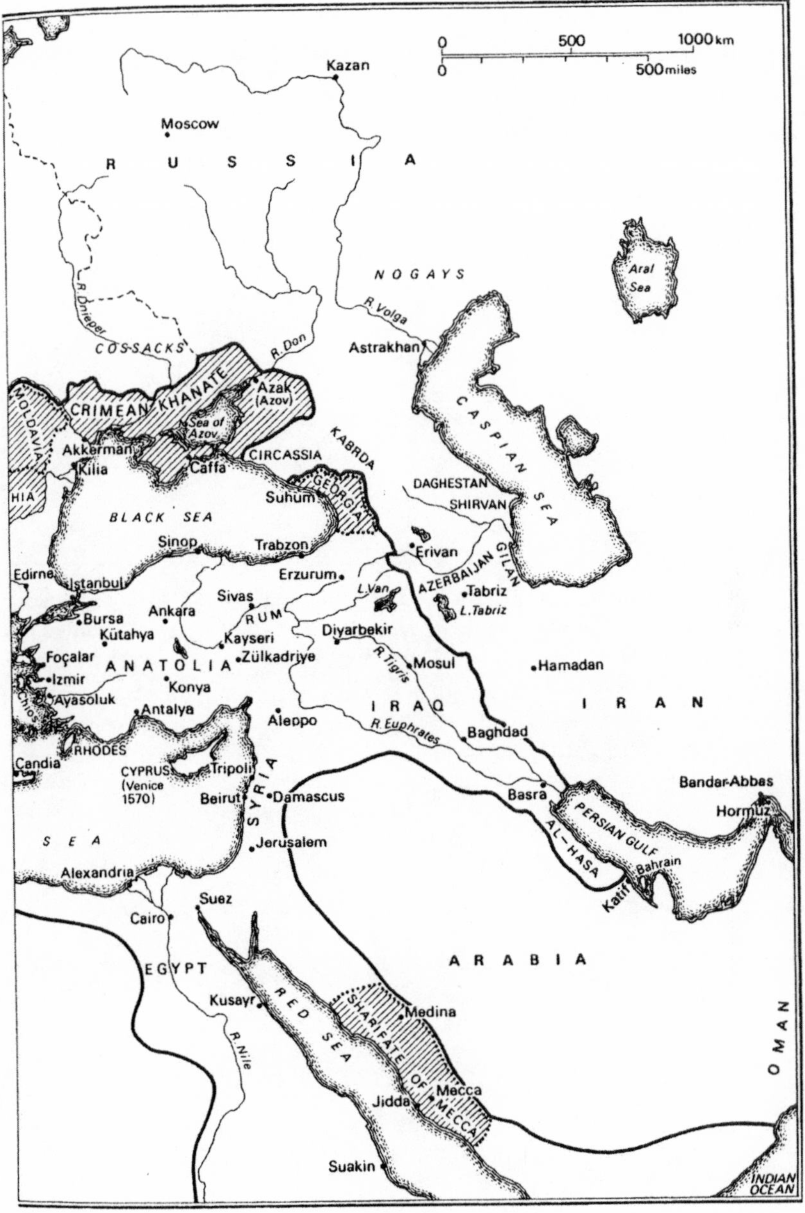

0
500
1000 km
0
500 miles
Kazan
Moscow
R U S S I A
NOGAYS
Aral Sea
R. Volga
R. Dnieper
COSSACKS
R. Don
Astrakhan
CRIMEAN KHANATE
MOLDAVIA
Azak (Azov)
Sea of Azov
CASPIAN SEA
KABRDA
Akkerman
Kilia
Caffa
CIRCASSIA
GEORGIA
DAGHESTAN
SHIRVAN
Suhum
BLACK SEA
Sinop
Trabzon
Erivan
GILAN
AZERBAIJAN
Edirne
Istanbul
Erzurum
Tabriz
L. Tabriz
L. Van
Sivas
Ankara
RUM
Bursa
Kütahya
Kayseri
Diyarbekir
Foçalar
Zülkadriye
Mosul
Hamadan
Izmir
ANATOLIA
R. Tigris
Konya
Ayasoluk
Chios
Antalya
IRAQ
IRAN
Aleppo
R. Euphrates
Baghdad
RHODES
Candia
CYPRUS (Venice 1570)
Tripoli
SYRIA
Basra
Bandar-Abbas
Hormuz
Beirut
Damascus
PERSIAN GULF
AL-HASA
SEA
Jerusalem
Bahrain
Alexandria
Katif
Suez
Cairo
ARABIA
EGYPT
Kusayr
RED SEA
SHARIFATE OF MECCA
Medina
OMAN
R. Nile
Mecca
Jidda
Suakin
INDIAN OCEAN

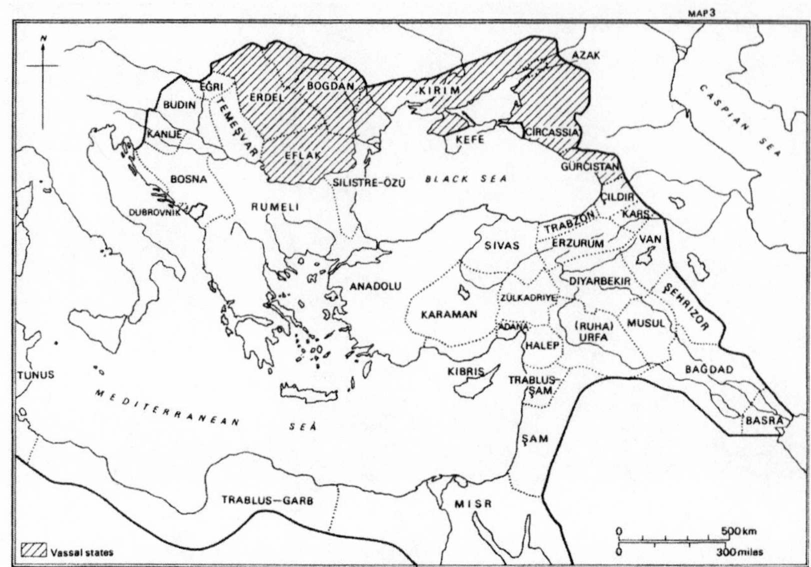

Ottoman provinces c. 1600. *Source:* Halil İnalcık and Donald Quataert, eds., *An Economic and Social History of the Ottoman Empire, 1300–1914* (New York: Cambridge University Press, 1994). Reprinted with permission.

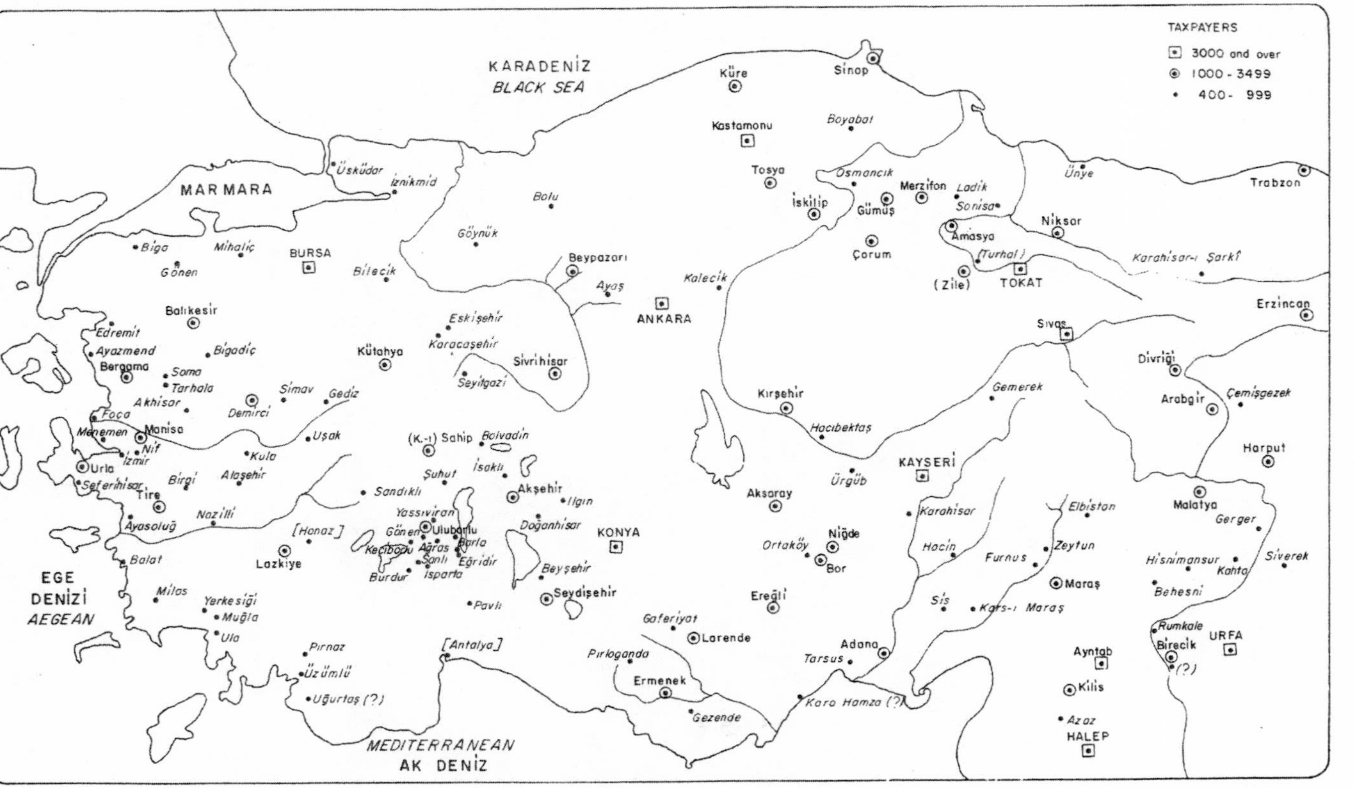

Anatolian towns of the late sixteenth century. *Source:* Suraiya Faroqhi, *Towns and Townsmen in Ottoman Anatolia* (New York: Cambridge University Press, 1984). Reprinted with permission.

INTRODUCTION

This is the story of how a climate event, the so-called "Little Ice Age," nearly brought down the Ottoman Empire around 1600 AD. And although that would be a story worth telling on its own, this study offers to explain much more. Through the narrative of climate and crisis, the following pages will explore the rise of an empire and its provisioning, settlement, and population. We will see how a complex set of circumstances conspired to create a climate-led catastrophe; and how the crisis of the Little Ice Age marked a critical conjuncture in the human ecology of Ottoman lands, as centuries of growth and expansion turned for a time to contraction and retreat. The story that follows describes much more than a single episode in the life of an empire. It represents nothing less than a turning point in the history of the Near East and by extension the making of the modern world.

In its simplest outlines, the plot runs as follows: In the fourteenth and fifteenth centuries, as the Ottoman Empire grew from a small band of warriors into a major world power, it instituted a number of systems for the management and provisioning of resources for its capital city and its military, all the while directing the expansion of settlement and cultivation across the region. In the sixteenth century, as Ottoman population soared, land and resources began to fall short. War and natural disasters, exacerbated by climate fluctuations, placed new pressures on peasant subsistence and imperial provisioning. Finally, in the last decade of the 1500s, the fierce cold of the Little Ice Age and the longest Eastern Mediterranean drought of the past six centuries brought unprecedented famine and mortality. As the imperial government continued to squeeze its subjects for supplies to support an ongoing war with the Habsburgs, central Anatolia erupted in a revolt – the Celali Rebellion – which pushed the empire into an intractable crisis. Over the following century, further climate disasters, nomadic invasion, rural insecurity, and flight from the land drove a vicious circle of demographic and agricultural contraction.

Despite some promising starts, the empire did not fully recover from the crisis for more than a hundred years, entering the nineteenth century still loosely governed and thinly populated.

The full story is considerably more complex. Climate certainly plays a leading role in the ensuing drama, and the onset of the Little Ice Age marks the turning point in our history. Nevertheless, climate shares the stage with many actors, whether environmental, geographic, economic, or political. The story that follows does not simply thrust the Little Ice Age into the usual narrative of Ottoman history. It represents a reinterpretation of that history, taking together both natural and human forces. Moreover, we see how at critical moments in our story even the leading figures of the drama – the Little Ice Age, provisioning, sultans, and war – were upstaged by something even more unexpected: the Ottoman sheep.

Unsurprisingly, few of these environmental factors (and least of all sheep) have so far played much part in Ottoman historiography. Despite its important place in world history, serious scholarly research on the Ottoman Empire remains a fairly new and cautious field of study, often hindered by extraordinary difficulties of language and sources. Apart from some older research influenced by the French Annales school, and the recent work of Faruk Tabak (discussed in Chapter 11), Ottomanists have yet to venture far into environmental history.[1] Many parts of this book have had to draw on numerous obscure, often regional studies published only in Turkish. Even the most central elements of our narrative such as the Ottoman provisioning system, population pressure, and the Celali Rebellion have so far received only a couple of dedicated monographs apiece. Other major developments – including those of critical importance such as the drought and famine of the 1590s – were virtually unknown, even among specialists.

Much of the story that follows, therefore, draws on wholly original or hitherto overlooked evidence. Remarkably, the usually parsimonious Ottoman and foreign archives and chronicles have proven a fairly generous source of information on environmental and particularly climatic affairs. This evidence, laid out in detail over the following chapters, has led me to draw up a new narrative of developments in the Ottoman

[1] This looks set to change. As this book goes to press, the *International Journal of Middle East Studies* is publishing an issue dedicated to environmental history, Oxford University Press is publishing a volume of collected essays on Middle East environmental history, and Cambridge University Press is publishing a monograph on the environmental history of Ottoman Egypt by Alan Mikhail.

Empire up to the eighteenth century – one that seriously incorporates environmental changes. Over the following pages, it will become clear just how much this perspective might contribute to the history of the region.

Not least, the narrative presented here offers a different approach to the ongoing historiographical debate over the so-called Ottoman "decline" of the seventeenth and eighteenth centuries. It has long been evident that once popular narratives of degenerate sultans and decadent political institutions relied too much on uncritical readings of a few primary sources.[2] Too often, authors wrote from an anachronistic or politicized perspective that equated modernity and progress with the kind of centralizing, secularizing, or etatist policies typical of nineteenth- and twentieth-century reformers.[3] And so, many widely accepted explanations of Ottoman stagnation or decay have been questioned or dismissed, and now a range of revisionist studies have emerged stressing the empire's resilience and adaptability and reinterpreting the sixteenth and seventeenth centuries as an era of "transformation" or even "privatization" and "proto-democratization."[4]

Suffice it to say, nothing in this book is intended to raise the old specter of "decline." In most respects, the evidence fully supports the reinterpretation of the seventeenth century as a period of turbulence and transformation rather than stagnation and decay. Likewise, I make the case that the eighteenth century represented a period of modest revival. Nevertheless, this book often parts company with the revisionist literature as well. The recent emphasis on the imperial flexibility and

2 See Cornell Fleischer, *Bureaucrat and Intellectual in the Ottoman Empire: The Historian Mustafa Âli (1541–1600)* (Princeton: Princeton University Press, 1986) and David Howard, "Ottoman Historiography and the Literature of 'Decline' in the Sixteenth and Seventeenth Centuries," *Journal of Asian History* 22 (1988): 52–76 for a critical analysis of Ottoman declensionist writing and its influence on modern historians.

3 Probably the most influential works in this regard have been Nizazi Berkeş, *The Development of Secularism in Turkey* (Montreal: McGill University Press, 1964) and Bernard Lewis, *The Emergence of Modern Turkey* (New York: Cambridge University Press, 1968), both of which tend to frame later Ottoman history as a struggle between reactionary (usually religious, provincial) and progressive (usually elite, centralizing) forces.

4 Among the more important works in this genre: Rifaat Abou-el-Haj, *The Formation of the Modern State* (Binghamton: State University of New York [SUNY] Press, 1991); Linda Darling, *Revenue-Raising and Legitimacy* (Leiden: Brill, 1996); Karen Barkey, *Bandits and Bureaucrats* (Ithaca, NY: Cornell University Press, Cornell University Press, 1994); Karen Barkey, *Empire of Difference* (New York: Cambridge University Press, 2008); Ariel Salzmann, "Measures of Empire: Tax Farmers and the Ottoman *Ancien Régime* 1695–1807" (PhD diss., Columbia University, 1995); and Baki Tezcan, *The Second Ottoman Empire* (New York: Cambridge University Press, 2010).

adaptation inaccurately minimizes both the degree of the empire's success in the sixteenth century and the depth of its crisis in the century that followed. As we see in the following chapters, after nearly doubling in the 1500s, parts of the Ottoman Empire may have lost half or more of their population in the early 1600s; and it appears that core Ottoman lands still held fewer subjects around 1830 than they had around 1590. This remains a crucial development that historians need to explain – not just explain away. As some Ottomanists have begun to argue, it is time to find a more balanced approach to this important middle period of Ottoman history.[5]

This work reevaluates the era of Ottoman crisis and transformation from the perspective of global environmental history, focusing on the decades from 1590 to 1610 as a key turning point. It makes the case that Ottoman troubles formed part of a world crisis borne of widespread ecological pressures and climate fluctuations, but that environmental factors particular to the Near East exacerbated both the extent and duration of that crisis in the Ottoman Empire. Consequently, this book embraces three broader world historical issues: the seventeenth-century "general crisis," the long-term environmental history of the Near East, and the role of climate events in history. These three topics, discussed here in the introduction, delineate the context of events and the themes of analysis in the chapters to follow.

The Seventeenth-Century Crisis

First, this book adds a significant chapter to the history of the seventeenth-century "general crisis," the common catastrophes that beset the world over the early to mid-1600s. Once confined to the historiography of Europe,[6] studies of this phenomenon now range from Mexico[7] to Ming

5 See Cemal Kafadar, "The Question of Ottoman Decline," *Harvard Middle East and Islamic Review* 4 (1997–98): 30–75 and Dana Sajdi, "Decline and Its Discontents" in *Ottoman Tulips, Ottoman Coffee: Leisure and Lifestyle in the Eighteenth Century*, ed. Dana Sajdi (London: I. B. Tauris, 2007), 1–40.

6 For the original debate on the "general crisis" among historians of early modern Europe, see T. H. Aston, ed., *Crisis in Europe, 1560–1660* (Garden City, NY: Anchor, 1967).

7 E.g., Jonathan Israel, "Mexico and the 'General Crisis' of the Seventeenth Century," *Past and Present* 63 (1974): 33–57 and Ruggiero Romano, *Conyunturas opuestas: Las crisis del siglo XVII en Europa e Hispanoamérica* (Mexico City: El Colegio de México, 1993). On Little Ice Age droughts and famines, see, e.g., Georgina Endfield, *Climate and Society in Colonial Mexico* (London: Blackwell, 2008).

China,[8] and demonstrate remarkable parallels and connections in the histories of these far-flung regions.[9] It is true that specialists of many regions (and not least the Ottoman Empire) have often been reluctant to acknowledge the global ties among these events. Nevertheless, the concept of a "general crisis" has gained traction in world history in recent years, as various regional and comparative studies have accumulated evidence for the synchronicity of demographic contraction, economic recession, and political upheaval across the globe.[10]

Two theories have emerged to offer an explanation for this worldwide outbreak of disasters, neither exclusive of the other. The first, advanced by Jack Goldstone, emphasizes the role of rising population pressure over the century building up to the general crisis.[11] As all parts of Eurasia recovered from the demographic disaster of the Black Death, and as new and more stable states and empires emerged, so each suffered from the common problems of diminishing land and rising inflation. As early modern agrarian-bureaucratic states struggled to adapt, this volatile combination of pressures blew up into conflicts and ultimately revolutions and rebellions, from the English Civil War to the Ming-Qing transition. The second theory, presented most forcefully in the recent work of Geoffrey Parker, concentrates on the role of extreme cold and droughts associated with the Little Ice Age – a phenomenon we explore in more depth in later chapters.[12] These climatic disasters provoked widespread shortages and famines, precipitating political violence and popular unrest.[13]

[8] See, e.g., William Atwell, "A Seventeenth-Century 'General Crisis' in East Asia?," *Modern Asian Studies* 24 (1990): 661–82; William Atwell, "Some Observations on the 'Seventeenth-Century Crisis' in China and Japan," *The Journal of Asian Studies* 45 (1986): 223–34; Richard von Glahn, "Myth and Reality of China's Seventeenth-Century Monetary Crisis," *The Journal of Economic History* 56 (1996): 429–54; and Frederic Wakeman, "China and the Seventeenth-Century Crisis," *Late Imperial China* 7 (1986): 1–26.

[9] See G. Parker and L. Smith, eds., *The General Crisis of the Seventeenth Century*, 2nd ed. (London: Routledge, 1997).

[10] For recent historiography, see Jonathan Dewald, "Crisis, Chronology, and the Shape of European Social History," *American Historical Review* 113 (2008): 1031–52 and Michael Marmé, "Locating Linkages or Painting Bull's-Eyes around Bullet Holes? An East Asian Perspective on the Seventeenth-Century Crisis," *American Historical Review* 113 (2008): 1080–99.

[11] Jack Goldstone, *Revolution and Rebellion in the Early Modern World* (Berkeley: University of California Press, 1991).

[12] See Geoffrey Parker, "Crisis and Catastrophe: The Global Crisis of the Seventeenth Century Reconsidered," *American Historical Review* 113 (2008): 1053–79. (My thanks to Prof. Parker for sharing parts of his forthcoming book manuscript as well.)

[13] See also William Atwell, "Volcanism and Short-Term Climate Climatic Change in East Asian and World History c.1200–1699," *Journal of World History* 12 (2001): 29–99.

Case studies from around the globe confirm the depth of the crisis and the prominent role of the two factors just described. At the turn of the seventeenth century, extreme cold and harvest failures plunged Russia into its "Time of Troubles," bringing flight, famine, and chaos in the midst of a serious succession crisis.[14] In 1618, central Europe erupted in the Thirty Years War, in which a third or more of Germany's population may have perished from violence and famine, exacerbated by Little Ice Age climate events.[15] In the 1630s and 1640s, the crisis reached England (the civil war), France (the Fronde and other uprisings),[16] and China (the Ming-Qing transition),[17] all of which suffered from severe climate and economic and political upheaval. Those same decades witnessed recurring drought and famine as far afield as West Africa[18] and Southeast Asia,[19] spelling the end of an era of flourishing trade and population growth in both regions.

However, these regional examples also illustrate the variations from one crisis to the next. Not all parts of the world suffered equally nor recovered in the same manner. For example, Mughal India also suffered a serious famine in the Deccan during the 1630s – yet it did not fall into serious political or economic turmoil until the waning years of the emperor Aurangzeb (r.1658–1707).[20] In Tokugawa Japan, the

[14] Chester Dunning, "Does Jack Goldstone's Model of Early Modern State Crises Apply to Russia?" *Comparative Studies in Society and History* 39 (1997): 572–92, fits this disaster into the "general crisis" model; and his history of the Time of Troubles – *Russia's Civil War* (University Park, PA: Penn State University Press, 2001) – refers frequently to the role of Little Ice Age weather events.

[15] Peter Wilson, *The Thirty Years War: Europe's Tragedy* (Cambridge, MA: Harvard University Press, 2009), 786–96. On Little Ice Age impacts in Central Europe, see Wolfgang Behringer et al., *Kulturelle Konsequenzen der "Kleinen Eiszeit"* (Göttingen: Vandenhoeck & Ruprecht, 2005) and Wolfgang Behringer, *A Cultural History of Climate* (Cambridge, UK: Polity Press, 2010).

[16] Emanuel Le Roy Ladurie, *Histoire humaine et comparée du climat, 1: Canicules et glaciers* (Paris: 2004), chapter 8, discusses the role of climate in these events.

[17] The role of the Little Ice Age in the Ming crisis is emphasized in Timothy Brook, *The Troubled Empire: China in the Yuan and Ming Dynasties* (Cambridge, MA: Harvard University Press, 2010), chapters 3 and 10.

[18] George Brooks, *Landlords and Strangers* (Boulder, CO: Westview, 1993) and James Webb, *Desert Frontier* (Madison: University of Wisconsin Press, 1995). For a more recent reconstruction of seventeenth-century West African droughts, see T. Shanahan et al., "Atlantic Forcing of Persistent Drought in West Africa," *Science* 324 (2009): 377–80.

[19] Anthony Reid, "The Seventeenth Century Crisis in Southeast Asia," *Modern Asian Studies* 24 (1990): 639–59; Anthony Reid, "Southeast Asian Population History and the Colonial Impact," in *Asian Population History*, ed. C. Liu (New York: Oxford University Press, 2001); and Peter Boomgaard, "Crisis Mortality in Seventeenth Century Indonesia," in ibid.

[20] John Richards, "The Seventeenth-Century Crisis in South Asia," *Modern Asian Studies* 24 (1990): 625–38.

so-called Kan'ei Famine of the same years may have left millions of victims in its wake; however, the Japanese quickly overcame the disaster and embarked on another two centuries of relative stability and economic development.[21] Furthermore, even regions that suffered real political and economic collapse often emerged stronger and more stable from the crisis than ever before. At opposite ends of Eurasia, both Britain and China recovered their losses in blood and treasure within two or three generations.[22] And even as Iberian empires and Mediterranean commerce retreated, Dutch wealth and population continued to grow, often picking up the losses of the former.[23]

By contrast, the Near East faced some of the worst and most enduring losses in the general crisis. As we see over the following chapters, the region suffered sooner and recovered less from the disasters of the age than perhaps any other part of the world. Therefore, this book makes a significant contribution to the study of the general crisis. The Ottoman case not only highlights the role of population pressure and climate disasters in this global event, but also emphasizes the importance of the general crisis as a turning point in world history.

Near East Environmental History

Second, this book offers an original contribution to the still emerging field of Near Eastern environmental history. Traditionally, most writings on the Near Eastern environment have grappled with the thorny issue of decline. Declensionist narratives of the region, emphasizing the degradation of the land and the desiccation of the climate, influenced Western perceptions even in ancient and medieval times. Starting in the seventeenth century, Enlightenment observers remarked on the

[21] Atwell, "Some Observations" and Alan Macfarlane, *The Savage Wars of Peace: England, Japan and the Malthusian Trap* (Oxford: Blackwell, 1997). Conrad Totman, in *Early Modern Japan* (Berkeley: University of California Press, 1993) and *A History of Japan* (Oxford: Blackwell, 2000), also puts particular emphasis on Japan's peculiar ecological path during this period.

[22] For studies of China's population and agricultural recovery in the wake of the crisis, see Robert Marks, *Rice Tigers Silt and Silk* (New York: Cambridge University Press, 1998) and Peter Perdue, *Exhausting the Earth* (Cambridge, MA: Harvard University Press, 1987).

[23] On climate events and social response in the Netherlands, see Leo Noordegraf, "Dearth, Famine, and Social Policy in the Dutch Republic at the End of the Sixteenth Century," in *The European Crisis of the 1590s*, ed. Peter Clark (London: Allen and Unwin, 1985). On Dutch social and economic history, see Jan de Vries, *The Dutch Rural Economy in the Golden Age 1500–1700* (New Haven, CT: Yale University Press, 1974); J. de Vries and A. van der Woude, *The First Modern Economy* (New York: Cambridge University Press, 1997); and Jan de Vries, "The Economic Crisis of the Seventeenth Century after Fifty Years," *The Journal of Interdisciplinary History* 40 (2009): 151–94.

supposed decay of Biblical landscapes;[24] in turn, this tendency found its way into the work of early environmentalists of the nineteenth century, such as George Perkins Marsh, who imagined that grazing and deforestation had provoked permanent desertification.[25] Then in the early twentieth century, climate determinist theories, particularly the work of Elsworth Huntington, argued simplistically for the rise and fall of Near Eastern empires based on long cycles of rainfall and drought.[26] In more recent decades, perceptions of degradation in the region have worked their way into the writings of environmental historians such as J. Donald Hughes[27] and J. V. Thirgood,[28] who have blamed irresponsible farming and grazing for the apparent decay of the landscape. Furthermore, a sense of long-term Near Eastern decline, whether climatic or man-made, has reentered the popular imagination through more recent popular histories such as the work of Jared Diamond.[29]

In response to some of these claims, other contemporary geographers and historians have painted an entirely different picture of the region, one emphasizing its long-term environmental stability. These works have challenged the declensionist models of landscape degradation and climatic deterioration, and have attacked the evidence and assumptions of earlier writers. The work of A. T. Grove and Oliver Rackham, in particular, has convincingly argued for the resilience of vegetation and

[24] C. J. Glacken, *Traces on the Rhodian Shore* (Berkeley: University of California Press, 1967); Richard Grove, *Green Imperialism* (New York: Cambridge University Press, 1995); Ann Thomson, "Perceptions des populations du Moyen-Orient," in *Orient et lumières*, ed. A. Moalla (Grenoble: Université de Grenoble, 1987).

[25] George Perkins Marsh, *Man and Nature* (Seattle: University of Washington Press, 2003), 161–2, 249–50, *et passim.*

[26] Elsworth Huntington, *The Pulse of Asia* (Boston: Houghton Mifflin, 1907). On the historiography of climate determinism, see A. Issar and M. Zohar, *Climate Change – Environment and Civilization in the Middle East* (Berlin: Springer, 2004), chapter 1, and James Fleming, *Historical Perspectives on Climate Change* (New York: Oxford University Press, 1998), chapter 8.

[27] J. Donald Hughes, *Ecology in Ancient Civilizations* (Albuquerque: University of New Mexico Press, 1975); *An Environmental History of the World* (London: Routledge, 2002); and *The Mediterranean: An Environmental History* (Santa Barbara, CA: ABC-CLIO, 2005).

[28] J. V. Thirgood, *Man and the Mediterranean Forest* (New York: Academic Press, 1981) and "The Barbary Forests and Forest Lands, Environmental Destruction and the Vicissitudes of History," *Journal of World Forest Management* 2 (1986): 137–84.

[29] Jared Diamond, *Guns, Germs, and Steel* (New York: Norton, 2001) discusses the decline of the region in terms of desiccation in the conclusion; and David Montgomery, *Dirt: The Erosion of Civilizations* (Berkeley: University of California Press, 2007) has recently argued for the collapse of Near Eastern civilizations in terms of soil salination and erosion.

soil in Mediterranean Europe, at least before the damage inflicted by modern development and industry.[30] Drawing on more empirical studies and archaeological evidence, these writers and others have made a strong claim that such landscapes can recover in the long term from human land use and, moreover, that the drought-prone terrain has evolved a native flora and fauna more naturally resistant to clearing, burning, and grazing than that of other lands. From the evidence, it would appear that the Mediterranean littoral, at least, has not somehow irrevocably degraded from what it was in ancient times, nor has it suffered from any steady desiccation of climate, at least in the past three millennia.[31] Furthermore, the recent work of Diana Davis has called into question the motivations and ideology of the declensionist narrative, particularly the way that accusations of environmental degradation may have been used to justify colonial rule and the expropriation of land in North Africa.[32]

Nevertheless, there may be problems with this revised interpretation as well, especially as we move from Mediterranean Europe to the more arid eastern shore. The evidence of long-term environmental continuity has not meant that the human ecology of the Near East has always been "stable or sustainable" or that the region has enjoyed an "environmental history without catastrophe" as claimed for the Mediterranean in general.[33] The arid and semiarid lands of the region have long proven a challenging environment for human societies, and the evidence of environmental continuity over the very long run does not mean that Near Eastern societies avoided ecological disasters in the shorter term. In other recent studies of the region, we might discern a third paradigm for the environmental history of the Near East: neither environmental decline nor stability, but recurring ecological crisis and protracted recovery.

Research in ancient history and archaeology offers some of the most compelling evidence for this historical pattern. Since the end of the last Ice Age, the Near East has witnessed dramatic fluctuations in temperature and rainfall with profound consequences for human population

[30] A. Grove and O. Rackham, *The Nature of Mediterranean Europe* (New Haven, CT: Yale University Press, 2001).

[31] E.g., B. D. Shaw, "Climate, Environment, and History: The Case of Roman North Africa," in *Climate and History*, ed. T. Wigley et al. (New York: Cambridge University Press, 1981). For an overview of the evidence from palynology and paleoclimatology, especially in Anatolia, see Neil Roberts, *The Holocene: An Environmental History* (Oxford: Blackwell, 1998).

[32] Diana Davis, *Resurrecting the Granary of Rome* (Athens: Ohio University Press, 2007).

[33] Quotes from P. Horden and N. Purcell, *The Corrupting Sea* (Oxford: Blackwell, 2000), 328–38.

and settlement, including the Younger Dryas of the eleventh millennium BC (associated with the collapse of Natufian culture and the eventual rise of agriculture) and the 8kya cooling event (associated with the collapse of late Neolithic societies and the mid-Holocene transitions to urban civilizations).[34] For early historical times, the work of Harvey Weiss and others has presented strong evidence for a spectacular collapse of civilizations throughout the Near East and beyond driven by a pronounced climate shift around 2200 BC.[35] From other research, it appears that similar albeit less severe episodes may have marked the later Bronze Age[36] and perhaps late Antiquity as well[37] – although these interpretations are not universally accepted.

Research on the medieval Near East has also presented less dramatic but better documented cases. In particular, the work of Peter Christensen has demonstrated a pattern of periodic crisis and protracted recovery across Mesopotamia and western Iran from late Antiquityy to the later Middle Ages. While explicitly rejecting the declensionist narrative, Christensen has argued forcefully that historians need to take environmental

34 For overviews of such climatic instability and its human consequences in the region, see, e.g., Frank Hole, "Agricultural Sustainability in the Semi-Arid Near East," *Climate of the Past* 3 (2007): 193–203; Arlene Rosen, *Civilizing Climate* (Lanham, MD: Altamira, 2007); and Issar and Zohar, *Climate Change.* For a summary of the literature on climate change and mid-Holocene transitions, see Nick Brooks, "Cultural Responses to Aridity in the Middle Holocene and Increased Social Complexity" *Quaternary International* 151 (2006): 29–49.

35 H. Dalfes, G. Kukla, and H. Weiss, eds., *Third Millennium BC Climate Change and Old World Collapse* (Berlin: Springer, 1997) and Harvey Weiss, "Beyond the Younger Dryas: Collapse as Adaptation to Abrupt Climate Change in Ancient West Asia and the Ancient Eastern Mediterranean" in *Environmental Disasters and the Archaeology of Human Response,* ed. G. Bawdon and R. Reycraft (Albuquerque, NM: Maxwell Museum of Anthropology, 2000).

36 Barry Weiss, "The Decline of Late Bronze Age Civilization as a Possible Response to Climatic Change," *Climatic Change* 4 (1982): 173–98; J. Neumann and S. Parpola, "Climatic Change and the Eleventh-Tenth-Century Eclipse of Assyria and Babylonia," *Journal of Near Eastern Studies* 46 (1987): 161–82; J. Neumann, "Climatic Changes in Europe and the Near East in the Second Millennium BC," *Climatic Change* 23 (1993): 231–45; and Neville Brown, *History and Climate Change: A Eurocentric Perspective* (London: Routledge, 2001), chapter 4.

37 E.g., I. Orland et al., "Climate Deterioration in the Eastern Mediterranean as Revealed by Ion Microprobe Analysis of a Speleothem That Grew from 2.2 to 0.9 kya Soreq Cave, Israel," *Quaternary Research* 71 (2009): 27–35. Other research has examined the connection between volcanic events, climate change, the Plague of Justinian, and the crisis of the middle Byzantine Empire: See J. Gunn, ed., *The Years without a Summer: Tracing A.D. 536 and Its Aftermath* (Oxford: Archaeopress, 2000) and Richard Stothers, "Volcanic Dry Fogs, Climate Cooling and Plague Pandemics in Europe and the Middle East," *Climatic Change* 42 (1999): 713–23.

factors into account to understand the long-term decline of power and population in parts of the Near East.[38] Above all, his work has stressed the challenges of maintaining and rebuilding agriculture in what he has described as "an ecological system sensitive to the smallest disturbance."[39] The recent work of Stuart Borsch on Egypt in the fourteenth century has advanced a similar argument, illustrating how the complex irrigation systems of Egypt collapsed in the wake of the Black Death. By comparing the Egyptian case to England, Borsch has further shown how this environmental vulnerability made the crisis far worse along the Nile, and how relative to other parts of the world, Egypt took far longer to recover.[40] Most recently, the work of Richard Bulliet on medieval Iran illustrates how a period of severe cold drove a nomadic invasion of the eleventh century, which hindered the recovery of Persian population and agriculture over the following generations.[41]

Judging from these and other examples, it would seem four basic factors have created this pattern of crisis and protracted recovery. First, the Near East – and in particular its large arid and semiarid tracts – has proven especially vulnerable to periodic fluctuations in climate and, most of all, severe droughts. Second, the region has historically relied on fragile systems of irrigated and marginal cultivation which have tended to break down during severe climate events and other natural and human disasters. These breakdowns have aggravated periods of crisis and obstructed the recovery of agriculture and population, sometimes for generations or centuries to follow. Third, times of crisis in the Near East have frequently set off population movements and upset the balance of rural and urban numbers. As refugees flocked to cities, agriculture and agricultural taxes would suffer from the flight, driving a downward spiral of instability and population loss.[42] Moreover, these population movements and relatively high rates of urbanization appear to have exacerbated the ravages of

[38] Peter Christensen, *The Decline of Iranshahr* (Copenhagen: Museum Tusculanum, 1993). See his discussion in the introduction and chapter 1.

[39] Ibid., 104.

[40] Stuart Borsch, *The Black Death in Egypt and England* (Austin: University of Texas Press, 2005) and "Environment and Population: The Collapse of Large Irrigation Systems Reconsidered," *The Journal of Interdisciplinary History* 46 (2004): 451–68.

[41] Richard Bulliet, *Cotton, Climate, and Camels in Early Islamic Iran* (New York: Columbia University Press, 2009).

[42] For further examples of this phenomenon, see Richard Bulliet, *Islam: The View from the Edge* (New York: Columbia University Press, 1994), chapter 4, and Eliyahu Ashtor, "The Economic Decline of the Middle East during the Later Middle Ages: An Outline," *Asian and African Studies* 15 (1981): 253–86. There are indications of similar problems in

plague and other epidemics, which have afflicted the Near East more than perhaps any other part of the world.[43] Fourth, and most characteristic of the region, major crises in the Near East have tended to upset the delicate balance between settled agriculture and pastoral nomadism, leading to periodic invasions of farmland. Whether violent or peaceful, these invasions often displaced agriculture from wide stretches of semi-arid territory, leading to a fundamental shift in the ecology of land use. Taken together over millennia of history, these four factors may help explain the eclipse of the Near East from the center of ancient civilization to the thinly populated and poorly developed land it would become by the dawn of the nineteenth century. In this model, the region did not simply "decline." Rather, it suffered more during periods of crisis and recovered more slowly from each than other parts of the world.

The story of Ottoman crisis presented here may offer the clearest and most detailed case yet for such a pattern of ecological crisis and protracted recovery. The following chapters take up all four of these factors and examine their role in more depth. Drawing on a wealth of historical evidence and climate data unavailable for ancient and medieval times, we also explore the ways in which human choices and historical contingencies interacted with these underlying environmental conditions in the making of crisis. Therefore, this book both builds on and contributes to this emerging paradigm in the region's environmental history.

Climate Events in History

Finally, this work advances the wider study of past climate events and their historical consequences. As global warming has drawn public interest, a growing number of works have come out in recent years that explore the role of these events throughout history.[44] At their best, these

classical times, as well, e.g., Robert Sallares, *The Ecology of the Ancient Greek World* (Ithaca, NY: Cornell University Press, 1991), 88–9.

43 On epidemics in the Near East, see Lawrence Conrad, "The Plague in the Early Medieval Near East" (PhD diss., Princeton University, 1981); Michael Dols, *The Black Death in the Middle East* (Princeton, NJ: Princeton University Press, 1977); Michael Dols, "The Second Plague Pandemic and Its Recurrences in the Middle East," *Journal of the Economic and Social History of the Orient* 22 (1979): 162–89; Daniel Panzac, *La peste dans l'Empire ottoman* (Paris: Peeters, 1985); Christen, *Decline of Iranshahr*; and Borsch, *Black Death.*

44 Such as the popular works of Brian Fagan or journalistic accounts such as Eugene Linden, *Winds of Change* (New York: Simon & Schuster, 2006). Other recent popular works on environmental crises, such as Jared Diamond, *Collapse* (New York: Norton, 2005) and Clive Ponting, *A Green History of the World* (London: Penguin, 1991) have also devoted chapters to climate-related disasters.

studies have offered fascinating new evidence and insights. However, the research has often been uneven and the authors have proven far too ready to reach hasty and dramatic conclusions. Consequently, climatic explanations have frequently met with skepticism from academic historians, and climate has yet to play to a major role in the mainstream historiography of most regions.

In general, climatic interpretations of history have faced two problems. First, many of these explanations have too readily proceeded from a *post hoc ergo propter hoc* line of reasoning. Once historical or archaeological data have revealed some sign of abnormal climate, some authors have been quick to blame any subsequent crises on the floods, droughts, heat, or cold just discovered.[45] This *post hoc* logic does not necessarily invalidate the climatic explanation, but neither does it prove causation. Even when the fit between climatic and historical events seems too perfect to dismiss as mere coincidence, simply coupling the two fails to explain how and why one development led to another, which constitutes the basic task of history. This issue raises the second major problem of current climatic explanations, namely that they are often dismissed as simplistic or monocausal. Of course, simple explanations are not necessarily wrong, nor are complex explanations necessarily right. Nevertheless, the criticism drives home the point that histories of climatic disaster often fail to consider social or political context or make adequate room for human agency.

Given these shortcomings, histories of climate have frequently focused on the dramatic collapse of ancient or early medieval civilizations, typically neglected by other historians. These works tend to recount such episodes as the disappearance of the Anasazi, the decline of the Maya, or the abandonment of Greenland – cases where written evidence is meager or nonexistent and where historians and archaeologists have been forced to draw broad inferences from limited information. For much the same reason, historians of regions such as Africa and Southeast Asia have generally made more extensive use of climatic explanations, while historians of better documented times and places have been inclined to resist similar arguments.[46] The trouble has arisen from integrating the role of climate into the current historiography wherever an abundance of evidence has already provided adequate social, economic, and political

45 Some popular examples include Brian Fagan, *Floods Famines and Emperors* (New York: Basic Books, 1999); Cesar Caviedes, *El Niño in History* (Gainesville: University Press of Florida, 2001); and David Keys, *Catastrophe* (New York: Ballantine, 2000).

46 For a discussion of this problem in the African context, see James McCann, "Climate and Causation in African History," *International Journal of African Historical Studies* 32 (1991): 261–80.

interpretations of events. In these cases, climatic developments have usually served as an incongruous subplot to the main historical narrative rather than a serious actor in the storyline. Unfortunately, this imbalance in the historiography has left us without clear and well-documented examples of how and why climate events could shift the course of human history.

This book seeks to meet that challenge by bringing climate into human history in a more nuanced way, neither simplifying its role nor neglecting its impact. In the Ottoman case, we have a rare example of a major empire that endured for centuries, but nevertheless arose in precarious ecological circumstances and suffered a clear and dramatic climate-led catastrophe. From the historian's perspective, we are even more fortunate that despite the gravity of the crisis, the Ottoman state itself managed to survive into modern times and has left us an almost unbroken record of its travails. Furthermore, the relatively recent nature of these events means that our climate data are more accurate and precise than any reconstructions from ancient times. Taking this historical and climatological evidence together, the following pages present perhaps the most detailed analysis of a major climatic crisis yet. The evidence and detail found here also permits us to integrate the effects of climate more thoroughly into the broader framework of the empire's political and economic history, and allows us to consider the role of human agency and historical accident all the more carefully.

These contributions to the historiography are not, however, the only reason for this work. Above all, this book tells a fascinating story about a critical part of the world – a story never told before. By taking a long-term perspective and drawing on new historical and scientific evidence, the following chapters offer an original history of momentous events. Some four hundred years ago, one of the world's most powerful empires endured climate-led catastrophes that changed the course of its history. The following pages tell how and why.

PART I

AN IMPERIAL ECOLOGY

Introduction to Part I: Rebuilding the Fleet

In October 1571, Sultan Selim II, successor to Süleyman the Magnificent, ruler of lands stretching from the Danube to the Nile, "lord of the two seas and two continents," received news of a devastating setback in his war with the Christians. In a battle in the Bay of Lepanto off the western shore of Greece, his navy had been crushed. Some 200 of his 230 ships had fallen victim to Spanish and Venetian galleys, and perhaps 59,000 men had been lost altogether in the single largest encounter on the Mediterranean Sea since Roman times.[1]

Without delay, the sultan rushed from his summer palace in Edirne to the capital to oversee the construction of a new fleet. Overlooking the imperial shipyards from his nearby garden, he remarked (so the chronicler İbrahim Peçevi has informed us) that they might complete seven or eight ships right away, "but to complete five or six hundred anchors and the other implements for two hundred new ships – cables, ropes, and sails – that would be impossible."

His chief minister Mehmed Paşa replied as follows:

> Your majesty, you still do not understand this great empire of ours. Believe me, this empire is such an empire that, were it your wish, every anchor of the fleet could be made of silver, every rope of silk thread, and every sail of satin without imposing the least hardship upon it.[2]

The minister, one imagines, had exaggerated. But he delivered on his promise nonetheless. In less than a year, the imperial navy was almost back

[1] Halil İnalcık, *The Ottoman Empire: The Classical Age, 1300–1600* (London: Weidenfeld and Nicolson, 1973), 41–2.

[2] Murat Uraz, ed., *Peçevi Tarihi* (Istanbul: Neşriyat, 1968), 260–1.

to full strength.[3] "The infidels," Peçevi remarked, with some hyperbole, "stood in amazement when they saw a perfect new fleet set out." Within a matter of months the Ottomans recovered most of their losses at sea, retaining the island of Cyprus and most of their hegemony over the eastern Mediterranean – at least for a time.[4]

It may be true that the Ottomans lacked something of the skill of Italian and Spanish sailors and shipbuilders of the era, particularly after their losses at Lepanto. Nor had they always taken up the latest advances in naval technology: These were still mostly simple galleys relying on oars for propulsion.[5] Yet whatever the Ottoman naval effort lacked in these respects, it more than made up with its wealth and size. By the 1570s, the Ottomans employed some 3,000 men in scores of specialized tasks in a dozen imperial shipyards from Istanbul to Alexandria, taking in a constant stream of matériel.[6] The Ottoman state could simply mobilize more labor, money, and supplies for the task than could its rivals.

Above all, the empire stood out among its neighbors for the natural resources it could command. Perhaps the imperial domains could not have delivered enough silver for anchors or satin for sails, yet it remains astounding enough that they could deliver all the necessary iron and sail-cloth. Even more impressive was the way they delivered so much timber. The great wooden ships of the day demanded staggering quantities of the stuff, the equivalent of small forests for each large galley.[7] And not just quantity, but quality, too: The wood had to have the right seasoning, the

3 See Colin Imber, "The Reconstruction of the Ottoman Fleet after the Battle of Lepanto," in *Studies in Ottoman History and Law* (Istanbul: Isis, 1996) for an overview of the reconstruction effort.

4 As Fernand Braudel has described it, the Battle of Lepanto is the classic example of a great event whose consequences were washed away by the stronger tides of history. While vulnerable to occasional attacks on the Eastern Mediterranean, the Ottoman Empire remained firmly rooted as a landed power with vast resources. See *The Mediterranean and the Mediterranean World in the Age of Philip II* (New York: Harper and Row, 1966), 1103–6 *et passim.*

5 See Colin Imber, "The Ottoman Navy of Süleyman the Magnificent," *Archivum Ottomanicum* 6 (1980): 211–82; John Pryor, *Geography, Technology, and War: Studies in the Maritime History of the Mediterranean* (New York: Cambridge University Press, 1988); and Carlo Cipolla, *Guns, Sails, and Empires* (New York: Minerva, 1965) for a comparative look at navies in this era. Some sources suggest that in the rush to rebuild so quickly, the quality of Ottoman construction suffered and some ships had improperly seasoned timber.

6 See İsmail Uzunçarşılı, *Osmanlı Devleti'nin Merkez ve Bahriye Teşkılatı* (Ankara: TTK, 1988), chapter IV.1.

7 Perhaps 2–3ha of hardwood and 2ha of pine. See Selçuk Dursun, "Forest and the State: History of Forestry and Forest Administration in the Ottoman Empire" (PhD diss., Sabancı University, 2007), 49–50.

right shape and texture. Dozens of specialized cuts and pieces demanded particular types of timber, with particular cuts and qualities.[8]

Yet the Ottomans appeared to face little difficulty meeting demand. With land and labor already set aside for the purpose, the empire could call on vast reserves of trees, hemp, tar, pitch, and other goods with an ease that put its European rivals to shame. Venice, by contrast, struggled throughout this period to secure enough naval supplies despite an elaborate procurement system of its own.[9] Meanwhile the demands of war drove Spain literally into bankruptcy by 1575. What was at issue here was not just the size of the Ottoman Empire, but its system of provisioning resources in the first place.

The state did not just purchase goods. With regulations and bureaucratic oversight, the empire effectively administered the resources of war. It kept protected forests, oversaw the extraction of timber and ores, and mobilized and transported workers. Though concerned like European states with fiscal obligations, the state was often just as concerned with the actual management of resources as with the money to buy them. In an age when mercantilist European states were encouraging exports and discouraging imports in order to store up bullion, the Ottomans let most imports flow in freely while actually forbidding many exports in order to keep resources at home. Within the empire, the state often guided the production and long-distance movement of commodities to meet its ends – above all the provisioning of the capital city and the army, and as in this case, the building of the fleet.

The success of the Ottoman Empire depended on a particular flow of resources and population directed by the imperial center, which I describe in Part I as its "imperial ecology." Goods had to keep pouring from the peripheries into the core; and settlement had to reach as far as possible for agriculture, extraction, and transportation. Resources had to be harvested, requisitioned, and managed to secure supply. The peasantry had to be taxed, cajoled, coerced, and sometimes moved about for imperial ends, and yet at the same time protected, secured, and held loyal to the imperial dynasty. The geographical diversity of Ottoman domains, the scale of military mobilization, and the imperial preference for the direct provisioning of many resources meant that this imperial ecology

[8] For the classic account of naval timber provisioning, including a detailed discussion of the varieties of cuts and difficulties of supply, see Robert Albion, *Forests and Sea Power* (Cambridge, MA: Harvard University Press, 1926).

[9] Karl Appuhn, "Inventing Nature: Forests, Forestry, and State Power in Renaissance Venice," *The Journal of Modern History* 72 (2000): 861–89.

would play a critical role in the rise of Ottoman power and in the crisis to follow at the close of the sixteenth century.

With regard to this imperial ecology, the Ottoman Empire was hardly unique but still remarkable. Despite its frequent association with the rising nation-states of Europe, the Ottoman Empire may be more properly compared with the other great agrarian empires of Eurasia that still dominated the sixteenth- and seventeenth-century world: Ming China, Mughal India, Safavid Persia, and later the Qing, Muscovy, and Tokugawa Japan, among the major players.[10] In varying measures, all relied on a top-down, increasingly bureaucratic control of settlement, land use, and raw materials to supply an expanding capital city and military. However, by geographical circumstance and ideological orientation, the Ottoman Empire proved especially apt at this sort of imperial management especially early in its history. Only Ming China and perhaps Mughal India moved resources on a larger scale at the time, but both had far larger populations and more productive land to draw on, and perhaps neither directed such a diverse range of materials over such varied territories.[11] By the eighteenth century, the Tokugawa would develop a more elaborate system of imperial forestry[12] and the Qing would embark on a more extensive scheme of agricultural settlement and nomadic control.[13] Nevertheless, at the time of Lepanto the Ottomans remained far ahead in both respects.

However, as they grew in scale and scope, Ottoman systems of provisioning and settlement faced mounting problems. Just as the Ottomans proved especially precocious at building these systems, so they became

[10] For a systematic comparison of state integration across early modern Eurasia, see Victor Lieberman, *Strange Parallels: Southeast Asia in Global Context*, 2 vols. (New York: Cambridge University Press, 2004–9). P. Perdue and H. İslamoğlu, eds., *Shared Histories of Modernity* (London: Routledge, 2009) also stresses the need for intra-Asian comparisons rather than binary comparisons with Europe.

[11] For a broader comparative look at Chinese management of environments and resources, see John McNeill, "China's Environmental History in World Perspective" in *Sediments of Time*, ed. M. Elvin and L. Ts'ui-jung (New York: Cambridge University Press, 1998). For Mughal agriculture, resources, and taxation, see Irfan Habib, *The Agrarian System of Mughal India*, 2nd ed. (New Delhi: Oxford University Press, 1999) and John Richards, *Mughal India* (Cambridge: Cambridge University Press, 1993), 185–204. On Mughal provisioning as environmental history, see M. Gadgil and R. Guha, *This Fissured Land* (New Delhi: Oxford University Press, 1992), 107–8 *et passim*. The Mughal state may have extracted an even larger portion of crops – up to one third of grains and one fifth of other crops – but its provisioning systems appear to have been less centralized and limited to a narrower range of commodities.

[12] Conrad Totman, *The Green Archipelago* (Athens: Ohio University Press, 1998).

[13] Peter Perdue, *China Marches West* (New Haven, CT: Yale University Press, 2005).

particularly dependent on their stability and susceptible to their failures. Already by the 1570s, the core Mediterranean lands of the empire had begun to suffer from population pressure, inflation, and diminishing returns from agriculture. Stretched by the growth of the capital and the rising scale of war on two fronts, imperial provisioning became subject to ever more frequent and troubling breakdowns. While not facing imminent decline, the empire proved increasingly vulnerable to external shocks as the century wore on, paving the way for a breakdown of this imperial ecology under the impact of extreme Little Ice Age climate events in the 1590s.

Part I explores the rise of this Ottoman imperial ecology and the buildup of forces that threatened to unravel the system by the late sixteenth century. Chapter 1 examines the distribution and exchange of resources among regions and the imperial direction of land-holding and settlement. Chapters 2 and 3 discuss issues of demographic change, population pressure, and natural and man-made disasters. Chapter 4, the final chapter of Part I, takes a closer look at the province of Karaman in south-central Anatolia, where ecological pressures would eventually reach a breaking point, setting the stage for rebellion and crisis.

1

REGIONS, RESOURCES, AND SETTLEMENT

The century leading up to Lepanto and above all the long reign of Süleyman the Magnificent (1520–66) marks the so-called Ottoman classical age when the empire's distinctive political and military system took root and flourished. The sultan, lodged in his imperial palace at Topkapı on the seaward tip of old Constantinople,[14] oversaw the decisions of his viziers and officers in the imperial divan, met with petitioners and ambassadors from the furthest corners of his empire and beyond, and personally led his soldiers year after year to distant fronts in Hungary and Persia, where the empire continued to expand decade after decade. His soldiers comprised, on the one hand, the *sipahis*, or prebendal cavalry, awarded grants of land for military service at the discretion of the sultan, and on the other hand, the Janissaries, the slave soldiers recruited from Balkan children, raised as Muslims and trained in the arts of war. The same slave recruitment provided for an elaborate palace staff and bureaucracy in the imperial capital, while the *kadıs*, the judge-administrators schooled in Islamic law, oversaw the day-to-day running of the provinces.[15]

Over the same period, the empire employed an equally distinctive, and for a time successful, management of resources and settlement. At the heart of this management lay the Ottoman systems for provisioning commodities from the far-flung lands of the empire to meet the

[14] The old city of Byzantium, renamed Constantinople in honor of the emperor Constantine in the fourth century AD, gradually took on the name "Istanbul" in the centuries following the Ottoman conquest of 1453, probably from the Greek *eis tin poli* ("to the city"). In the sixteenth century, as often as not, official documents still refer to the city as "Kostantiniyye" or some similar variant, while the pious corruption "Islambol" ("full of Islam") comes up frequently as well. The change of name to Istanbul (as celebrated in song) did not become official until the modern Republic of Turkey. This book will use the names interchangeably, as the Ottomans themselves did.

[15] For an overview of the Ottoman political and military systems in the sixteenth century, see İnalcık, *Ottoman Empire* and Colin Imber, *The Ottoman Empire, 1350–1650: The Structure of Power* (New York: Palgrave, 2002).

insatiable demands of its imperial capital and of its massive army and navy, perhaps the most formidable military in the world at the time. As imperial domains expanded, Ottoman officials developed ways to direct the varied resources of diverse lands across three continents for imperial ends. At the same time, as their subjects multiplied, imperial officials employed novel methods to orchestrate movements in population and land use.

While considered a "classical" age, however, it is important to bear in mind that this period actually proved exceptional in terms of its ecological possibilities. Ongoing conquests continued to open new lands for settlement, agriculture, and extraction, while the empire's rapidly growing but still sparse population had not yet put severe strains on natural resources. Central authority remained strong, and the pressures and temptations of the wider global economy had barely begun to siphon commodities from Ottoman lands. The sultans from Mehmed II (1451–81) to Selim II (1566–74) enjoyed an unparalleled opportunity to direct the resources of the Near East for imperial purposes. This first chapter explores the ideology, development, and workings of these provisioning systems as they reached their zenith around the time of the Battle of Lepanto.

Provisionism

Modern historians have usually recognized three guiding principles of Ottoman economic strategy: fiscalism, traditionalism, and provisionism.[16] The first was straightforward enough: The Ottoman Empire, like any other government of its day, looked for policies that could maximize revenue to its treasury while minimizing expenses. The second principle was also typical of most states at the time. Like the other great landed Eurasian empires – and perhaps more than most – the Ottoman realm was an amalgam of peoples, religions, and customs, the outcome of centuries of conquest and acquisition. Rather than bringing all under a single law and status, the Ottomans preferred to compromise with different traditions of regulation and taxation in the various polities it absorbed. If a group could show it had possessed some right

[16] Descriptions of Ottoman economic theory in the classical age may be found in Mehmet Genç, *Osmanlı İmparatorluğunda Devlet ve Ekonomi* (Istanbul: Ötüken, 2000), part I; H. İnalcık and D. Quataert, eds., *An Economic and Social History of the Ottoman Empire* (New York: Cambridge University Press, 1995), v.1, section A; and Cemal Kafadar, "When Coins Turned into Drops of Dew and Bankers into Robbers of Shadows: The Boundaries of the Ottoman Economic Imagination" (PhD diss., McGill University, 1988).

or privilege "from ancient times" (*kadimden*), then it would usually be upheld under Ottoman law.

Provisionism remains a more difficult and controversial concept, and yet the most crucial for understanding the Ottoman management of empire. As coined by historian Mehmet Genç, "provisionism" in its most basic sense refers to the way that the Ottomans geared economic relations in favor of the consumer, "to provide goods as cheap, high quality, and plentiful as possible."[17] Yet in a broader way the concept also captures the Ottoman concern for the continuous, centrally directed provisioning of key commodities. As described in the introduction to Part I, the empire took a direct interest in the movement of vital resources throughout the empire, not just in obtaining the money to buy them. At times, this management might involve state ownership: After all, by right of conquest most of the empire's territory fell under the sultan's eminent domain. However, the Ottoman Empire was far from a modern socialist state or command economy. It had neither the means nor the incentive to take direct control of most agriculture or industry.

What lay at the heart of Ottoman provisionism was not statism per se but simply a different approach to obtaining and distributing important resources. When it came to vital public functions, Ottoman rulers had little confidence in an unregulated market to deliver goods when and where they were needed. Furthermore, they had little or no interest in leaving prices up to the market, in order to boost production or encourage innovation (even if innovation was something to be desired – by no means a certainty). To let a commodity grow expensive would not encourage producers to make more, it was supposed, but would only drive speculation and harm consumers. Similarly, to export goods to the Christians, even at a higher price, meant giving ground in a zero-sum contest for resources. The bullion Ottoman merchants could receive in return for such trade might not be considered just compensation but rather illegitimate gain by scheming profiteers. Prices in Venice could reach twice or even three times those in nearby Ottoman Greece, but only on rare occasion would the sultan grant his special permission for the sale of grain or other basic goods.[18] When he did, the decision was

17 Mehmet Genç, "Osmanlı İktisâdi Dünya Görüşünün İlkeleri," in *Osmanlı İmparatorluğunda Devlet ve Ekonomi* (Istanbul: Ötüken, 2003), 45.

18 Such export restrictions may go back as far as the fourteenth century. See Kate Fleet, "Ottoman Grain Exports from Western Anatolia at the End of the Fourteenth Century," *Journal of the Economic and Social History of the Orient* 40 (1997): 283–94. For a detailed examination of the Mediterranean grain trade in the period, see Maurice Aymard, *Venise, Raguse, et la commerce de blé pendant la seconde moitié du XVIe siècle* (Paris: SEVPEN, 1966).

presented as a gift to the Christian nations, offered as much from strategic as economic motives.[19]

Broadly speaking, Ottoman officials usually acted on the assumption that production would flourish not when prices were highest or markets largest, but when the state created the best conditions of justice and fairness, and when it ensured manufacturers ready access to materials. In the countryside, officials tried to ensure that settlement extended as far as possible and agriculture produced as much food as possible. In the cities, the state regulated crafts and industry to produce as plentifully and cheaply as the techniques of the day allowed. On the administrative level, the Ottomans assigned *muhtesibs*, overseers of the markets, to regulate the quality of manufactures and the honesty of sales, while the *kadıs* enforced contracts and regulations. At the market level, producers were organized into dozens of guilds, which enforced standards and negotiated with officials over sales, wages, and practices. The state even arranged for direct transfers of goods from guild to guild for processing. For example, city slaughterhouses delivered their tallow straight to the candlemakers' guild and their hides straight to the tanners.[20]

Prices nevertheless played a key role in the Ottoman economic system. In the sixteenth century, the state often set a fixed price, or *narh*, for basic goods. The *narh* was not meant to be an arbitrary figure, but rather an approximation of what local prices ought to be, given that the buyer should have the goods as cheaply as possible while the seller should have fair compensation for his expenses.[21] In practice, when times were good, the *narh* more or less reflected market rates. When times were not so good, as discussed in later chapters, the *narh* could diverge widely from black-market prices, leading the sultan and men of state to rant against "profiteers" and "swindlers." However, the *narh* represented more than a

19 As when the French were at war with their mutual enemy the Habsburgs in the 1550s – see Gilles Veinstein, "Un achat français de blé dans l'Empire ottoman au mileu du XVIe siècle," in *L'Empire ottoman, la République de Turquie et la France*, ed. H. Batu and J. Bacqué-Grammont (Istanbul: Isis, 1986).

20 Suraiya Faroqhi, *Towns and Townsmen of Ottoman Anatolia* (New York: Cambridge University Press, 1984), 157 *et passim*. For orders to sell fat to candlemakers, see Ahmet Refik, *Hicrî On Birinci Asırda İstanbul Hayatı* (Istanbul: Devlet Matbaası, 1931), documents 42 and 58.

21 On the operation of Ottoman price regulation, see Mustafa Öztürk, "Osmanlı Dönemi Fiyat Politikası ve Fiyatların Tahlili," *Belleten* 55 (1991): 87–100. For more on the intellectual underpinnings of price regulation and unraveling of the system in times of crisis, see Cemal Kafadar, "Les troubles monétaires de la fin du XVIe siècle et la prise de conscience ottomane du déclin," *Annales: Economies, sociétés, civilisations* 46 (1991): 381–400 and "When Coins Turned into Drops of Dew," chapter 3.

medieval "just price."[22] Setting the *narh* was also a tool to direct the flow of resources. Favored regions like the capital did not always have lower prices, as is sometimes assumed, but often *higher* prices. The idea was that this price gradient could nudge goods along from lower-price regions in the provinces to higher-price cities and ultimately to the capital itself, as in the case of meat provisioning (discussed below) or in the event of shortages (as explained in Chapters 3 and 6). In other words, these prices served as stimuli to *distribution* rather than production.

Recently, some Ottomanists have begun to question this "provisionist" paradigm. In particular, economic historian Şevket Pamuk has pointed out that official records used by historians have been biased toward evidence of interventionism rather than unregulated markets.[23] He emphasizes the flexibility and pragmatism of Ottoman monetary regimes, belying the supposedly statist orientation of the Ottoman economy.[24] Furthermore, he argues that Ottoman interventionism applied mainly to key resources for the capital, military, and major cities and that price controls were only employed in "wars, crop failures, and other difficulties in provisioning the city and monetary instabilities."[25] Finally, citing the rise of provincial market towns, Pamuk concludes that the empire was tending away from provisionism throughout the sixteenth century.

On the one hand, critics such as Pamuk are right to dismiss exaggerated notions of a centralized command economy or fixed interventionist mentality. While the Ottoman central government had truly reached a peak of authority in these years that other sovereigns of the age might have found enviable, it was no "oriental despotism" that could dictate

[22] Even medieval "just prices" could also be more sophisticated than often presumed. For a comparative analysis of European and Ottoman price regulation, see Seven Ağır, "From Welfare to Wealth: Ottoman and Castilian Trade Policies in a Time of Change" (PhD diss., Princeton University, 2009), chapter 2.

[23] Şevket Pamuk, "Ottoman Interventionism in Economic and Monetary Affairs," *Revue d'histoire maghrebine* 25 (1998): 361–7 and "Osmanlı Ekonomisinde Devlet Müdaheleciliğine Yeniden Bakış," *Toplum ve Bilim* 83 (1999/2000): 133–45.

[24] Baki Tezcan has made a related argument that the volume of long-distance gold-silver arbitrage in the late sixteenth century should be seen as evidence of a monetized, market-oriented economy. See "Searching for Osman," chapter 1. However, a wider perspective reveals that gold-silver arbitrage was really an exceptional case. As the Flynn-O'Rourke debate in the *European Review of Economic History* (*EREH*) has shown, gold-silver arbitrage spanned the globe by the late 1500s, even though nothing like a world-wide market economy emerged until the 1800s. See K. O'Rourke and J. Williamson, "When Did Globalization Begin?" *EREH* 6 (2002): 23–50 and D. Flynn and A. Giraldez, "Path Dependence, Time Lags, and the Birth of Globalization," *EREH* 8 (2003): 81–108.

[25] Pamuk, "Ottoman Interventionism," 364.

the entire economy.[26] Furthermore, there is no reason to assume that it actually wanted to do so, and no reason to dismiss signs of flexibility or openness to local market activity.

On the other hand, Pamuk and other critics of provisionism have overstated their case and overlooked some important developments of the late sixteenth century. First, although the available evidence does tend to focus on cases of state involvement, it would be just as presumptuous to fill in the spaces between the documents with an unregulated market as with an interventionist administration. As discussed in the following sections, imperial direction of provisioning involved a wide array of regular commodity movements, often mentioned only when they demanded particular official attention. Moreover, Pamuk minimizes the tremendous volume and range of provisioning necessary to maintain the empire's major cities, army, and navy – enterprises that, taken together, consumed a major proportion of the empire's annual production of food and extraction of natural resources. Furthermore, his argument that the state only regulated prices in times of emergency overlooks the fact that by the late 1500s, war, natural disaster, and other such "difficulties in provisioning" were not the exception but the norm. As Chapters 2 and 3 demonstrate, rising population pressure and frequent famine actually led to greater imperial intervention in provisioning in the late 1500s, not a gradual liberalization. While it is true that the economy was increasingly monetized and that local market towns flourished in the general growth and prosperity of the sixteenth century, these developments actually demanded more, not less, imperial oversight of long-distance movements of major commodities, because they increased opportunities for profitable smuggling and black-market sales.

Shorn of any simplistic exaggerations, provisionism remains a vital concept for understanding certain key developments of the sixteenth century. As the reader will see, the language of official documents, and more importantly the course of events leading up to the Little Ice Age crisis, demonstrate that the imperial government remained committed to provisionist policies, only to abandon them under force of necessity. Moreover, it is crucial not to dismiss provisionism in this period as just some detour from a supposed European capitalist rationality, as Ottomanists have tended to do. For a time, Ottoman provisioning worked

[26] See I. Metin Kunt, *The Sultan's Servants* (New York: Columbia University Press, 1983) and Barkey, *Empire of Difference* for analyses of the evolving relationship among Ottoman central and provincial powers.

remarkably well, keeping the empire's population adequately fed and its military well equipped. Its breakdown came less from inherent failures in the system than from ecological pressures and natural disasters beyond anyone's control.

Regions

The scale and scope of Ottoman provisioning systems were born from the empire's wide expanse and geographical diversity. By the late 1500s, Ottoman lands extended outward from the capital, Istanbul, at the junction of the Black and Mediterranean seas, to encompass the Balkans, Anatolia, Iraq, the Levant, Egypt, the Hijaz, and beyond. At times, orders would go out as far as the Crimea, the Maghreb, Yemen, and Ethiopia. In total, the empire ruled or claimed suzerainty over all or part of some thirty present-day countries, with lands ranging from fertile river valleys to empty deserts to rugged mountains. Yet in some respect, each region had something to offer and something to demand from other parts of the empire.

To be precise, the late-sixteenth-century empire consisted of thirty-two provinces, each with its own peculiarities with regard to revenue and organization. In very simplified terms, however, one could say the empire comprised administratively and geographically a core and two peripheries.[27] The core, generally speaking, consisted of lands within easier reach of the capital and under more direct Ottoman control. Administratively, these provinces received officials appointed from the capital, they shouldered the greatest share of land revenue and wartime taxes, and their settlement and landholding systems were regulated from the center. Geographically, these were Mediterranean lands: present-day Greece and southern Bulgaria, western and central Anatolia, Syria and Palestine – lands of sufficient rainfall for pasture and the dry farming of cereals, but often little besides. More fertile territory along rivers or streams, or those in rich alluvial valleys, might provide some diversity of crops and some surplus for provisioning, but scarcely enough to feed a great empire.

Most provisioning of basic resources, especially foodstuffs, remained the task of what might be called the first periphery of the empire: the rich lands of the northern Balkans, Egypt, and the Crimea. Administratively,

[27] For an overview of Ottoman provincial administration and differences among types of provinces, see Gabor Agoston, "A Flexible Empire: Authority and Its Limits on the Ottoman Frontiers," *International Journal of Turkish Studies* 9 (2003): 15–31.

these were regions of vital interest to the Ottomans but under less direct imperial control. Traditional legal systems and systems of land-holding remained largely intact. Although Hungary was more directly administered, the principalities of the Danube and the Tatar Khan of the Crimea even preserved their nominal independence as Ottoman vassals. Geographically, these lands differed a great deal, but all produced a significant agricultural surplus. These were the regions that gave the Ottomans an ecological windfall of farmland and other natural resources as they conquered outwards from Anatolia. From Egypt came rice and grain, as it had for millennia, although less to supply the capital than to feed the holy lands of the Hijaz. From present-day Serbia, Hungary, Bulgaria, and Romania came goods such as wheat, honey, timber, and above all sheep. From the Crimea came mostly hides, tallow, butter, and lard – the last particularly important among Turks who had not yet developed a taste for olive oil. By this time, the Ottomans had turned the Black Sea into a virtual Ottoman lake, locking up its rich resources for consumption within the empire.[28]

The second periphery, as I have labeled it, comprised the more marginal lands of the empire. Administratively, the state preferred to rule such regions indirectly, often giving the preconquest rulers a nominal Ottoman title, and sometimes asking no more than token signs of tribute and submission. Geographically, these were typically arid or mountainous places inhabited largely by pastoral tribes and practically impossible to govern directly – lands such as Kurdistan, Albania, Yemen, and the Arabian Desert. These territories (and Iraq, still thinly populated and lightly administered at the time)[29] play a lesser role in this book. Yet no part of the empire escaped entirely from the reach of Ottoman administration; and in the coming pages, even lands as far afield as Libya and Macedonia appear from time to time in contexts as diverse as timber supply and famine management.

The main focus of this book, however, remains the Ottoman "core." Despite the vital economic and ecological role played by lands such as Egypt and the Danube, the rise and crisis of the empire ultimately hinged on the fate of lands from the southern Balkans through Anatolia and the

[28] Halil İnalcık, "The Question of the Closing of the Black Sea under the Ottomans," *Archeion Pontou* 35 (1979): 74–110 and Victor Ostapchuk, "The Human Landscape of the Ottoman Black Sea in the Face of Cossack Naval Raids," *Oriente Moderno* 20 (2001): 23–95.

[29] For long-term population trends in Iraq, and its decline since medieval times, see Robert Adams, *Land Behind Baghdad* (Chicago: University of Chicago Press, 1965).

Levant. It was this region that would enjoy the fastest growth, face the most acute population pressure, and suffer the worst effects of the Little Ice Age to come. Furthermore, as the center of Ottoman administration, these provinces have also left the best historical record over the period concerned. Nevertheless, the environmental history of these core lands only makes sense within the context of resources and their redistribution across the entire empire.

Resources

To manage these resources and their movement over three continents, the empire developed extensive systems of provisioning. Over and above the regulation of quality, pricing, and sales, the state could take a more or less direct management of supply, storage, transportation, and distribution for a range of key commodities. As these systems demanded constant attention from the central administration, they figure prominently in the Ottoman imperial orders (*mühimme defters*). Although the records fail to provide precise accounting for the sixteenth century, these documents offer enough information to outline the management of several major items. The archival evidence paints a picture of diverse and often peculiar provisioning systems, each with particular strengths and vulnerabilities.

Timber

Timber constituted the single largest commodity by bulk and the one most often featured in the documents.[30] Contrary to popular misimpressions that the Turks had ravaged an already deforested Near Eastern landscape,[31] the Ottoman Empire inherited extensive forest reserves along its mountainous coasts and it managed them to good effect.

[30] The study of Ottoman forestry is still in its infancy. So far, two interesting collections of Ottoman documents on the subject have come out – Halil Kutluk, *Tükiye Ormancılığı ile İlgili Tarihi Vesikalar 893–1339 (1487–1923)* (Istanbul: Tarım Bakanlığı, 1948) and *Osmanlı Ormancılığı ile İlgili Belgeler* (Ankara: T. C. Orman Bakanlığı, 1999) – as well as one unpublished dissertation – Dursun, "Forest and the State." For ship-building and related timber supplies generally, see Uzunçarşılı, *Osmanlı Devleti'nin Merkez ve Bahriye Teşkılatı*; İdris Bostan, *Osmanlı Bahriye Teşkilâtı* (Ankara: TTK, 1992); and Murat Çızakça, "Ottomans and the Mediterranean: An Analysis of the Ottoman Shipbuilding Industry as Reflected by the Arsenal Registers of Istanbul 1529–1650," in *Le genti del Mare Mediterraneo*, ed. R. Ragosta (Naples: Lucio Pironti, 1981).

[31] E.g., Thirgood, *Man and the Mediterranean Forest*; Maurice Lombard, "Le bois dans la Méditeranée musulmane (VIIe-XIe siècles)," *Annales* (1959): 234–55; and Steven Pyne, *Vestal Fire* (Seattle: University of Washington Press, 1997), chapter 4.

Foreign travelers marveled at the extent and size of trees,[32] and imperial records have left evidence of vast, if by no means limitless, supplies.

By the age of Lepanto, the imperial government had set aside widespread tracts of the best timber as protected state forests, called *miri koru*. While concentrated around the Sea of Marmara,[33] imperial orders mention *miri koru* up and down the Mediterranean and Black Seas and at times as far afield as Romania, Syria, and Albania.[34] Forbidding its subjects from any unauthorized cutting, grazing, or charcoal-making,[35] the imperial government appointed Janissaries to serve as forest rangers[36] and imposed penalties as harsh as galley service for interfering with the timber supply.[37]

The state regulated not only the forests themselves but also the selection, cutting, and delivery of timber. Trees for ships, for instance, had to be felled "in their season" so as to have the right sap and potential for seasoning.[38] Other orders regulated the species of trees used for specific purposes, such as gun stocks and wheel felloes of elm[39] and galley oars from a particular stand of protected hornbeam trees.[40] More often, orders specified cuts from certain regions: masts from Akyazı,[41] barrel stays from Kocaeli,[42] or capstans from İznikmid, and so forth.[43] Even ordinary pine had to be cut to specific standardized measures before delivery to the shipyards or construction sites in cities.[44] Given the often remote, mountainous terrain of the best forests, long-distance delivery proved

[32] Visiting the imperial forests on the Bay of Izmit, for instance, the Venetian envoy Aurelio Santa Croce wrote that "there was infinite wood to make vessels of combat and above all trees for galleys and ships," perhaps as much a comment on the relative deforestation of Italy as the quantity of wood in Anatolia – quoted in Maria Pedani-Fabris, ed., *Relazioni di ambasciatori veneti al Senato XIV* (Turin: Bottega d'Erasmo, 1996), 179.

[33] E.g., MD 3/285 and MD 3/1552. See also Bostan, *Osmanlı Bahriye Teşkilâtı*, 102–3 *et passim*.

[34] E.g., MD 12/67, MD 3/846, MD 3/846, MD 5/1292, MD 7/658, MD 7/658, MD 7/1800, and MD 7/2330.

[35] E.g., MD 12/815, MD 12/683, MD 39/352, MD 24/672, and MD 16/428. However, other orders confirm traditional rights to certain forest resources, such as permission to collect loose wood (MD 14/541) or to hunt with bow and arrow (MD 10/561).

[36] E.g., MD 39/163 and MD 40/753.

[37] MD 6/185.

[38] E.g., MD 7/1710, MD 12/1020, and MD 12/1054.

[39] MD 70/218.

[40] MD 7/1795.

[41] MD 6/626.

[42] MD 6/627.

[43] E.g., MD 7/2093.

[44] E.g., MD 7/1425.

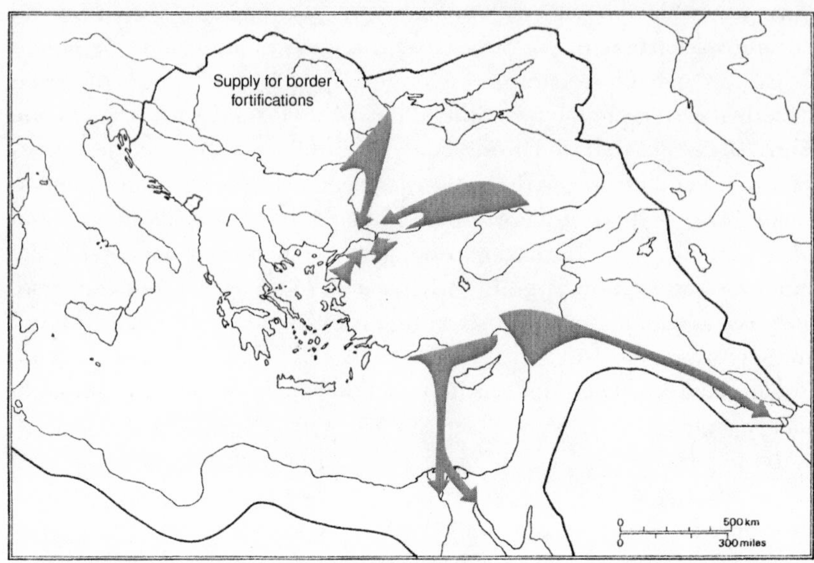

Approximate flows of Ottoman timber provisioning in the late sixteenth, based on the mühimme defters.

even more challenging. When local means proved inadequate, the state would send hundreds of oxcarts or buffalo from nearby provinces to get the timber to the coast, then hire rented ships for delivery over water.[45]

Although the archives fail to give comprehensive figures, anecdotal accounts leave some impression of the scale of consumption. Factoring in not only naval timber but also wood for military and civilian construction, hundreds of shiploads and thousands of wagonloads must have gone out annually under imperial instructions. Some individual orders give a sense of this volume: 50,000 barrel stays from Kocaeli in 1564/5;[46] 5,000 hornbeam galley oars from İznikmid in 1570;[47] 5,000 *çeki* (about 1,250 tons) of naval timber from Kite in 1571;[48] another order for 5,000 *çeki* of ship timber along with 250 cannon stocks and 10 masts from Akyazı the same year;[49] 3,000 trees from Moldovia to repair Akkırman Castle in Hungary in 1574[50] – and then another 2,000 trees for the

45 E.g., MD 3/185, MD 3/1174, and MD 14/1052.
46 MD 6/627.
47 MD 14/935.
48 MD 10/305.
49 MD 14/135.
50 MD 26/798.

same task less than six years later.[51] The treeless Nile Valley received continuous shipments from southeastern Turkey and sometimes Yemen or Ethiopia;[52] and nearly treeless southern Iraq took in shipments overland from eastern Anatolia and northern Syria that passed down the Tigris and Euphrates.[53] In the sixteenth century, as the Ottomans built Indian Ocean fleets to challenge the Portuguese, these shipments swelled to supply new naval yards at Suez and Basra.[54] Furthermore, Istanbul in general and the imperial palace in particular demanded a tremendous and continuous supply of firewood from nearby forests specifically set aside for the purpose.[55] Again, exact figures are lacking, but the city's demand for fuel must have been staggering, given that one document records an annual demand of 6,720 tons for the imperial palace alone.[56]

Grain

The provisioning of grain – the most vital commodity of all – operated on nearly the same scope and scale as timber.[57] While not entirely under state control, the Ottoman grain market came under heavy regulation and direction from the Porte. Beyond the usual oversight of price and quality, the imperial government took active steps to secure supply,

[51] MD 39/657. For more on local timber demand for military construction in Hungary, see Lajos Rácz, "The Price of Survival: Transformations in Environmental Conditions and Subsistence Systems in Hungary in the Age of Ottoman Occupation," *Hungarian Studies* 24: 21–39, at 26–7.

[52] E.g., MD 7/612 and MD 7/1973. Egypt had imported its wood from the Alanya region since at least the fourteenth century: See Ibn-Battuta, in *Travels in Asia and Africa*, ed. H. Gibb (New Delhi: Manohar, 1992), 124.

[53] E.g., MD 3/1249, MD 7/2371, and MD 32/71.

[54] On Ottoman strategy in the Indian Ocean, see Giancarlo Casale, *The Ottoman Age of Exploration* (New York: Cambridge University Press, 2010).

[55] E.g., MD 31/161 and MD 6/122. See also Dursun, "Forest and the State," 59–63.

[56] Faroqhi, *Towns and Townsmen*, 79–81 (figure for the year 1643/4).

[57] Grain provisioning has also received more attention from Ottomanists than any other commodity: For a review of the historiography, see Ahmet Uzun, "Osmanlı Devleti'nde Şehir Ekonomisi ve İaşe," *Türkiye Araştırmaları Literatür Dergisi* 3 (2005): 211–35. Among the studies consulted here: Lütfi Güçer, *Osmanlı İmparatorluğunda Hububat Meselesi ve Hububattan Alınan Vergiler* (Istanbul: İstanbul Üniversitesi, 1964); Lütfi Güçer, "İstanbul'un İaşesi İçin Lüzumlu Hububatın Temini Meselesi," *İstanbul Üniversitesi İktisat Fakültesi Mecmuası* 11 (1950): 397–416; Rhoads Murphey, "Provisioning Istanbul: The State and Subsistence in the Early Modern Middle East," *Food and Foodways* 2 (1988): 217–63; Lynne Sasmazer, "Provisioning Istanbul: Bread Production, Power, and Political Ideology in the Ottoman Empire" (PhD diss., Indiana University, 2000); and Ağır, "From Welfare to Wealth."

deliveries, and distribution. Given its geographical extent, the empire as a whole seldom faced shortfalls, at least until the onset of the Little Ice Age. However, the imperial government rarely relied on market forces to balance areas of surplus and areas of deficit, preferring an active management of shipments among the provinces.

Above all, the Ottoman grain supply depended on the rich Danube and Black Sea regions and the bounty of the Nile. The former sent its surplus as taxes and tribute either directly to Istanbul or to army depots and imperial warehouses, especially in the Thracian port of Rodosçuk (also known as Tekirdağ or Rodosto), from where the capital drew much of its supplies, including the largest shipments during wars and emergencies.[58] In extreme cases, individual orders from the northern Balkans could reach about 4,000 tons of grain,[59] while total annual imports of cereals and other foodstuffs from the region must have reached tens of thousands of tons altogether.[60] Egypt, though the breadbasket of empires since Roman times, had suffered greatly under the later Mamluks[61] and had not quite eclipsed the northern provinces and principalities as a source of food and raw materials. Each year, the Nile sent more than a thousand tons of grain, along with hundreds more of rice, sugar, and other commodities to Constantinople – a significant sum if only a fraction of total supply.[62] Just as importantly, Egypt also provided the bulk of foodstuffs for the Holy Cities of the Hijaz, a distribution called *deşişe*, of

[58] E.g., MD 5/595.

[59] In 1586, for instance, we find a single emergency order for 40,000 *kile* (roughly 40,000 bushels or 1,500 tons) of wheat, 50,000 of barley, and another 20,000 of millet from Wallachia and Moldovia (MD 61/208).

[60] Peter Sugar, *Southeastern Europe under Ottoman Rule, 1354–1804* (Seattle: University of Washington Press, 1977), 125, cites a figure of 80,000 *kile* (around 3,000 tons) of barley delivered from the Danubian provinces annually by the 1560s just for the imperial stables.

[61] By the time of the Ottoman conquest in the 1510s, Egypt may have been a net *importer* of foodstuffs. See Leonor Fernandes, "The City of Cairo and Its Food Supply During the Mamluk Period," in *Nourir les cités de Mediterranée – Antiquité-temps moderns*, ed. B. Marin and C. Virlouvet (Paris: Maisonneuve, 2003) and Borsch, "Environment and Population."

[62] Murphey, "Provisioning Istanbul," 232, gives a figure of 20,000 *ardabs* (about 1,400 tons). Alan Mikhail, "The Nature of Ottoman Egypt: Irrigation, Environment, and Bureaucracy in the Long Eighteenth Century" (PhD diss., University of California Berkeley, 2008), chapter 3, finds that shipments from Egypt to Istanbul in the eighteenth century may have varied from a few thousand *ardabs* (a few hundred tons) to over 40,000 *ardabs* (nearly 3,000 tons) annually. For an example of imperial management of Egyptian granaries and accounts, see, e.g., MD 5/601.

several thousand tons each year. When the Nile flood fell short, it meant almost certain famine for Mecca and Medina.[63]

However, imperial management of grain reached deep into the provinces of the core as well. The Porte expected each *kaza* (the administrative unit defined by the jurisdiction of a *kadı*) to be essentially self-sufficient in basic foodstuffs, neither importing nor exporting until called on to meet imperial requisitions.[64] These typically took the form of a forced purchase at the *narh* from reserves stocked in public and private granaries. Each transfer across regions then met with painstaking precautions to discourage loss and smuggling. Carriers had to provide guarantors or collateral, register transactions, and collect receipts. While never as vital as Egypt or the North, these Mediterranean lands still provided regular long-distance deliveries of basic grains, especially barley, for military campaigns, urban consumption, and sometimes famine relief.[65]

As with timber, transportation and processing presented nearly as many difficulties as supply. Most shipments moved by sea on state or rented private ships with costs running in the millions of *akçe*, totaling perhaps 15 percent to 25 percent of the value of cargo.[66] Diversion and smuggling posed constant risks, provoking incessant threats and inspections from imperial officials. To tap inland regions, the state would have to arrange vast wagon or camel caravans to convey grain, especially during military preparations or emergencies;[67] but given the much higher costs of overland transport – at least twice that of shipping – these deliveries rarely played a major role.[68] Given the dangers and expense of transport,

[63] Murphy, "Provisioning Istanbul," 232, gives a figure of 48,000 *ardabs* (3,341 tons) in the seventeenth to eighteenth centuries; Michel Tuchscherer, "Approvisionnement des villes saintes d'Arabie en blé d'Egypte d'après des documents ottomans des années 1670," *Anatolia Moderna* 5 (1994): 79–99, at 80, claims the total was over 70,000 *ardabs* in the 1670s, once deliveries from *vakıfs* were included. For more on the *deşişe* administration, see Jane Hathaway, *A Tale of Two Factions* (Albany: SUNY Press, 2003), 145–6. For examples from the imperial orders, see MD 5/895 and MD 61/262.

[64] For an overview of this system see Lütfi Güçer, "XVI. Yüzyıl Sonlarında Osmanlı İmparatorluğu Dahilinde Hububat Ticaretinin Tâbi Olduğu Kayıtlar," *İstanbul Üniversitesi İktisat Fakültesi Dergisi* 12 (1951): 79–98 and *Osmanlı İmparatorluğunda Hububat Meselesi.*

[65] E.g., MD 58/431 and MD 27/935. For more on famine relief, see Chapter 3.

[66] Murphey, "Provisioning Istanbul," 226.

[67] E.g., MD 27/935.

[68] On the logistics of overland transport, see Suraiya Faroqhi, "Camels, Wagons, and the Ottoman State in the Sixteenth and Seventeenth Centuries" *International Journal of Middle East Studies* 14 (1982): 523–39.

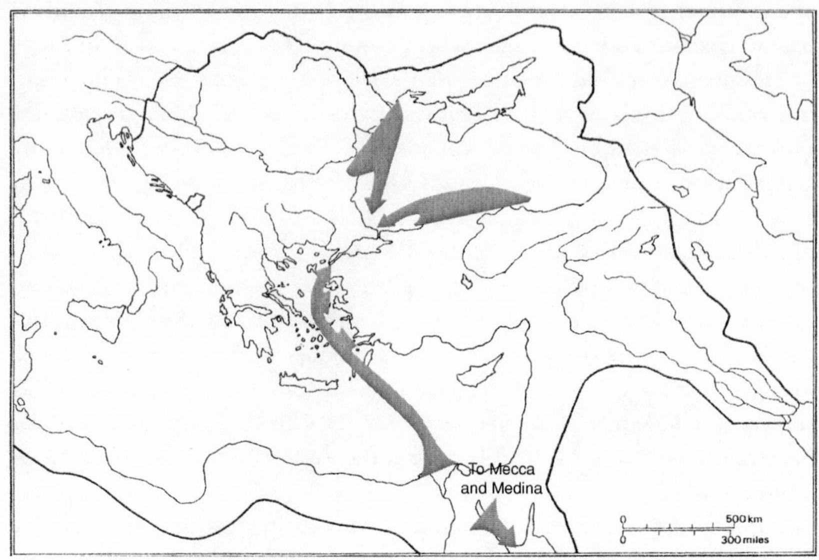

Approximate flows of Ottoman grain provisioning in the late sixteenth, based on the mühimme defters.

the grain administration worked with grain merchants through the guild system to spread risk, and at the same time required bakers and millers to keep extra stocks on hand to see through the inevitable breakdowns in supply.[69] Even once raw grain reached its destination, milling and baking presented additional obstacles requiring further state oversight: For example, the simple undershot watermills of the period suffered such frequent breakdowns in drought or freezing weather that the sultan had to order the construction of extra horse-powered mills to preserve a constant supply of flour for the capital.[70]

Sheep

Imperial sheep provisioning, known as the *celep-keşan* system, deserves particular attention here, both for its unusual nature and for the key role it would play in the crisis of the 1590s.[71] Given the low status of chicken

[69] Eyüp Özveren, "The Black Sea and the Grain Provisioning of Istanbul in the *Longue Durée*," in *Nourir les cités de Mediterranée – Antiquité-temps moderns*, ed. B. Marin and C. Virlouvet (Paris: Maisonneuve, 2003).

[70] MD 7/230, MD 7/273, and Ahmet Refik, *Onaltıncı Asırda İstanbul Hayatı* (Istanbul: Devlet Basımevi, 1935), chapter 8, document 22.

[71] The only detailed studies on sheep provisioning remain Anthony Greenwood, "Istanbul's Meat Provisioning: A Study of the Celep-Keşan System" (PhD diss., University of

and goats, religious taboos on pigs, and the rarity of beef cattle, sheep supplied most of the meat, lard, and dairy of the empire. Figures on Istanbul's meat consumption vary widely, but by the time of the Little Ice Age crisis the total was probably in the range of 1.5 million sheep annually, with 70,000 destined for the imperial kitchen alone.[72] Figures for other Ottoman cities remain unknown, but may have amounted altogether to another million head. Meanwhile, sheep sent on the hoof supplied the principal source of protein for soldiers away on campaign.

Rather than centrally manage supplies and delivery for imperial sheep provisioning, the state left the task to contractors pressed into service. Periodically, the central administration had provincial officials designate men as "*celeps,*" who had to provide a particular number of sheep each year at the *narh* as a kind of special tax. Strangely, the records do not describe most *celeps* as sheep farmers but rather as wealthy men from all walks of life, especially "usurers," suggesting that officials may have assigned them the tax as punishment for the disreputable practice of money-lending.[73] The only particular qualification was that they had the proper "means of support" (*tahammül*), a term that would come up repeatedly as the system started to break down in the Little Ice Age crisis. To ensure year-round supply, the sheep administration appointed *celeps* by season, giving most attention to the difficult winter deliveries.[74] In theory, a sliding scale of fixed prices between the provinces, major cities, and the capital allowed the *celeps* to buy up flocks where they lived and sell at Istanbul and other key destinations for enough profit to cover the cost of delivery. Moreover, when it worked, the price gradient encouraged additional private sales of sheep from the countryside to the right urban markets.

Despite the high price of drovers and the dangers of the drive, sheep had some of the lowest transportation costs of any commodity since they could deliver themselves on the hoof. As with grain, the Danube region met the greatest share of demand. Comprehensive accounts are lacking,

Chicago, 1988); Faroqhi, *Towns and Townsmen,* chapter 9; and Bistra Cvetkova, "Le service des celep et le ravitaillement en bétail dans l'Empire ottoman (XVe–XVIIIe s.)," *Études historiques* 3 (1966): 145-72.

72 Greenwood, "Istanbul's Meat Provisioning," 8–16. For comparison, London in the early eighteenth century is thought to have consumed about 600,000 sheep, 100,000 beeves, and 100,000 calves – figure cited in Keith Thomas, *Man and the Natural World* (New York: Oxford University Press, 1983), 26.

73 Greenwood, "Istanbul's Meat Provisioning," chapter 3.

74 Ibid., 121–3.

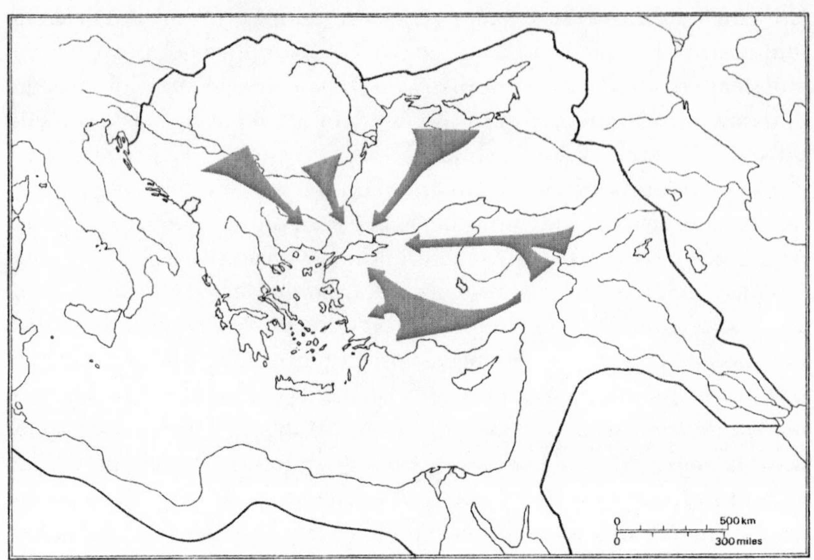

Approximate flows of Ottoman sheep provisioning in the late sixteenth, based on the mühimme defters.

but Balkan historians have estimated that the region delivered around 440,000 sheep annually in this period,[75] and one imperial order implies the area delivered 472,000 sheep just in 1582.[76] Others suggest that by then Moldovia alone sent some 300,000 per year,[77] while anecdotally, the other Balkan principalities often supplied about 200,000 at a time.[78] The autonomous Crimea, another rich pastoral region, typically sent its tax and tribute in animal products, especially lard and clarified butter, constituting the next major source. Given the relative ease of transport, the state could also reach deep into central and eastern Anatolia for supplies as well, sometimes from settled farmers and sometimes from nomadic Türkmen tribes. These requisitions reached significant totals – tens of thousands annually, and near a hundred thousand in emergencies – but never the hundreds of thousands regularly sent from up north.[79] Once deliveries arrived, the administration regulated the shares of meat to be allotted first among the designated slaughter-houses outside the

75 Figure cited in Sugar, *Southeastern* Europe, 125.
76 MD 48/705.
77 MD 53/294.
78 Greenwood, "Istanbul's Meat Provisioning," 22–7.
79 E.g., MD 14/180.

city gates and next among the butcher shops for sale to the public at the official fixed price.[80]

The three commodities studied here play the largest role in the story to follow, but Ottoman provisioning systems encompassed far more still. Virtually all war matériel involved imperial management drawing on a range of resources from across the empire.[81] The state owned mines of precious metals and important ores throughout Anatolia and the Balkans.[82] Imperial gunpowder brought together saltpeter from state-directed mines in Karaman (south-central Anatolia)[83] and charcoal from specialized sources in unlikely places: the *palamud* oak of Anatolia, the Lebanese willow, and the Syrian poplar.[84] Horses and camels, whether for transportation or for war, demanded considerable state oversight in matters such as grazing lands[85] and supplies for the imperial stables,[86] along with management of the nomadic tribes who bred and reared the animals in the first place (see the following section). For the navy, tar, resin, lead, iron, sailcloth, and hemp were each just as indispensable as timber, and each demanded additional measures of procurement.[87] Even commodities without obvious strategic value could come under state systems of regulation: At times, the empire banned exports of goods as diverse as fruit,[88] goat hides, wax, and honey.[89] It set fixed prices and forbade speculation in commodities such as oil, lard, and even onions,[90] and occasionally restricted the making of wine to save grapes for pickles and grape molasses (*pekmez*).[91] It made special arrangements for the supply of various goods from alum[92] to sugar.[93] Salt provisioning demanded

80 Greenwood, "Istanbul's Meat Provisioning," 45–8.

81 On military materiel in general, see Gabor Agoston, *Guns for the Sultan* (New York: Cambridge University Press, 2004).

82 Ibid., chapter 6.

83 Although other sources are occasionally mentioned in the imperial orders, the Karaman mines figure by far the most frequently. The most complete discussion of saltpeter supply in the documents occurs in MD 12/800–810.

84 V. J. Parry, "Materials of War in the Ottoman Empire," in *Studies in the Economic and Social History of the Middle East*, ed. M. Cook (London: Oxford University Press, 1970).

85 E.g., MD 12/57.

86 E.g., MD 3/187.

87 Faroqhi, *Towns and Townsmen*, 126–31, and Bostan, *Osmanlı Bahriye Teşkilâtı*, 121–46.

88 E.g., MD 61/172.

89 E.g., MD 6/71.

90 E.g., MD 5/129.

91 E.g., MD 5/484. The empire's Jews and Christians could usually make wine for their own consumption.

92 Faroqhi, *Towns and Townsmen*, 145–6.

93 E.g., MD 71/565.

heavy state investment, record-keeping, and tax incentives;[94] and rice production involved a complex system all to itself.[95]

While this provisioning functioned smoothly, the end result was a well-fed capital of around half a million inhabitants and perhaps the most powerful military in the sixteenth-century world. Although Istanbul remained in the words of one historian a "stomach capital" ("*capitale-ventre*")[96] – an engine of pure consumption, producing little of its own – its people seldom faced serious shortages before the onset of the Little Ice Age. Ottoman armies reached over 100,000 men, with tens of thousands more auxiliaries, while the fleet might hold as many as 50,000 at a time.[97] However, the empire's soldiers remained among the best supplied in the world.

During major military mobilizations, imperial demands could soar, pushing the system to its limits.[98] Preparations began months before the start of the spring campaign season, getting underway by the previous autumn at the latest. The imperial government took inventory of ships and other transportation and planned the stocking of supply stations for the army's outward march.[99] For the navy, the first task was to outfit the fleet, and next to provide the hardtack that served as the staple provision for the 200 to 300 men aboard each vessel.[100] Army provisioning demanded a balance of goods shipped in from the farthest corners of empire and local supplies for ready use. Both demands were met primarily by extraordinary taxes in cash and kind (*avarız* and *nüzul*) and forced purchases (*sürsat*) of grain, sheep, and other goods, typically

94 See Lütfi Güçer, "XV.–XVII. Asırlarda Osmanlı İmparatorluğunda Tuz İnhisarı ve Tuzlaların İşletme Nizamı," *İstanbul Üniversitesi İktisat Fakültesi Mecmuası* 23 (1962/63): 81–143.

95 Halil İnalcık, "Rice Cultivation and the *Çeltükçi-Re'âyâ* System in the Ottoman Empire," *Turcica* 14 (1982): 69–141. Chapter 2 will consider rice agriculture in more detail.

96 Robert Mantran, *Istanbul dans la seconde moitié du XVIIe siècle* (Paris: Maisonneuve, 1962), part II, chapter 1.

97 For calculations of military manpower, see Rhoads Murphey, *Ottoman Warfare 1500–1700* (New Brunswick, NJ: Rutgers University Press, 1999), 35–49; and for naval strength, see Çızakça, "Ottomans and the Mediterranean."

98 For details of Ottoman warfare and administration, see Agoston, *Guns for the Sultan*; Murphey, *Ottoman Warfare*; and Caroline Finkel, *The Administration of Warfare* (Vienna: VWGÖ, 1988).

99 Gilles Veinstein, "Some Views on Provisioning in the Hungarian Campaigns of Suleyman the Magnificent," in *Osmanistische Studien zur Wirtschafts- und Sozialgeschichte in Memoriam Vančo Boškov*, ed. H. Majer (Wiesbaden: O. Harrassowitz, 1986).

100 E.g., MD 6/643 and MD 6/1469. For the size of crews on various vessels see Çızakça, "Ottomans and the Mediterranean."

coming from the provinces of the core.[101] Horses still had to find grazing land locally, and in hard times it proved impossible to stop soldiers from extorting from provincial populations. Nevertheless, the Ottoman system, though far from perfect, probably delivered a better provisioned army at less cost to the local inhabitants than any other from Spain to India at the time.[102]

Settlement

Yet whether in war or peace, the most important resource of all was people: people to cut the timber, to grow the grain and herd the sheep, and to extract the resources and transport them for the demands of the imperial capital and military.[103] As their empire expanded rapidly in the fifteenth and early sixteenth centuries, the Ottomans inherited lands depopulated by centuries of war and plague.[104] Wages in the empire remained high in relation to other costs, compelling the Porte to conscript, mobilize, move around, and otherwise coerce and cajole labor as much as any other resource.[105] Where skilled labor or large projects were called for, the imperial government might send for workers from halfway across the empire. However, for the basic tasks of working the land and extracting raw materials, the state needed to extend settlement far and wide, dealing with the distribution of subjects almost as it dealt with the distribution of key commodities. Over time, the empire developed systems of landholding and settlement to promote agriculture and manage land use and labor while maximizing imperial oversight and taxation, particularly in the core provinces.

[101] E.g., MD 12/397, MD 12/517, MD 44/262.

[102] For logistical problems in early modern Europe, see Martin van Creveld, *Supplying War: Logistics from Wallerstein to Patton* (New York: Cambridge University Press, 2004), chapter 1. On military provisioning in Mughal India, see Stewart Gordon, "War, the Military, and the Environment: Central India, 1560–1820" in R. Tucker and E. Russell, eds., *Natural Enemy, Natural Ally* (Eugene: University of Oregon Press, 2004).

[103] For another view on people as "the ultimate resource" in the Mediterranean, see Horden and Purcell, *Corrupting Sea*, 377–80.

[104] Uli Schamiloglu, "The Rise of the Ottoman Empire: The Black Death in Medieval Anatolia and Its Impact on Turkish Civilization," in *Views from the Edge: Essays in Honor of Richard Bulliet*, ed. N. Yavari et al. (New York: Columbia University Press, 2004).

[105] For more on labor, see Suraiya Faroqhi, "Labor Recruitment and Control in the Ottoman Empire (16th-17th Centuries)," in *Manufacturing in the Ottoman Empire and Turkey*, ed. D. Quataert (Binghamton: SUNY Press, 1994).

Despite the size and number of Ottoman cities, peasant farmers and pastoralists still constituted the great majority of the empire's population. The Ottoman sultans termed these subjects the *reaya*, roughly translated as the "flock"; and in many respects, it proved an apt metaphor for an imperial government that sought to herd its people to favorable land and earn the most from their products. To be sure, it fleeced them too – but not too harshly. Ottomans rulers had inherited the traditional Islamic concept of a "circle of justice," in which the peasantry provided revenues for the sultan and his army, who in turn provided security and justice for the peasantry.[106] Although more an ideal than a practical principle, in the Ottomans' better days this "circle" resembled the truth much more than any European notion of "oriental despotism." So long as circumstances permitted, rulers and their officials willingly compromised and adapted policies to secure their subjects' consent to Ottoman rule.[107] There are even indications that some Christians from the "abode of war" beyond the empire sought a better life in Ottoman lands during the classical age.[108]

Legally speaking, the *reaya* held the status of free peasantry, released from the servile conditions that had prevailed in much of pre-Ottoman Anatolia and the Balkans.[109] Most became, in practice, hereditary tenants of the sultan's crown land (*miri*), which comprised most of the empire's territory.[110] Theoretically immune from the arbitrary exactions

[106] For more on the "circle of justice" in the context of Ottoman state consolidation, see Linda Darling, "Political Change and Political Discourse in the Early Modern Mediterranean World," *Journal of Interdisciplinary History* 38 (2008): 505–31.

[107] Amy Singer, *Palestinian Peasants and Ottoman Officials* (New York: Cambridge University Press, 1994), 2–3 *et passim*, draws a similar conclusion based on a detailed case study of the Jerusalem area.

[108] MD 7/166, for instance, orders local authorities in the Balkans to allow some of these Christians to resettle in Ottoman territory. Another example would be the mass relocation of Spanish Jews to Salonica in 1492.

[109] See İnalcık, *Economic and Social History*, vol. 1, for an overview of the system and Ömer Lütfi Barkan, *Türkiye'de Toprak Meselesi* (Istanbul: Gözlem Yayınları, 1980) for the classic study of its origins and development. Suraiya Faroqhi has also written extensively on the historiography of Ottoman agriculture and land use. See "Agriculture and Rural Life in the Ottoman Empire (ca. 1500–1878)," *New Perspectives on Turkey* 1 (1987): 3–34; "Rural Society in Anatolia and the Balkans During the Sixteenth Century, I," *Turcica* 9 (1977): 161–95; "Rural Society in Anatolia and the Balkans During the Sixteenth Century, II," *Turcica* 11 (1979): 103–53; and "Ottoman Peasants and Rural Life: The Historiography of the 20th Century," *Archivum Ottomanicum* 18 (2000): 153–82.

[110] See İnalcık, *Social and Economic History*, vol. 1, 110–14.

of landlords, they usually paid moderate taxes and held an inalienable and hereditary right of usufruct over their farms. Nevertheless, any land uncultivated for three years could be taken away and registered to another peasant, and the *reaya* were bound to their farms on penalty of a sharp fine (*çift-bozan akçesi*), unless they could ensure that someone else would work the fields and pay their taxes in their absence.[111] In each province, law codes (*kanunname*) offered further regulations on agriculture and property, often codifying local practice.

The independent peasant household (*hane*) working enough land to plow with a single pair of oxen (*çift*) constituted the building-block of the Ottoman agricultural economy. This *çift-hane* system, as it is known, was not often realized in practice. (See Chapter 2 for calculations of actual landholdings.) However, it served as the model for the Ottoman agrarian system (comparable in some respects to the equal-field ideal in imperial China). Such a holding would be held and inherited intact, with brothers working the land together in the case of multiple heirs. The goal was a self-sufficient peasant household that produced a healthy surplus to provide taxes and resources for the state.[112]

These taxes were mainly collected by *sipahis*, the prebendal cavalry force that constituted most of the Ottoman army until the seventeenth century. These soldiers held the land not as property, but as *tımars* – grants of land revenue given at the sultan's discretion in return for military service. The first level of taxation consisted of a tithe on grain and similar shares of other agricultural products (sheep, honey, oil, and so forth) paid out in kind to *tımar*-holders, who typically sold off the goods for cash, bringing food to the towns and coin into the rural economy. The second level was a fee (*çift resmi*) levied according to the size of farms (one *çift*, half a *çift*, or less) with a special rate levied on unmarried men (*mücerred*) – an assessment that demanded comprehensive cadastral surveys, allowing later historians to reconstruct the outlines of Ottoman population and land use.

From the rise of the empire in the fourteenth century to its early modern peak around 1590, the imperial government pursued a variety

[111] E.g., MD 5/18, MD 7/463, MD 36/915, and MD 51/105. See also Amy Singer, "Peasant Migration: Law and Practice in Early Ottoman Palestine," *New Perspectives on Turkey* 8 (1992): 49–65.

[112] For an overview of the *çift-hane* system and peasant tenure, see İnalcık, *Economic and Social History* vol. 1, chapter 6.

of policies to promote settlement and agriculture.[113] On the legal level, the Ottomans interpreted sharia creatively to encourage cultivation and reclamation. In Islamic law, the "improvement" (*ihya*) of "empty" (*mevat*) land conferred certain rights of use or ownership, growing out of traditions that encouraged irrigation and the planting of fruit trees in the desert. In Ottoman times, officials continued to grant land to men who established irrigation for rice, for instance,[114] while legal pronouncements (*fetvas*) established land rights for planting orchards on unused territory.[115] However, in the early Ottoman Empire, unlike the lands of classical Islam, the trouble was more often too many trees than too few, and Ottoman practice effectively extended the idea of improvement to include clearing and cultivation in woodlands and waste.[116] Among dozens of legal pronouncements on the topic from the fifteenth and sixteenth centuries, the following give a sense of the process:

> Question: A *sipahi*, Zeyd, has an empty forest on his *tımar* and has Amr clear the forest with his axe without paying him. If Amr clears the forest, plants and plows it, can Zeyd still say, "Give me a fee for it or I will give it to another"?
>
> Answer: No.
>
> Question: If Zeyd, one of the people of a village, clears and cultivates a parcel of forest in that village without the permission of the landlord, can the landlord register and give away that field?
>
> Answer: Yes. However, it is preferable he give it to Zeyd.[117]

Islamic law also handed the sultan control of most imperial land simply by right of conquest, permitting the imperial government to use land grants strategically in order to promote permanent settlement.[118] In the earlier years of expansion, these grants came in a manner known

[113] Remarkably little has been written about Ottoman settlement policies per se. For an overview and examples from the *mühimme defters*, see Hüseyin Arslan, *Osmanlı'da Nüfus Hareketleri* (Istanbul: Kaknüs, 2001).

[114] İnalcık, "Rice Cultivation and the *Çeltükçi-Re'âyâ* System."

[115] See Colin Imber, "The Status of Orchards and Fruit-Trees in Ottoman Law," in *Studies in Ottoman History and Law* (Istanbul: Isis, 1996).

[116] See Ronald Jennings, "The Society and Economy of Macuka in the Ottoman Judicial Registers of Trabzon, 1560–1640," in *Continuity and Change in Late Byzantine and Early Ottoman Society*, ed. A. Bryer and H. Lowry (Birmingham: University of Birmingham, 1986).

[117] Kutluk, *Tükiye Ormancılığı ile İlgili Tarihi Vesikalar*, chapter 2. This sort of question and answer format is standard for *fetvas*, and "Zeyd" and "Amr" are the sharia equivalent of John Doe.

[118] Barkan, "Türkiye'de Toprak Meselesinin Tarihi Esasları" in *Türkiye'de Toprak Meselesi.*

as *temlik*, wherein the sultan gave large tracts to elite followers as freehold. In some cases, these grants targeted border regions to encourage conquest and settlement of the frontiers, and in other cases the sultan chose unpopulated or rebellious lands, the better to secure new imperial acquisitions.[119] In time, partible inheritance, escheatment, and occasionally confiscation would break up the large freeholds, unless the families converted their property to permanent pious endowments (*vakıfs*).[120]

By the sixteenth century, sultans tended to grant land directly as *tımars* rather than freehold, often with the same explicit intention to promote settlement. A typical order from 1564/5 targeted the thinly populated lands of western Iraq:

> To the provincial governor (*beylerbey*) of Baghdad:
>
> You have sent the following letter: "In the newly surveyed district (*sancak*) of Kurdistan and elsewhere in the province (*vilayet*) of Baghdad there are some empty and ruined lands. These are places that do not belong to the sultan's lands nor the district governor's lands nor to holders of any *tımar*, and that are capable of cultivation. If they were granted as *tımars*, then in due course they might be rendered flourishing as they ought." The provincial secretary has declared, "As it is, the appointment of these empty lands as *tımars* would be highly advantageous to the province." Now, as has been reported, the empty lands belong to no one. In order to cultivate unregistered and uncontested lands, let them be given as *tımars. So ordered*...[121]

Other examples include the creation of 230 *tımars* to improve empty land in the district of Mosul in 1568,[122] and another 120 in the district of Ardahan (near the present border between Turkey and Georgia) around the same time.[123] In other cases still, we find the land granted not to *tımars* but to pious foundations, although in a similar manner and with a similar goal.[124]

More often, the imperial government promoted settlement by offering special privileges and exemptions to colonists. Of particular note was the system of *derbends*, a type of colony originally created to secure key

[119] For more on this system, see the articles "Mülk Topraklar ve Sultanların Temlik Hakkı," "Osmanlı İmparatorluğu'nda Kuruluş Devrinin Toprak Meseleri," and "İmparatorluk Devrinde Toprak Mülk ve Vakıflarının Hususiyeti," in Barkan, *Tükiye'de Toprak Meselesi.*

[120] See the articles "Malikâne-Divânî Sistemi" and "İmparatorluk Devrinde Toprak Mülk ve Vakıflarının Hususiyeti," in Barkan, *Türkiye'de Toprak Meselesi.*

[121] MD 6/282.

[122] MD 7/2166.

[123] MD 7/462.

[124] E.g., MD 58/535.

nodes along the transportation network, especially bridges and mountain passes.[125] By the 1500s, at the latest, the Ottomans had adapted the system to plant strategically placed villages to secure critical areas around the empire. In a typical case, provincial authorities would identify an appropriate location and a number of households for settlement and then ask the provincial governor to recruit the settlers by offering permanent, hereditary exemption from extraordinary taxes. In turn, the new settlers remained bound to the land in perpetuity and forfeited the option to pay a fine and relocate like other peasants. On occasion, when assigned to dangerous areas, the *derbend* settlers also had the right to carry firearms and other weapons normally forbidden to *reaya*.

Ottoman authorities used such colonists to create a critical mass of population to tip the balance between wild and settled territory. As a number of reports attested, thinly settled lands tended to harbor bandits and rebellious tribes, driving out ordinary settlers and creating a downward spiral of depopulation and disorder.[126] *Derbends*, as fortified permanent colonies, were a way to reverse the cycle by creating a nucleus of settlement to attract more population and create security for agriculture and commerce. Examples from the imperial orders demonstrate the process at work in regions spread over the Balkans, Anatolia, and Syria.[127]

When incentives failed, the imperial government could take more stringent measures, including the forcible relocation of whole populations, known as *sürgün*.[128] Beginning as early as the 1350s, with the transfer of men from Anatolia to newly conquered lands in the Balkans, the practice expanded dramatically in the late fifteenth century as Sultan Mehmed II brought in hundreds of thousands of men to repopulate the city of Constantinople conquered in 1453.[129] Most

[125] Cengiz Orhonlu, *Osmanlı İmparatorluğunda Derbend Teşkilâtı* (Istanbul: İstanbul Üniversitesi, 1967) and Arslan, *Osmanlı'da Nüfus Hareketleri*, chapter 5.

[126] E.g., MD 6/337.

[127] E.g., MD 26/909, MD 35/452, and MD 36/229. See also Arslan, *Osmanlı'da Nüfus Hareketleri*, 260–75.

[128] For more on forced population transfers, see Ömer Lütfi Barkan, "Bir İskân ve Kolonizasyon Metodu Olarak Sürgünler," *İktisat Fakültesi Mecmuası* 11–15 (1949–1954); İlhan Tekeli, "Osmanlı İmparatorluğu'ndan Günümüze Nüfusun Zorunlu Yer Değiştirmesi ve İskân Sorunu," *Toplum ve Bilim*, 50 (1990): 49–71; and Arslan, *Osmanlı'da Nüfus Hareketleri*, chapter 6.

[129] Heath Lowry, "Pushing the Stone Uphill: The Impact of Bubonic Plague on Ottoman Urban Society in the Fifteenth and Sixteenth Centuries," *Osmanlı Araştırmaları* 23 (2003): 93–132.

examples, however, dealt with rural colonization, including the improvement of the land (*şenlendirmek*), the establishment of transportation networks (*seyahatı teşkilatlandırmak*), or the forced removal of dangerous elements including the transfer of some Anatolian tribes into the Balkans.[130]

The practice slowed somewhat by the sixteenth century, but it still proved useful on occasion. In the summer of 1568, for instance, the provincial governor of Baghdad complained that nearby Yazidi tribes were making trouble, so the sultan ordered him to "remove the Yazidis from the aforementioned villages and have them migrate to another land (*âhar yire göçürüp*)."[131] Likewise, when Christians on the island of Andıra oppressed the local Greeks and Albanians, the sultan ordered the provincial governor, "If there is an empty place on the island, have them migrate and settle there. If there is not, have them resettle on the island of Rhodes."[132] With the conquest of Cyprus in 1571, the use of *sürgün* expanded once more as the sultan turned to forced population transfers in order to resettle the island quickly, secure the new territory, and repopulate it with Muslims.[133]

However, the task of settlement involved much more than just bringing colonists to newly conquered lands. The empire had to deal with its diversity of terrain and land use, and to maximize taxes and resource extraction while still maintaining control of its widely dispersed and mobile population. To borrow a concept from James Scott's work, the Ottomans like other premodern agrarian empires faced the basic problem of keeping its population and land use "legible." As Scott explains for precolonial Southeast Asia, "The role of statecraft in this context becomes that of maximizing the productive settled population in such state spaces while at the same time drawing tribute from, or at least neutralizing, the nonstate spaces."[134] In the Ottoman case, there were not quite "nonstate spaces" but still vast stretches of territory at the margins of imperial control: the rugged mountains, the remote forests, and the arid lands fit only for nomadic pastoralism. While these lands offered vital resources – horses, camels, game, pasture, charcoal, ores, and so forth – they posed critical challenges for imperial administration

130 Barkan, "Bir İskân ve Kolonizasyon Metodu Olarak Sürgünler."

131 MD 7/1942.

132 MD 6/252.

133 Faroqhi, *Towns and Townsmen*, 282–4. For more on the settlement of Cyprus, see Chapter 4.

134 James Scott, *Seeing Like a State* (New Haven, CT: Yale University Press, 1998), 187.

and security.[135] Other empires of the time faced similar difficulties, but the Ottomans proved particularly tenacious at tackling the problem.[136]

The empire dealt especially harshly with mountain villagers, above all in the Balkans, where the difficult terrain harbored bandits and rebellious tribes.[137] Although the problem reached across the mountains of the Mediterranean, the Ottomans were probably unique in their determination to impose order as settlement advanced into difficult terrain. As Rhoads Murphey has observed, the Ottoman officials thought in terms of "taming the wildness of the landscape" in its northern frontiers.[138] Besides the use of *derbends* to control mountain passes,[139] the state sometimes engaged in the wholesale removal of troublesome mountain villages, forcibly resettling them in the valleys. In typical cases, imperial orders would outline the depredations of mountain bandits and follow with a command to "bring them down to the lowlands and make them settle" (*düzi yerlere indürüp iskân itdüresin*).[140]

The settlement of Macedonia has left us the most dramatic examples. In 1564, following complaints from the *kadı* of İşpat, the sultan issued an order revealing the tenacity of the conflict:

> You have sent a letter with the following information: "The village of Dardas in the *kaza* of İşpat occupies mountainous land. Previously, when my envoy (*çavuş*) Koçi brought down many rebellious villages from mountainous ground and settled them in the valley, the inhabitants of the aforementioned village did not obey. They gathered and broke into the houses of the *sipahis* and the *reaya*, murdered men, and plundered their goods and animals. When ordered by the court they still refused to obey. We cannot obtain justice from them, nor can the *reaya* resist their evil-doing."

135 Braudel, *Mediterranean*, part I, offers the classic description of this geography and its relation to settled society in the lowlands.

136 Cf. Chetan Singh, "Forests, Pastoralists, and Agrarian Society in Mughal India," in *Nature, Culture, and Imperialism*, ed. D. Arnold and R. Guha (Delhi: Oxford University Press, 1995).

137 E.g., MD 9/44, MD 22/65, and MD 48/424. See also Arslan, *Osmanlı'da Nüfus Hareketleri*, 217–20.

138 Rhoads Murphey, "Evolving Versus Static Elements in Ottoman Geographical Writing between 1598 and 1729: Perceptions, Perspectives and Real-Life Experience of 'The Northern Lands' (*Taraf Al-Shimali*) over 130 Years," *International Journal of Turkish Studies* 10 (2004): 73–82.

139 E.g., MD 40/323.

140 E.g., MD 14/832, MD 27/298, MD 27/353, and MD 58/126.

> *Urgently, so ordered:*
>
> When this command arrives, go to the aforementioned village unannounced. As a precaution, block all possible means of escape. Capture all the law-breaking, rebellious bandits and evil-doers and bring them under the sword. Plunder their wives and children and punish them as necessary so they might serve as a warning, so the other trouble-makers will obey. In the days of my reign, let the country and the *reaya* be secure from their depredations and let them live in peace and security . . .[141]

In the very same year in another *kaza* of the province, the state resorted to taking women and children hostage in order to force mountain villagers to capitulate.[142] In some cases, the same villagers would try to head back into the hills years later, only to meet new reprisals.[143]

Like mountains, dense forests also tested imperial control. Favored by the peasants for fuel, hunting, and gathering, they also served as a haven for bandits and anyone seeking escape from the reach of the state. Other countries around the Mediterranean faced similar challenges, but once again the Ottomans proved exceptional in their determination to advance settlement and preserve order, sometimes destroying entire forests.[144] "Around Leş (Albania)," one such order went, "there is a great forest. Thieves and criminals come and take shelter there constantly, nor do they refrain from crime and evil-doing. I command you immediately to burn the trees and make fields. *So ordered* . . ."[145] Likewise in 1577, a *kadı* near Edirne reported "that since there is empty land and a great forest, criminals are committing robbery," and so the sultan simply ordered him to "have the forest cut, make fields and improve the land to ward off crime and evil-doing."[146] On the military frontiers, Ottoman soldiers might also cut down forests where rebels or enemy forces could hide.[147]

Arid and semiarid pastoral land presented a more delicate challenge. At the time of conquest, nomadic and seminomadic tribes dominated the landscape: Türkmen in central and eastern Anatolia, Bedouin in

[141] MD 6/365.
[142] MD 6/677.
[143] MD 27/353 and MD 35/472.
[144] Cf. Roland Bechman, *Trees and Man: The Forest in the Middle Ages* (New York: Paragon House, 1990), 262–8 *et passim*.
[145] MD 26/636.
[146] MD 30/519.
[147] E.g., MD 10/224. Cf. John McNeill, "Woods and Warfare in World History," *Environmental History* 9 (2004): 388–410.

the Arab provinces, Tatars on the north shore of the Black Sea, and smaller mountain tribes in the Balkans.[148] As a rule, the empire preferred settled agriculture over pastoral nomadism, since agriculturalists generally provided more population, taxation, and resources. Nevertheless, vast tracts of the Near East remained unsuitable or marginal for cultivation, especially in the mountainous reaches of southern and eastern Anatolia and the desert lands of Arabia. Only nomadic pastoralists could make adequate use of the thin soil and rugged terrain by grazing sheep, goats, camels, and horses, often crossing hundreds of miles to reach upland pastures in the summer and lowland pastures in the winter. Furthermore, mobile nomadic tribes could provide vital transport and auxiliary services for Ottoman armies on the march.[149] Thus nomadic tribes presented a serious challenge to orderly administration and taxation, but also the only effective means to tap the resources of a harsh landscape.

The Ottomans pursued the twin goals of neutralizing the nomadic threat to settled agriculture while extracting the most it could from the tribes in animals, animal products, and military recruitment. It took registers of the nomads and their livestock, taxed their herds accordingly, and assigned specific winter and summer pastures and migration routes, punishing violations by sharp fines and the threat of military action.[150] The empire also called on some tribes, mostly Anatolian Türkmen, for the delivery of sheep for the capital and the military – on occasion up to 60,000 at a time.[151] Meanwhile, other groups such as the Atçeken of southern Anatolia and some Bedouin of the Hijaz provided the imperial stables with horses and the army with camels.

[148] On the ecology of nomads in the region, see Frederik Barth, *Nomads of South Persia* (New York: Humanities Press, 1964); Anatoly Khazanov, *Nomads and the Outside World* (Madison: University of Wisconsin Press, 1994); Lawrence Krader, "The Ecology of Nomadic Pastoralism," *International Social Science Journal* 11 (1959): 499–510; Xavier de Planhol, "Les nomades, la steppe, et la foret en Anatolie," *Geographische Zeitschrift* 52 (1965): 101–16; and Xavier de Planhol, *De la plaine pamphylienne aux lacs pisidiens: Nomadisme et vie paysanne* (Paris: Maisonneuve, 1958). For a summary of major nomad migration routes, see also Xavier Planhol, *Les fondements geographiques de l'histoire de l'Islam* (Paris: Flammarion, 1968), 235–43, and Güçer, *Osmanlı İmparatorluğunda Hububat Meselesi*, 14–16.

[149] Reşat Kasaba, *A Moveable Empire* (Seattle: University of Washington Press, 2009), 35 *et passim*.

[150] Rudi Lindner, *Nomads and Ottomans in Medieval Anatolia* (Bloomington: Indiana University Press, 1983).

[151] E.g., MD 12/927.

For these reasons, the Porte did not always side with agriculturalists at the expense of nomads as the expansion of settlement began to put the two sides into conflict. Rather, officials had to strike a fair balance, usually appealing to the traditional rights of both parties. In 1564, for instance, when a *kadı* from Kavala (northern Greece) wrote to complain that nomads (*yörük*) had come and "claiming it as their pasture, they have chewed up the fields and cut down fig trees to graze their sheep and goats," the sultan replied:

> . . . *So ordered*:
>
> When this command arrives personally go to the location in question. Bring the litigants together and that way investigate according to law. Let it be known where the aforementioned tribe has traditionally pastured its animals and what are the limits of the land where the abovementioned villagers have cultivated their fields. Apportion the traditional boundary in between and do not let the aforementioned tribe transgress from their pastures . . .[152]

In another case, the imperial government actually ordered the summary expulsion of *tımar*-holders around Diyarbakır who had moved into tribal land and started farming illegally, driving the nomads out of their summer pastures.[153] As Chapter 9 explains, tensions over land were building up gradually and would eventually reach a breaking point in the Little Ice Age crisis. However, in the meantime, successive Ottoman rulers managed more or less to preserve the delicate balance between the desert and the sown.

Conclusion: Ecology and Empire

The rebuilding of the fleet after Lepanto represented the culmination of decades, if not centuries, of imperial expansion and development. Every plank of every ship and every soldier and sailor gave testament to a working imperial management of resources and population. Taken together, Ottoman systems of provisioning and settlement had provided the imperial government an ever larger and more extensive command of commodities and labor, above all for the conduct of war. Although successive rulers had worked out these systems piecemeal and developed

[152] MD 6/300.

[153] MD 6/445–46. In this case, the imperial administration was also responding to warnings that the nomadic tribes in question might go over to the enemy Persians if the Ottomans could not entice them to remain on their side.

them pragmatically, together they reflected a common conception of provisionism and drove a far-reaching imperial ecology.

This Ottoman imperial ecology by no means constituted conservationism or resource management in the modern sense. Nor were the Ottomans environmentalists *avant la lettre.* Ottoman writings have left few traces of environmental sensibilities, or for that matter, little insight on how they viewed the natural world. Works of geography tended to focus on cartography, trade, and military campaigns,[154] while studies of Ottoman art history and architecture have revealed little more than a taste for public spaces and Persian-style gardens. Despite a growing body of literature on contemporary Islam and the environment, there are few indications that such ideas shaped perceptions or policies in Ottoman times.[155] Pre-Islamic traditions, including elements of shamanism and a cult of sacred trees,[156] may have influenced some Alevi groups, especially the heterodox sect of *Tahtacıs* (literally "woodcutters").[157] However, as the history of imperial China demonstrates,[158] spiritual beliefs about nature may have little practical consequence when it comes to human impact on the environment. Ottoman documents reveal, for instance, that even protected state forests might be logged to excess and erosion when the need arose.[159] If they deemed it necessary, imperial authorities could violate even the most basic environmental precepts of traditional

154 For an overview of Ottoman geographical literature, see Mustafa Ak, "Osmanlı Coğrafya Çalışmaları," *Türkiye Araştırmaları Literatür Dergisi* 2 (2004): 163–211.

155 E.g., Oğuz Erdur, "Reappropriating the "Green": Islamist Environmentalism," *New Perspectives on Turkey* 17 (1997): 151–66; M. Izzi Dien, *The Environmental Dimensions of Islam* (Cambridge, UK: Lutterworth, 2000); and J. Khalid and F. O'Brien, eds., *Islam and Ecology* (New York: Cassell, 1992). Yunus Macit, "Osmanlı Türklerinde Çevre Bilinci," *Türkler* 10 (2002): 589–97 and Ahmed Akgündüz, *İslam ve Osmanlı Çevre Hukuku* (Istanbul: Osmanlı Araştırmaları Vakfı, 2009) have looked for these approaches in Ottoman law and policy, but the only major "environmental" policies of the empire appear to those related to urban street cleaning, discussed in Chapter 10.

156 See Jean-Paul Roux, *Les traditions des nomades de la Turquie méridionale* (Paris: Maisonneuve, 1970) and Pervin Ergun, *Türk Kültüründe Ağaç Kültü* (Ankara: Atatürk Kültür Merkezi Başkanlığı, 2004).

157 İsmail Engin, "Tahtacılar: Kimdir ve Kökenleri Nereden Gelir?" *Toplumsal Tarih* 4–5 (1995–1996) and Ali Selçuk, *Tahtacılar* (Istanbul: Yeditepe, 2004).

158 Yi-Fu Tuan, "Discrepancies between Environmental Attitude and Behaviour: Examples from Europe and China," *Canadian Geographer* 12 (1968): 176–91 and Mark Elvin, "The Environmental Legacy of Imperial China," *China Quarterly* 156 (1999): 733–56.

159 E.g., MD 3/1255.

Islam, as when they uprooted desert date palms to punish recalcitrant Arab tribes.[160]

Yet however anachronistic it may appear to discuss imperial "ecology" among the Ottomans, the term captures the nature of their rule far better than the usual discussion of imperial "economy." Ottoman rulers had even less sense of abstract economic concepts like GDP than they had of ecosystems. Every transaction was bound up in matters of society, religion, and tradition; or as Mehmet Genç has put it, "in the tangled skein of religious, political, moral, family, social, and sectarian relations, to disentangle *purely economic dealings* would be as difficult as separating the sugar dissolved in a glass of tea."[161] Under the paradigm of ecology, with its appreciation of complex and unanticipated interactions and the dense interrelationships among populations and natural resources, we may actually come closer to the holistic Ottoman notion of imperial rule and its management of provisioning and settlement.

Likewise, it would prove equally anachronistic to think of the Ottoman Empire in the terms of a modern nation-state, as a set of boundaries, standardized institutions, and citizenship. The Ottomans belonged to no well-defined system of international law, and their empire had no official limits or membership. Not until the institution of quarantine in the nineteenth century did the Ottomans even lay down a precise border with Persia, and then only to prevent the spread of disease.[162] The Ottoman Empire was not so much an abstract entity of constitutions, laws, and treaties, as a working circulation of money, goods, soldiers, ships, and so forth. In this respect, the empire was actually defined by the resources it could command, including people; and the success or failure of Ottoman rule remained closely bound to the proper functioning of its provisioning and settlement systems. In 1571, as the empire rebounded from disaster at Lepanto, these systems appeared to function at their peak. Nevertheless, beneath the surface, the first signs of trouble were already stirring.

[160] Suraiya Faroqhi, *The Ottoman Empire and the World Around It* (Leiden: Brill, 2004), 87 (citing Uzunçarşılı).

[161] Genç, *Osmanlı İmparatorluğunda Devlet ve Ekonomi*, 44 (italics in original).

[162] Daniel Panzac, "Politique sanitaire et fixation des frontieres: l'exemple ottoman (XVIIe-XIXe siècles)," *Turcica* 31 (1999): 87–108. For more on the empire's integration into the modern state system, including the adoption of boundaries, see Richard Horowitz, "International Law and State Transformation in China, Siam, and the Ottoman Empire during the Nineteenth Century," *Journal of World History* 15 (2004): 445–86.

2

GROWTH AND ITS LIMITS

By the late sixteenth century, the Ottoman imperial ecology had begun to fall victim to its own success. After working for generations to settle a land ravaged by centuries of war and plague and to build up its military and capital city, the empire started to face problems of population pressure and resource scarcities. Ottoman numbers soared in the classical age, and agriculture in the core Mediterranean provinces expanded to the limits of arable land. As environmental, social, and technological barriers left the peasantry unable to keep up with rising demand, food production ran up against diminishing marginal returns. While the empire as a whole did not yet face a Malthusian crisis, some regions were approaching the limits of subsistence by the 1580s, and the margin of surplus for provisioning began to dwindle. In the meantime, landlessness, inflation, and unemployment were breeding a new class of desperate and potentially dangerous men.

Numbers

With few exceptions, the years from the late fifteenth to the late sixteenth centuries marked an era of growth across the Old World.[1] The Black Death had done its worst by the 1450s, and in spite of frequent new outbreaks, plague would never again kill off such a large proportion of the population as it had in the late Middle Ages. Man-made disasters proved less deadly as well. The Mongol and Timurid invasions had passed, the

[1] For a summary of demographic trends, see Massimo Livi-Bacci, *A Concise History of World Population*, 4th ed. (Malden, MA: Blackwell, 2006) and C. Liu, ed., *Asian Population History* (New York: Oxford University Press, 2001). The main exception here is Japan, where political fragmentation and warfare delayed growth until the era of unification around the turn of the seventeenth century. In the New World, the invasion of European microbes had devastated the population, which would not recover for at least another century.

Hundred Years War had come to an end, and stronger, more stable states had emerged from Tudor England to Ming China. New World resources, particularly New World crops like potatoes and maize, began trickling in over the Atlantic and Pacific. Above all, as discussed in Chapter 5, the Northern Hemisphere was enjoying a period of relatively warm and mild climate.

Broadly speaking, Ottoman demography fit into a characteristic Mediterranean pattern. Decades ago, Braudel demonstrated that populations around the sea roughly doubled over the course of the century, totaling perhaps some 60 million or 70 million by the Battle of Lepanto in 1571.[2] When Braudel first published his estimates, however, Ottoman demography remained a mystery, or at best, a subject for mere conjecture. His own estimates yielded about 8 million for Turkey and the Levant, perhaps a little more for the Balkans, and maybe 2 million to 3 million apiece for Egypt and the Maghreb, bringing the total to some 22 million for the eastern Mediterranean in the late sixteenth century.[3] Braudel did not even venture guesses as to the population of Iraq, the Hijaz, Yemen, Habesh, and the Crimea, but these would not likely have added much to the total.

However, as Braudel acknowledged, research in the Ottoman archives had already begun to revise those estimates upward. The key to this new research was the discovery of vast numbers of comprehensive regional cadastral surveys covering most of the empire's core provinces.[4] The more detailed among these, called *mufassal tahrir defters*, enumerated every household in a region, its landholding, the productivity of farming, and all its tithes and taxes. The empire undertook such surveys beginning in the late fifteenth century, usually on the conquest of new land, following up about once every generation. At the least, we tend to have *tahrirs* of greater or lesser detail from the 1520s or the 1530s, and again from the 1560s or the 1570s for most districts from Bulgaria to Palestine.[5]

[2] Braudel, *Mediterranean*, vol. 2, 394–417.

[3] Braudel, *Mediterranean*, vol. 2, 395–6.

[4] On the origin and compilation of the *tahrirs*, see Halil İnalcık, "Ottoman Methods of Conquest," *Studia Islamica* 2 (1954): 103–29.

[5] For the original work on *tahrirs*, see Ömer Lütfi Barkan, "'Tarihî Demografi' Araştırmaları ve Osmanlı Tarihi," *Türkiyat Mecmuası* 10 (1953): 1–26; "Türkiye'de İmparatorluk Devirlerinin Nüfus ve Arazi Tahrirleri ve Hâkana Mahsus İstatik Defterleri (I)," *İktisat Fakültesi Mecmuası* 2 (1940): 20–59; and "Türkiye'de İmparatorluk Devirlerinin Nüfus ve Arazi Tahrirleri ve Hâkana Mahsus İstatik Defterleri (II)," *İktisat Fakültesi Mecmuası* 2 (1941): 214–47.

Table 2.1. *Barkan's Population Estimates*

Region	1520s–1530s	1570s–1580s	Change
Total Empire	12 million–12.5 million (excl. Egypt, etc.)	30 million–35 million	**~150% (incl. new provinces)**
Anadolu (west-central Anatolia)	2.4 million	3.4 million	**42%**
Karaman (south-central Anatolia)	0.75 million	1.3 million	**73%**
Zülkadriye (inner Anatolia)	300,000	550,000	**83%**
Rum (east-central Anatolia)	500,000	900,000	**80%**
Rum-i Hadis (north-east Anatolia)	380,000	570,000	**50%**
Balkans (total)	4.7 million	8 million	**70%**

While by no means a modern census, these surveys allow us to make some reasonably accurate counts of taxable households in both rural and urban areas. Assuming a multiplier of five persons per household,[6] Ömer Lutfi Barkan arrived at estimates of 12 million to 12.5 million for the empire in the 1520s, excluding Iraq, Egypt, and the other more distant provinces. Looking at *tahrirs* from the 1570s, and adding in the estimated populations of Egypt and Iraq, Barkan then arrived at a figure of some 30 million to 35 million by the later date.[7] Table 2.1 summarizes his findings.

6 This issue of the "household multiplier" has grown complicated and contested, but it seems Barkan's estimate was basically correct. For various examples of Ottoman household size, see Leila Erder, "The Measurement of Pre-Industrial Population Changes: The Ottoman Empire from the 15th to the 17th Century," *Middle East Studies* 11 (1975): 284–301; Tomoki Okawara, "Size and Structure of Damascus Households in the Late Ottoman Period as Compared with Istanbul Households," in *Family History in the Middle East*, ed. Beshara Doumani (Binghamton: SUNY Press, 2003); Ömer Demirel, "1700–30 Tarihlerinde Ankara'da Ailenin Niceliksel Yapısı," *Belleten* 54 (1990): 945–61; Nejat Göyünç, "'Hâne' Deyimi Hakkında," *İstanbul Üniversitesi Edebiyat Fakültesi Tarih Dergisi* 32 (1979): 331–48; and Kemal Karpat, "The Ottoman Family: Documents Pertaining to Its Size," *International Journal of Turkish Studies* 4 (1987): 137–45. This book presents some new evidence on the issue in Chapter 10.

7 Ömer Lütfi Barkan, "Essai sur les données statistiques de régistres de recensement dans l'Empire ottoman aux XVe et XVIe siècles," *Journal of the Economic and Social History of the Orient* 1 (1958): 9–36 and "Research on the Ottoman Fiscal Surveys," in *Studies in the Social and Economic History of the Middle East*, ed. M. Cook (London: Oxford University Press, 1970).

Barkan's research remained incomplete on his death, and his estimates for the 1570s never gathered the same foundation of evidence as his survey of the 1520s. The higher estimate of 30 million to 35 million in particular has garnered some criticism.[8] Nevertheless, more recent work on the *tahrirs* has tended to support his figures, at least in the core provinces covered by the surveys. In the decades since Barkan, dozens of lesser-known Ottomanists have undertaken research into the same documents, and their findings have generally matched his. Despite some imperfections in methodology and inconsistencies in results, these *tahrir* studies have left an overwhelming impression of rapid demographic growth.[9] In fact, most suggest that the increase actually exceeded the roughly 70 percent growth Barkan had estimated for Anatolia and the Balkans between the 1520s and 1580s. Some areas scarcely grew at all, but most grew rapidly – in some cases doubling or even tripling in sixty years – reaching well over the 1 percent annual growth often considered the maximum for preindustrial populations.[10] By sampling regional surveys from different parts of the empire, Table 2.2 gives a sense of the overall pattern.

Outside of Anatolia, the data are less comprehensive, but the results still point in the same direction. In the region of Tatar Pazarcık, for example, *tahrirs* indicate that population doubled over the century,[11] and that pattern seems to hold true in most of the rest of Bulgaria and Bosnia as well.[12] In Greece, the picture is more mixed: Some regions more than doubled their population in the late fifteenth to late

[8] Halil İnalcık, "Impact of the *Annales* School on Ottoman Studies and New Findings," *Review* 1 (1978): 69–96.

[9] For a survey of these works, see Erhan Afyoncu, "Türkiye'de Tahrir Defterlerine Dayalı Olarak Hazırlanmış Çalışmalar Hakkında Bazı Görüşler," *Türkiye Araştırmaları Literatür Dergisi* 1 (2003): 267–86.

[10] Sallares, *Ecology of the Ancient Greek World*, 95 *et passim*, finds a similar pattern of growth in ancient times, which suggests that regional population could grow much faster while still expanding into uncultivated lands.

[11] Machiel Kiel, "Tatar Pazarcık: A Turkish Town in the Heart of Bulgaria, Some Brief Remarks on Its Demographic Development 1485–1874," in *X. Türk Tarih Kongresi* (Ankara: TTK, 1986).

[12] Machiel Kiel, "Ottoman Sources for the Demographic History and the Process of Islamisation of Bosnia-Hercegovina and Bulgaria in the Fifteenth–Seventeenth Centuries," *International Journal of Turkish Studies* 10 (2004): 93–119; Machiel Kiel, "The Ottoman Imperial Registers: Central Greece and Northern Bulgaria in the 15th–19th Century, the Demographic Development of Two Areas Compared," in *Reconstructing Past Population Trends in Mediterranean Europe (3000BC–1800AD)*, ed. K. Sbonias and J. Bintliff (Oxford: Oxbow, 1999); and Hatidza Car Drnda, "Pljevlja'd (Taşluca) Nüfusun Yapısı – 15. Yüzyılın İkinci Yarısı ve 16. Yüzyıl," *Belleten* 74 (2010): 113–26.

Table 2.2. *Population and Growth Estimates for Various Regions of the Empire (figures in households)*

Region	1520s–1530s	1570s–1580s	Change
Northern Anatolia			
Gedegra (*kaza*)[a]	3,605	8,712	142%
Samsun (*kaza*)[b]	2,321	3,597	55%
Kafirni (*nahiye*)	1,094	3,286	73%
Çorumlu (*nahiye*)	1,974	3,522	78%
Niksar (*nahiye*)[c]	2,181	6,100	180%
Western Anatolia			
Aydın (5 *kazas*)	4,666	6,181	32%
Hamid (13 *kazas & nahiyes*)[d]	9,907	17,240	74%
Uluborlu (*nahiye*)	1,706	4,042	150%
İznik (*nahiye*)	962	1,104	15%
Eastern Anatolia			
Mindaval (*nahiye*)[e]	413	861	109%
South/Central Anatolia			
Kayseri (*kaza*)[f]	2,364	8,251	261%
Larende (*kaza*)[g]	6,104	14,810	143%

[a] Mehmet Öz, "Tahrir Defterlerine Göre Vezirköprü Yöresinde İskân ve Nüfus (1485–1576)," *Belleten* 57 (1993): 509–31.

[b] Mehmet Öz, "XVII. Yüzyıl Ortasına Doğru Canik Sancağı," in *Prof. Dr. Bayram Kodaman'a Armağan*, ed. Mehmet Ali Ünal (Samsun: n.p., 1993).

[c] Huri İslamoğlu, *State and Peasant in the Ottoman Empire* (Leiden: Brill, 1994), appendices.

[d] Michael Cook, *Population Pressure in Rural Anatolia, 1450–1600* (London: Oxford University Press, 1972), appendices.

[e] H. İslamoğlu and S. Faroqhi, "Crop Patterns and Agricultural Production Trends in Sixteenth-Century Anatolia," *Review* 2 (1979): 401–36.

[f] Ronald Jennings, "The Population, Society, and Economy of the Region of Erçiyes Dağı in the 16th Century," in *Contributions á l'histoire économique et sociale de l'Empire ottoman*, ed. J. Bacqué-Grammont and P. Dumont (Louvain: Peeters, 1983).

[g] Osman Gümüşçü, *Tarihî Coğrafya Açısından Bir Araştırma* (Ankara: TTK, 2001), chapter 3. NB: This figure includes all tax-paying males (*nefer*) rather than households (*hane*).

sixteenth centuries,[13] while others made few gains at all.[14] The population of Hungary, the furthest region for which we have *tahrirs*, held steady from the late 1400s to the 1580s – a remarkable achievement considering the constant warfare along the Habsburg

[13] Kiel, "Ottoman Imperial Registers."

[14] F. Zarinebaf, J. Bennet, and J. Davis, *A Historical and Economic Geography of Ottoman Greece* (Athens: American School of Classical Studies, 2005), 10–20.

border.[15] A survey of the tri-border region around Syria, Turkey, and Iraq has also found characteristically rapid growth.[16] For example, the *tahrirs* of Jabal Sima'an outside of Aleppo indicate the number of households grew some 85 percent from 1519 to 1570.[17] Population estimates for southern Syria and Palestine are less consistent, often growing rapidly in the first half of the century before gradually leveling out.[18] Data for other parts of the Arab world, unfortunately, are slender to nonexistent. Nevertheless, these exceptions do little to alter the overall impression of strong demographic growth throughout the empire.

Moreover, we have every reason to believe that these numbers are, if not perfect, at least highly indicative of overall population trends. Although some Ottomanists have pointed out shortcomings in the *tahrirs*, none of these flaws are fatal, and no one has yet proposed why the empire would have gone through the time and expense of compiling the figures every generation if they did not serve a real need.[19] Furthermore, regional surveys of past settlement patterns by both historical geographers[20] and archaeologists[21] have supported the picture of

[15] Geza David, "16.–17. Yüzyıllarda Macaristan'ın Demografik Durumu," *Belleten* 59 (1995): 341–52; Geza David, "Data on the Continuity and Migration of the Population in 16th Century in Ottoman Hungary," *Acta Orientalia Hungarica* 45 (1991): 219–52; Geza David, "Demographische Veranderungen in Ungarn zur Zeit der Türkenherrschaft," *Acta Historica* 39 (1988): 79–87; and Rácz, "Price of Survival," 28–9.

[16] N. Göyünç and W. Hütteroth, *Land an der Grenze* (Istanbul: EREN, 1997).

[17] Margaret Venzke, "The Question of Declining Cereals Production in the 16th Century: A Sounding on the Problem-Solving Capacity of the Ottoman Cadastres," *Journal of Turkish Studies* 8 (1984): 251–64, at 254.

[18] W. Hütteroth and K. Abdulfattah, *Historical Geography of Palestine, Transjordan and Southern Syria* (Erlangen: Fränkische Geographische Ges., 1977), chapter 3, and Singer, *Palestinian Peasants*, 30–2. Note that the later *tahrirs* in Palestine date from 1595–6 rather than the 1580s, and so they may already reflect some of the flight and mortality that started with the Great Drought of 1591–6 (see Chapter 6).

[19] For more views on the reliability of the *tahrirs*, see Afyoncu, "Türkiye'de Tahrir Defterlerine Dayalı Olarak Hazırlanmış Çalışmalar Hakkında Bazı Görüşler"; Bekir Kemal Ataman, "Ottoman Demographic History (14th–17th Centuries): Some Considerations," *Journal of the Economic and Social History of the Orient* 35 (1992): 187–98; Erder, "Measurement of Pre-Industrial Population Changes"; Dariusz Kolodziejczyk, "The Defter-i Mufassal of Kamaniçe from ca. 1681 – An Example of Late Ottoman Tahrir, Reliability, Function, Principles of Publication," *Osmanlı Araştırmaları* 13 (1993): 91–8; and Mehmet Öz, "Tahrir Defterlerindeki Sayısal Veriler," in *Osmanlı Devleti'nde Bilgi ve İstatik*, ed. H. İnalcık and Ş. Pamuk (Ankara: DİE, 2000).

[20] E.g., Wolf-Dieter Hütteroth, *Ländliche Siedlungen im südlichen Inneranatolien in den letzen vierhundert Jahren* (Göttingen: Universität Göttingen, 1968).

[21] E.g., Tony Wilkinson, "Demographic Trends from Archaeological Survey: Case Studies from the Levant and Near East," in *Reconstructing Past Population Trends in Mediterranean Europe (3000BC–1800AD)*, ed. J. Bintliff and K. Sbonias (Oxford: Oxbow, 1999).

growth painted by the cadastral surveys. The strongest objection to the *tahrirs* has been that they just captured more population as census techniques improved.[22] However, in that case we would expect the largest gains in population to fall between the earliest *tahrirs*, while the process was still developing, whereas the greatest increases typically come in the later 1500s. Others have suggested that the increases reflect migration rather than growth, but the numbers do not seem to match up,[23] and the region usually cited as the chief source of migrants – eastern Anatolia – also witnessed a considerable rise in population.[24]

The growing number of households may even understate the rise in real population. First, as growth accelerated, we would expect to find more children in each household and therefore a larger household multiplier.[25] Second, as the number of unmarried and landless men rose (see below), we would also expect to find more daughters living with parents and more extended families living together. Third, as vagrancy and migration accelerated in response to population pressure, the number left uncounted may have risen, too. Finally, we must consider that the *tahrirs* almost all stop in the 1570s or 1580s at the latest, while as we will see, the real crisis came in the 1590s. Taking all these factors into account, Barkan's higher estimate seems entirely reasonable.[26]

Finally, there may be one more reason to accept a peak of around 35 million for the late sixteenth century: The figure would more or less bring the population of Ottoman lands back to levels of Roman and early Byzantine times, when a strong empire had last kept the Eastern Mediterranean in security and prosperity.[27] The Ottoman classical age, in other words, represented one more cyclical upswing in the region's long cycle of crisis and recovery described in the introduction. Therefore, as

[22] See Göyünç and Hütteroth, *Land an der Grenze*, 123–6.

[23] Osman Gümüşçü, "Internal Migrations in Sixteenth Century Anatolia," *Journal of Historical Geography* 30 (2004): 231–48.

[24] According to Öz, "Tahrir Defterlerindeki Sayısal Veriler," the district of Harput nearly doubled and Canik grew some 60%–70%, while according to Jennings, "Urban Population in Anatolia," Erzurum, which was practically deserted at the turn of the century, had some 548 tax-paying adult males by 1585.

[25] Erder, "Measurement of Pre-Industrial Population Changes."

[26] Yunus Koç, "The Structure of the Population of the Ottoman Empire," in *The Great Ottoman-Turkish Civilization*, vol. 2, ed. Kemal Çiçek, 538, arrives at an estimate of closer to 30 million, even assuming a somewhat lower population for the newly conquered territories and only 60% growth in the core.

[27] For various estimates of ancient population levels, see Angus Maddison, *Contours of the World Economy, AD 1–2030* (New York: Oxford University Press, 2007), 32–7. In Ottoman times, populations may have been much higher in the northern Balkans, lower in Iraq and Egypt, and roughly similar elsewhere.

their population peaked, the Ottomans came face-to-face with the same ecological limitations as empires past.[28]

Population Pressure

The Ottoman Empire exemplified a general Eurasian and specifically Mediterranean pattern of early modern population pressure. From England to China, as growth accelerated in the late 1500s, the numbers of the landless and destitute rose even faster, and inflation and shrinking economic opportunities began to destabilize states and societies.[29] As Braudel first proposed, the situation proved especially dire in the Mediterranean, where diminishing marginal returns to agricultural land set in early, and food prices began rising by the 1550s or the 1560s. At some point in the 1590s, he argued, the pressure turned to crisis, and Italy and Spain were forced to open up to northern ships and northern grain, precipitating the relative decline of the region.[30] Studies of the Mediterranean grain trade[31] and regional studies of agriculture and population[32] have born out Braudel's conclusions for Mediterranean Europe; and for the last thirty years, research on Ottoman historical demography has largely pointed in the same direction.

In the 1970s, Michael Cook became the first to test Braudel's thesis against the *mufassal tahrir defters* previously described, offering some tentative support.[33] In the following two decades, Ottoman historians and historical demographers such as Leila Erder, Suraiya Faroqhi, and Huri İslamoğlu pursued a number of further regional studies, producing more evidence of population pressure and diminishing marginal returns on agriculture.[34] In the years since, a number of new Turkish historians

[28] For a detailed look at demographic growth and population pressure in the ancient world, see Sallares, *Ecology of the Ancient Greek World.*

[29] Goldstone, *Revolutions and Rebellions.*

[30] Braudel, *Mediterranean,* vol. 1, 505–6 *et passim.*

[31] E.g., Aymard, *Venise, Raguse, et la commerce de blé.*

[32] E.g., Emmanuel Le Roy Ladurie, *The Peasants of Languedoc* (Urbana: University of Illinois Press, 1976).

[33] Cook, *Population Pressure.*

[34] Erder, "Measurement of Pre-Industrial Population Changes"; Erder and Faroqhi, "Population Rise and Fall"; Suraiya Faroqhi, "Urban Development in Ottoman Anatolia (XVI.–XVII. Centuries)," *ODTÜ Mimarlık Fakültesi Dergisi* 7 (1982): 35–51; Suraiya Faroqhi, "Towns, Agriculture and the State in Sixteenth-Century Ottoman Anatolia," *Journal of the Economic and Social History of the Orient* 33 (1990): 125–56; and Huri İslamoğlu and Suraiya Faroqhi, "Crop Patterns and Agricultural Production Trends," *Review* 2 (1979): 401–36.

have also taken up the issue, usually in smaller local studies, often reaching stronger, more Malthusian conclusions, especially for the semi-arid regions of the empire.[35]

All of these studies draw on one or more of three key patterns in the cadastral surveys, all pointing to mounting population pressure in the later decades of the century. First, nearly everywhere populations rose, landholdings per household shrank, often drastically. While the *tahrirs* do not give a measure for every property in every survey, they generally indicate whether a family posessed a full *çift*, half a *çift*, or less. By this measure, it becomes apparent that the *çift-hane* ideal had completely broken down in most regions by the late 1500s as families parceled out their holdings among heirs in spite of imperial law. Cook's original study found that the *çift*:household ratio fell from 0.66 to 0.53 in Aydın, from 0.42 to 0.34 in Hamid, and from 0.44 to 0.27 in Rum between the 1520s and 1570s–80s. Virtually everywhere in Anatolia, the proportion of families with a full farmstead fell off dramatically, while those registered with little or no land grew at an accelerating pace.[36] The pattern holds for Greece and Bulgaria as well: According to Machiel Kiel's study of Boeotia, "In 1516 almost all peasants possessed a full farm (*çift*). In 1580 only a quarter of them still had one and a whole class of landless peasants had come into being."[37] Likewise, by one estimate, more than half the rural population of Mosul (northern Iraq) was already landless by mid-century, a problem that only grew worse in the following decades of population growth.[38]

Second, the *tahrirs* record a sudden increase in the number of registered "bachelors" (*mücerred*), suggesting an alarming rise in landlessness. Again, the Ottoman Empire appears to exemplify a typical sixteenth-century pattern: As land distribution grew more unequal, the number of the dispossessed multiplied far more quickly than the population as a whole.[39] In the extreme case of Aydın (in western Anatolia), records show the number of bachelors rising from 3 percent to 48 percent of

[35] Afyoncu, "Türkiye'de Tahrir Defterlerine Dayalı Olarak Hazırlanmış Çalışmalar." The most thorough, and also the most Malthusian, of these studies have come from Osman Gümüşçü and Oktay Özel.

[36] Oktay Özel, "Population Changes in Ottoman Anatolia: The 'Demographic Crisis' Reconsidered," *International Journal of Middle East Studies* 36 (2004): 183–205.

[37] Kiel, "Ottoman Imperial Registers," 199.

[38] Dina Khoury, *State and Provincial Society in the Ottoman Empire* (New York: Cambridge University Press, 1997), chapter 2.

[39] Goldstone, *Revolution and Rebellion*, 32–3.

adult male taxpayers over the course of the century. Likewise, in Hamid these *mücerred* figures rise from 2,353 to 10,037 over the course of the century – a 300 percent increase – even as the number of family households rose "only" 81 percent (from 9,519 to 17,240).[40] The pattern repeats itself across Anatolia: By 1576, the proportion of unmarried men to total households had reached 45.8 percent in Canik and 44.8 percent in Amasya. When adding in married but landless men (*caba*), then the proportions become truly depressing at 80 percent and 76 percent, respectively.[41] Of course, undercounting in the early *tahrirs* may exaggerate the apparent growth in numbers of *mücerreds*; and the term does not always translate as "bachelor" in the modern sense, because registration typically began at around twelve to fifteen years of age[42] and men probably married in their late twenties.[43] Nevertheless, the number of newly registered adolescents could at best account for only part of the total. Instead, the unmistakable impression is that more and more rural men suffered from a lack of land and other economic opportunities, and simply found it impossible to start a new household. Comparable findings for parts of early-seventeenth-century Spain[44] suggest that the Ottoman figures were not an exaggeration, but rather an indication of the same early modern Mediterranean pattern.

The third and most telling indicator of population pressure comes from records of tax yields and productivity. Despite some limitations in the data, careful analysis seems to provide a reasonably accurate view of food production, and it paints a grim picture of declining per capita output.[45] Almost everywhere figures are available, agriculture lagged far

40 Cook, *Population Pressure*, 25–7 and 84.

41 Özel, "Population Changes in Ottoman Anatolia."

42 See Geza David, "The Age of Unmarried Male Children in the *Tahrir Defters* (Notes on the Coefficient)," *Acta Orientalia Hungarica* 31 (1977): 347–57 and Cook, *Population Pressure*, appendix on *mücerreds*.

43 Ottoman records provide rather limited data for family reconstructions before the nineteenth century, but most anecdotal evidence points in the same direction. See Ö. Demirel et al., "Osmanlılarda Ailenin Demografik Yapısı," in *Sosyo-Kultürel Değişme Sürecinde Türk Ailesi* (Ankara: T. C. Başbakanlık Aile Kurumu, 1993); Alan Duben, "Turkish Families and Households in Historical Perspective," *Journal of Family History* 10 (1985): 75–97; A. Duben and C. Behar, *Istanbul Households: Marriage, Family and Fertility 1880–1940* (New York: Cambridge University Press, 1991); and Maria Todorova, *Balkan Family Structure and the European Pattern* (Washington, DC: American University Press, 1993).

44 See Geoffrey Parker, *Europe in Crisis, 1598–1648*, 2nd ed. (London: Blackwell, 2001), 16–17.

45 See Venzke, "Question of Declining Cereals Production" and "The Ottoman Tahrir Defterleri and Agricultural Productivity," *Osmanlı Araştırmaları* 17 (1997): 1–61.

behind population, at times falling to a fraction of previous levels. In one survey of ten districts of northern Anatolia, where the *tahrirs* suggest that populations doubled or even tripled from 1520 to 1574, wheat and barley production inched up only 30 to 40 percent in most cases. No district saw overall grain output grow even half as fast as the number of mouths to feed.[46] The same pattern holds true for other parts of Anatolia as well: In Mindaval, located in the east, population roughly doubled while wheat and barley revenues rose only 11.4 percent and 21.9 percent, respectively. In Uluborlu, within the lake region, population grew around 150 percent while barley revenues rose only about a quarter and wheat revenues even fell slightly.[47] Likewise in central Greece, production of grain per household dropped by about a third.[48]

In spite of this evidence, some Ottomanists have still resisted notions of population pressure and diminishing marginal returns. Huri İslamoğlu, in particular, has objected to any Malthusian implications, arguing instead that peasants could adapt to changing circumstances. Drawing on the comparative research of Ester Boserup,[49] İslamoğlu has advanced two main arguments: First, her work has put a great deal of emphasis on areas of intensive horticulture around Ottoman cities and towns and on the diversification of crops in certain parts of the empire. Second, pointing to the registration of new fields and villages in the *tahrirs*, İslamoğlu has argued that Ottoman peasants still had the option of clearing new land for farms and pastures.[50]

There is certainly no a priori reason why İslamoğlu should be wrong. As Boserup has pointed out, peasants the world over typically respond to population pressure by intensifying agriculture. In fact, the *tahrirs* offer no shortage of examples for crop diversification and intensified horticultural production, even in the core Mediterranean lands. Around

46 İslamoğlu, *State and Peasant*, 141–2.

47 İslamoğlu and Faroqhi, "Crop Patterns and Agricultural Production Trends."

48 Kiel, "The Ottoman Imperial Registers."

49 Ester Boserup, *The Conditions of Agricultural Growth* (London: Allen and Unwin, 1965).

50 These arguments are developed throughout a number of İslamoğlu's works: "M. A. Cook's *Population Pressure in Rural Anatolia 1450–1600*: A Critique of the Present Paradigm in Ottoman History," *Review of Middle East Studies* 3 (1978): 120–35; "Die osmanische Landwirtschaft im Anatolien des 16. Jahrhunderts: Stagnation oder regionale Entwicklung?" *Jahrbuch zur Geschichte und Gesellschaft des Vorderen und Mittlern Orients* (1985–1986): 165–212; "State and Peasants in the Ottoman Empire: A Study of Peasant Economy in North-Central Anatolia During the 16th Century," in *The Ottoman Empire and the World-Economy* (Cambridge: Cambridge University Press, 1987); and "Les paysans, le marché et l'état en Anatolie au XVIe siècle," *Annales* 43 (1988): 1025–43.

Jerusalem, for example, the number of vineyards rose tenfold and the number of orchards roughly doubled over the course of the century, while a significant number of villages reported irrigated summer crops for the first time in the mid- to late 1500s.[51] Similarly, records show that Bigadiç in western Anatolia diversified into sesame and Adana in the southeast moved into cotton over the same period.[52] Furthermore, İslamoğlu is correct to point out that the Ottoman population should have had room to grow. At the end of the century, Anatolia may have had as few as 20 people per square mile and the Balkans only 41, compared to roughly 100 per square mile in England and Italy.[53]

Nevertheless, the signs of population pressure in the *tahrirs* and other documents are simply overwhelming. Theoretical arguments as to why Ottomans *should* have intensified production and moved to unused land cannot explain the fact that they simply *did* not – or at least, not enough to ward off significantly diminishing marginal returns. If shrinking holdings, rising landlessness, and declining per capita food production do not constitute population pressure, then nothing does. Clearly, certain forces were working against the continued increase of food production in Ottoman lands.

Barriers to Growth

Throughout the sixteenth century and beyond, Ottoman agriculture in the core provinces remained bound by severe environmental and technological limitations, often exacerbated by unfavorable economic and political conditions. The largely mountainous, arid land presented relatively few opportunities for investment, diversification, or intensification; and the Ottomans rarely had adequate means or incentives to take advantage of even those. Instead, population growth tended to drive extensive rather than intensive practices, encouraging a move into ever more marginal land, which in turn only aggravated certain resource shortages, such as timber.

The often harsh Near Eastern environment left Ottoman farmers with limited options. Even at the height of the classical age, most peasants in more arid lands remained overwhelmingly dependent on a single crop

51 A. Makovsky, "Sixteenth-Century Agricultural Production in the Liwa of Jerusalem: Insights from the *Tapu Defters* and an Attempt at Quantification," *Archivum Ottomanicum* 9 (1984): 91–127.

52 İslamoğlu and Faroqhi, "Crop Patterns and Agricultural Production Trends."

53 İnalcık, *Economic and Social History of the Ottoman Empire*, vol. 1, 31.

of winter wheat or barley. Highly seasonal and variable precipitation precluded most crop rotations or diversification. Fields dried out in the hot months of summer, and farmers had to wait for moistening autumn rains to break ground and sow their seeds at all. (The Turkish name for October, *ekim*, literally means "planting.") If the second, spring rains proved adequate, then the harvest would be ready in early summer. Then the region descended into its regular seasonal drought again, precluding a second crop except in pockets of irrigated or exceptionally well-watered lands.[54]

Apart from the richer alluvial valleys, soils in the region tend to be thin and light. The mountainous, uneven terrain that covered most of the southern Balkans and Anatolia suffered easily from erosion, historically limiting the extent and intensity of land use in the uplands. In the worst cases, miscalculations could aggravate soil loss, runoff, and siltation, and contribute to the formation of malarial swamps downstream.[55] Most agriculture congregated in the valleys and plains, where ground could easily bake and dry out in the harsh summer sun if tilled too often or too deep.

Such a challenging environment seems to have bred a cautious resistance to change. While evidence on Ottoman farming techniques remains scarce, what little we know suggests they remained quite basic. It is true that absence of evidence is not evidence of absence when it comes to developments in agriculture; yet the almost total silence of contemporaries on the matter, whether Ottoman or Western, argues strongly against significant technological innovation. European observers of the time could report with interest and enthusiasm on the agricultural marvels of China and Japan. Therefore, their disinterest with Ottoman cultivation implies that they found little worth reporting, or perhaps that it merely resembled practices in neighboring countries. Quite possibly, cultivation in the Eastern Mediterranean had changed little for hundreds, if not thousands, of years.[56] If Ottoman population arrived at roughly the

54 The first scientific studies on Turkish agriculture, conducted when the U.S. began to give Marshall Aid to its new ally at the start of the Cold War, revealed a country still dependent on grain for about 90% of cultivated land and about 71% of calories and protein. See Jacques May, *The Ecology of Malnutrition in the Far and Near East* (New York: Hafner, 1963), 348–51.

55 J. R. McNeill, *The Mountains of the Mediterranean* (New York: Cambridge University Press, 1992). See Chapter 11 for a more detailed discussion of erosion.

56 Mehmet Öz, "Agriculture in the Classical Period," in *The Great Ottoman-Turkish Civilization*, ed. Kemal Çiçek (Ankara: Yeni Türkiye, 2000), vol. 2, 37–8, describes this as "a period of no fundamental changes in agricultural technology."

same peak that Roman and Byzantine populations had reached before, then that may be because little had changed in the intervening centuries to permit a larger basis for subsistence.[57]

Our first detailed accounts of agriculture in the region come from anthropologists and geographers of the early twentieth century, writing just before modern inputs began to transform rural life in the 1950s.[58] All describe the same basic broadcast planting, harvesting with sickles, and threshing and winnowing by hand, and the same simple wooden agricultural tools. Pairs of oxen continued to drag the same light scratch-plows as they had for millennia. Deep coulters and mouldboards to turn the earth would have exposed the soil to erosion anyway, and the team of horses to pull a heavier plow would have been too expensive to feed.[59]

Terracing was very simple when present at all, and manuring was rare except in garden plots.[60] Into modern times, farmers in many parts of the empire saved precious manure for fuel, drying it out in patties called *tezek*. Some Ottoman peasants may have plowed back in the stubble after harvest as a sort of fertilizer,[61] but in general it appears they simply relied on long fallows to restore the fields. Without manure or crop rotations, the ground had to go unplanted more often than not. While most accounts of Mediterranean agriculture point to a biennial rotation, it seems some Ottoman lands were left untilled as much as two years in three, especially in the more arid regions of inner Anatolia.[62]

57 Following Andrew Watson, *Agricultural Innovation in the Early Islamic World* (New York: Cambridge University Press, 1983) some writers have assumed that an "Islamic agricultural revolution" underpinned post-classical Middle Eastern demographic growth. However, that view has been seriously challenged. See Bulliet, *Islam: The View from the Edge*, chapter 4, and Michael Decker, "Plants and Progress: Rethinking the Islamic Agricultural Revolution," *Journal of World History* 20 (2009): 187–206.

58 E.g., Planhol, *De la plaine pamphylienne aux lacs pisidiens*; Hütteroth, *Laendliche Siedlungen*; Paul Stirling, *Turkish Village* (New York: Wiley, 1965); and Walter Ruben, *Kırşehir: Eine altertümliche Kleinstadt Inneranatoliens* (Würzburg: Ergon, 2003). For more on the long-term history of farming and agricultural implements, see J. M. Wagstaff, *The Evolution of Middle Eastern Landscapes* (London: Croom Helm, 1985).

59 On the relative merits of the light wooden plow, see S. Erinç and N. Tunçdilek, "The Agricultural Regions of Turkey," *Geographical Review* 42 (1952): 179–203; and Lynn White, *Medieval Technology and Social Change* (Oxford: Clarendon, 1962), 41–7.

60 Erinç, "The Agricultural Regions of Turkey" and Planhol, *De la plaine pamphylienne aux lacs pisidiens*, 145–6.

61 At least it would appear that way from a document of 1630 complaining about those tearing the stubble out of the ground (MD 85/497). Even if this were so, the method only supplies about one-fifth the nitrogen that needs to be replenished for traditional wheat agriculture: See Vaclav Smil, *Enriching the Earth* (Boston: MIT Press 2001), 23–4.

62 For instance, in one Ottoman document of the early seventeenth century describing possession of a certain farm, we find that the owner had held the tract for twenty years

The inevitable consequences were low yields and even thinner margins of surplus once settlement expansion had already occupied the best land. Ottoman records have left us two ways of estimating the productivity of agriculture. The first simply uses the yield ratios mentioned in the *tahrirs*, and the second divides taxed production by the seed planted per unit of land, as prescribed in local law codes. The results vary considerably. Some fertile river valleys might have yielded as much as 6:1, but most of Anatolia was in the range of 3:1 to 4:1. In some cases, yields fell as low as 2:1 – that is, farmers could supposedly harvest only twice the seed they planted.[63] The precise numbers may be misleading, but the overall impression is clear. Ottoman agriculture was altogether even less productive than that of contemporary Europe[64] (let alone China or India), and probably no better than that of ancient Greece or Rome if not actually worse.[65]

To intensify and diversify in such terrain, farmers needed to improve the land and develop irrigation. As İslamoğlu has shown, some Ottomans did actually manage to create pockets of intensive garden and orchard production around some villages and many towns and cities. Doubtless, this local intensification helped ease what would otherwise have been a real shortage of provisions as the surplus of the countryside dried up. However, there is no sign that these pockets of intensive horticulture managed to do more than keep up with local growth. That is to say, there is no sign that population in these pockets grew faster than regional populations as a whole, at least not in the sixteenth century. Nor does it appear that irrigation ever spread far into the Ottoman countryside or offered a viable alternative to the basic subsistence of dry farming on most Mediterranean lands until modern times.[66]

and plowed it only six times (MD 82/39). Ruben, *Kırşehir,* chapter 3, part A, mentions even longer fallows in more marginal land.

63 See Mehmet Öz, "XVI. Yüzyılda Anadolu'da Tarımda Verlilik Problemi," in *XIII. Türk Tarih Kongresi* (Ankara: TTK, 1999) and Öz, "Agriculture in the Classical Period." Calculations from *tahrirs* in one of the richer regions of the Peloponnese in the early eighteenth century have come up with slightly higher yields, in the range of 4:1 to 5:1. See Stefka Pareva, "Agrarian Land and Harvest in Southwest Peloponnese in the Early 18th Century," *Études Balkaniques* (2003): 83–123. Unfortunately, there has not been enough research to determine whether these ratios were going up or down.

64 For European yield ratios, see Fernand Braudel, *The Structures of Everyday Life* (New York: Harper & Row, 1981), 120–3; and B. H. Slicher van Bath, *Agrarian History of Western Europe* (London: E. Arnold, 1963).

65 For the productivity of ancient Greek and Roman agriculture, see Sallares, *Ecology of the Ancient Greek World,* chapter III.12. It appears ancient farmers made much more productive use of fertilizer.

66 Marsh, *Man and Nature,* 313–15, makes this observation for the nineteenth century as well.

Again, the major obstacles were environmental and technological. The Mediterranean provinces possessed relatively few sites with the right combination of workable water and irrigable land. For the most part, the Ottomans had to rely on easily utilized, fast-running streams located away from malarial swamps, leaving the flat coastal plains largely undercultivated and underpopulated until the late nineteenth century.[67] The Çukurova valley in the alluvial plain of the Seyhan and Ceyhan rivers in southeastern Anatolia offers the most striking example. Today perhaps the richest agricultural region in Turkey, it remained relatively unimportant in early and classical Ottoman times. Until the great settlement expansion of the 1500s, it had served as little more than winter pasture for sheep and goats. Even in the late sixteenth century, agriculture mostly huddled about state-directed rice farms on the smaller streams and tributaries, while the larger rivers were left unused. Given the vulnerability of even these modest irrigation systems to disruption, Çukurova farms were all but abandoned in the Little Ice Age crisis, many reverting to swamps and forests by the 1700s, leaving few sixteenth-century settlements that could still be identified today.[68]

Even where viable opportunities presented themselves, the local *reaya* frequently lacked the means to improve the land or even preserve irrigation systems already in place. Rural capital was scarce and large investments impractical. Construction costs for a major irrigation project could run into the hundreds of thousands of *akçes*, which could prove unattainable even for an entire village. Annual maintenance, moreover, could run up to a quarter the value of produce, even on good lands.[69]

If the *reaya* lacked the means to undertake such works, then the wealthier *tımar*-holders lacked the motivation. The military landlords rotated in and out too quickly to take a long-term interest in improvement of the land. Not only did they fail to build new works, but in some cases they may have let the old systems fall into disrepair. For example, a 1583 report from around Aksaray (south-central Anatolia) described how the irrigation system had deteriorated under the *sipahis*:

> ... since ancient times the aforementioned villages have drawn water from three places in the river. While it was freehold (*eşkincilü mülk*) the peasantry and their livestock benefitted, their fields and gardens were irrigated, and their harvests were great. Afterwards, once it was granted

[67] İnalcık, "Rice Cultivation and the *Çeltükçi-Re'âyâ* System," 81.

[68] Mustafa Soysal, *Die Siedlungs- und Landschaftsentwicklung der Çukurova* (Erlangen: Fränkische Geographische Gesellschaft, 1976), chapter 3.

[69] İnalcık, "Rice Cultivation and the *Çeltükçi-Re'âyâ* System," 82–3.

> to *tımar*-holders, the waterways were not cleared, and the water lost its flow. Now the *reaya* are suffering and the former harvests cannot be reaped...[70]

Outside of Egypt,[71] the state did not offer much help either. For all its efforts to manage land use and resources, the imperial government rarely invested in large-scale public works in the countryside. In 1568 the Ottomans attempted a Suez canal, and a year later they tried to link the Don and Volga rivers, but neither project came to fruition.[72] Provincial officials did play a role in some irrigation schemes over this period,[73] but apparently nothing on a major scale. Even in Iraq, apart from the construction of a dike at Kerbala and an expansion of the Hasaniyya canal in the 1530s, the governors from Istanbul failed to undertake any large projects, remaining content to leave waterworks to private charities and local initiative.[74] Among tens of thousands of imperial orders from the late sixteenth century, I have only been able to uncover a few examples of simple flood control[75] and a single case of draining swamps.[76]

The state went further with the promotion of irrigated rice, but the crop never realized its potential to transform agriculture in the region. Rice had entered the Near East in ancient times and its cultivation had spread gradually under the Arabs.[77] In the late fifteenth and sixteenth centuries, as the Ottomans converted servile labor into free peasantry, they created a system to turn former serfs into rice-growing sharecroppers, known as *çeltükçi reaya*.[78] Using tax incentives and land grants to encourage investment and settlement, the system spread in parts of western Anatolia and Syria, helping rice become a staple item among

70 MD 51/222.

71 For irrigation projects on the Nile, see Mikhail, "Nature of Ottoman Egypt."

72 Caroline Finkel, *Osman's Dream* (New York: Basic Books, 2005), 155–7, and Casale, *Ottoman Age of Exploration*, 135–7.

73 İnalcık, "Rice Cultivation and the *Çeltükçi-Re'âyâ* System," 80–3.

74 Rhoads Murphey, "The Ottoman Centuries in Iraq: Legacy or Aftermath? A Survey Study of Mesopotamian Hydrology and Ottoman Irrigation Projects," *Journal of Turkish Studies* 11 (1987): 17–29 and Wolf-Dieter Hütteroth, "Between Dicle and Firat: Turkey, Northeastern Syria and Northwestern Iraq in the 16th Century," in *VIIIth International Congress on the Economic and Social History of Turkey*, ed. Nurhan Abacı (Morrisville: Lulu Press, 2006).

75 E.g., MD 7/1550.

76 MD 7/1872.

77 Watson, *Agricultural Innovation*, 15–19.

78 See İnalcık, "Rice Cultivation and the *Çeltükçi-Re'âyâ* System"; M. Venzke, "Rice Cultivation in the Plain of Antioch in the 16th Century," *Archivum Ottomanicum* 12 (1992): 175–276; and N. Beldiceanu and I. Beldiceanu-Steinherr, "Riziculture dans l'Empire ottoman (XIVe–XVe siècles)," *Turcica* 10 (1978): 9–28.

the urban elite. Nevertheless, the Ottomans never expanded the *çeltükçi reaya* system outside of a few small areas, and peasants never took to the crop spontaneously on a large scale. Even within the system, production was limited and rice cultivation was often part-time, employing the less labor-intensive method of broadcast planting rather than the far more productive nursery preparation of seedlings.[79] In fact, population pressure in the late 1500s may have actually turned peasants away from rice and back to grains, since the former was considered a luxury cash crop and not a staple like wheat or barley.[80] Furthermore, peasants may have resented the harsh labor of growing rice and the high taxes of the *çeltükçi reaya* system, to judge from frequent reports of theft and flight.[81]

Rather than intensify, the peasants appear to have spread outward into ever more marginal land. After all, Ottoman settlement expansion was not a colonization of virgin soil. The Near East did not enjoy an open frontier in the American or Russian sense – nor even in the more limited sense of Han Chinese expansion to the south,[82] Japanese expansion to the north,[83] or Mughal expansion into Bengal.[84] Apart from some sparsely populated territory in eastern Anatolia and the northern Balkans, Ottoman lands had been cultivated on and off for millennia. In most cases, settlers were not crossing into uncharted wilderness, but radiating outward from zones of permanent habitation into surrounding lands of temporary fields and pastures, and sometimes into forests that had grown back during the depopulation of the Black Death. This was particularly true in Anatolia, where despite the ebb and flow of population over centuries and millennia, the basic geography of settlement had held steady and farmers had returned time and again to the same favorable locations.[85] Indeed, the pattern would repeat itself once more when settlements deserted in the Little Ice Age crisis would be repopulated by refugees and migrants in the late nineteenth century.[86]

79 Venzke, "Rice Cultivation in the Plain of Antioch," 232.

80 This was apparently the case in Bigadiç in western Anatolia: See İslamoğlu and Faroqhi, "Crop Patterns and Agricultural Production Trends."

81 İnalcık, "Rice Cultivation and the *Çeltükçi-Re'âyâ* System," 106–13.

82 Elvin, *Retreat of the Elephants*, chapter 8.

83 Brett Walker, *The Conquest of Ainu Lands* (Berkeley: University of California Press, 2001).

84 Richard Eaton, *The Rise of Islam and the Bengal Frontier* (Berkeley: University of California Press, 1993).

85 Necdet Tunçdilek, *Türkiye İskân Coğrafyası* (Istanbul: İstanbul Üniversitesi, 1967), 17, and Hütteroth, *Laendliche Siedlungen*, chapter 3.

86 Hütteroth, *Laendliche Siedlungen*, chapter 4, and Wagstaff, *Evolution of Middle Eastern Landscapes*, chapter 10.

The *tahrirs* help illustrate this pattern. First, they recorded a rising number of assarts in the late 1500s, as peasants cleared woodlands to expand cultivation.[87] More often, they mentioned peasants moving into *mezraas*, or previously uninhabited fields used for seasonal cultivation or pasture.[88] Not only did peasants come to rely heavily on *mezraas* for subsistence,[89] but many of the temporary fields eventually became registered villages, suggesting that once occasional clearings had come under permanent cultivation.[90] While there is no direct evidence that these *mezraas* always occupied worse land than the original villages, it would seem reasonable that peasants would have selected the most fertile fields for permanent cultivation first and then left more marginal terrain for occasional use. Furthermore, regional patterns in the *tahrirs* also indicate that population rose fastest at the margins of rain-fed cultivation. Central Anatolia, in particular, recorded some of the greatest growth, as agriculture moved into former nomad grazing lands (see Chapter 4). On a more local level, a recent study comparing the Gaza *tahrirs* with reconstructed precipitation data reveals that the *reaya* tended to push cultivation to its limits in semiarid lands, with farming expanding in times of favorable climate only to contract again in times of drought.[91]

This movement into marginal land only aggravated the tendency toward extensive rather than intensive land use. Poorer soil and more arid or rugged terrain benefited even less from investment in irrigation. Moreover, the dangers of marginal land exacerbated the general preference for risk avoidance over output maximization that seems to have characterized the region's peasantry. As observed by Planhol among other anthropologists, farmers in the semiarid lands tended to scatter their plots at varying locations and elevations and preferred to mix garden crops, agriculture, and husbandry wherever possible.[92] From the cadastral surveys, we can also see how the late sixteenth-century *reaya* were switching from wheat to barley, a lower-yielding but hardier and more

87 Cook, *Population Pressure*, 79–80 and 101.

88 For a discussion of this term, see Tunçdilek, *Türkiye İskân Coğrafyası*, 124–9, and Hütteroth, *Laendliche Siedlungen*, 169–70.

89 See Venzke, "Ottoman Tahrir Defterleri and Agricultural Productivity."

90 Yunus Koç, "XVI. Yüzyılın İkinci Yarısında Köylerin Parçalanması Sorunu: Bursa Kazası Ölçeğinde Bir Araştırma," in *XIII. Türk Tarih Kongresi* (Ankara: TTK, 1999).

91 Haggay Etkes, "The Impact of Short Term Climate Fluctuations on Rural Population in the Desert Frontier Nahiye of Gaza (ca. 1519–57)" (paper presented at the National Bureau of Economic Research conference "Climate Change: Past and Present," 5/30/2008).

92 Planhol, *De la plaine pamphylienne aux lacs pisidiens*, chapter 6.

drought-tolerant crop.[93] Given the frequency of drought and famine, as we see in Chapter 3, the *reaya*'s caution may have made sense in individual terms, even if it left a smaller surplus for a rapidly growing population as a whole.

Settlement expansion may also have encouraged a growing dependence on pastoralism, further extensifying land use. At the most basic level, all Ottoman farmers needed a pair of oxen to plow their land; and in that, they differed little from their counterparts in Europe or for that matter India, although it did distinguish them from intensive rice-planting ecologies in East Asia, which had little need for livestock at all. What really set the Ottomans apart was their relative numbers of sheep and goats, even around urban areas and even as population densities soared. Around Kayseri, for example, *tahrirs* still recorded three to four sheep per person toward the end of the century, even after regional population had tripled.[94] In İslamoğlu's study of northern Anatolia, the number of sheep per capita continued to rise while population doubled.[95]

For the peasantry as a whole, it would seem greater density should have discouraged extensive pasturing and encouraged investment in more intensive farming. Nevertheless, the best course for everyone together was not necessarily the best option for any one individual, and population pressure may have actually accelerated the trend toward pastoralism. On the one hand, growing urban markets and rising prices encouraged wealthier landholders – whether *tımar*-holders or just better-off peasants – to invest more in livestock. The market for animal products, such as wool and hides, appears to have been more lucrative than the market for grains, probably due to the relative ease of transporting animals on the hoof.[96] Meanwhile, for the poorer peasantry, grazing animals on common, public, or in some cases even protected land probably still proved more profitable than working to maximize yields on a small or marginal

93 For a comparison of wheat and barley yields in Turkey, see A. Wahbia and T. Sinclair, "Simulation Analysis of Relative Yield Advantage of Barley and Wheat in an Eastern Mediterranean Climate," *Field Crops Research* 91 (2005): 287–96.

94 Jennings, "Population, Society, and Economy of the Region of Erçiyes Dağı." Animals also figured in about one in ten Kayseri court cases, often in bitter ownership disputes. See Gönur Karaduman, "Kayseri in the End of the 16th Century in Light of the Court Records, 988-1002/1580–1592" (PhD diss., Boğaziçi University, 1995), 95–8.

95 İslamoğlu, *State and Peasant*, 152 *et passim.*

96 For instance, Akdağ, *Celâlî İsyanları*, 42–9, points to instances of landlords dispossessing *reaya* to make room for pasture and argues that a preference for livestock may have undermined food production.

plot. Furthermore, diversification into livestock offered more security than a total investment in agriculture. For rich and poor alike, animals would have seemed like something to to fall back on when the harvest failed, or a source of portable wealth in times of uncertainty and unrest.[97] Although, as we will see, this calculation would prove disastrously wrong in the Little Ice Age crisis.

By the late sixteenth century, there are further indications that population had run up against the limits of natural resources in the core provinces. As clearing for farmland continued apace, wood became increasingly scarce. By the 1570s, repeated imperial orders complained of illegal cutting and burning in protected forests[98] – in some cases, even fruit trees cut down for charcoal[99] and cemeteries logged for timber.[100] As fuel grew more expensive, farmers probably had to burn even more manure as *tezek*, further undermining the land's productivity. Meanwhile, the (black) market price of wood had soared well above the official fixed price, creating incentives to smuggle away lumber purchased at the *narh*.[101] By the 1580s, official orders began to acknowledge looming shortages in some of the *miri koru*, and referred to cutting "the remaining trees"[102] or "if there are any trees left."[103]

Other evidence suggests that extensive pasturing had begun to create conflicts over land use, as owners sought out new land for their animals. As early as 1568, for example, the imperial government warned against grazing in protected wetlands that served as flood control.[104] By the 1570s, complaints of livestock in *miri koru* and even in tombs and cemeteries became almost as frequent as complaints of illegal logging and charcoal-making.[105] Across Anatolia, farmers and pastoralists also

97 Cf. Michel Sivignon, *Les pasteurs du Pinde septentrional* (Lyon: Centre d'études et de recherches sur la géographie de l'Europe, 1968).

98 E.g., MD 3/86, MD 3/1018, MD 3/1494, MD 6/813, MD 6/949, MD 7/1447, MD 7/1800, MD 7/2674, MD 12/53, MD 14/27, MD 14/226, MD 14/367, MD 14/541, MD 16/428, MD 26/808, MD 29/96, MD 40/535, and MD 42/309.

99 MD 30/29.

100 MD 7/1643.

101 E.g., MD 6/799 and MD 6/1445. See also Faroqhi, *Towns and Townsmen*, 78–9. In MD 7/1589, the sultan even refers to "speculation" (*madrabazlık*) in timber, much like orders condemning speculation on grain in times of famine (see Chapter 3).

102 MD 19/274.

103 MD 26/830.

104 MD 7/1550.

105 E.g., MD 5/1292, MD 5/1396, MD 6/1405, MD 16/22, MD 24/672, and MD 62/26.

fell into disputes as the latter led livestock into farmland or as their wandering animals chewed up crops.[106] Judging from incidents in the wake of the Little Ice Age crisis, Ottoman pastoralists were also looking for opportunities to set fire to woods and fields to create more pasture, fitting a general Mediterranean pattern.[107]

Economic Turmoil and Unrest

By the late 1500s, population pressure in the core provinces aggravated the empire's economic troubles as well. As in other parts of the early modern world, demographic expansion and the influx of American silver drove up inflation over the late sixteenth century.[108] By the 1580s, prices had nearly doubled from a century before, even absent famines and other breakdowns in supply.[109] As costs rose, the imperial government began to debase the silver coinage to raise funds and cut debts,[110] culminating in a major devaluation of the *akçe* in 1585 (see Chapter 3). These debasements only ignited more instability and speculation in coinage; and the process tended to exacerbate a persistent

106 E.g., MD 41/249 and MD 72/769. Other instances may be found in regional court records: See Fatih Bursa, "Manisa'nın 14 Numaralı H.1002 Tarihli Şeriyye Sicil Defteri" (PhD diss., Niğde Üniversitesi, 2002) documents 26/1 and 57/18.

107 E.g., MD 90/58. On burning in the Mediterranean region in general, see Pyne, *Vestal Fire*, 81–146, and Grove and Rackham, *Nature of Mediterranean Europe*, chapter 13.

108 David Hackett Fischer, *The Great Wave* (New York: Oxford University Press, 1996) and Harry Miskimin, *The Economy of Later Renaissance Europe* (New York: Cambridge University Press, 1977).

109 The classic work on the subject remains Ömer Lütfi Barkan, "The Price Revolution of the Sixteenth Century: A Turning Point in the Economic History of the Near East," *International Journal of Middle East Studies* (1975): 3–28. Barkan's figures have since been refined by the research of Şevket Pamuk: See "The Price Revolution in the Ottoman Empire Reconsidered," *International Journal of Middle East Studies* 33 (2001): 69–89 and "Prices in the Ottoman Empire," *International Journal of Middle East Studies* 36 (2004): 451–68. While Pamuk tries to the play down the magnitude and impact of the "Price Revolution," it seems his main conclusion is that the inflation took place later and more suddenly than Barkan had presumed. For our purposes, Pamuk's practice of smoothing annual fluctuations and the impact of harvest failures also misrepresents the human experience of this period of inflation: To the average Ottoman, the fact that decade-to-decade changes were not especially severe would not have been much comfort when famines might double the cost of basic foodstuffs in a year.

110 Mustafa Akdağ, *Türkiye'nin İktisadi ve İçtimai Tarihi* (Ankara: TTK, 1971). Baki Tezcan, "Searching for Osman," chapter 1, has argued that the imperial treasury was also trying to solve difficulties related to the incorporation of Egypt, which had long maintained a different silver:gold ratio.

wage-price lag that dragged down real incomes in Ottoman towns and cities.[111]

Meanwhile, the shortage of good land and the dwindling opportunities in the countryside drove a stream of new migrants into urban areas. The population of the capital and other cities continued to keep pace with rural numbers, putting an increasing burden on dwindling agricultural surpluses. At the same time, tax records have left the impression that urban economic growth also fell far short of demographic growth, leaving many newcomers to swell the ranks of the unemployed. The problem grew worst in Istanbul, where the imperial government began restricting immigration, clearing out squatters, and demanding that newcomers provide guarantors from among the established inhabitants. However, the very repetition of these orders only suggests that enforcement had failed and the problem was getting worse (see Chapter 9).

While some of the landless and desperate drifted to the cities, others turned to theft and banditry. A considerable portion of the imperial orders from the late 1500s dwell on crime and insecurity, especially in the core provinces of the empire. Small bands of men plundered the countryside throughout Anatolia and the Balkans, typically stealing money and food from nearby villages. By the 1580s, reports from the provinces also began to mention gangs of *sohtas* – unemployed madrasah students who often turned to violence and extortion.

The first modern historian of the Celali Rebellion and the Ottoman crisis, Mustafa Akdağ, focused heavily on these cases of vagrancy and crime in his seminal work of the 1950s and 1960s.[112] Pouring over thousands of imperial orders and court records, Akdağ argued that inflation, economic turmoil, and banditry had swelled into widespread social unrest by the 1580s, and that the crisis of the 1590s was not a sudden outbreak, but the culmination of decades of pressure. There are certainly shortcomings in Akdag's explanation for rebellion and crisis: At times, his work overstates the degree of unrest and colors events with an element of class conflict not entirely justified by the evidence, at least before the 1590s. Most importantly, lacking any sense of how chance and exogenous factors like the Little Ice Age would influence developments in the empire, his narrative endows the crisis with a sort of

[111] S. Özmücür and Ş. Pamuk, "Real Wages and Standards of Living in the Ottoman Empire, 1489–1914," *The Journal of Economic History* (2002): 293–321.

[112] Mustafa Akdağ, *Celâlî İsyanları* (Ankara: Ankara Üniversitesi Basımevi, 1963) and *Türkiye'nin İktisadi ve İçtimai Tarihi.*

inevitable, snowballing momentum. As we see in the following chapters, the course of events would prove more complex and less predictable. Social and economic pressures did not just operate smoothly and inexorably toward rebellion; and incidents of banditry and other troubles often came in sporadic bursts as the empire faced natural and man-made disasters. Nevertheless, Akdağ was correct in pointing to population pressure and inflation as underlying causes of Ottoman troubles.

Conclusion: A Malthusian Crisis?

Even before the disasters of the Little Ice Age, demographic growth and environmental limitations had begun to create serious problems for the empire. Land was running short, per capita harvests had fallen, and parts of the population had turned to banditry, all raising the specter of a Malthusian crisis. This interpretation, moreover, would seem to fit with traditional notions that the empire was in steady decline and that the rebellion and crisis of the 1590s were just the culmination of mounting pressures. The full picture, however, proves more complicated.

On the one hand, the empire as a whole was not facing starvation. In matters of food availability, the evidence from the *tahrirs* paints a picture of striking contrasts within and among regions, even in the late 1500s.[113] Where water was readily available, Ottomans farmers could sometimes work wonders. One study of the *tahrirs* from what is now southwestern Georgia has described a land of irrigated terraces paying out a tithe of one-fifth of the harvest and still producing extra wheat, barley, honey, flax, and vegetables.[114] Cadastres of the Danubian provinces likewise reveal a healthy surplus even in the later part of the century.[115] Cyprus[116]

113 See Mehmet Öz, "XVI. Yüzyıl Anadolusu'nda Köylülerin Vergi Yükü ve Geçim Durumu Hakkında Bir Araştırma," *Osmanlı Araştırmaları* 17 (1997): 77–90.

114 Mihail Svanidzé, "L'Économie rurale dans le *Vilâyet* d'Akhaltzıkhé (Çıldır) d'après le "Registre Détaillé" de 1595," in *Contributions à l'histoire économique et sociale de l'Empire ottoman*, ed. J. Bacqué-Grammont and P. Dumont (Leuven: Peeters, 1983).

115 Bruce McGowan, "Food Supply and Taxation on the Middle Danube (1568–79)," *Archivum Ottomanicum* 1 (1969): 139–96.

116 Ronald Jennings, "The Population, Taxation, and Wealth in the Cities and Villages of Cyprus According to the Detailed Population Survey (*Defter-i Mufassal*) of 1572," in *Raiyyet Rüsûmu: Essays Presented to Halil Inalcik*, ed. Carolyn Gross (Cambridge, MA: Harvard University Press, 1986) and Ronald Jennings, "Village Agriculture in Cyprus," *Bulletin of the School of Oriental and African Studies, University of London* 51 (1988): 279–313.

and also parts of the Black Sea coast[117] still had land to spare. In short, the Ottoman population had not yet reached the absolute limits of food supply, when averaged out across the empire. Even given the simple technologies of the day, the same territory could probably have held more people; and if the total produce of Ottoman lands had been divided evenly among all its inhabitants every year, then each would probably have enjoyed more than enough to eat, at least until the worst of the Little Ice Age.

On the other hand, in some of the core provinces the peasantry faced rapidly diminishing food supplies in the late 1500s. Calculations of per capita consumption suggest that even as some districts still enjoyed a moderate surplus, many others were on track to reach bare subsistence by the end of the century. The threat was particularly severe in central Anatolia, where production had scarcely diversified beyond wheat, barley, sheep, and goats.[118] Furthermore, the figures in the *tahrirs* assumed normal years, ignoring the ever-present dangers of dearth and banditry.[119] Uneven tax rates and frequent extraordinary wartime requisitions only compounded the problem, stripping some lands of what little they had to spare.[120]

What troubled the empire, therefore, was not so much population growth in general as the rapid growth of marginal populations on marginal land in particular. Large parts of the empire, though still productive enough to see through average years, really did face famine in times of drought and other disasters, as we see in the following chapter. Furthermore, these same lands, unable to provide for all their inhabitants, began to export a growing number of landless, unmarried, and potentially dangerous men.

The empire was not starving or declining, but it was increasingly vulnerable. In good years, the state could still easily support its basic systems of provisioning and mobilize for war. However, in bad years – years of

[117] Ronald Jennings, "The Society and Economy of Maçuka in the Ottoman Judicial Registers of Trabzon, 1560–1640," in *Continuity and Change in Late Byzantine and Early Ottoman Society*, ed. A. Bryer and H. Lowry (Birmingham: University of Birmingham Centre for Byzantine Studies, 1986).

[118] İslamoğlu and Faroqhi, "Crop Patterns and Agricultural Production Trends."

[119] Faroqhi, *Towns and Townsmen*, 201.

[120] Some authors have assumed that different rates of tax actually reflected different levels of productivity (e.g., Makovsky, "Sixteenth-Century Agricultural Production"), but Öz, "XVI. Yüzyıl Anadolusu'nda Köylülerin Vergi Yükü ve Geçim Durumu" suggests that this was not the case.

drought, famine, or military setbacks – population pressure in parts of the empire exacerbated the impact of disasters and aggravated the risk of instability, unrest, and ultimately the breakdown of Ottoman provisioning systems. Unfortunately for the Ottomans, as the century wore on the good years were becoming more rare and the bad years more threatening.

3

DISASTERS OF THE LATE SIXTEENTH CENTURY

It was not population pressure alone, but population pressure combined with natural disaster and imperial missteps that drove the empire into rebellion and crisis. To understand how the catastrophe unfolded, we need first to examine the empire's vulnerabilities and responses to natural disaster more closely. In the generation leading up to the crisis of the 1590s, the Ottomans weathered a number of violent storms, both literal and metaphorical. These events tested the strength of imperial authority and its systems of population and resource management against the vagaries of man and nature. The threats came from the usual suspects: famine, pestilence and death, and war – the classic Four Horsemen of the Apocalypse. The underlying causes of disaster, however, were frequently meteorological, above all the severe winters and spring droughts that characterized the onset of the Little Ice Age.

These disasters proved fatal not only for Ottoman subjects but also for Ottoman provisioning systems. In theory, the empire's interconnected imperial ecology allowed it to balance out deficits in one area with surpluses in another, while preserving a range of options for supplying the capital and the military. And in most years, that is precisely how the system worked. However, by the late 1570s population pressure and escalating military and civilian requirements placed rising demands on the empire's dwindling surplus of foodstuffs and other raw materials. Therefore, provisioning systems became even more dependent on every part of the empire for supplies, creating the risk of generalized shortages whenever one region suffered from disaster. Meanwhile, the imperial government was slow to adjust its demands and its prices for commodities, even as provisioning systems ran into difficulties. By examining this development in some detail, we can understand how an empire that had survived and even flourished after a setback like Lepanto would eventually face a serious rebellion and crisis in the 1590s on account of Little Ice Age weather events and a disruption to the supply of sheep.

Famine

In the sixteenth century, no part of the world had yet entirely escaped from the chronic danger of harvest failures and food shortages. However, with rapid population growth on often marginal land, the Ottoman Empire of the late 1500s proved even more vulnerable than most.[1] Severe food shortages struck in one or another part of the empire almost every other year from the late 1560s through the 1580s, usually on a local scale but sometimes in great famines spanning large regions. While Ottomanists have often overlooked these events, the registers of imperial orders from those decades include scores of documents dealing with food shortages and famine, many providing useful insights into the nature of the problem and the Ottoman response.[2] Appropriate to the size and scale of its provisioning systems, the empire had developed fairly comprehensive methods of famine management; yet even these measures proved to have severe limitations that would become all too apparent during the Little Ice Age crisis.

Ottoman imperial orders describe a range of threats to agriculture. Hordes of mice could devour crops.[3] Locusts could strip fields bare: In Cyprus they unleashed a general famine in 1572–6, in spite of major eradication schemes.[4] At times, the insects could reach as far north as Anatolia and even the Crimea, where a swarm in the late 1570s devastated the region's grain and pasture.[5] At other times, the Eastern Mediterranean

[1] The classic work on the subject, Güçer, *Osmanlı İmparatorluğunda Hububat Meselesi*, gives an overview of Ottoman agriculture and the threat of famine but focuses more on the nature of imperial grain tithes. Sabri Ülgener, *Darlık Buhranları ve İslam İktisat Siyaseti* (Ankara: Mayaş, 1984), originally published in 1951, covers famine in the Islamic world more generally, while Mehmet Erler, *Osmanlı Devleti'nde Kuraklık ve Kıtlık Olayları (1800–1880)* (Istanbul: Libra, 2010) covers famines of the nineteenth century. Mustafa Akdağ, *Türk Halkının Dirlik ve Düzenlik Kavgası* (Ankara: Bilgi Yayınevi, 1975), 74–85, briefly discusses some of the famines and breakdowns of provisioning described in this chapter.

[2] In the following paragraphs, I have built off of the helpful research of Orhan Kılıç, "Osmanlı Devleti'nde Meydana Gelen Kıtlıklar," *Türkler* 10 (2002): 718–30, which displays a table of famine events and relevant documents, contributing my own findings from the archives.

[3] E.g., MD 73/602.

[4] MD 28/104. On the locust problem in Cyprus, see Benjamin Arbel, "Sauterelles et mentalités: Le cas de la Chypre vénitienne," *Annales* 44 (1989): 1057–74; Ronald Jennings, "The Locust Problem in Cyprus," *Bulletin of the School of Oriental and African Studies* 51 (1988): 279–313; and Gilles Veinstein, "Sur les sauterelles à Chypre, en Thrace et en Macédonie à l'époque ottomane," in *Armağan: Festschrift für Andreas Tietze* (Prague: Enigma, 1994).

[5] MD 12/618, MD 12/983, MD 14/1619, MD 60/579, MD 32/401, and MD 35/340. See also Singer, *Palestinian Peasants*, 115–16, for locusts and other natural disasters in

was struck by serious earthquakes or sudden storms.[6] Flooding could prove particularly destructive along the fertile banks of the Danube and the Black Sea, drowning crops and submerging fields in unusually heavy downpours.[7]

However, the leading cause of harvest failure and famine by far was drought. Among documents specifying the reason for a shortage or famine, about two-thirds point to a lack of rainfall.[8] As explained in Chapter 2, far too many Ottoman peasants relied on fickle autumn and spring precipitation in marginal Mediterranean land to yield a single crop of winter wheat or barley for their subsistence. In the later decades of the sixteenth century, as erratic Little Ice Age climate swings set in, cold dry winters and springs became increasingly frequent and severe, with devastating consequences for the region's agriculture. While accustomed to local shortages, the Ottoman Empire now had to cope with serious widespread harvest failures.

In the generation building up to the Little Ice Age crisis of the 1590s, major droughts and famines came in waves about once every five years, notably in 1564–5, 1570–1, 1574, 1579, and 1583–5. In the first wave, drought struck the Aegean basin, inflicting famine on the Greek islands and western Anatolia.[9] Meanwhile, whether for related or unrelated causes, districts as far north as Salonica and Dubrovnik[10] and as far east as Lake Van[11] faced shortages; and to make matters worse, the Nile flood fell short that year, bringing famine to Egypt and the Hijaz.[12] The next wave of drought, in 1570–1, reached further south, this time

Palestine. Locusts remained a major problem in Anatolia into the nineteenth century: See Ertan Gökmen, "Batı Anadolu'da Çekirge Felâketi (1850–1915)," *Belleten* 74 (2010): 127–80.

6 For examples, see Orhan Kılıç, "Mühimme Defterlerine Göre 16. Yüzyılın İkinci Yarısında Osmanlı Devleti'nde Doğal Afetler," in *Pax Ottomanica, Studies in Memoriam Prof. Dr. Nejat Göyünç* (Haarlem: SOTA, 2001). For further studies of such natural disasters, see Elizabeth Zachariadou, ed., *Natural Disasters in the Ottoman Empire* (Heraklion: Crete University Press, 1999).

7 E.g., MD 19/40 and MD 41/704. See also Bruno Simons, "Le blé dans les rapports vénéto-ottomans au XVIe siècle," in *Contributions à l'histoire économique et sociale de l'Empire ottoman*, ed. J. Bacqué-Grammont and P. Dumont (Paris: Peeters, 1983) and Aymard, *Venise, Raguse, et la commerce de blé*, 138.

8 E.g., MD 7/174, MD 23/424, MD 24/197, MD 58/309, and MD 60/112. See also Kılıç, "Osmanlı Devleti'nde Meydana Gelen Kıtlıklar."

9 MD 5/106, MD 5/488, MD 6/312, MD 6/344, MD 6/539, MD 6/731, MD 6/926, and MD 6/1382.

10 MD 5/106, MD 6/226, and MD 6/266.

11 MD 6/690.

12 MD 5/813, MD 5/895, and MD 6/485.

afflicting Rhodes, Cyprus, Damascus, and Jerusalem,[13] where corrupt officials aggravated the shortages by stealing grain.[14] The Mosul area and parts of Greece and Macedonia also suffered shortages,[15] and the Nile may have fallen short of its mark again.[16] That same year, locust swarms reached Rhodes and even İznik, in northwestern Anatolia, possibly driven north of their usual range by the dry weather.[17]

Periodic local shortages[18] continued up to the drought of 1574–5, which turned into one of the most severe famines in memory. As the chronicler Mustafa Ali described it (no doubt with some exaggeration), "In fact that year there was such a famine that historians studied the famine of the prophet Joseph and found that the famine this time was even worse. There had not been such suffering and famine since the time of Sultan Osman."[19] The Edirne area was the worst affected, but other regions as far afield as Jerusalem and Baghdad also reported severe shortages.[20] In Istanbul, the sultan and men of state arranged great processions and prayers for rain in the principal mosques.[21] The following wave of drought, in 1579, was apparently more localized, affecting mainly Syria, eastern Anatolia, and northern Iraq.[22]

The last wave of drought, starting in Syria in the summer of 1583,[23] proved even worse. By 1585, famine extended into Anatolia, the Aegean, and eventually the Balkans, creating generalized shortages across the empire.[24] As far north as Tamışvar (today's Timişoara, in western

[13] MD 12/237, MD 12/348, and MD 12/1066.

[14] MD 12/1162.

[15] MD 14/70–71, MD 14/249, MD 14/599, and MD 17/34–35.

[16] MD 14/1101.

[17] MD 12/618, MD 12/983, and MD 14/1619. For the relation between climate and locust migrations, see D. Camuffo and S. Enzi, "Locust Invasions and Climatic Factors from the Middle Ages to 1800," *Theoretical and Applied Climatology* 43 (1991): 43–73.

[18] E.g., MD 17/34–35 and MD 19/57.

[19] Gelibolu Mustafa Âlî, *Künhü'l-Ahbâr*, ed. Faris Çerçi (Kayseri: Erçiyes Üniversitesi, 2000), 240–1.

[20] MD 24/197, MD 24/503, MD 25/128, MD 26/394, MD 26/669, and MD 26/931. The famine was also recorded by Venetian representatives: See Aymard, *Venise, Raguse, et la commerce de blé*, 138.

[21] Ebru Boyar and Kate Fleet, *A Social History of Ottoman Istanbul* (New York: Cambridge University Press, 2010), 66.

[22] MD 36/70, MD 36/142, MD 36/220, MD 36/271, MD 36/717, MD 36/941, and MD 40/296.

[23] MD 44/443, MD 51/213, and MD 52/261.

[24] MD 52/604, MD 52/752, MD 52/800, MD 55/118, MD 55/191, MD 55/253, MD 55/346, MD 55/409, MD 58/309, MD 58/441, MD 58/602, MD 58/642, MD 58/643, MD 58/736, MD 58/746, MD 58/752, MD 58/791, MD 59/182, MD 60/93, MD

Romania), a petition noted that "this year it has not rained for six or seven months."[25] Reports from Lepanto claimed that "this blessed year the rains never came, and even the lands we planted yielded no harvest"[26] – a plea echoed in dispatches from as far away as Kos (in the Aegean)[27] and Berkofça (in Bulgaria).[28] Around Edirne the rivers dried up, leaving the watermills stranded and creating a shortage of flour.[29] The drought apparently lifted by late 1585, leaving the empire relatively free of famine until the crisis of the 1590s.

Throughout these disasters, the imperial government responded with various measures of famine relief depending on the location and scale of the disaster. Certain districts, usually described as "harsh and stony" (*saab u sengistan*), already faced frequent shortfalls and usually had traditional rights to purchase fixed quantities of grain from neighboring lands at the *narh*, bypassing some of the usual restrictions on the grain trade described in Chapter 1.[30] Rhodes figured prominently among these examples,[31] as did the various Aegean islands like Chios,[32] Andros,[33] Imbros,[34] and Limni,[35] and parts of mainland Greece like İnebahtı (Lepanto)[36] and the Peloponnese.[37]

More often, the Porte issued special ad hoc measures redirecting the flow of grain to relieve shortages. As described in Chapter 1, the imperial government expected most districts in the core provinces to remain self-sufficient in foodstuffs until called on for imperial needs. For less urgent cases, the state might respond by simply offering tax breaks or extensions on current requests for provisions.[38] On more pressing

60/112, MD 60/131, MD 60/498, MD 60/579, MD 61/9, MD 61/16, MD 61/70, MD 61/71, MD 61/138, and MD 61/262.

25 MD 58/746.

26 MD 60/131.

27 MD 55/409.

28 MD 60/112.

29 MD 58/309.

30 E.g., MD 5/488 and MD 58/602. See also Faroqhi, *Towns and Townsmen*, 84–5.

31 E.g., MD 5/513, MD 5/851, MD 14/1619, MD 19/57, MD 43/220, and MD 61/9.

32 MD 4/699.

33 MD 6/824.

34 MD 58/736.

35 MD 40/468.

36 MD 27/562 and MD 60/131.

37 MD 5z/373.

38 E.g., MD 7/418, MD 26/669, and MD 40/296. See also Michael Ursinus, "Natural Disasters and *Tevzi*: Local Tax Systems of the Post-Classical Era in Response to Flooding, Hail, and Thunder," in *Natural Disasters in the Ottoman Empire*, ed. E. Zachariadou (Heraklion: Crete University Press, 1999).

occasions, orders might go out to distribute stocks from local granaries, as was the case during a severe famine in Van (eastern Anatolia) in 1576, when the peasants lacked even seed corn for the next sowing.[39] When local supplies fell short, the Porte might also authorize limited purchases from surrounding regions, granting the special permission required to move grain between districts.[40]

In the worst cases, the state could take the further step of organizing large-scale deliveries of foodstuffs to famine-stricken areas. These shipments proved especially important during the major regionwide droughts already described, when the empire had to arrange significant transfers from areas of surplus to areas of deficit. In most cases, orders went directly from the capital along with the ship coming to purchase the grain. In other words, the area of supply had to be ready with stocks on hand (*der anbar* or *der mahzen*) to load onto boats as they arrived.[41] Given the high transportation costs involved, relief typically came from the nearest available supply. For example, relief for Dubrovnik could come from Albania,[42] relief for the Aegean islands from Euboia,[43] relief for Lapseki from nearby Gelibolu,[44] and relief for Uzeyr (on the Syrian–Turkish border) from Cyprus.[45] Evidently, requests for deliveries among the most far-flung reaches of the empire still passed through Istanbul for approval, as seen in imperial orders for relief from Tunisia to Libya in 1592[46] and from Egypt to Ethiopia in 1573.[47] Only rarely did orders call for famine relief directly from the major imperial grainaries that supplied Istanbul, such as Rodosçuk.[48]

In most cases, these measures appear to have worked. (Or at least, the documents did not record any further famine once relief arrived.) However, Ottoman famine relief efforts suffered two serious shortcomings that would come to play an important role in the crisis of the 1590s.

[39] MD 28/797.

[40] E.g., MD 4/699, MD 5/106, MD 5/513–14, MD 6/266, MD 14/70–71. For more examples of tax breaks and local distribution in famines, see also Murphey, "Provisioning Istanbul."

[41] E.g., MD 6/226 and MD 43/220.

[42] MD 5/106.

[43] MD 6/226.

[44] MD 6/731.

[45] MD 36/70.

[46] MD 69/312.

[47] MD 21/980.

[48] One of these rare exceptions would be MD 55/118 authorizing Saruhan to purchase grain there during a famine.

First, given the limits of transportation, the empire faced considerable obstacles relieving inland areas. During the drought and famine around Damascus in 1583–4, for example, supplies had to be relayed from the Aegean and the western Black Sea coast to Tripoli and then hauled by pack animals some distance into the Syrian interior.[49] Supplying the famine-prone lands of eastern Anatolia proved more challenging still. In the case of the 1576–7 famine in Van, all supplies had to come overland, probably by camel, on difficult roads from Diyarbakır, which was not exactly a fertile breadbasket itself. As it turns out, Diyarbakır could supply only half the 100,000 *kile* (about 100,000 bushels or 1,400 tons) needed in this case; and moreover, it appears the delivery may have gone to relieve the Ottoman garrison rather than the *reaya*.[50] Two years later, another report confirmed that wheat and barley were still at famine prices around the Van area.[51] Similarily, in Erzurum during the drought and famine of 1585, the sultan had to call off *sipahis* from military duty so they could stay behind and furnish relief supplies of grain instead.[52]

Second, serious famines could unleash flight and unrest, spreading chaos into surrounding territories while the imperial government struggled to impose order. In 1560 and again in 1579, starvation in the Crimea reached such a pitch that Tatar refugees flooded into the Balkans offering to sell their families for food, spreading famine and disorder into Romania and Bulgaria.[53] In other cases, failed harvests could leave the *reaya* unable to meet their assigned tax burdens, creating a sudden downward spiral of famine and flight. In the autumn of 1570, for example, the governor of Ioannina (northwestern Greece) wrote the sultan warning, "In the past year there has been a great famine in these parts, and many of the villages have scattered (*perakende olup*). Now the *reaya* cannot meet the obligations on their harvest. Most cannot support [the taxes in] the new cadastral surveys, and they are decided upon flight."[54] Worse still, times of desperation and disorder could attract the unwanted attention

49 MD 49/456, MD 49/477, MD 51/213, MD 52/261, MD 52/604, MD 52/752, and MD 52/800.

50 MD 28/9–10, MD 28/797, MD 29/30, MD 30/47–48, MD 30/71, and MD 30/200. The order may have actually been for 200,000 *kile*, but because two different *kile* measures are mentioned (Edirne *kiles* and Istanbul *kiles*), the figure is uncertain.

51 MD 36/717.

52 MD 61/16, MD 61/70–71, MD 61/75, and MD 61/138.

53 MD 3/822, MD 3/849, MD 3/863, MD 3/894, MD 3/949, MD 3/1321, MD 3/1478, MD 3/1500, MD 39/291, and MD 40/500.

54 MD 14/499. A similar development seems to have taken place in Romania during the famine of 1585 as well: See MD 58/746.

of unruly tribes. Bedouin raids were implicated in a famine in Silifke (southern Anatolia) in 1568,[55] and a decade later Kurdish tribes aggravated a Mosul famine by stealing grain shipments.[56] Likewise, the 1585 drought in Syria gave surrounding Arab tribes a pretext to plunder the peasantry and graze their animals on farmland.[57] Finally, in the worst cases, famine and flight could breed outbreaks of epidemic disease that preyed on the poor conditions of refugees,[58] as proved to be the case in Baghdad during the famine of 1579.[59]

Plague

Ottoman lands also proved unusually susceptible to the ravages of disease – if not exactly for the reasons historians have supposed.[60] The standard historiography, which relied mainly on Arabic medical treatises and European reports, focused overwhelmingly on the impact of bubonic plague, thought to spread episodically from endemic rodent populations and their fleas. Muslim societies, bound by religious scruples to accept the will of God, were supposed to have accepted these epidemics with stoic fatalism, refusing even to flee their towns and cities. And so, plague broke out in inevitable cycles, steadily draining the population of the region.

New research into Ottoman sources has recently revealed a more complex and interesting picture.[61] First, it now appears bubonic plague was

55 MD 7/1752.

56 MD 36/142.

57 MD 55/253.

58 Studies of better documented famines in early modern Europe have usually found that the worst mortality arose not from starvation itself, but from diseases that thrived among the poor sanitary conditions and weakened immune systems of famine refugees. See for example Andrew Appleby, "Epidemics and Famine in the Little Ice Age," in *Climate and History*, ed. R. Rotberg and T. Rabb (Princeton, NJ: Princeton University Press, 1981); Massimo Livi-Bacci, *Population and Nutrition* (New York: Cambridge University Press, 1991); and John Post, *Food Shortage, Climatic Variability, and Epidemic Disease in Preindustrial Europe* (Ithaca, NY: Cornell University Press, 1985). This book returns to the issue of famine mortality in more depth in Chapters 6 and 8.

59 MD 40/296.

60 On the evolving historiography of Ottoman disease, see Sam White, "Rethinking Disease in Ottoman History," *International Journal of Middle East Studies* 42 (2010): 549–67. Among the most influential studies, see Conrad, "Plague in the Early Medieval Near East"; Dols, *Black Death in the Middle East*; Dols, "Second Plague Pandemic"; Biraben, *Hommes et la peste*; and Panzac, *Peste dans l'Empire ottoman.*

61 White, "Rethinking Disease." These new studies include: Orhan Kılıç, *Genel Hatlarıyla Dünya'da ve Osmanlı Devletinde Salgın Hastalıklar* (Elazığ: Fırat Üniversitesi Basımevi,

just one of many deadly pathogens in a complex disease environment. While past authors readily translated every Ottoman reference to "*taun*" as bubonic plague (in contradistinction to "*veba*," or just "epidemic"), its meaning was apparently more flexible. Not even classical Arabic accounts of "*taun*" always referred to bubonic plague,[62] and Ottoman writers were not really so careful with medical terminology. The sixteenth-century chronicler Selaniki, for example, described "a great *taun* and *veba*" that caused people to swell up before apparently it "roasted their livers" (*ciğerlerin biryan eyledi*);[63] and he mentioned two further outbreaks of "*taun*" wherein victims apparently died of "a stomach sickness" (*maraz-ı su-ı mide*).[64] Elsewhere in two different copies of his history, one Ottoman scribe has recorded a certain outbreak as a "*mübarek maraz*" (a blessed sickness), while another copyist has written "*maraz-ı taun*" (a sickness of *taun*), suggesting the term was not used very precisely.[65] Official documents also employed the word metaphorically for any great scourge, as in descriptions of bandits as a "*taun-ı ekber*" ("a great plague").[66] In fact, "*taun*" seems to equate rather closely with the English "plague" in all its variety of meaning; and precisely the same goes for "*peste*" – whether in French or Italian – which could also refer to a range of maladies.

Second, there is little to suggest that plague was just a natural condition of the region tied to endemic populations of rodents. When the Ottomans did finally introduce quarantine beginning in 1838, plague diminished immediately.[67] If constant plague outbreaks were really responsible for most excess mortality, then population in the region should have been consistently low for centuries. Although that proved

2004); C. Yılmaz and M. Yılmaz, ed. *Osmanlılarda Sağlık* (Istanbul: Biofarma, 2006); Birsen Bulmuş, "The Plague in the Ottoman Empire, 1300–1838" (PhD diss., Georgetown University, 2008); Nukhet Varlık, "Disease and Empire: A History of Plague Epidemics in the Early Modern Ottoman Empire (1453–1600)" (PhD diss., University of Chicago, 2008); Alan Mikhail, "The Nature of Plague in Late Eighteenth-Century Egypt," *Bulletin of the History of Medicine* (2008): 249–75; Aaron Shakow, "Marks of Contagion: Bubonic Plague in the Early Modern Mediterranean" (PhD diss., Harvard University, 2009); and Miri Shefer-Mossensohn, *Ottoman Medicine* (Binghamton: SUNY Press, 2009).

62 Conrad, "Plague in the Early Medieval Near East," 79–80, and Lawrence Conrad, "Ta'un and Waba Concepts of Plague," *Journal of the Economic and Social History of the Orient* 25 (1982): 268–307, at 271–3.

63 Selânikî Mustafa Efendi, *Tarih-i Selânikî*, ed. Mehmet İpşirli (Ankara: TTK, 1999), 759.

64 Ibid., 178–9 and 229.

65 *Tarih-i Selânikî*, 768.

66 E.g., MD 7/974.

67 Panzac, *La peste dans l'Empire ottoman*, 504–7.

true for the eighteenth century – the period of Daniel Panzac's influential study – we have already seen how the empire's inhabitants nearly doubled in the sixteenth century despite ongoing outbreaks of "*taun*." Furthermore, in the rare cases where the seasonality of mortality is known, the numbers are not what we would expect from a flea-borne disease. Urban mortality peaks typically appear in August–September rather than June–July, a pattern more consistent with gastrointestinal infections or malaria than rat- and flea-borne bubonic plague (see Chapter 10). In other words, given the skepticism that surrounds "plague" diagnoses even in better-documented European cases,[68] we should be very cautious assigning a particular pathogen to most epidemics in Ottoman history. Most of the supposed plagues of the sixteenth- and seventeenth-century Ottoman Empire would just as well meet the description of typhus, another serious epidemic of the period, and one that occasionally spread to Europe from Ottoman lands.[69] Epidemics in the Ottoman Empire, as throughout the early modern world, involved a complex mix of pathways and pathogens, sensitive to human and environmental disturbances.

Finally, evidence from the period overturns older ideas of Muslim fatalism in the face of plague. When Muslims saw the hand of God in outbreaks of disease or other natural calamities, they differed little from their Byzantine predecessors or their Christian contemporaries. All three tended to view natural disasters as divine judgment; and yet religious notions did not prevent any of them, including Ottoman Muslims, from perceiving that disease had natural causes, too, and from taking action accordingly.[70] As the English traveler John Covel observed during a plague in Edirne in 1679:

> The best sort of people fled to other places, as the Turkes likewise themselves did from Adrianople to their houses here [in the countryside], for that same is a story that they are not afraid of the plague, because their fortunes are wrote on their forehead; for all fled, but such as were poor, or had offices about Court, and could not get away. There dyed that year about 100 persons out of the Vizier's own house; and really,

68 E.g., Samuel Cohn, "The Black Death: End of a Paradigm," *American Historical Review* 107 (2002): 703–38 and J. Theilman and F. Cate, "A Plague of Plagues: The Problem of Plague Diagnosis in Medieval England," *Journal of Interdisciplinary History* 37 (2007): 371–93.

69 Hans Zinsser, *Rats, Lice and History* (New York: BD&L, 1935), chapter 15, and Frederick Carwright, *Disease in History* (New York: Crowell, 1972), 83–5.

70 See especially M.-H. Congourdeau and M. Melhaoui, "La perception de la peste en pays chrètien byzantin et musulman," *Revue des études byzantines* 59 (2000): 95–124.

> those that are forc't to stay value it no more than we do an ague. But this is the same amongst Jewes, Greeks, Armenians, and every body else.[71]

As with other natural disasters, the imperial government employed a range of measures to contain epidemics and relieve afflicted areas. By the limited standards of the time, Ottoman medical practice was reasonably sophisticated and its system of public health rather extensive. Thanks to the number and wealth of Ottoman pious foundations, hospitals were fairly widespread and well-endowed, and by the sixteenth century the better-off among them employed large staffs of surgeons, doctors, and orderlies.[72] By the 1590s, even the army and navy had their own medical staffs, with a doctor or surgeon assigned to every thousand soldiers.[73] Moreover, it would appear the Ottomans possessed at least a basic notion of contagion and sometimes took active steps to prevent the spread of disease. For example, some Ottoman cities maintained leper colonies (*miskinler tekyesi*) to isolate victims, and it would appear that local officials kept watch for new outbreaks.[74] Likewise, it was the Ottomans who pioneered variolation for smallpox, another major affliction of the early modern Near East.[75]

Incidents from imperial orders and court records offer at least anecdotal evidence that the state could take active measures to contain epidemics. In one case from 1579, the sultan ordered the governor of Alexandria to prevent pilgrims and merchants from leaving by ship to Istanbul, apparently to keep them from bringing a plague to the capital.[76] Other examples suggest that local governments usually took the initiative.

71 John Covel, "Extracts from the Diaries of John Covel, 1670–1679," in *Early Voyages and Travels in the Levant*, ed. J. Bent (New York: Ben Franklin, 1972), 244.

72 C. Yılmaz and N. Yılmaz, "Osmanlı Hastahane Yönetmelikleri: Vakfiyelerde Osmanlı Dârüşşifâları," in *Osmanlılarda Sağlık*, ed. C. Yılmaz and N. Yılmaz (Istanbul: Biofarma, 2006). See also Amy Singer, "Ottoman Palestine (1516–1800): Health, Disease, and Historical Sources," in *Health and Disease in the Holy Land*, ed. M. Wasserman and S. Kottek (Lewiston: Edwin Mellen, 1996) for hospitals in Palestine.

73 Abdülkadir Özcan, "Osmanlı Ordusunda Sağlık Hizmetlerine Bir Bakış," in *Osmanlılarda Sağlık*, ed. C. Yılmaz and N. Yılmaz (Istanbul: Biofarma, 2006) and İdris Bostan, "Osmanlı Bahriyesinde Sağlık Hizmetleri," in ibid.

74 E.g., Yılmaz and Yılmaz, eds., *Osmanlılarda Sağlık*, vol. 2, documents 328, 377, 407, 458, and 488.

75 Europeans only adopted the practice after Lady Mary Wortley Montagu, the clever wife of an English diplomat, wrote home describing its use among Anatolian peasants in the 1710s. See J. N. Hays, *The Burdens of Disease* (New Brunswick, NJ: Rutgers University Press, 1998), 123.

76 Yılmaz and Yılmaz, eds., *Osmanlılarda Sağlık*, vol. 2, document 188.

One document from 1566, for example, makes it clear that the island of Chios continued its pre-Ottoman practice of quarantine well after Ottoman conquest, isolating merchants who came from plague-infested areas for twenty-five days after arrival.[77] Likewise, in a study of two epidemics recorded in the court records of Trabzon, the *kadı* had suspected cases investigated, and in some instances he ordered infected persons carried to the outskirts of town and left to die. Meanwhile, the *sipahis* fled the town, and Ottoman ships avoided Trabzon harbor.[78] Moreover, it appears walled cities tried to exclude unwanted vagrants, and the practice could also be used deliberately to keep out carriers of infection.[79]

More importantly, the imperial government's general restrictions on unauthorized flight and migration may have helped isolate major outbreaks. Most Ottoman subjects had to stay put during a plague for the same reason they had to stay put any time: not because flight violated divine law, but because it violated imperial law. Unless they paid their taxes or the *çift-bozan akçesi*, the peasantry remained bound to the land.[80] During an epidemic that struck Diyarbakır in 1544–5, for example, imperial orders specifically forbade anyone to "flee saying that there is plague" (*taun vardır diyü kaçup*),[81] and later orders included similar refrains, usually in response to complaints from *tımar*-holders.[82]

Collectively, these practices may have done the Ottomans some good, limiting the spread of major epidemics that would otherwise have threatened sixteenth-century population growth. Early modern European quarantine had also evolved from piecemeal steps that gradually constrained the spread of plague even before its disappearance there in the eighteenth century.[83] Local responses had often played a key role in

77 MD 5/1334.

78 Ronald Jennings, "Plague in Trabzon and Reactions to It According to Local Judicial Registers," in *Humanist and Scholar: Essays in Honor of Andreas Tietze*, ed. H. Lowry and D. Quataert (Istanbul: Isis, 1993).

79 E.g., MD 7/1706. See also Kılıç, *Genel Hatlarıyla Dünya'da ve Osmanlı Devleti'nde Salgın Hastalıklar*, 83–4.

80 The policy even applied to Jews and Christians. The Jews of Salonica, in particular, had a customary right to reside outside the city during plague outbreaks, but even they had to fulfill their tax quota of broadcloth first. See MD 3/172, MD 7/1626, MD 7/1828, MD 19/417, and MD 36/738.

81 H. Sahillioğlu and E. Ihsanoğlu, *Topkapı Sarayı Arşivi H.951–952 Tarihli ve E-12321 Numaralı Mühimme Defteri* (Istanbul: IRCICA, 2002), documents 311 and 369.

82 E.g., MD 12/534 and MD 14/120.

83 Biraben, *Les hommes et la peste*, 309–10; Paul Slack, "The Disappearance of Plague: An Alternate View," *The Economic History Review* 34 (1981): 469–76; and Paul Slack, "The Response to Plague in Early Modern England: Public Policies and Their Consequences,"

containing epidemics, since city officials could react more quickly than central authorities.[84]

Nevertheless, Ottoman practices fell far short of real quarantine, and disease remained an ever-present threat in Ottoman lands. Even if imperial measures reduced mortality overall, deadly epidemics remained a constant feature of Ottoman life. Like food shortages, plagues seemed to strike somewhere in the empire about every other year, usually in isolated incidences, but occasionally as serious epidemics. From the 1560s, Ottoman documents record plagues in Aleppo in 1564;[85] Karaman in 1565;[86] and Salonica, Alacahisar, and the nearby *yörük* nomads in 1568.[87] In 1571, plagues struck Caffa[88] and Samakov;[89] then, over 1572–4 a series of epidemics apparently spread from Cyprus[90] to Salonica,[91] Edirne,[92] and Uzeyr.[93] In 1576, the Romanian districts of Erdel and Tamışvar were afflicted;[94] and the following year plague appeared in Erzurum, in eastern Anatolia.[95] The last significant epidemic before the crisis of the 1590s apparently began in Salonica in 1579[96] and then spread to Bosnia[97] and Herzegovina[98] over the following two years. Ottoman chronicles also mention a serious plague in Istanbul during the summers of 1584 and 1585,[99] perhaps tied to that year's major drought and famine. Given the lack of consistent recordkeeping, these examples could be only the tip of the iceberg.

As in cases of famine, epidemics could spread in synergy with famine and disorder. Had the Ottomans actually proven as fatalistic and

in *Famine, Disease and the Social Order in Early Modern Society*, ed. J. Walker and R. Schofield (Cambridge: Cambridge University Press, 1989).

84 Gary Magee, "Disease Management in Pre-Industrial Europe: A Reconsideration of the Efficacy of the Local Responses to Epidemics," *Journal of European Economic History* 26 (1997): 605–26.

85 MD 6/114.

86 MD 5/369.

87 MD 7/1626, MD 7/2186, and MD 12/572.

88 MD 14/120.

89 MD 14/1224.

90 MD 19/407 and MD 23/372.

91 MD 19/417.

92 MD 22/82.

93 MD 24/262.

94 MD 28/843 and MD 29/269.

95 MD 33/352 and MD 33/360.

96 MD 36/738.

97 MD 43/547.

98 MD 46/715.

99 *Tarih-i Selânikî*, 148 and 173–4.

indifferent as historians once imagined, the *reaya* might have stayed calm and spared the empire some of the worst outbreaks of flight and contagion. High mortality or disorder could also create openings for tribes and bandits to prey on afflicted populations, driving a downward spiral of insecurity and depopulation. The situation was especially precarious when the initial death toll left remaining peasants unable to meet their assigned tithes and requisitions, compelling them to escape ahead of the tax collector.[100] The imperial government often made efforts to relieve afflicted populations and revise down their tax and conscription quotas, but frequently it responded too late.[101] During the Little Ice Age crisis, refugees from disease, disorder, and taxation would become another major vector for infection.

War and Banditry

In the later decades of the sixteenth century, war was as much the natural state of affairs as shortages and epidemics. Conflict raged somewhere on the Ottoman frontiers nearly every year from the 1560s through the 1590s. From 1567–71, Ottoman troops were putting down revolt in Yemen; in 1569, they campaigned in the north in Astrakhan; and in 1571, they entered the Mediterranean war described in the introduction to Part I, which flared up periodically until a formal treaty with Spain in 1580. By then, the empire had already launched another campaign to the east against Safavid Persia, which it pursued to a successful conclusion, capturing Tabriz in 1589. After four scant years of peace, the Ottomans would launch another campaign against the Habsburg Empire, whose consequences would prove altogether more fateful, as we see in Part II. Others have already written about Ottoman warfare itself, and the Ottoman military rarely faced defeat abroad in these years, so the purpose of this section is to consider the impact of war at home and, above all, how the demands of major campaigns enflamed unrest in the core provinces.

Other authors have already commented on the strong association between war and banditry in the sixteenth-century empire, but this connection has been misunderstood. Mustafa Akdağ argued that the *sipahis* only stirred up trouble at home, and that the *reaya* breathed a sigh of relief when they went on campaign. The trouble started when they stayed back

[100] E.g., MD 7/2186, MD 22/82, MD 29/269, and MD 43/537.

[101] E.g., MD 5/369, MD 24/262, and MD 28/843.

from the front to sponge off the peasantry.[102] More recently, Ottomanists have tended to follow Halil İnalcık's approach, which ties rural violence to the spread of firearms and the recruitment of irregular infantry, the so-called *sekbans*, from the swelling ranks of the landless and unemployed – men who would turn to banditry as soon as they were released from campaign.[103]

These interpretations imply that it was demobilization after war, rather than war itself, that fueled the banditry and unrest afflicting the empire, especially Anatolia. Based on the imperial orders, however, it appears just the opposite was true. Even though *kadıs* provided regular law enforcement and administration, the empire still relied on military governors commanding *sipahis* to keep order in the countryside.[104] Rather than ridding the empire of menacing officers and irregulars, major campaigns stripped the provinces of their protection against banditry, leaving them exposed to waves of violence. Whereas in normal years the imperial orders might mention a dozen significant incidents of banditry and a couple complaints of general lawlessness, years of major campaigns could produce scores of reports complaining of pillaging and theft in the absence of soldiers. Moreover, as we see in Part II, relatively few documents make any mention of clashes with private armies or militias until the 1590s and even fewer mention gun-toting "*sekbans*" until the 1600s. As Chapter 7 explains, both these phenomena were more the consequence than the cause of the Little Ice Age crisis.

Prior to the crisis of the 1590s, perhaps the worst outbreak of unrest came in 1583–4. Already mentioned as a time of drought and famine, these years also witnessed a major campaign on the eastern front in a deepening war with Persia. One of the first descriptions of this wave of banditry came in a letter from the *kadı* of Uluborlu (in southwestern Anatolia) discussing "the punishment of criminals and bandits who have appeared here while the soldiers are away on the eastern campaign."[105] Then in rapid succession, reports followed from

[102] Akdağ, *Celali İsyanları*, 82–3 *et passim*.

[103] Halil İnalcık, "The Socio-Political Effects of the Diffusion of Firearms in the Middle East," in *War, Technology and Society in the Middle East*, ed. V. Parry and M. Yapp (New York: Oxford University Press, 1975) and Barkey, *Bandits and Bureaucrats*.

[104] See Ronald Jennings, "Limitations of the Judicial Powers of the Kadi in 17th-Century Ottoman Kayseri," *Studia Islamica* 50 (1979): 151–84, especially 155.

[105] MD 44/334. This *defter* has been transcribed and published as Mehmet Ali Unal, *Mühimme Defteri 44* (İzmir: Akademi Kitabevi, 1995).

Tripoli (Lebanon);[106] Canik (northeastern Anatolia);[107] Bolu, Kastamonu, Kangırı, and Ankara (west-central Anatolia);[108] Menteşe (southwestern Anatolia);[109] and Akşehir (south-central Anatolia).[110] Almost all included similar phrases to the effect that bandits were taking advantage of the soldiers' absence. From Canik, for example, the *kadı* warned that "since the land is mountainous and stony, bandits settle here and commit crime. In previous years, the *sipahis* have stayed and defended the *reaya* from criminals, and they lived in peace. Now that the *sipahis* of the aforementioned district have gone on campaign, there can be no doubt that these bandits have taken again to crime."[111]

Meanwhile, the departure of soldiers left the empire vulnerable to other sorts of lawlessness. Predatory nomadic tribes used the opening left by war to pillage settled communities along the border of the desert and steppe. An uprising of tribes around Diyarbakır (eastern Anatolia) killed more than thirty men.[112] From Gaza came reports of Bedouin raids on the *reaya*; and a little to the north around Nablus and Jerusalem, a group of fifteen Arab tribes pillaged the towns, killing over a hundred.[113] In the Black Sea region, the distraction of war gave the Cossacks a chance to attack Tatars and other Ottoman allies.[114] Meanwhile, gangs of unemployed religious students – the *sohtas* alluded to in the previous chapter – took advantage of the lawlessness to terrorize parts of Anatolia. One such gang appeared in western Anatolia, plundering villages around Aydın, Saruhan, and Menteşe.[115] Two more gangs of eighty to ninety men each turned up in northern Anatolia, one in the province of Rum, and the other in Kırşehir south of Ankara, while a third appeared subsequently around Denizli, further west.[116] Finally, warnings came to the capital that bandits were actually crossing over from Persia into Ottoman territory around Van.[117]

106 MD 44/337.
107 MD 44/356.
108 MD 44/384.
109 MD 44/394.
110 MD 44/434.
111 MD 44/356.
112 MD 44/164.
113 MD 44/393.
114 MD 44/352–53.
115 MD 44/373. For more on the *sohta* uprisings of 1584, see Akdağ, *Celali İsyanları*, 100–6.
116 MD 44/412 and MD 44/417.
117 MD 44/376.

In response to such outbreaks of lawlessness, the imperial government developed certain standard precautions. As far back as 1570, the state started appointing local leaders called *yiğitbaşıs* to raise militias for domestic security,[118] and it appears the tactic became more widespread in response to rising incidents of banditry over the following two decades.[119] Furthermore, when militias proved inadequate to keep the peace, the imperial government would order lower-ranked *sipahis* to stay behind and defend the homeland as well. For instance, during the same campaign of 1583–4, the following order went out to the provincial governor of Anadolu:

> It was my command that "Each of the commanders subject to your governorship shall receive my order, and every *tımar*-holder shall be equipped for war and ready to join my campaign first thing this spring." That command remains unchanged and in force as before. However, since it has become customary (*adet-i kamdime olmağın*) to appoint a number of *sipahis* each from among the lesser *tımar*-holders to defend every district from bandits, criminals, and *sohtas*, so this time, too, I command you to appoint *sipahis* for protection as you did last year. *So ordered*...[120]

However, it remains unclear whether either measure proved effective; and both policies proved to have unintended consequences in the long run. The local militias could easily turn into gangs that differed little from the bandits whom they were ordered to suppress. Likewise, the *sipahis* ordered to clear the land of bandits could themselves turn into the worst offenders. Although we have far more documents dealing with regular, run-of-the-mill criminals taking advantage of wartime distress, there are a number of orders that discuss theft and extortion by soldiers[121] – a problem that would become particularly acute during the crisis of the 1590s.

Furthermore, both measures only added to the rising cost of warfare, as Ottoman armies fought to keep ahead of rivals in Europe and Asia.

118 The earliest description I have found comes from a report of the *kadı* of İznik in 1571: "...when criminals and thieves appeared in the mountains and passes of Yalak, the governor (*bey*) of Bursa came with an order to appoint a certain Mustafa as *yiğitbaşı*, and he warned the people of the surrounding villages to go up into the mountains with guns and other weapons and get the thieves and criminals whenever they appeared" (MD 12/148).

119 E.g., MD 35/75 and MD 44/334.

120 MD 44/264.

121 E.g., MD 51/78.

As in most early modern states, military expenditures already devoured the lion's share of the Ottoman budget – perhaps two-thirds in normal years.[122] During major campaigns, the *reaya* bore the additional burden of forced purchases and requisitions, as well as extraordinary cash taxes levied almost every year by the end of the century. During years like 1583–4, when these demands came on top of drought and famine, general desperation and disaffection must have played an important part in the spread of theft and violence. As Amy Singer has described in Palestine:

> Annual rhythms were predictably interrupted by unanticipated natural crises and disasters. Any common concerns over the vicissitudes of nature, however, were not enough to unite the peasants and Ottoman officials in a harmonious provincial polity. The two groups stood at opposite sides of the tax chest: the peasants filled it while the officials drained its contents.[123]

And so, for regions already facing population pressure, shortages, and natural disaster, the heavy demands of war could prove another major cause of unrest. As we see in Part II , this potent combination would come to play a critical role in the outbreak of rebellion in the 1590s.

Breakdowns in the Provisioning System

The empire's struggle to support the costs of war represented just one way in which provisioning systems were coming unraveled after the peak of their efficiency in the early 1570s, when the Ottomans rebuilt their fleet in the aftermath of Lepanto. Squeezed by population pressure and price inflation, the empire faced growing problems getting basic commodities to feed its major cities and military. Like the other disasters of the late sixteenth century, these problems were partly natural and partly man-made. Inherent shortcomings in Ottoman provisioning systems exacerbated an already difficult situation as growth in demand outpaced supply. Faced with a combination of ecological pressures and rising costs, the imperial government often proved unyielding and inflexible, failing to fix the system before it became too late.

The shortfalls struck first at the heart of the provisioning system, the shipments of basic foodstuffs to Constantinople. As the city's population ballooned to some half a million, it appears that regular shipments from

[122] Barkan, "Price Revolution" and İnalcık, *Economic and Social History of the Ottoman Empire*, vol. 1, 77–102.

[123] Singer, *Palestinian Peasants*, 89.

the Danube and Nile began to fall short of demands. Every couple years from the late 1560s onward, the imperial government began to complain of chronic "shortages" (*müzayaka*), turning increasingly to emergency purchases and requisitions from other regions. In late 1568, for example, the sultan ordered half a ten-ship consignment of grain bound for Caffa rerouted to ease a shortage in Istanbul;[124] and at the same time, Euboia, Salonica, and Karasu also had to make extra shipments to balance a shortfall in the capital granaries.[125] Then in the winter of 1574–5, there came a "severe shortage" (*ziyade müzayaka*) of provisions, and Istanbul ordered stocks from Yenişehir (northwest Anatolia),[126] Çorlu (eastern Thrace),[127] and Ereğli (south central Anatolia).[128] A year later similar shortages led to sweeping demands for provisions from the Black Sea coast[129] and huge overland shipments by camel from parts of central and western Anatolia.[130]

As the shortages piled up, the state attempted to restrict the consumption and export of basic commodities in order to enhance the flow of supplies to the capital. Orders went out in 1564 and 1565 banning the use of grapes for wine, so that the juice could go to make Istanbul's vinegar and grape molasses.[131] Meanwhile, grain exports, which had peaked in the 1550s during a series of poor Italian harvests, declined sharply during and after the shortages of 1565–7.[132] Apparently, the restrictions on exports were intended to protect the self-contained imperial provisioning system and to free up surplus for Istanbul and the army.

These consumption and export controls may have only aggravated problems of smuggling and speculation. A number of documents from the mid-1560s onward make it clear that Ottoman official food prices had started to drift away from (black) market values; and in the inflationary years of the later sixteenth century this gap put increasing strains on suppliers. By 1563, it seems Ottomans in Greece could illegally sell grain to foreign ships for almost twice the official price – that is to say

[124] MD 7/2077.
[125] MD 7/2489.
[126] MD 26/873.
[127] MD 26/885.
[128] MD 26/886.
[129] MD 28/231.
[130] MD 27/935–36 and MD 28/899.
[131] MD 5/484 and MD 6/41.
[132] Aymard, *Venise, Raguse, et la commerce de blé*, part II, chapter 2; and Simons, "Le blé dans les rapports vénéto-ottomans."

twenty-five to thirty *akçe* per *kile*, instead of the usual fifteen.[133] Along the Adriatic and Aegean coasts, smugglers started to deliver grain, honey, wax, hides, and leather to the Christian states,[134] and imperial orders began to accuse officials of diverting the major grain shipments from Egypt and the Balkans.[135]

The problem was not just Western demand or the price differential between the two halves of the Mediterranean. Ottoman official prices had simply become unrealistic, encouraging evasion and speculation. As early as the famine of 1564–5, the *kadı* of Bursa warned of "swindlers" stockpiling grain,[136] and meanwhile hoarding in İznik (northwest Anatolia) and Samsun (a port on the Black Sea) created a shortage of onions in the capital.[137] Even in times of natural disaster, the imperial government sometimes failed to adjust prices accordingly. After a severe snowstorm in November 1573, for example, the bread-makers of Istanbul petitioned for an increase in the fixed price "claiming that there are no provisions." However, the sultan, in an imperial order, rejected the whole claim as "excuses" arguing that "two days of snow is no reason to raise the official price of provisions."[138] Yet at just this time speculators were already stockpiling grain in Rodosçuk, apparently betting that either the sultan would cave in and raise the price or, alternatively, that they could smuggle out the grain or sell it on the black market for a sizeable profit.[139] Not surprisingly, reports of the 1570s and 1580s increasingly lay the blame for grain shortages on speculators and hoarders.[140]

Meanwhile, the imperial sheep supply fell into even greater difficulties – and given the role that sheep would play in the outbreak of crisis in the 1590s, this aspect of imperial provisioning deserves closer study. As with other foodstuffs, the meat supply ran into shortfalls every couple of years starting in the late 1560s, with serious breakdowns in exceptionally bad seasons. As with grain, the imperial government tried to curtail consumption and step up forced purchases and deliveries from outside the usual range of supply. The problems appear within the famine

133 MD 6/621.
134 E.g., MD 6/24–26, MD 6/71, and MD 6/125.
135 E.g., MD 6/531, MD 6/419, MD 10/80, and MD 14/65.
136 MD 6/297 and MD 6/384–85.
137 MD 6/190 and MD 5/129.
138 Refik, *Onaltıncı Asırda İstanbul Hayatı*, chapter 8, document 26.
139 Ibid., chapter 8, document 27.
140 E.g., MD 5/811, MD 6/425, MD 6/1353, MD 7/213, MD 39/631, MD 51/67, MD 51/218.

years of 1564–5, when the imperial government had to make extra requisitions from Anatolia.[141] Then in the winter of 1567–8, the meat crisis reached the point that the state ordered first the Jews of Salonica and then the entire population of Rumeli not to slaughter sheep, but only to eat cattle and goats.[142] Eight years later in 1576, the sultan again promulgated a similar order over an even larger part of the empire.[143] The year after that the supply fell so short that some regions were sending in female sheep for slaughter – a desperate practice that the sultan sensibly outlawed, since it would cut into the reproductive stock.[144] Even so, some regions were still sending ewes instead of lambs as late as 1579.[145] By the 1580s, supplies of livestock were getting so tight that some soap manufacturers of western Anatolia were forced to abandon their trade for want of animal fat, and even well-endowed *imarets* had to serve goat instead of mutton, unless they could get special access to supplies.[146]

As explained in Chapter 2, the per capita supply of sheep and goats had not fallen as quickly as the per capita supply of grains. However, the animal provisioning system of the late sixteenth century suffered from two major shortcomings that left it especially vulnerable to natural disasters and inflation. First, the unusual method of purchase and delivery through the *celep-keşan* system proved far more sensitive to disruptions and price shocks than the larger grain supply system. As described in Chapter 1, grain shipments were usually large-scale, state-directed enterprises with risk spread out among merchants, guilds, and the imperial government. Sheep deliveries, on the other hand, placed the burden not on the state or guilds but on individuals who could easily exhaust their capital and go bankrupt during hard times, interrupting the supply of provisions for years to come.

Second, the supply of animals suffered longer from natural disasters than the supply of grains. As seen in the discussion of famine, the the harvest of one region could usually compensate for the failure of another. Furthermore, wheat and barley could be stocked over a period of years to see through annual fluctuations. Although flocks lived on, their

141 MD 6/47, MD 6/72, MD 6/165, MD 6/953, MD 6/1333, MD 6/1334, MD 6/1406, MD 6/1407, MD 6/1408–10, and MD 6/1430.

142 MD 7/834 and MD 7/1996. This practice is also described in Greenwood, "Istanbul's Meat Provisioning," 22–3.

143 MD 28/237, MD 28/274, and MD 28/328.

144 MD 30/320 and MD 33/133.

145 MD 35/479, MD 36/119, MD 36/464, MD 40/260, and MD 40/327.

146 Faroqhi, *Towns and Townsmen*, 224–5.

harvest, so to speak, consisted of the increment of births over deaths from to year to year. Since that "harvest" was a living animal, it could not be warehoused like grain or other crops, and so the good years could not always compensate for the bad. Moreover, when crops were lost in drought or floods, famers could always plant new seeds and hope for the best next season; but when animals died off in large numbers it was as though pastoralists had lost their accumulated capital stock, which could take years to recover. Finally, the onset of the Little Ice Age with its cold winters and dry springs proved as deadly for livestock as for cereals. As early as 1571–2, reports came back from northern Anatolia and Bulgaria of many animals freezing to death in heavy snows;[147] and seven years later, severe cold and disease combined to kill off an even larger number of livestock, fueling the shortages already described for that year.[148]

As with grain, the imperial government may have aggravated the situation by refusing to adjust the *narh* in line with market prices. Consequently, hoarding and speculation developed into a chronic problem by the 1570s. The failure of an emergency shipment of clarified butter (*sadeyağ*) from the Crimea in 1571, for example, provoked the following reply from the sultan:

> To the governor (*bey*) of Caffa:
>
> Some speculators and others over there have come, and claiming that "there is a shortage and the price should go up," they have not sent their butter here but have apparently stockpiled it. Now how many times have I warned you and ordered, "Do not let speculators or others their stockpile fat but send it immediately." What is the reason there is still stockpiled fat?[149]

Therefore, by the time the Persian war got underway in the 1580s, Ottoman provisioning systems had already run into significant difficulties. Military demands on top of civilian needs tested the limits of Ottoman resources, exacerbating shortages driven by population pressure and natural disaster. Matters came to a head by 1584, when as described, drought and famine struck in the midst of a major Ottoman campaign. For the first time, hitherto manageable problems of shortages, hoarding, and speculation threatened to boil over into widespread crisis,

[147] MD 10/217 and MD 16/570.

[148] MD 32/468, MD 35/74, and MD 35/462.

[149] MD 12/664. Akdağ, *Celali İsyanları*, 50, also discusses the shortages caused by the misalignment of official prices.

giving a preview of the much greater catastrophe that would befall the empire a decade later.

Starting in 1581, the imperial government began to arrange extraordinary shipments of supplies from all over the empire to meet the burgeoning demands of the army on the eastern front. Wallachia shipped out around a thousand tons of flour and barley,[150] while the provinces of Anadolu and Karaman raised levies of two *müds* (perhaps half a ton) of barley and one of flour from every thirty households.[151] Many local *sipahis* also received exemptions from military service in return for extra grain contributions to the campaign.[152] Meanwhile, the Porte sent out sharp threats to all the governors of Anatolia and Syria, demanding prompt delivery of the year's requisitions and reprimanding them for excuses such as "there is famine and the delivery is impossible."[153]

In spite of these efforts and ongoing requsitions throughout the provinces, the shortages mounted, reaching famine proportions by 1585.[154] The garrison at Tiflis (in present-day Georgia) suffered first from a shortfall of grain that eventually progressed to hunger and sickness. The sultan demanded extra supplies from Erzurum – already saddled with the cost of feeding the army's camels – and then called in reinforcements from Diyarbakır.[155] Within a couple of years, Diyarbakır itself was facing want, as part of the general trend of drought and famine spreading across the empire.[156] By 1585, this famine reached Erzurum, too, just as the army was passing through on its way to another campaign in Persia. The chronicler İbrahim Peçevi described the tense situation that followed:

> The winter that year had been passed quietly in Kastamonu. In the spring, they prepared to go to Tabriz and along the way they arrived at Erzurum in July. So God willed it that up until that time there had been plenty, but suddenly such a famine started that the soldiers began to

150 MD 44/92.

151 MD 44/262.

152 MD 44/61.

153 MD 44/46.

154 See also Orhan Kılıç, "1585 Yılında Tebriz Serferi'ne Çıkan Osmanlı Ordusunun İkmal ve İaşesi," *Askeri Tarih Bülteni* 46 (1999): 109–36 for a list of supplies ordered that year, as registered in MD 59. Joseph von Hammer-Purgstall, *Histoire de l'Empire ottoman* (Paris: 1838–39) vol. 7, 209, claims that the Ottoman army originally contained some 200,000 men that year, but that the vizier "reduced it by 40,000 for fear of an imminent famine." However, the source of this information is not clear.

155 MD 44/47, MD 44/102, MD 44/103, and MD 44/147–49.

156 MD 44/446.

> grow insolent. One day, indeed, a unit of soldiers perishing with hunger came to the grand vizier and not only spoke out of line, but even took the bags of fodder out from under the feeding horses. But what can solve famine? Despite this incident, they continued on their way to the front...[157]

In a desperate response to the escalating costs of war, the sultan debased the silver coinage by some 45 percent that year, sparking destabilizing inflation and cutting soldiers' real pay by almost half. The move did not so much affect the prebendal cavalry, who were paid in land revenues, but it enraged the Janissaries and other elite soldiers who received salaries in cash.[158] In 1589, after four more years of shortages, late wages, and monetary instability, these Janissaries staged their first mutiny against the Ottoman sultan, forcing him to depose the imperial treasurer.[159] In the few years of peace that followed, the situation calmed down again, but the uprising proved an ominous sign of things to come.

Meanwhile, on the home front, grain supplies and prices suffered serious shocks, leaving dearth in Istanbul and other major cities. In 1585, the sultan sent out a command to all the *kadıs* of the Black Sea and Mediterranean coasts ordering that "while there is need for provisions in Istanbul, however much barley, wheat, and other provisions that are found in your *kaza*, I command that none be sent elsewhere and all be sent here."[160] For the next year, however, the capital continued to face "severe shortages" (*ziyade müzayaka*) in provisions, until the imperial government finally ordered an extraordinary shipment of around 2,500 tons of grain along with cheese, honey, and other commodities from Wallachia and Moldavia.[161]

At the same time, the sheep supply was in serious turmoil. Over the 1580s, the official price of meat diverged widely from the real market value, creating huge losses for the *celeps* and fueling rampant smuggling and hoarding. In 1584, the sultan began to complain of suppliers going bankrupt, issuing threats to provincial officials who failed to find new

[157] *Peçevî Tarihi*, 324–5.

[158] *Tarih-i Selânikî*, 427, gives a dramatic description of the lawlessness and insubordination of salaried soldiers and officials following the debasement. For a detailed discussion of the debasement, its causes, and consequences, see Baki Tezcan, "The Ottoman Monetary Crisis of 1585 Revisited," *Journal of the Economic and Social History of the Orient* 52 (2009): 460–504.

[159] See Kafadar, "Les troubles monétaires" for more on the economic and political context of the uprising.

[160] MD 58/431.

[161] MD 61/208.

celeps able to meet their quotas.[162] By 1588, the widening gap between the *narh* and the market price for meat had driven many of Istanbul's suppliers out of business, and the important supply from Rumeli to the capital was getting diverted to more profitable illegal markets.[163]

Even as the Persian war came to a close, the imperial government refused to revise the *narh*, fueling shortages into the following decade. As late as 1591, the sultan continued to warn *kadıs* in Salonica, Silistre (Bulgaria), Skopje, and Beyşehir (south-central Anatolia) that:

> While in Istanbul presently there is a severe shortage of meat, the *kadıs* of the surrounding cities and towns have been implored by the administrators of pious foundations (*ehl-i vukuf*); and in order to have excess meat, they have raised the price to three, four, or even five *akçe* per *vukiye* (about 1.25kg). So now the *celeps*, drovers, and others with sheep do not come to Istanbul but go take them to those cities and towns instead. If the cities and towns around here set the *narh* at two *akçe* per *vukiye*, enough sheep would come to Istanbul and it would not suffer a shortage.[164]

Yet just a few months later, another report in the *mühimmes* mentions that in Edirne, meat was selling illegally for up to eight *akçe* per *vukiye* – that is, four times the price that Salonica and other cities were supposed to charge.[165] Had the *kadıs* followed orders, their cities would have lost their meat supply altogether and their *celeps* would have simply gone bankrupt. Instead, sheep prices remained chaotic and Istanbul continued to suffer shortages until developments in the impending Little Ice Age crisis conspired to undermine the *celep-keşan* system altogether.

Conclusion: Was Crisis Inevitable?

The reader may be tempted to conclude from this catalogue of disasters that Ottoman lands were headed toward inevitable catastrophe by the 1590s. However, looking over the same evidence, one could just as well draw the opposite conclusion: If the empire had already weathered so many storms and still come out intact, it must have been more resilient than observors have given it credit for. Conditions around 1589–91 might only confirm that opinion. In these few years of peace, the empire remained relatively free of famine, disease, or other disturbance.

[162] MD 55/992.
[163] MD 64/256, MD 64/363, and MD 64/383.
[164] MD 68/33.
[165] MD 69/84 and MD 69/89.

For a brief window, the sultan even authorized grain exports to Venice again.[166] By the time the Ottomans went to war with the Habsburgs again in 1593, they appeared to have more or less recovered from the disasters of the preceding decades. After a slow start, the empire launched a series of large, well-equipped campaigns to the Hungarian front starting in 1594.[167]

Had the war been short and victorious like previous Ottoman campaigns, it may not have put any extraordinary strains on the empire. Had nature cooperated and the climate remained relatively benign, even the expenses of a prolonged conflict might still have been tolerable. Instead, the 1590s would bring military setbacks and natural catastrophes far surpassing even the worst years of the 1580s. This combination would expose the underlying weaknesses in the Ottoman response to disasters – especially the empire's vulnerability to synergies of famine, disease, and disorder, and their potential to undermine imperial provisioning. Before moving on to this narrative, however, we need to turn our attention to the one particular region where the tipping point would be reached, sending the empire into rebellion and crisis.

[166] MD 67/114.

[167] Murphey, *Ottoman Warfare*, 6–9. For details of the administration of the 1593–1606 war, see Finkel, *Administration of Warfare*.

4

LAND AT THE MARGINS

KARAMAN AND LARENDE

By the late 1580s, the empire faced systemic threats to its stability and the functioning of its provisioning systems. However, the crisis and rebellion that would sweep Ottoman lands in the following decade was also rooted in the problems of one particular region: the province of Karaman in south-central Anatolia, especially its southeastern district of Larende. In order to understand how the crisis broke out here in this poor, inland province rather than in one of the major urban or agricultural centers of the empire, this chapter takes a closer look at Karaman's peculiar history and geography. A relatively late and difficult conquest, Karaman had once been the seat of an independent empire and had long resisted Ottoman rule. By the late sixteenth century, this region of south-central Anatolia also exemplified the worst effects of population pressure and economic turmoil in the empire, creating an explosive situation that would blow up in the Celali Rebellion of the 1590s.

The Semiarid Steppe

In geographical terms, Karaman province lay in the semiarid steppe, which occupies the land between the Mediterranean coastal ranges of Anatolia and Syria to the south and west and the mountains and desert to the east. Today, this semiarid steppe is "land at the margins" in the literal sense that it straddles the Turkish, Iraqi, and Syrian borders.[1] In Ottoman times, of course, these political lines did not yet exist, nor even the concepts of nationalism and nation-states that divide the region today. However, the steppe was still land at the margins in three important respects: First, it lay at the edge of aridity, hovering near the isohyet of 300 millimeters precipitation that generally marks the boundary of rain-fed agriculture. During the demographic expansion of the sixteenth century,

[1] The expression is taken from Göyünç and Hütteroth, *Land an der Grenze.*

cultivation in this region reached its pre-modern limits, pressing farther than it would again until the coming of modern irrigation and tractors.[2] Second, the steppe occupied the margin between settled and nomadic societies. In these parts – unlike the true deserts of Arabia – land shifted among cultivation, pastoralism, or an overlap of the two; and over the course of millennia, nomads had forced out farmers and in turn farmers nomads many times according to the prevailing political or demographic balance.[3] Third, the land lay at the limits of Ottoman political control, situated at the furthest boundary of territory that the empire could administer directly and call on for extraordinary taxes and levies in times of war. The reader might imagine Anatolia as "Turkish" and so somehow more integral to the Ottoman Empire than the Balkans, Egypt, or the Black Sea; but that impression would be highly misleading. The tenacity of local dynasties and the difficulties of overland communications had made these lands as tough to conquer and even tougher to rule in Ottoman times than most of the territory that would eventually break away to form separate nation-states.

It should be noted that these lands are not remote desert, but simply lie in the rain shadow of coastal mountain chains. As humid air masses pass from the central Mediterranean over the eastern littoral in the winter and spring, they deposit most of their moisture on the uplands through what is known as the orographic effect. The leeward side of the mountain chains is inevitably drier than the coast or seaward slopes. For example, a journey today by bus or plane from Istanbul to the modern Turkish capital of Ankara gives the impression of sudden change from well-watered hills to dry rolling plains. In a matter of minutes, it seems the green of the landscape gives way to dusty brown, and substantial modern farms to shepherds herding flocks of sheep.

The journey to Ankara reveals another striking feature of the semiarid steppe of Anatolia: the legacy of so many important cities and imperial capitals rising out of a seemingly unpromising landscape. It was not just modern nationalism that built Ankara in the middle of Anatolia. The city has been almost continually inhabited since the days of the Hittites in the late Bronze Age. Not far to the east lies the even older Hittite capital of Hattuşa on a flat hill around similar land. Another short trip away, one might visit the ancient Pontic capital of Amasya in a beautiful

[2] Hütteroth, "Between Dicle and Firat," 21.

[3] Khazanov, *Nomads and the Outside World*, 62 *et passim*, explains this distinct "Middle East" type of nomadism.

river gorge, or the Seljuk capital Sivas in the hills to the southeast, and so forth. Most of these cities have gone under many names over many centuries without altering their basic geography – a testament to the long history of the lands in question and the ebb and flow of their population depending on environmental and political circumstances. The endurance of the same cities over millennia also bears witness to the paucity of both fertile and defensible locations and their potential to command the flatter surrounding countryside and the overland trade of Anatolia.

Many of these centers had seen their fortunes wax with the rise of the caravan trade during the rule of the Seljuks, the first great Turkic dynasty of the Middle East, which had invaded through Iran in the eleventh century, driven from Central Asia by a period of extreme climate.[4] During the political fragmentation of the Seljuks in the following centuries, several of these cities emerged as the capitals of successor dynasties, who built many of the mosques and monuments which still decorate these urban centers today. Although all of these dynasties eventually fell to the rising Ottoman power in the fifteenth century, many put up a lengthy and spirited resistance, and their capitals later revived as centers of regional trade and provincial government. Under Ottoman rule, populations in the semiarid region rose especially fast, bringing many towns and villages there to the extremes of population pressure and famine described in the preceding chapters.

Karaman

The province of Karaman illustrates these patterns perfectly. Occupying a relatively flat and fertile valley, the province comprised roughly that area in the bowl of the Taurus Mountains along the curving south-central Anatolian coast, stretching east to the almost lunar landscape of Cappadocia, west to the Pisidian lakes, and north to the desert region of the Salt Lake and the steppe around Kırşehir. Settled since Neolithic times and ruled successively by Hittites, Phrygians, Lydians, Greeks, Romans, and Byzantines, in the eleventh century it became the seat of the Rum Seljuk Sultanate, which placed its capital in Konya (the ancient Iconium). As the home of the famous mystic Mevlana Celaleddin Rumi, and as the site of important caravan networks, the region flourished until succumbing to the chaos and tribal migrations that followed the Mongol invasion

[4] Bulliet, *Cotton, Climate, and Camels.*

of the Middle East in the 1250s. In the following years, the territory was overrun by the Karamanid Turks, who installed their capital first in Larende in 1256 and then in Konya in 1312, from where they ruled the region for nearly two centuries. In the late 1300s, a rapid invasion by the Ottoman Sultan Bayezid (known as Yıldırım, or "Thunderbolt") had taken most Karamanid lands. However, with the defeat of the Ottomans by Timur the Lame in 1402, the Karamanids recovered their old territory and more, at least for a time. Beginning in the 1440s, a new series of wars with the Ottomans again reduced the Karamanids to vassalage and eventually to a mere province of the expanding empire. Karamanid resistance, however, continued through the fifteenth century, ending only after the Ottomans crushed a revolt over a new tax assessment in the first decade of the 1500s.[5] Even then, the Ottomans were forced to grant tax exemptions and leave most of the old Karamanid notables in place to keep the province pacified.[6] Over the following century, as trade and agriculture flourished under the *pax Ottomanica,* the region recovered some measure of its former importance. Konya revived as a major provincial center; and Kayseri, Karahisar (today's Afyon), and eventually Larende and other Karamanid towns witnessed decades of growth and prosperity.

Today the Konya plain is Turkey's breadbasket, producing a healthy surplus of wheat on heavily irrigated and fertilized land. Ottoman documents, however, paint a very different picture of the province some four hundred years ago. Quite by chance, we happen to know more of the historical geography of Karaman than most other regions of the empire. Thanks to a number of studies on Karaman's law codes, court records, and tax registers and the observations of early modern travelers and modern anthropologists and geographers, we can reconstruct some of the main developments in land use and population in Ottoman south-central Anatolia.[7] From these studies it is clear that even more than in

5 On the Karamanids, see Faruk Sümer, "Karaman-Oghullari (Karamanids)," in *Encyclopedia of Islam Online,* ed. P. Bearman, http://www.brillonline.nl; Claude Cahen, *Pre-Ottoman Turkey* (London: Sidgwick and Jackson, 1968); and İ. H. Konyalı, *Karaman Tarihi* (Istanbul: Baha Matbaası, 1967).

6 İnalcık, "Ottoman Methods of Conquest."

7 Among these studies see: Alâadin Aköz, "Şeriye Sicillerine Göre XVI. Yüzyıl Sonunda ile XVII. Yüzyıl Başlarında Karaman" (PhD thesis, Selçuk Üniversitesi, 1987); N. Beldiceanu and I. Beldiceanu-Steinherr, "Recherches sur la province de Qaraman au XVIe siècle, étude et actes," *Journal of the Economic and Social History of the Orient* 11 (1968): 1–129; Irene Beldiceanu-Steinherr, "Un transfuge qaramanide aupres de la Porte ottomane: Reflexions sur quelques institutions," *Journal of the Economic and Social History of the Orient*

other parts of the empire, population growth had outstripped the limits of land and agriculture by the end of the century.

Items in the provincial law code provide indications of local land use. One regulation rated a full-sized farm, or *çift*, at sixty *dönüms* (turns of the plow) for the best land, eighty or ninety for average land, and one hundred twenty for the worst: about five to ten hectares in modern terms. These were fairly typical numbers for Anatolia as a whole, but small for such dry land, especially because so few households still owned a full *çift* in the late 1500s (as discussed in the following section). Law codes required farmers to plant each *çift* with four Bursa *müd* of seed (about 450 liters), imposing tax penalties on unplanted or underplanted land to encourage the maximum cultivation of grains. So even assuming a higher yield ratio of 4:1, a family of five would have needed nearly a full *çift* for a comfortable subsistence after taxes and seedcorn. A family with half a *çift* would have relied on income from livestock, horticulture, or cultivation in *mezraas* to make ends meet; and families with less than that may well have been in desperate circumstances.

Elsewhere the law codes make reference to flax, hemp, and vegetables on *suğlas*, or irrigated land. For the most part, this irrigation received little regulation apart from local custom. The practice in Karaman apparently consisted of damming floodwaters and releasing them into artificial lakes. However, the extent of irrigation appears to have been limited, since the regulations can be rather specific about particular irrigated tracts. To judge by one lengthy catalogue of the region's historical waterworks, most Ottoman effort had been expended on urban drinking water and rather little on rural irrigation, which was widely developed only at the end of the nineteenth century.[8] Moreover, irrigated land could be taxed at a far higher rate, perhaps discouraging private investment in new waterworks.[9]

16 (1973): 155–67; Süleyman Demirci, "*Avârız* and *Nüzul* Levies in the Ottoman Empire: A Case Study of the Province of Karaman, 1620s–1700," *Belleten* 70 (2007): 561–88; Akıf Erdoğru, "Some Observations on the Urban Population of Karaman Province," in *Histoire économique et sociale de l'Empire ottoman et de la Turquie*, ed. D. Panzac (Paris: Peeters, 1995); Akıf Erdoğru, "Karaman Vilayeti Kanunnameleri," *Ankara Üniversitesi Osmanlı Tarihi Araştırma ve Uygulama Merkezi Dergisi* 4 (1993): 467–516; Semavi Eyice, *Karadağ ve Karaman Çevresinde Arkeolojik İncelemeler* (Istanbul: İstanbul Üniversitesi, 1971); Gümüşçü, *Tarihî Coğrafya*; Hütteroth, *Laendliche Siedlungen*; Jennings, "Urban Population in Anatolia"; and Planhol, *De la plaine pamphylienne aux lacs pisidiens*.

8 Mehmet Bildirici, *Tarihi Su Yapıları: Konya, Karaman, Niğde, Aksaray, Yalvaç, Side, Mut, Silifke* (Ankara: T. C. Bayındırlık ve İskân Bakanlığı, 1994).

9 Beldiceanu, "Recherches sur la province de Qaraman" and Erdoğru, "Karaman Vilayeti Kanunnameleri."

In the case of Aksaray, earlier irrigation schemes deteriorated under Ottoman rule, as disinterested *tımar*-holders failed to make the necessary investments for maintanence. Without careful control, as one geographer has noted, the prevailing karstic topography of the region tends to drain away streams, leaving mostly poor, isolated, and seasonal pools of water.[10]

To judge by the cadastral surveys of the sixteenth century, agriculture in Karaman underwent considerably less diversification than in other parts of the empire. Describing the region, one study concluded tentatively that "grain was almost a monoculture, possibly complemented by a certain amount of husbandry."[11] Although the soil of the region is fairly fertile, the balance of evidence suggests that peasants did not always have the means to realize its potential. Trapped by environmental, technological, and economic constraints, the *reaya* had little opportunity or incentive to boost productivity in line with rising population.

Observations by Western visitors second this conclusion. Traveling through the region in the 1550s, the ambassador Ogier Ghiselin de Busbecq made the following comment on the diet:

> The Turks are so frugal and think so little of the pleasures of eating that if they have bread and salt and some garlic or an onion, and a kind of sour milk ... which they call *yoghoort*, they ask for nothing more ... Thus their food and drink costs them very little – so little that I dare say that a man of our country spends more on food in one day than a Turk in twelve.[12]

Nearly four hundred years later, an anthropologist living in Kırşehir made similar observations.[13] By his estimations, yields were still in the range of 24 cwt/ha in the watered lands about the town, falling to only 14 cwt/ha in the unwatered lands in the village fields. (If we take the Ottoman figures for seed planted, and assume about two and a half hectares were planted on a *çift* in a given year, 14 cwt/ha would give a yield ratio of around 4:1.) Dry fields in the plains were fallowed every other year, while those at higher elevations might be left unplowed for three to five years at a stretch. Irrigation was simple, where present at all, and designed as much to prevent flooding as to water the crops. Terracing was rare or nonexistent. Agricultural technologies showed no evident signs of

[10] Hütteroth, *Laendliche Siedlungen*, 21.
[11] İslamoğlu and Faroqhi, "Crop Patterns and Agricultural Production Trends," 420.
[12] E. Forster, ed., *The Turkish Letters of Ogier Ghiselin de Busbecq* (Oxford: Clarendon, 1927), 52–3.
[13] Ruben, *Kırşehir*, chapter 3, part A.

The landscape around Konya during a season of drought (author's photo).

change for centuries or perhaps millennia. Years of drought and crop failure struck about once a decade, creating disaster when two or more followed in close succession.

Nevertheless, in the sixteenth century the region witnessed some of the most rapid population growth in the empire. According to Barkan's original estimates (see Chapter 2), the number of inhabitants in Karaman expanded by some 80 percent from the 1520s to the 1570s alone, nearly double the 40 percent to 50 percent growth in other parts of Anatolia.[14] To take an extreme case, the region of Erçiyes Dağı (around Kayseri) grew by some 261 percent from 1500 to 1584, more than doubling in the last thirty years alone. Although immigration clearly played a role here, the even increase in both villages and towns suggests that most of the growth remained natural.[15] Moreover, the growth here and elsewhere in the region owed much to the settlement of nomads and the conversion of

[14] Barkan, "Research on the Ottoman Fiscal Surveys."

[15] Jennings, "Population, Society, and Economy of the Region of Erçiyes Dağı."

once pastoral land to arable, and presumably former waste and forest land into pasture. The Karaman law code of 1575, for example, noted how many nomads (*yörük*) had already settled in the lands near Kayseri and how they were to be newly registered as *reaya*.[16] The region's rapid growth represented yet another sudden swing of the pendulum from nomadism to settled agriculture – a turn of fortune that proved all too brief.

Studies of Karaman cadastral surveys leave an overwhelming impression of mounting population pressure and rapidly diminishing marginal returns by the 1570s. In the fast-growing Erçiyes Dağı region, for example, a few areas apparently maintained a decent agricultural surplus but others saw per capita yields fall to bare subsistence.[17] Around Akşehir on the Konya plain, to take another example, the number of adult male taxpayers nearly doubled from 922 to 1,727 between the 1520s and 1580s while efforts to extend cultivation late in the century appeared to have failed: "Thus, there was no alternative but to try and squeeze a larger harvest out of the agricultural lands available. In this respect, success was only moderate. The value of the wheat harvest increased by 15.8 percent, barley by 22.3 percent."[18] The Konya area followed a similar pattern, with population up by over 80 percent and the overall grain harvest rising scarcely a quarter as much.[19] After relative stability in mid-century, the price of grains in the city started to edge upwards in the mid-1570s, multiplying several times over even before the crisis of the 1590s.[20] Regions near the provincial center demonstrated a similar pattern of diminishing land holdings and per capita food supplies, with many inhabitants working less land than could reasonably provide their subsistence.[21] It probably did not help either that much of the Karaman peasantry labored under the so-called *malikâne-divani* system, which gave more landlords a claim to their produce and probably raised the overall burden of taxation.[22]

[16] Erdoğru, "Karaman Vilayeti Kanunnameleri."

[17] Jennings, "Population, Society, and Economy of the Region of Erçiyes Dağı."

[18] Faroqhi, *Towns and Townsmen*, 196–7.

[19] Ibid., 200.

[20] Ibid., 208–10.

[21] E.g., Suraiya Faroqhi, "The Peasants of Saideli in the Late Sixteenth Century," *Archivum Ottomanicum* 8 (1984): 215–50.

[22] For more on the workings of *malikane-divani* in the Karaman region, see Suraiya Faroqhi, "The Tekke of Haci Bektaş: Social Position and Economic Activities," *International Journal of Middle East Studies* 7 (1976): 183–208.

Imperial efforts to colonize Cyprus in the 1570s offer further evidence of Karaman's plight. After capturing the island in 1570, Sultan Selim II seized the opportunity to try and rid central Anatolia, especially Karaman, of surplus population.[23] Around early 1571, the imperial government ordered the *kadıs* of Karaman to let migrants depart for the island;[24] and a few months later another command directed the *kadıs* of Konya, Larende, Kayseri, and Niğde in particular to send more settlers, particularly landless craftsmen, offering tax exemptions to new arrivals.[25] Shortly thereafter, a broader order went out to the provinces of Karaman, Anadolu, Rum, and Zülkadriye boasting of the bounties of Cypriot farms and giving a roll call of new migrants to send:

> ... *reaya* settled on harsh and stony land and thus suffering from want; and those who are known for being troublesome; and *reaya* and their children who are not recorded in the provincial tax surveys; and those who have come from another land and resettled; and *reaya* who do not have their own land and are holding land for a fee; and those who have been quarreling over land rights or pastures or gardens for a long time; and those who have left their land and home and settled in the towns and cities; and those in either towns or cities without work or employment; and those doing day labor...[26]

The suggestion is that not only were there many such people to be found, but that the best place to find them was now the struggling provinces of the semiarid zone. Eventually, some 20,000 persons from inner Anatolia, mostly landless and unemployed, would be deported to the island, but without any apparent impact on population pressure.[27]

Migration accelerated within the region as well, particularly as peasants left in search of land or work. Even as villagers lost their farms and moved to nearby towns, townsmen packed up and headed for nearby cities, and some city-dwellers moved on to Konya or Constantinople.[28] Workers from Kayseri, in particular, figure heavily among labor rolls for public works in Istanbul.[29] Other documents suggest that Karaman had more than its

[23] For more on the colonization of Cyprus, see Faroqhi, *Towns and Townsmen*, 282–4, and Gümüşçü, "Internal Migrations."

[24] MD 12/302.

[25] MD 10/378–79.

[26] MD 19/669.

[27] Gümüşçü, "Internal Migrations," 242.

[28] Ibid.

[29] Jennings, "Population, Society, and Economy of the Region of Erçiyes Dağı."

share of crime and banditry, too. Akşehir[30] and Afyon,[31] for example, became targets of *sohtas* in the 1570s, and the former also fell victim to banditry in the general outbreak of lawlessness during the campaign of 1583–4.[32] Meanwhile, Larende became a target of bandits and predatory tribes from the Taurus Mountains.[33] The most troubling sign of violence, however, comes from a document of 1584 describing a gang of seventy to eighty men on horseback plundering from village to village across the province.[34] Such attacks – still rare at the time – offered a preview of events to come in the Little Ice Age crisis.

Larende

Larende, the eventual epicenter of the Celali Rebellion, exemplified some of the worst of this population pressure and associated problems. Located on the southern edge of the Konya plains at the Taurus foothills, Larende encircles Karaman Castle, seated on a small, prominent hill. Settlement of the area had begun in Neolithic times, and the town itself can trace its history all the way back to the Bronze Age Hittite fort of "Laranta" and to subsequent Phrygian and Byzantine settlements on the same location, before the Karamanids chose it as their first capital. Given the limited area suitable for dry cultivation, local settlements tended to surface and resurface in the same sites over centuries despite the flux of population. Even now it remains possible to identify some 165 of the 194 villages recorded for the Larende region in the sixteenth-century Ottoman *tahrirs*,[35] even though the region suffered from some of the most catastrophic violence and flight of the Little Ice Age crisis. The soil itself is fertile, and today it is thickly planted with wheat and other staple crops. However, without the heavy irrigation and liberal doses of fertilizer that characterize modern Turkish agriculture, it must have looked very different in Ottoman times. With an annual average precipitation of just 340 millimeters, the land barely exceeds the threshold for reliable dry farming of cereals.

30 MD 12/925.
31 MD 10/37.
32 MD 44/434.
33 MD 10/48 and MD 10/173.
34 MD 53/250.
35 Gümüşçü, *Tarihi Coğrafya*, 48–55.

The view from Karaman Castle toward the Taurus foothills (author's photo).

As the seat of the Karamanid Empire, Larende had been a significant hub of administration and overland trade. Even after the Karamanids moved their capital to Konya in the fourteenth century, Larende remained an important imperial city, particularly during the fifteenth-century revival of the dynasty that followed Timur's defeat of Sultan Bayezid in 1402. After the Ottoman conquest, however, both the major east-west trade routes and the seat of administration shifted north to Konya, leaving Larende in temporary economic decline. The latter regained its position after the Ottoman conquest of Cyprus in 1570, since Larende lay on the road to Silifke, the main port of trade with the island. As the city recovered, surrounding settlement expanded and the region's population soared. By the late 1500s, the district (*sancak*) of Larende was facing some of the most acute population pressure in the empire.[36]

The *sancak*'s inhabitants nearly tripled from 1500 to 1584, sustaining well over 1 percent annual growth in the latter half of the century. In the meantime, the area of cultivation barely grew, creating a tremendous squeeze on landholdings. Over the 1500s, the number of adult male taxpayers holding a full *çift* of land fell from 905 to 309, and the number holding half a *çift* remained roughly constant, between 2,200 and 2,300. At the same time, the number holding less than half a *çift* (*bennak*) rose from only 482 to a remarkable 3,786; and the number of unmarried

[36] On the history and geography of the region, see Gümüşçü, *Tarihî Coğrafya*, 15–47, and A. de Groot and J. Rogers, "Laranda," in *Encyclopedia of Islam Online*, ed. P. Bearman, http://www.brillonline.nl.

A Karamanid mosque in Larende (modern Karaman) (author's photo).

and landless men (*caba* and *mücerred*) rose from fewer than 800 to over 4,400 between the years 1500 and 1584.[37] Accordingly, the production of grain per taxpaying individual decreased by more than two thirds, with especially steep shortfalls in wheat.[38]

Over the same period, the town of Larende also received a steady stream of landless migrants from the surrounding countryside.[39]

[37] Gümüşçü, *Tarihî Coğrafya*, 202–3.
[38] Ibid., 184.
[39] Gümüşçü, "Internal Migrations in Sixteenth Century Anatolia."

Furthermore, the district's location on the edge of the Taurus Mountains made it a destination for emigrants from the rugged İçel region, described in documents of the time as "harsh and stony" and short of places to settle and farm.[40] The region has already been mentioned as a source of bandit raids, adding to the troubles of Larende and the port of Silifke.[41] During the crisis of the 1590s, migrants from the Taurus Mountains would also play a part in the outbreak of the Celali Rebellion.

Center and Periphery

From documents of the 1500s, it seems clear that Karaman province formed part of the geographic and administrative core of the Ottoman Empire. Frequent *tahrirs* and assessments for wartime levies indicate that the province ranked among the dozen or so routinely called on to the meet the empire's fiscal and logistical requirements, especially in wartime. Furthermore, the *sipahis* of Karaman earned a number mentions among imperial orders preparing for military campaigns, not least due to their proximity to Cyprus. In these important respects, Karaman would deserve to be considered part of the imperial center, especially when compared to outlying or autonomous regions, such as Kurdistan, Albania, or the Crimea.

However, with respect to its role in the Ottoman imperial ecology, Karaman like much of the empire was more peripheral. It was certainly never a major region of supply worthy of close imperial inspection in the manner of the Nile or Danube. Neither was it a region that could make traditional claims to the produce of other lands in the manner of Edirne or Bursa or the capital itself. The province was expected to remain mostly self-sufficient apart from the occasional imperial demand for grain, meat, or other basic goods; and its landlocked position reinforced this self-sufficiency.

Given the high cost of shipments overland, Karaman's contribution to imperial provisioning consisted mostly of high-value commodities and goods that were easy to transport. Of the former, saltpeter was probably the most significant, because it formed a crucial ingredient in gunpowder and Karaman was evidently one of the most critical areas of supply.[42] Of bulk goods, Karaman's chief contribution lay in its famous fat-tailed

[40] Gümüşçü, *Tarihî Coğrafya*, 187–8.

[41] MD 7/1752. See the section on famine in Chapter 3.

[42] See Chapter 1. For examples of Karaman saltpeter supply, see, e.g., MD 12/800–10.

Fat-tailed Karaman sheep (author's photo).

sheep. The ambassador Busbecq, previously mentioned, marveled at the unfamiliar breed:

> In this country is also frequently found (indeed their flocks consist of little else) the breed of sheep with fat, heavy tails, weighing three or four, and sometimes even eight or ten, pounds. In the older sheep they sometimes reach such a size that they have to be laid on a little platform on two wheels, so that the sheep may drag what they cannot carry. You will not, perhaps, believe this, but it is quite true. While it cannot be denied that such tails may serve a good purpose on account of the fat which they yield, yet the rest of the meat seemed to me tougher and less tasty than our mutton.[43]

Indeed, the sheep today are raised primarily for wool and lamb, and present-day Konya sheep farmers informed me that the mutton is relatively cheap and low-quality. Olive and sunflower oil – neither much used in sixteenth-century Anatolia – have long since replaced tail fat in cooking.

In Ottoman times, however, these sheep were evidently raised for meat and fat and they were sent off to Istanbul in considerable numbers. Although the Danube provided the principal meat supply of the

43 Forster, ed., *Turkish Letters*, 46–7.

capital and army, central and eastern Anatolia also contributed tens of thousands of sheep on occasion. Most orders came from the nomadic or seminomadic Türkmen. In 1571, for example, these tribes were called on for a levy of 60,000 sheep[44] – perhaps their largest contribution in these decades, but still much less than the 200,000 or more regularly contributed by Moldavia and Walachia. The *reaya* of Karaman also made contributions, whether as *celeps* or as ordinary taxpayers assigned with extraordinary wartime levies and forced purchases. Again in 1571, the district governor of İçel wrote complaining of a very wealthy usurer in Larende who had failed to meet his quota of 50,000 sheep – by far the highest I have found for the region.[45]

However, that particular year appears to have marked a turning point for the region and its role in Ottoman provisioning. The Cypriot campaign had evidently stretched the supplies of Karaman as far as they would go. The unlucky *celep* who failed to find 50,000 sheep was not alone. The empire had levied extraordinary wartime contributions across a number of goods in Karaman including barley and flour,[46] and the province apparently fell short of its quotas. That year, officials received the sultan's harshest reprimand: "When an imperial order has been written and something has been demanded and your neglect is reported," he concluded, "there is no doubt you will not only be dismissed but chastised with the severest punishments (*eşedd-i ukûbet ile mu'âkab olmanuz mukarrerdür*)."[47]

Such failures to meet imperial demand were hardly unique, but the intensity of the sultan's threat in this case was exceptional. Moreover, the outcome of the contest this time was almost unprecedented: In the same year, the sultan actually cancelled his order for sheep from the province, settling instead for a consignment of archers for the Cypriot campaign.[48] An imperial order even ordered sheep already requisitioned from the Konya-Silifke road (that is, the way to Cyprus) to be returned to their owners.[49] Although we cannot find out exactly what transpired between imperial officials and the people of Karaman, it would appear that local

44 MD 12/927.

45 MD 12/334. This particular *celep* appears to be one of the region's notorious "usurers" (*ribahor*): See Akdağ, *Celali İsyanları*, 37.

46 MD 12/397 and MD 12/517.

47 MD 12/409.

48 MD 14/365.

49 MD 14/167.

forces successfully resisted imperial demands – if only, perhaps, because such demands were unrealistically high in the first place.

The significance of the event could easily be overstated. For one thing, the timing of the documents is not entirely clear.[50] And it may well be that other forces were at play this year which the surviving records fail to reveal. Nevertheless, these documents do raise the important question of whether and how imperial demands may have created tension between the capital and provinces. The problem takes on a further dimension when we consider how some of these provinces, such as Karaman, had until recently been independent kingdoms resisting Ottoman expansion. Although the Turkish dynasties of central Anatolia shared important commonalities of culture, they were nonetheless distinct polities and not merely the forerunners of the Ottoman Empire – much less the Republic of Turkey.[51] Ottoman historiography has outgrown many of its nationalist biases in recent years, especially with regard to Arab and Balkan legends of Turkish oppression. However, concerning the present-day lands of Turkey itself there often persists, as Cemal Kafadar has stated in another context, "the assumption of a continuous national identity, a linear nationhood or national essence that underlies even [the Ottomanists'] own non-chauvanistic history."[52]

It is not the intention here to consider national identity in the Ottoman context. What matters for the purpose of our discussion is to recognize that these assumptions may have colored the usual narrative of Ottoman development, and perhaps blinded historians to the role of local resistance to demands of the center, especially in Anatolia. Political ideas and activities in the Ottoman provinces have received only scant attention thus far from historians of the classical age. The nature of our sources, coming overwhelmingly from the imperial center, often leaves us at a loss with regard to independent developments in places like Karaman. Yet as we see in Part II , this underlying tension between capital and province and between core and periphery, exacerbated by ecological pressures,

50 The orders found in the *mühimme defters* are dated by the day on which they were copied into the records, not the day on which they were actually issued or delivered. In cases where we have access to both dates, however, the two rarely differ by much. For more on this problem, see the introduction to Uriel Heyd, *Ottoman Documents on Palestine 1552–1615* (Oxford: Clarendon, 1960).

51 See, e.g., Cahen, *Pre-Ottoman Turkey*, 361.

52 Cemal Kafadar, *Between Two Worlds* (Berkeley: University of California Press, 1995), 26.

may provide a key to understanding the outbreak of crisis at the close of the 1500s.

Conclusion: Karaman and the Climate of Rebellion

The history of Karaman illustrates the most troubling weaknesses in the classical Ottoman imperial ecology. By the late sixteenth century, conditions in the province were difficult at best and dangerous at worst. Population pressure had eroded its ecological spare capacity. Simple agricultural techniques and marginal, semiarid farmland left it exposed to the slightest fluctuations in climate. As a landlocked region, it still had to supply animals, but in hard times it was too remote to reprovision with imported grain. Poverty and landlessness had bred a volatile class of desperate men migrating across the countryside and into towns and cities. Generations later, its Karamanid tradition of independence and resistance lingered beneath the surface. These factors would all come together in the outbreak of rebellion and crisis in the Little Ice Age.

Conclusion to Part I: Ottoman Imperial Ecology in Perspective

In a single year, 1571, we can see both the apogee of the Ottoman imperial ecology and the first symptoms of the crisis to come. In that same year, the empire's management of territory and resources accomplished the awesome task of rebuilding an entire fleet and salvaging military victory from disaster at Lepanto. The steady advance of Ottoman settlement and population had brought land and commodities under imperial control sufficient to support the largest city and most powerful army in Europe. Even though the Ottoman economy remained relatively underdeveloped and its lands thinly populated by comparison with Northern Europe or China, the empire had without a doubt joined the ranks of major world empires, and its growth continued almost unchecked.

At the same time, some of its regions began to show the strains of meeting wartime demands. Population growth proved a mixed blessing for the empire as the available surplus of resources began to shrink in line with diminishing marginal returns. The semiarid territories suffered more than others and the province of Karaman perhaps most of all. Recurring famine, epidemics, and banditry, and the constant stress of campaigning began to expose weaknesses in the Ottoman management of human and natural resources.

In some respects, these problems were hardly unique to the Ottoman Empire. Population pressure, natural disasters, and the strains of war afflicted all of the major powers of late sixteenth-century Eurasia. Furthermore, all of these states faced difficulties of provisioning, especially military provisioning, in an age of escalating expenses and mounting inflation. Nevertheless, the Ottoman Empire faced exceptional challenges associated with its ecological conditions. The tremendous size of its capital city, army, and navy put a heavier burden on the empire's extensive systems of resource management. As population rose, Near Eastern lands provided relatively few opportunities for agricultural intensification, and the Ottomans lacked new frontiers to colonize, accelerating problems of landlessness and resource shortages. The Near East also proved especially vulnerable to epidemic outbreaks and climatic fluctuations, particularly spells of severe cold and drought.

For these reasons, the Ottoman Empire would be among the first to suffer a crisis as the Little Ice Age set in. While the empire had not entered into inevitable decline, it clearly needed a break from the periodic natural disasters and constant warfare that tested the means of its impoverished peasantry. At the end of the 1580s, during a brief window of peace, it appeared that such a respite might have arrived. However, by the time the Ottomans marched off to war again in 1593, a chain of events had already begun that would nearly bring the empire to ruin.

PART II

THE LITTLE ICE AGE CRISIS

Introduction to Part II: The Freezing of the Bosphorus

In February 1621,[1] the chronicler İbrahim Peçevi observed a "very rare event." After several days of taking ice, the Istanbul Bosphorus had frozen over completely.[2] For a brief window of time, a bridge of ice covered the narrow strip of water separating Europe and Asia, uniting the two continents and the two halves of the empire. In memory of the occasion, Peçevi quoted a poem composed that year:

> By the will of God, the winter in Istanbul this year has been colder than any winter since the world began. Between Üsküdar and Istanbul it has frozen, the sea gone dry . . . Who has seen so many walk over the ice on the sea fearless as though it were dry land?[3]

However another witness, the chronicler Hasan Beyzade, penned a more somber description of the event. Noting how the sea ice blocked the

[1] The exact day was probably February 9, as this was the date of the Venetian dispatch describing the event and the date given by later chroniclers, including Naima and Katip Çelebi. Unfortunately, our three Ottoman eyewitnesses only refer generally to the winter of AH 1030 (1620/21 AD). See also William Griswold, "Climatic Change: A Possible Factor in the Social Unrest of Seventeenth Century Anatolia," in *Humanist and Scholar: Essays in Honor of Andreas Tietze*, ed. H. Lowry and D. Quataert (Istanbul: Isis, 1993), ff.33.

[2] At least one similar event has been recorded in historical times: In the winter of 763–4 AD, Byzantine chroniclers observed large ice flows from the Black Sea passing through the Bosphorus and crashing into the walls of Constantinople: See I. Telelis and E. Chrysos, "The Byzantine Sources as Documentary Evidence for the Reconstruction of Historical Climate," in *European Climate Reconstructed from Documentary Data: Methods and Results*, ed. B. Frenzel (Stuttgart: Fischer, 1992). Other possible cases are described in Y. Vural et al., "The Frozen Bosphorus and Its Paleoclimatic Implications Based on a Summary of the Historical Data," in *The Black Sea Flood Question: Changes in Coastline, Climate, and Human Settlement*, ed. V. Yanko-Hombach et al. (Dordrecht: Springer, 2007).

[3] *Peçevî Tarihi*, 459.

provisioning of Istanbul, he focused on the famine and suffering in the capital that winter:

> And in the year 1030 (1620/1 A.D.) there was such a cold that the Istanbul Bosphorus froze, and without ships many men crossed over the ice to Üsküdar, Galata, and Kasımpaşa on foot. In that same city some men froze from the severe cold and died. The earth was covered in snow. Famine invaded, and the man who could get any bread for a *dirhem* counted himself lucky. The reason for this terrible famine was that once the sea froze, the İskender Bosphorus along Yöros castle was closed and no ship could come from the Black Sea. With no ship coming to the neighborhood of Istanbul from the Mediterranean either, no one was capable of getting provisions to Istanbul.[4]

As recently as 2007, the *Cambridge History of Turkey* dismissed the freezing of the Bosphorus as a "so-called event."[5] In fact, there is every reason to believe it was real. Not only were both these chroniclers probably eyewitnesses to the occurrence, but they were writing for an Istanbul audience that had most certainly lived through that winter and would have laughed at a make-believe freezing of the straits. The contemporary chronicler Hüseyin Tuği has left us an account as well,[6] and the Venetian ambassador Almoro Nani described the event in a dispatch, along with a harrowing account of the unbelievable cold and snows that plagued the city that winter.[7]

Furthermore, this was hardly the only incidence of severe cold in those years that would stretch the bounds of credulity today. In these decades of the so-called "Little Ice Age," there were years when the Thames froze so solid that Londoners set up fairs and festivals on the ice, and seasons when armies marched back and forth over the Hungarian Danube. One hundred years later, when Antonio Vivaldi composed the winter concerto of his "Four Seasons," he had in mind the real winter of 1708–9, during a second phase of Little Ice Age weather, when the Venetian lagoon froze over so thick that revelers skated on the canals.[8] As described

4 *Hasan Bey-Zâde Târîhi*, 928–9.

5 Wolf-Dieter Hütteroth, "Ecology of the Ottoman Lands," in *The Cambridge History of Turkey*, vol. 3, ed. S. Faroqhi (New York: Cambridge University Press, 2007), 19–25.

6 See Fahir İz, "XVII. Yüzyılda Halk Dili ile Yazılmış Bir Tarih Kitabı: Hüseyin Tuği 'Vak'a-i Sultan Osman Han,'" *Türk Dili Araştımaları Yıllığı Belleten* (1967): 119–55 at 142–3. (Hereafter: "Tuği/İz".)

7 *A.S.V. Dispacci-Costantinopoli* 90 (9 Feb.1621).

8 A contemporary painting depicting the event may be found in the Museo del Settecento in Venice. For a complete record of years when the lagoons froze, see D. Camuffo,

in the introduction, this Little Ice Age was a global event – the same that hastened the end of the Ming Dynasty in China and produced the freezing winters that killed so many early colonists and Pilgrims settling in distant America.

In the 1590s and 1600s, climate events were the trigger for the largest rebellion in Ottoman history. Once the uprising was underway, the freezing winters of the Little Ice Age propelled hundreds of thousands, or even millions, of Ottomans into famine, flight, and death. Of course, climate was not the only reason for the disaster. In Part I, we have already seen how a number of forces pushed the empire to the brink of crisis by the late sixteenth century; and in the following chapters we see how errors of judgment and accidents of chance helped turn a climatic disruption into a human catastrophe. Nevertheless, these events would never have happened as they did but for the Little Ice Age; and in that sense, climate really was the cause of the Ottoman crisis.

Part II covers the climatology and the main narrative of the crisis period. We begin in Chapter 5 with a look at the climatic forces at work in the Near East in general, and the Little Ice Age in particular. Chapter 6 narrows in on the Great Drought of the 1590s, particularly how war and famine undermined peasant subsistence and imperial provisioning. Chapter 7 explains how these pressures drove the people of Anatolia into a widespread rebellion, and Chapter 8 explores the role of climate in the ongoing political and social crises of the seventeenth century.

"Freezing of the Venetian Lagoon since the 9th Century AD in Comparison to the Climate of Western Europe and England," *Climatic Change* 10 (1987): 43–66. For other anecdotes of extreme Little Ice Age cold, see Fagan, *Little Ice Age*.

5

THE LITTLE ICE AGE IN THE NEAR EAST

For centuries, scholars have speculated about the nature of climate fluctuations and their consequences in historical times. However, only recently have historians and climatologists found ways to reliably and accurately reconstruct these changes. Global warming, in particular, has inspired the creation of ever longer and more comprehensive climate histories based on proxy data, such as tree rings and ice cores, and on events recorded in historical sources. While such efforts have focused principally on early modern Europe, the wealth of weather-related information in Ottoman writings and documents, together with contemporary European reports and modern climatology studies, permit a similar if less detailed reconstruction of climate in the Near East. This climate history reveals both likenesses and disparities with Little Ice Age weather in Europe and in other parts of the world. Both factors – the local forces at work in Near Eastern climate and the global forces that created the Little Ice Age – played a key role in the atmospheric and human drama of the Ottoman crisis.

Climatic Factors in the Near East

As described in Chapter 1, the lands at the core of the Ottoman Empire were essentially "Mediterranean." In the popular imagination, this adjective conjures up images of particular landscapes: rolling hills, light soil, fields of wheat and olives, gardens of herbs, and pastures of goats and sheep. Underlying these landscapes, however, is a peculiar climatic pattern unique to only a small fraction of the earth's surface. The lands in question are essentially defined by hot dry summers and cold wet winters, whereas most of the temperate and subtropical world receives as much or more precipitation in the warmer months. Travelers to the region in autumn and winter, accustomed to the endless sunshine of the holiday season, may be surprised to encounter the frequent chill, damp weather that prevails the other half of the year. Yet if not for the rains that come from October to March, the region would be no different from the deserts to its south and east.[9]

The reasons for this peculiar weather lie in the shifts of high and low pressure cells over the Atlantic Ocean and the Mediterranean Sea. Simplifying a great deal, we may say that during the summer hot dry air settles over the region in a mass of high pressure that blocks wet air masses from the north and west and inhibits the formation of cyclones over the Mediterranean itself. When in the autumn this high pressure cell dissolves, prevailing westerly winds bring in storms from the Atlantic and cyclogenesis resumes over the Mediterranean Sea. For the eastern half of the sea, it is these midlatitude cyclones, tracking east from the Gulf of Genoa or the seas southwest of the Peloponnese or Cyprus, which bring most of the year's rains.[10] In the case of Anatolia, there are several paths these cyclones may take, bringing wet weather to different sections of the peninsula.[11]

On any given occasion, local factors play the principal role in the distribution of precipitation. The mountainous and uneven coastline of the sea ensures that moisture gets deposited unevenly across the land, producing wide variations in regional rainfall. Furthermore, the farther east one travels, the more that winds from the colder, wetter north and the harsh, dry Sahara compete with the prevailing westerlies for influence over temperature, humidity, and precipitation.[12] In Istanbul, as one Turkish climatologist has remarked, the real seasons are not just winter and summer, but Poyraz (the north wind) and Lodos (the south wind).[13] Indeed, by the time we reach the middle Black Sea coast of Turkey, the weather is generally wet and mild, controlled more by influences from the north than from the Mediterranean itself.[14]

[9] For overviews of Mediterranean climate, see Grove and Rackham, *Nature of Mediterranean Europe*, chapter 2, and J. Thornes and J. Wainwright, *Environmental Issues in the Mediterranean* (London: Routledge, 2004), chapter 3.

[10] For a more detailed explanation of pressure patterns and cyclogenesis in the Mediterranean, see Wainwright and Thornes, *Environmental Issues in the Mediterranean*, 59–69.

[11] M. Karaca et al., "Cyclone Track Variability over Turkey in Association with Regional Climate," *International Journal of Climatology* 20 (2000): 1225–36.

[12] For more analysis of regional factors in Eastern Mediterranean precipitation, see H. Kutiel et al., "Circulation and Extreme Rainfall Conditions in the Eastern Mediterranean during the Last Century," *International Journal of Climatology* 16 (1996): 73–92.

[13] Mikdat Kadıoğlu, *Küresel İklim Değişimi ve Türkiye* (Istanbul: Güncel Yayınları, 2001), 201.

[14] For an overview of climate regions in Turkey, see Erinç, "Agricultural Regions of Turkey."

Nevertheless, in spite of this local variation in the short term, forces on a regional or even global level can display a powerful influence across the entire Eastern Mediterranean during annual or longer timescales. Recent work in climatology has highlighted these connections, gradually bringing the region into climate models that once only covered Western Europe.[15] One case in point has been the role of the North Atlantic Oscillation (NAO). The NAO concerns the annual difference in pressure between the semipermanent cell of high pressure over the Azores and that of low pressure over Iceland, as measured by the North Atlantic Oscillation Index (NAOI). In simple terms, this pressure difference guides the masses of air that bring mild rainy weather to Europe in the spring and summer. Climatologists have long understood that generally speaking a high NAOI means a wet year for northern and western Europe. What they have discovered more recently is that the oscillation correlates inversely with precipitation in the Balkans and Turkey – in other words, that some rainy springs and summers in northern and western Europe can be very dry in the southeast. It now appears that the NAO may account for a great deal of the variance in precipitation of what were once Ottoman lands, and especially the Aegean basin – a factor which may have played an important role in some of the climate events this book describes.[16]

Other factors, such as the El Niño Southern Oscillation (ENSO) and pressure oscillations over Asia, appear to play a less direct role in the climate of the Near East. Some of these forces, particularly ENSO, may

[15] See H. Cullen and P. DeMenocal, "North Atlantic Influence on Tigris-Euphrates Streamflow," *International Journal of Climatology* 20 (2000): 853–63; H. Cullen et al., "Impact of the North Atlantic Oscillation on Middle Eastern Climate and Streamflow," *Climatic Change* 55 (2002): 315–38; T. Felis et al., "A Coral Oxygen Isotope Record from the Red Sea Documenting NAO, ENSO, and North Pacific Teleconnections on Middle East Climate Variability since the Year 1750," *Paleoceanography* 15 (2000): 679–94; Michael Mann, "Large-Scale Climate Variability and Connections with the Middle East in Past Centuries," *Climatic Change* 55 (2002): 287–314; and E. Xoplaki et al., "Wet Season Mediterranean Precipitation Variability: Influence of Large-Scale Dynamics and Trends," *Climate Dynamics* 23 (2004): 63–78.

[16] M. Türkeş and E. Erlat, "Climatological Responses of Winter Precipitation for the Eastern Mediterranean in Turkey to Variability of the North Atlantic Oscillation During the Period 1930–2001," *Theoretical and Applied Climatology* 81 (2005): 45–69 find the highest negative correlation between NAOI and Turkish precipitation, and Ü. Akkemik and A. Aras, "Reconstruction (1689–1994) of April-August Precipitation in the Southern Part of Central Turkey," *International Journal of Climatology* 25 (2005): 537–48 also finds a good fit. R. Touchan et al., "Preliminary Reconstructions of Spring Precipitation in Southwestern Turkey from Tree-Ring Width," *International Journal of Climatology* 23 (2003): 157–71 finds a weaker negative correlation.

play more of a role in summer than winter weather; and given that the vital rains come during the other half of the year, disturbances in the dry season can be of relatively little consequence.[17] (It is important to note, however, that the Little Ice Age witnessed a high frequency of strong El Niños,[18] possibly triggered by volcanic activity,[19] which may account for some weak monsoons and low Nile floods described in the following chapters.[20] Unfortunately, most Nilometer readings for the period have been lost, so the strength of the connection is uncertain.)[21] What matters for the purpose of our discussion is that, taken together, these variations in local, regional, and global forces create a highly variable climate in Mediterranean lands from year to year. Over the course of decades or centuries, the Mediterranean can also be sensitive to global climate events. That is to say, the Mediterranean has certainly felt the effects of global warming in recent years, and the effects of global cooling in centuries past.

[17] J. Reddaway and G. Bigg, "Climatic Change over the Mediterranean and Links to the More General Atmospheric Circulation," *International Journal of Climatology* 16 (1996): 651–61; B. Ziv et al., "The Factors Governing the Summer Regime of the Eastern Mediterranean," *International Journal of Climatology* 24 (2004): 1859–71; M. Jones et al., "Eastern Mediterranean-Indian-African Summer Climate Connections through the Past 2000 Years," *Geophysical Research Abstracts* 6 (2004): 00418; and M. Karabörk and E. Kahya, "The Teleconnections between Extreme Phases of the Southern Oscillation and Precipitation Patterns over Turkey," *International Journal of Climatology* 23 (2003): 1607–25.

[18] See, e.g., W. Quinn et al., "El Niño Occurrences over the Past Four and a Half Centuries," *Journal of Geophysical Research* 92 (1987): 14449–63; R Grove and J Chappell, "El Niño Chronologies and the History of Global Crises during the Little Ice Age," in *El Niño: History and Crisis*, ed. R. Grove and J. Chappell (Cambridge: White Horse Press, 2000); V. Markgraf and H. Diaz, "The Past ENSO Record: A Synthesis," in *El Niño and the Southern Oscillation*, ed. H. Diaz and V. Markgraf (Cambridge: Cambridge University Press, 2000); and Michael Mann, "Volcanic and Solar Forcing of the Tropical Pacific over the Past 1000 Years," *Journal of Climate* 18 (2005): 447–56. Unless otherwise noted, I have relied on the following recent multi-proxy reconstruction for ENSO events: J. Gergis and A. Fowler, "A History of ENSO Events since A.D. 1525: Implications for Future Climate Change," *Climatic Change* 92 (2009): 343–87.

[19] See, e.g., J. Adams, M. Mann, and C. Amman, "Proxy Evidence for an El Niño-Like Response to Volcanic Forcing," *Nature* 426 (2003): 274–8 and Julien Emile-Geay, "Volcanoes and ENSO over the Past Millennium," *Journal of Climate* 21 (2008): 3134–49.

[20] See, e.g., William Quinn, "A Study of Southern Oscillation-Related Activity for AD 622–1900 Incorporating Nile River Flood Data" in H. Diaz and V. Markgraf, eds., *El Nino: Historical and Paleoclimate Aspects of the Southern Oscillation* (Cambridge: Cambridge University Press, 1992) and Fekri Hassan, "Historical Nile Floods and Their Implications for Climatic Change," *Science* 212 (1981): 1142–5.

[21] William Popper, *The Cairo Nilometer* (Berkeley: University of California Press, 1951) and P. Whetton and I. Rutherford, "Historical ENSO Teleconnections in the Eastern Hemisphere," *Climatic Change* 28 (1994): 221–53.

Reconstructing the Little Ice Age

Although historians of Europe were long aware that weather had once been colder than in modern times, it was not until the 1950s that a combination of historical and climate research established the existence of a "Little Ice Age." Broadly dated from either the fourteenth or the late sixteenth centuries until the mid-1800s, this time of cold was measured by the gradual progression of those same Alpine glaciers whose visible retreat today makes such a powerful case for global warming.[22] In the 1960s, the French historian Emmanuel Le Roy Ladurie became the first to define the Little Ice Age as a historical event and not just a climatic phenomenon in Europe. Carefully pouring over French records, his research traced several periods of glacial advance in the Alps from the late 1500s until the mid-nineteenth century. Furthermore, he noticed a gradual delay of the French grape harvest, revealing the onset of cold summers from 1560 onward. Looking through diaries and other descriptive sources, Le Roy Ladurie also pointed out that the real threat to northern Europe came from persistent wet and cold weather, while the Mediterranean suffered instead from the severe winter frosts and droughts of the period. On the whole, however, his conclusions were narrow and cautious, constrained by the limits of climate data at the time.[23] Thanks in no small part to Le Roy Ladurie's doubts, the role of the Little Ice Age in history has traditionally met with skepticism from Europeanists, particularly from those looking for precise correlations between weather and events.[24] Through the 1970s and 1980s, researchers in European historical demography and interdisciplinary history compiled further studies on the Little Ice Age and its impacts, but their work has still not had much influence on scholarly understanding of major historical developments.[25]

[22] For a complete account of glacier movements, see Jean Grove, *Little Ice Ages: Ancient and Modern* (London: Routledge, 2004).

[23] Emanuel Le Roy Ladurie, *Times of Feast, Times of Famine* (Garden City, NY: Doubleday, 1971). In his more recent work, *Histoire humaine et comparée du climat*, the author has presented a much stronger role for climate in human affairs.

[24] E.g., Jan DeVries, "Measuring the Impact of Climate on History: The Search for Appropriate Methodologies," in *Climate and History*, ed. R. Rottberg and T. Rabb (Princeton: Princeton University Press, 1981).

[25] For examples of this research, see R. Rotberg and T. Rabb, eds., *Climate and History* (Princeton, NJ: Princeton University Press, 1981) and J. Walter and R. Schofield, eds., *Famine, Disease and Social Order in Early Modern Society* (Cambridge: Cambridge University Press, 1989).

Among Ottomanists, the Little Ice Age has usually been overlooked and occasionally misunderstood. Braudel made the first venture into this field with an offhand suggestion that climate events may have played a role in the Mediterranean's turn to north Atlantic grain in the 1590s – a correct surmise, as we see in the following chapter.[26] Building on Braudel's work, a few years later the Swedish historian Gustav Utterström made a more forceful case for climate-related disaster in the Mediterranean world around 1600, albeit on rather circumstantial evidence.[27] In the early 1980s, William Griswold became the first historian to uncover Ottoman evidence for Little Ice Age impacts in the Near East, which he first mentioned in his monograph on the Celali Rebellion.[28] Taking advantage of some preliminary work on Aegean tree rings (see the following discussion), Griswold wrote an article ten years later making the case that climate change set off the Ottoman crisis of the 1590s.[29] Generally speaking, his conclusions have turned out to be accurate, but his data were very limited, and his argument lacked a narrative that could tie together climatic and human events. His article also came out in a specialist *festschrift*, where its conclusions received insufficient attention until the present. Although several Ottomanists since Griswold have casually raised the question of climate, none have pursued the matter at any length.[30] As mentioned, the recent *Cambridge History of Turkey* – relying on out-of-date, low-resolution climate data – has argued against any climate change at all. Some Ottomanists have even made the error of suggesting that Little Ice Age weather may have been beneficial for Ottoman lands, because after all, cold wet weather should have brought relief to a region known to suffer from heat and drought.[31]

Until recently, such errors and omissions were understandable. Both our knowledge of climate history and our appreciation of climate change

[26] Braudel, *Mediterranean*, vol.1, 267–76.

[27] Gustaf Utterström, "Climatic Fluctuations and Population Problems in Early Modern History," *The Scandinavian Economic History Review* 3 (1955): 3–47.

[28] William Griswold, *The Great Anatolian Rebellion, 1591–1611* (Berlin: K. Schwarz, 1983), 48–50 (see footnotes), 182, 190, and 214.

[29] Griswold, "Climatic Change."

[30] E.g., Abraham Marcus, *The Middle East on the Eve of Modernity* (New York: Columbia University Press, 1989), 131–2, and Darling, *Revenue-Raising and Legitimacy*, 44. Finkel, *Osman's Dream* also gives brief descriptions of some extreme weather events, although without any reference to the climatology of the Little Ice Age.

[31] E.g., Haim Gerber, *The Social Origins of the Modern Middle East* (London: Mansell, 1987), 15–16.

still had a long way to go. However in the past few years, spurred on by interest in global warming, both climatologists and historians have returned to the Little Ice Age problem with far more creativity and sophistication. Working from various sorts of proxy data – such as tree rings, ice cores, and sediment layers – climate experts have begun to reconstruct weather patterns on an annual or even seasonal basis.[32] Meanwhile, historians working with written material have devised ever more elaborate and comprehensive indices of past weather, confirming and clarifying the physical evidence.[33] What they have discovered revolutionizes our perspective on the era and offers important lessons for the role of climate in Ottoman history. For the sake of clarity, we may group the new findings under five headings:

First, historical climatologists need no longer write of the Little Ice Age as an undifferentiated era of cold or glacial advance. Instead, experts now study its fluctuations and variability, putting particular emphasis on concentrated episodes of frequent Little Ice Age-type weather events, such as cold summers or extreme winters.[34] Among these periods, the generation from the 1580s to the 1610s and that from the 1680s to the 1700s stand out as the two most severe, particularly in Europe.[35] As new studies constantly refine our knowledge of weather events from year to year, so researchers have been able to draw more convincing connections between climate and history, especially in parts of Europe.[36] Current research on sources such as ships' weather logs and early

[32] For an overview of new research and methods, see P. D. Jones, "High-Resolution Palaeoclimatology of the Last Millennium: A Review of Current Status and Future Prospects," *The Holocene* 19 (2009): 3–49.

[33] For overviews of document-based historical climatology, see R. Brázdil et al., "Historical Climatology in Europe: The State of the Art," *Climatic Change* 70 (2005): 363–430 and R. Brázdil et al., "European Climatology of the Past 500 Years: New Challenges for Historical Climatology," *Climatic Change* 101 (2010): 7–40.

[34] Christian Pfister has pioneered this methodology, particularly the construction of annual and decadal thermal and wetness indices. See Christian Pfister, "The Little Ice Age: Thermal and Wetness Indices for Central Europe," *Journal of Interdisciplinary History* 10 (1980): 665–96.

[35] See, e.g., J. Luterbacher et al., "European Seasonal and Annual Temperature Variability, Trends, and Extremes since 1500," *Science* 303 (2004): 1499–1503 and J. Luterbacher et al., "Circulation Dynamics and Its Influence on European and Mediterranean January-April Climate over the Past Half Millennium: Results and Insights from Instrumental Data, Documentary Evidence and Coupled Climate Models," *Climatic Change* 101 (2010): 201–34.

[36] For an overview of this research, see Christian Pfister and Rudolf Brázdil, "Climatic Variability in Sixteenth-Century Europe and Its Social Dimension: A Synthesis," *Climatic Change* 43 (1999): 5–53. Two in-depth studies of Central Europe deserve

instrumental data promise to take these climate reconstructions to new levels of accuracy and detail in the coming years.[37]

Second, along with more detailed reconstructions of climate events, recent investigations have also done more than ever before to explain the causes of the Little Ice Age. Variations in solar output, possibly related to sunspot cycles, appear to account for much of the general cold of the period. This may have been the case particularly during the late seventeenth-century "Maunder Minimum," when observers found few or no sunspots at all.[38] However, fluctuations in solar output appear insufficient to account for all of the severe cooling and particularly the large annual variations in temperature, and so far it has been difficult to establish a direct link between sunspots and particular climate episodes.[39] Therefore, climatologists have also turned to the role of volcanic eruptions to account for much of the period's anomalous cold. As analyzed by H. H. Lamb, major eruptions can create dust veils and release sulphates into the stratosphere that reflect back solar radiation, cooling the lower atmosphere. During the Little Ice Age, observers recorded a number of these episodes, which Lamb compiled into a historical dust veil index.[40] More recent studies have uncovered further evidence of eruptions in the form of sediments and acids embedded in ice cores, many corresponding to extreme phases of the Little Ice Age, such as the major eruption of Huaynaputina in 1600, thought to be responsible for the extreme cold of the early seventeenth century.[41] Taken together, the combined effects

particular mention: Christian Pfister, *Wetternachhersage: 500 Jahre Klimavariationen und Natur Katastrophen (1496–1995)* (Bern: Paul Haupt, 1999) and Rüdiger Glaser, *Klimageschichte Mitteleuropas* (Darmstadt: Primus Verlag, 2001).

37 E.g., R. García-Herrera et al., "Description and General Background to Ships' Logbooks as a Source of Climatic Data," *Climatic Change* 73 (2005): 13–36.

38 See John Eddy, "Solar History and Human Affairs," *Human Ecology* 22 (1994): 23–36; D. Rind, "The Sun's Role in Climate Variations," *Science* 296 (2002): 673–7; and Drew Shindell et al., "Solar Forcing of Regional Climate Change during the Maunder Minimum," *Science* 294 (2001): 2149–52.

39 See, e.g., M. Free and A. Robock, "Global Warming in the Context of the Little Ice Age," *Journal of Geophysical Research* 104 (1999): 19057–70.

40 H. H. Lamb, "Volcanic Dust in the Atmosphere; with a Chronology and Assessment of Its Meteorological Significance," *Philosophical Transactions of the Royal Society of London (Series A., Mathematical and Physical Sciences)* 266 (1970): 425–533. For a variety of new volcanic indices, see the appendix to Atwell, "Volcanism and Short-Term Climatic Change."

41 K. Briffa et al., "Influence of Volcanic Eruptions on Northern Hemisphere Summer Temperature over the Past 600 Years," *Nature* 393 (1999): 450–5 and S. De Silva and G. Zielinski, "Global Influence of the AD 1600 Eruption of Huaynaputina, Peru," *Nature* 393 (1998): 455–8.

of solar and volcanic forcing can account for most of the unusual cold and variability of the period.[42]

Third, moving beyond their European focus, historians and climatologists have begun studying the Little Ice Age across the globe. In the past two decades, historians of lands from Mexico to China have discovered new evidence for these extreme weather events contemporary with, and comparable to, those in Europe. As described in the introduction, this discovery has led to a new interpretation of the so-called "general crisis of the seventeenth century" as a global event driven by climate change.

Fourth, recent work on atmospheric circulation and climate patterns in the Eastern Mediterranean has provided us with better models to understand the impact of the Little Ice Age in the Ottoman Empire. It was only natural that some past historians might imagine that since the era was marked by cool, wet springs and summers in Europe that it should have been the same in Ottoman lands. The climatology of the Near East was in its infancy and its relations to climate in Europe remained unclear. Now new studies suggest that, if anything, just the opposite should have been the case. As previously noted, atmospheric shifts associated with the North Atlantic Oscillation often have a contrary effect in parts of the Near East. In other words, the same rainy springs and summers that rotted new seedlings in England may have killed the winter wheat and barley with drought in Greece and Turkey. Furthermore, it appears that the impact of volcanic dust veils may differ in important respects between northern Europe and the Near East. In the former region, these events have been associated with cloudy, cool weather from spring to autumn, such as the famous "year without a summer" in 1816, when Mary Shelley whiled away the dark days by writing *Frankenstein*. In the Near East, however, eruptions have not had the same impact on summer weather, but have led to freezing dry winters instead, as explained in recent circulation models.[43] Furthermore, periods of volcanic activity have been known to

[42] Drew Shindell, "Volcanic and Solar Forcing of Climate Change during the Preindustrial Era," *Journal of Climate* 16 (2003): 4094–107 and Michael Mann, "Global Signatures and Dynamical Origins of the Little Ice Age and Medieval Climate Anomaly," *Science* 326 (2009): 1256–60. For more on the causes of the Little Ice Age, see Heinz Wanner, "Die Kleine Eiszeit – mögliche Gründe für ihre Enstehung," in *Nachhaltige Geschichte: Festschrift für Christian Pfister*, ed. Andre Kirchhofer (Zurich: Chronos, 2009).

[43] Shindell, "Dynamic Winter Climate Response"; C. Mass and D. Portman, "Major Volcanic Eruptions and Climate: A Critical Evaluation," *Journal of Climate* 2 (1989): 566–93; and A. Robock and J. Mao, "The Volcanic Signal in Surface Observations," *Journal of Climate* 8 (1995): 1086–103.

create strange "dry fogs" in the Mediterranean, historically associated with crop failures, famine, and disease.[44]

Finally, the past decade has seen the publication of numerous new documentary and proxy climate reconstructions of the Eastern Mediterranean, providing strong confirmation for Ottoman descriptions of extreme cold and drought.[45] New evidence and techniques have proven capable of accurately calculating changes in climate over hundreds or thousands of years. Although much of this work once relied on low-resolution proxies such as pollen samples,[46] more recent studies have turned to more high-resolution proxies capable of verifying Little Ice Age temperature and precipitation fluxuations on a centennial or even decadal scale.[47] Moreover, beginning with the work of Peter Kunniholm in the 1980s,[48] several teams have completed tree ring sequences for various parts of the Near East. Correlating the tree growth to modern weather data, experts have used this dendrochronology to construct much more detailed measures of annual spring and summer rainfall over the past several hundred years for parts of Anatolia and Jordan and for the Eastern Mediterranean overall.[49] Finally, working from archival sources,

44 D. Camuffo and S. Enzi, "Chronology of 'Dry Fogs' in Italy, 1374–1891," *Theoretical and Applied Climatology* 50 (1994): 31–3 and Stothers, "Volcanic Dry Fogs."

45 For an overview of Mediterranean historical climatology, see J. Luterbacher et al., "Mediterranean Climate Variability over the Last Centuries: A Review," in *The Mediterranean Climate: An Overview of the Main Characteristics and Issues*, ed. P. Lionello et al. (Amsterdam: Elsevier, 2006).

46 E.g., Sytze Bottema, "A Pollen Diagram from the Syrian Anti-Lebanon," *Paleorient* 3 (1975/7): 259–68; W. van Zeist and H. Woldring, "A Postglacial Pollen Diagram from Lake Van in Eastern Anatolia," *Review of Paleobotany and Palynology* 26 (1978): 249–76; and N. Roberts and H. Wright, "Vegetational, Lake-Level, and Climatic History of the Near East and Southwest Asia," in *Global Climate since the Last Glacial Maximum*, ed. H. Wright et al. (Minneapolis: University of Minnesota Press, 1993).

47 E.g., L. Wick et al., "Evidence of Late Glacial and Holocene Climatic Change and Human Impact in Eastern Anatolia: High-Resolution Pollen, Charcoal, Isotopic and Geochemical Records from the Laminated Sediments of Lake Van, Turkey," *The Holocene* 13 (2003): 665–75; T. Felis et al., "A Coral Oxygen Isotope Record from the Red Sea Documenting NAO, ENSO, and North Pacific Teleconnections on Middle East Climate Variability since the Year 1750," *Paleoceanography* 15 (2000): 679–94; and M. Bar-Matthews, A. Ayalon, and A. Kaufman, "Middle to Late Holocene (6,500 Yr. Period) Paleoclimate in the Eastern Mediterranean Region from Stable Isotopic Composition of Speleothems from Soreq Cave, Israel," in *Water, Environment and Society in Times of Climatic Change*, ed. A. Issar and N. Brown (Dordrecht: Kluwer Academic Publishing, 1998).

48 Peter Kunniholm, "Archaeological Evidence and Non-Evidence for Climate Change," *Philosophical Transactions of the Royal Society of London* 330 (1990): 645–55.

49 R. D'Arrigo and H. Cullen, "A 350-Year (AD 1628–1980) Reconstruction of Turkish Precipitation," *Dendrochronologia* 19 (2001): 853–63; R. Touchan and M. Hughes, "Dendrochronology in Jordan," *Journal of Arid Environments* 42 (1999): 291–303; R. Touchan

historians and historical climatologists have begun to create comprehensive charts of weather events in lands in or near the Ottoman Empire, particularly Venice, Greece, Crete, and Hungary.[50] These studies offer information on extreme temperatures often lacking in the physical record. Furthermore, they provide insights into the human dimensions of Little Ice Age weather events, particularly the suffering created by spring droughts and freezing winters.

Taken together, the data present some remarkable findings. The Eastern Mediterranean, though never uniformly cold and dry, began to suffer from recurring drought and freezing winters in the 1560s. From 1591 to 1596, as colder temperatures set in, Ottoman lands entered their

et al., "A 396-Year Reconstruction of Precipitation in Southern Jordan," *Journal of the American Water Resources Association* 35 (1999): 49–59; R. Touchan et al., "Preliminary Reconstructions of Spring Precipitation in Southwestern Turkey from Tree-Ring Width," *International Journal of Climatology* 23 (2003): 157–71; R. Touchan et al., "Standardized Precipitation Index Reconstructed from Turkish Tree-Ring Widths," *Climatic Change* 72 (2005): 339–53; R. Touchan et al., "Reconstructions of Spring/Summer Precipitation for the Eastern Mediterranean from Tree Ring Widths and Its Connection to Large-Scale Atmospheric Circulation," *Climate Dynamics* 25 (2005): 75–98; Ü. Akkemik and A. Aras, "Reconstruction (1689–1994) of April-August Precipitation in the Southern Part of Central Turkey," *International Journal of Climatology* 25 (2005): 537–48; Ü. Akkemik et al., "A Preliminary Reconstruction (AD 1685–2003) of Spring Precipitation Using Oak Tree Rings in the Western Black Sea Region of Turkey," *International Journal of Biometeorology* 49 (2005): 297–302; Ü. Akkemik et al., "Anadolu'nun Son 350 Yılında Yaşanan Önemli Kurak ve Yağışlı Yıllar," *Türkiye Kuvarterner Sempozyumu* 5 (2005): 129–35; Ü. Akkemik et al., "Tree-Ring Reconstructions of Precipitation and Streamflow for Northwestern Turkey," *International Journal of Climatology* 28 (2008): 173–83; and C. Griggs et al. "A Regional High-Frequency Reconstruction of May-June Precipitation in the North Aegean from Oak Tree Rings, A.D. 1089–1989," *International Journal of Climatology* 27 (2007): 1075–89.

50 J. Grove and A. Conterio, "The Climate of Crete in the Sixteenth and Seventeenth Centuries," *Climatic Change* 30 (1995): 223–47; J. Grove and A. Conterio, "Climate in the Eastern and Central Mediterranean, 1675 to 1715," in *Climatic Trends and Anomalies in Europe 1675–1715*, ed. B. Frenzel et al. (Stuttgart: Fischer, 1994); J. Grove and A. Grove, "Little Ice Age Climates in the Eastern Mediterranean," in *European Climate Reconstructed from Documentary Data: Methods and Results*, ed. B. Frenzel (Stuttgart: Fischer, 1992); E. Xoplaki et al., "Variability of Climate in Meridional Balkans During the Periods 1675–1715 and 1780–1830 and Its Impact on Human Life," *Climatic Change* 48 (2001): 581–615; C. Repapis et al., "A Note on the Frequency of Occurrence of Severe Winters as Evidenced in Monastery and Historical Records from Greece During the Period 1200–1900 A.D.," *Theoretical and Applied Climatology* 39 (1988): 213–17; Lajos Rácz, "The Climate of Hungary During the Maunder Minimum (1675–1715)," in *Climatic Trends and Anomalies in Europe*, ed. B. Frenzel et al. (Stuttgart: Fischer, 1994); Lajos Rácz, "Variations of Climate in Hungary (1540–1779)," in *European Climate Reconstructed from Documentary Data: Methods and Results*, ed. B. Frenzel (Stuttgart: Fischer, 1992); and Lajos Rácz, *Climate History of Hungary Since 16th Century: Past, Present and Future* (Pécs: Centre for Regional Studies of the Hungarian Academy of Sciences, 1999).

longest drought in the past 600 years. Around the time that Huaynaputina erupted in 1600, weather grew extraordinarily wet and winter temperatures plunged even further. In 1607, severe drought struck once more, and a succession of freezing dry winters brought on the worst suffering of the entire crisis. While cold persisted over the following years, particularly during the freezing of the Bosphorus in 1621, the next serious drought came in the late 1650s. Finally, from the late 1670s to the 1700s the so-called "Late Maunder Minimum" brought new extremes of precipitation and probably the worst winters since the 1620s.

This published climate data receive ample confirmation in the Ottoman and Venetian sources I have employed in this book. With uncanny reliability, the small blips on the dendroclimatology charts indicating a year or two of drought find some echo in reports of shortage or famine. With a few exceptions, years that the climate models would predict as extremely cold or dry turn out just so. Sensitized as we are today to the importance of climate change, it seems remarkable that the Little Ice Age impact in the Ottoman Empire went undiscovered for so long. Dramatic descriptions of extreme climate events fill the records and chronicles of the period, leaving no doubt about their impact on Ottoman lives. Recent climatology not only alerts us to these climate changes but also provides objective backing to the subjective impressions found in historical sources.

Conclusion: The Onset of the Little Ice Age

Taking these new findings into account, we can now review the development of the Ottoman Empire in light of historical climatology. Unfortunately, the scarcity of pre-Ottoman and early Ottoman sources has left us with relatively little information on the climate of the Near East until the mid-sixteenth century. Byzantine historians have only just begun to look for records of climate events,[51] and older Mediterranean tree-ring data can be uncertain and unreliable. From the limited evidence at hand,

51 Dionysios Stathakopoulos, "Reconstructing the Climate of the Byzantine World: State of the Problem and Case Studies," in *People and Nature in Historical Perspective*, ed. J. Laszlovsky and P. Szabo (Budapest: Central European University, 2003); Telelis, "Byzantine Sources"; Ioannis Telelis, "Medieval Warm Period and the Beginning of the Little Ice Age in the Eastern Mediterranean: An Approach of Physicial and Anthropogenic Evidence," in *Byzanz als Raum: Zu Methoden und Inhalten der historische Geographie des östlichen Mittelmeerraumes*, ed. Klaus Belk (Vienna: Österreichischen Akademie der Wissenschaften, 2000); and Ioannis Telelis, "Climatic Fluctuations in the Eastern Mediterranean and

it appears the region experienced much of the same cold, wet weather that often plagued northern Europe from the mid-fourteenth to early fifteenth centuries, while the Ottomans established their dominion over western Anatolia and the southern Balkans. Around the time of Mehmed II's conquest of Constantinople in 1453, the region was apparently struck by dry weather,[52] although the first major climate events in Ottoman records do not show up until the 1490s, when parts of Anatolia suffered from drought, famine, and epidemics.[53]

For the following half century, as Ottoman rule expanded up to Hungary and down to Egypt, it seems the eastern Mediterranean enjoyed some of the most temperate weather of early modern times. The tree ring charts smooth out appreciably, and the historical evidence makes few mentions of famine and shortages. It was this mild climate that formed the backdrop to the reign of Süleyman the Magnificent and the settlement and demographic growth described in Chapters 1 and 2.

From the 1560s onward, however, the climate became considerably more erratic. In the proxy reconstructions, 1561, 1570, and 1585 all stand out as years of serious widespread spring drought;[54] and as we have seen in Chapter 3, all but the first were years of serious famine. On the other hand, 1565 marked the wettest year on record,[55] with Edirne and Sofia reporting major floods and heavy snowfall,[56] and 1572 and 1574 brought serious inundations as well.[57] Meanwhile, the same years witnessed the first signs of freezing Little Ice Age weather, including

the Middle East AD 300–1500 from Byzantine Documentary and Proxy Physical Paleoclimatic Evidence – A Comparison," *Jahrbuch der Österreichischen Byzantinistik* 58 (2008): 167–208.

52 Touchan et al., "Reconstructions of Spring/Summer Precipitation."

53 Akdağ, *Türk Halkının Dirlik ve Düzenlik Kavgası*, 75; and Yılmaz and Yılmaz, eds., *Osmanlılarda Sağlık*, vol. 2, documents 14–27 and 41–47.

54 Region-wide dendroclimatology reveals nearly two standard deviations below normal precipitation for each of these years in Touchan et al., "Reconstructions of Spring/Summer Precipitation." For extreme drought in 1585, see also Griggs et al., "Regional High-Frequency Reconstruction."

55 Touchan et al., "Reconstructions of Spring/Summer Precipitation."

56 MD 5/314, MD 5/410; see Kılıç, "Mühimme Defterlerine Göre 16. Yüzyılın İkinci Yarısında Osmanlı Devleti'nde Doğal Afetler."

57 On the floods of 1572, see MD 19/40 and *Peçevî Tarihi*, 261. For the floods of the mid-1570s see, for example, MD 26/128 and Kılıç, "Mühimme Defterlerine Göre 16. Yüzyılın İkinci Yarısında Osmanlı Devleti'nde Doğal Afetler." The spring–summer of 1574 registers nearly 2 standard deviations above normal in Touchan et al., "Reconstructions of Spring/Summer Precipitation."

notably severe winters in Bulgaria in 1565–6,[58] Greece in 1577–8,[59] and eastern Anatolia in 1578–9.[60] In nearby Crete, Venetian officials began to write of severe winters or drought and famine nearly every year from 1585 onward.[61]

With the benefit of this data, we see how the disasters of the late sixteenth century, described in Chapter 3, marked the empire's uneven descent into the Little Ice Age. The relatively stable climate in the reigns of Selim I (1512–20) and Süleyman I (1520–66) had permitted an expansion of population and settlement that would prove unsustainable in the coming decades of severe cold and drought. Isolated incidents of extreme weather began to form a pattern of freezing winters and erratic precipitation that would come to characterize the region over much of the following century. Of course, the Ottomans themselves could have had no idea they were entering a Little Ice Age, nor could they have guessed at the scale and swiftness of the disasters that would come in the final years of the sixteenth century.

58 MD 5/410–11 and Kılıç, "Mühimme Defterlerine Göre 16. Yüzyılın İkinci Yarısında Osmanlı Devleti'nde Doğal Afetler."

59 Repapis, "Note on the Frequency of Occurence of Severe Winters."

60 MD 41/1069 and *Peçevî Tarihi*, 301–3.

61 Grove and Conterio, "Climate of Crete."

6

THE GREAT DROUGHT

What we regard as the final decade of the 1500s was for the Ottomans the dawn of a new era, in more than one sense of the word. Overlapping with the years 1591 and 1592 AD came the thousandth anniversary of Mohammed's flight from Mecca to Medina, as reckoned in lunar years. In other words, the Muslim world entered upon the year 1000 AH: the beginning of the new millennium. Although the year 1000 inspired a wave of millenarian prophecies in the Muslim world as it had among Christians some six hundred years before,[1] the calendrical revolution passed without a corresponding revolution in human affairs, at least at first.

Yet, quite literally, there was change in the air. In the very same year that Ottoman lands entered the new millennium, they also entered their longest drought in the past six centuries. Scarcely noticed at first, the dryness gradually swelled into a crisis of terrible proportions. Ottoman lands could expect droughts of a year or two every decade or generation, and the peasantry had learned to adapt. A dry spell of five or six years in a row, however, was unprecedented. Inexorable want and famine invaded the land, followed by banditry, flight, and epidemics. Worse still, the drought overlapped with a major war in Hungary, placing tremendous new burdens on supplies of food and matériel. Faced with such disasters, Sultans Murad III (1574–95) and Mehmed III (1595–1603) responded all too often with a mix of denial and desperation. In the end, this combination of natural calamity and human folly drove the empire into the very crisis so many had also predicted toward the millennium's end.

[1] On millenarianism and the declensionist trend in Ottoman writing in the 1590s, see Griswold, *Great Anatolian Rebellion*, 13–14, and Sanjay Subrahmanyam, "Du Tage au Gange au XVIe siècle: Une conjoncture millénariste à l'echelle eurasiatique," *Annales* (2001): 51–84.

The Drought

The drought of the 1590s was the longest in the Eastern Mediterranean for the past six centuries and by far the worst in the empire's history. The dry spring and summer months show up most clearly in two recent tree ring studies: one covering the Eastern Mediterranean in general, where the drought appears from 1591 to 1595,[2] and one for southern Anatolia in particular, where it appears over the years 1592 to 1596.[3] The authors of these studies also mention in passing the close association of drought with human calamities; but concerned as they are with long-term climate dynamics, the articles do not go into any more depth concerning the causes or consequences of the event.

From other climate studies, it is apparent that the northern hemisphere as a whole witnessed significant irregularities in atmospheric circulation from the 1590s to the 1610s, probably associated with volcanic eruptions and ENSO activity. Quite possibly, the cooling from dust veils weakened Hadley cells – the rise of tropical heat and its subsidence in subtropical latitudes – leading to a southward displacement of the westerly (zonal) circulation that would normally bring precipitation to the Eastern Mediterranean.[4] Recent NAOI reconstructions also reveal a peak in the 1590s, followed by a drop in the early 1600s, timing well with the drought and then the years of heavy precipitation that followed, although the data are not quite precise enough to justify a direct causal connection.[5] One tentative reconstruction of atmospheric patterns for the winter of 1594–5 actually has strong high pressure over the Baltic region driving cold dry air from Asia west across Europe, reversing the moist and mild westerlies that normally keep the continent temperate.[6] If correct, such a pattern might help to explain much of the freezing weather that afflicted not only Ottoman lands but parts of Europe as well.

[2] Touchan et al., "Reconstructions of Spring/Summer Precipitation."

[3] Touchan et al., "Preliminary Reconstructions."

[4] See A. Schimmelmann, "A Large California Flood and Correlative Global Climatic Events 400 Years Ago," *Quaternary Research* 49 (1998): 51–61. In support of this hypothesis, the authors point out that Morocco experienced its highest precipitation in centuries, just as Anatolia and Greece descended into their worst drought in at least 600 years.

[5] V. Trouet et al., "Persistent Positive North Atlantic Oscillation Mode Dominated the Medieval Climate Anomaly," *Science* 324 (2009): 78–80.

[6] J. Jacobeit et al., "European Surface Pressure Patterns for Months with Outstanding Climate Anomalies During the Sixteenth Century," *Climatic Change* 43 (1999): 201–21.

Historical sources suggest that the drought began gradually, increasing in extent and intensity from 1591 to 1596, accompanied by the onset of Little Ice Age cold. A traveler's description has recorded drought in Palestine as early as the winter of 1590,[7] and the first indications in Ottoman records appeared the following spring, when the sultan complained to the inspector of water shortages in Istanbul.[8] At the same time, drought began to destroy harvests in the more arid agricultural regions: Karabağ (near Konya)[9] and the Peloponnese reported famine,[10] and Libya suffered shortages and sought grain relief from the Balkans and Tunisia,[11] perhaps contributing to the serious unrest in North Africa that year.[12] By 1592, the Damascus region also reported "much famine,"[13] leading the sultan to remove the current *kadı*.[14] The following year, the shortages spread to Baghdad[15] and then the Hijaz, where officials in Medina pleaded for more grain from Egypt: "Since it has not rained for a few years, there is famine . . . The poor settled in Medina are suffering a total shortage (*kemal müzayaka*)."[16] Yet the Nile flood failed as well in 1593, and the *deşişe* must have fallen short.[17]

Starting that winter, volcanic dust veils plunged Europe and the Near East into some of the coldest weather of the Little Ice Age.[18] Anatolia was particularly hard hit, enduring heavy snows that closed roads and killed off livestock.[19] By January 1595, even the new sultan Mehmed III struggled through the freezing weather on his way from Manisa to Istanbul to claim the throne.[20] Meanwhile, as the following narrative explains, Ottoman soldiers began to suffer from floods and frosts on the Hungarian front.

7 Cippora Klein, "Fluctuations of the Level of the Dead Sea and Climatic Fluctuations in Erez Israel During Historical Times" (PhD thesis, Hebrew University of Jerusalem, 1986), 89.

8 MD 68/86.

9 MD 67/59.

10 MD 5z/373.

11 MD 67/61 and MD 69/312.

12 Finkel, *Osman's Dream*, 180.

13 MD 67/300.

14 *Tarih-i Selânikî*, 237.

15 MD 71/771.

16 MD 70/141.

17 *Tarih-i Selânikî*, 335.

18 See Lamb, "Volcanic Dust Veils" and Atwell, "Volcanism and Short-Term Climatic Change."

19 *Tarih-i Selânikî*, 444, and MD 75/31.

20 *Tarih-i Selânikî*, 433.

By that time, the drought had reached the Aegean region and into Anatolia, as described in Venetian dispatches.[21] From 1594 to 1596, dangerous storms plagued the Adriatic, too, adding to the disruption in supplies and eventually forcing the Venetian grain administrators to begin importing from the Atlantic.[22] In the meantime, taxes, war, and banditry came to play as much a role as Little Ice Age weather in the famines, plagues, and disorder that swept the empire from Syria to the Balkans and beyond.

The Hungarian War

Turning a meteorological disaster into a human crisis, the Great Drought happened to coincide with one of the empire's longest and most difficult wars. The Ottomans had been locked in conflict with the Habsburgs ever since the later fifteenth century, when both states had emerged as leading European powers. Even intervals of supposed peace were marked by constant raiding, maneuvers, and the erection of fortifications. In the years leading up to this particular round of warfare, the Habsburgs had stepped up their provocations as they sensed weakness in their Ottoman opponents and sought to take advantage of French caution in the wake of that country's long civil war. During the struggle with Persia throughout the 1580s, the Ottomans had been careful to avoid hostilities on a second front, but by 1593 the expansionist faction in Ottoman political circles gained the upper hand, convincing Sultan Murad III to embark upon another round of warfare with the old enemy.[23]

However, the Ottoman statesmen seriously miscalculated this time. By the 1590s, improved infantry and heavy fortifications had begun to transform the nature of warfare in Europe, sharply raising the costs of conflict.[24] Following the lead of Northern Europe, the Austrian Habsburgs had modernized their fortresses and weaponry, acquiring solid frontier defenses and superior infantry firepower.[25] No longer could the

[21] *A.S.V. Dispacci-Costantinopoli* 43 (19 May 1596) and (6 Jun. 1596).

[22] *A.S.V. Dispacci-Costantinopoli* 38 (1 Dec. 1593), 39 (6 Mar. 1594), and 40 (11 Feb. 1595); and *Provveditori alle Biave* 4.

[23] Griswold, *Great Anatolian Rebellion*, 4–10.

[24] For an overview of these changes, see Geoffrey Parker, *The Military Revolution* (New York: Cambridge University Press, 1996).

[25] Gabor Agoston, "Habsburgs and Ottomans: Defense, Military Change, and Shifts in Power," *Turkish Studies Association Bulletin* 22 (1998): 126–41 and Colin Imber, "İbrahim Peçevi on War: A Note on the European Military Revolution," in *Frontiers of Ottoman Studies: State, Province, and the West*, vol. 2, ed. C. Imber, K. Kiyotaki, and R. Murphey (London: I. B. Tauris, 2005).

Ottomans rely on rapid advances and decisive charges to bring their campaigns to a swift and successful conclusion. The war in Hungary, known for good reason as the "Long War," would drag thirteen more years with few notable gains or losses. The worst of the fighting centered around the city of Pest and the fortress of Esztergom, which each changed hands twice over the period of hostilities. Advances and retreats across the frontier resulted in few permanent gains for either side. Peace came about by mutual exhaustion in 1606, and the resulting treaty did little more than restore the *status quo ante.*

The trouble was not that the Ottomans had failed to adjust to the new tactics. Although by no means technological leaders, the empire more or less kept pace with European military innovation until the eighteenth century.[26] What defeated the Ottomans, like so many other powers during this period of the "military revolution," was logistics rather than battles. A generation before, the empire had far outclassed its rivals in the resources and manpower it could put to war. Now, as described in the conclusion to Part I, the empire of the 1590s found itself at a critical conjuncture. Population pressure had squeezed supply, and the growth of cities and the military had raised demand for basic commodities. Moreover, an unprecedented drought was bringing famine to the same core provinces presently called upon to meet the extraordinary exactions of war – and not just any war, but a drawn-out war of sieges and counter-sieges.

Meanwhile, severe Little Ice Age cold plagued the Ottoman army at the front. The initial campaign season went well enough: A few years' breathing room since the last war with Persia had left the empire ready again with provisions. Furthermore, the soldiers were fortunate to have an exceptionally mild first winter.[27] Troubles mounted swiftly as the weather turned in late 1594. As that winter grew unusually harsh,[28] the Janissaries began to complain of famine.[29] In Hungary, meanwhile, the Danube froze for three months from February to April of 1595, and armies raided

[26] Jonthan Grant, "Rethinking Ottoman 'Decline': Military Technology Diffusion in the Ottoman Empire, 15th to 18th Centuries," *Journal of World History* 10 (1999): 179–201 and Günhan Börekçi, "A Contribution to the Military Revolution Debate: The Jannissaries' Use of Volley Fire during the Long Ottoman-Habsburg War of 1593–1606 and the Problem of Origins," *Acta Orientalia* 59 (2006): 407–38.

[27] *Peçevî Tarihi*, 348–9.

[28] Ibid., 355–6; Naîmâ Mustafa Efendi, *Târîh-i Naîmâ* (Istanbul: Danışman Yayınevi, 1967), 117; Rácz, *Climate of Hungary*, 29–30 and 94.

[29] *Tarih-i Selânikî*, 419–20, 423–4.

back and forth over the ice.[30] That spring the harvest in the northern Balkans failed,[31] and that summer as the ice melted, the Danube flooded and fevers broke out among the famished Ottoman soldiers.[32] Then the winter of 1595–6 proved just as awful as the last with more severe cold, heavy snows, and flooding.[33] Famine broke out again, first in Bosnia and then along the Hungarian frontier.[34] As soldiers without adequate provisions turned to living off the land, the local *reaya* began to flee.[35] By the spring, reports had begun to filter back to Istanbul of rampant shortages and insubordination at the front,[36] even though in one chronicler's words, the imperial government drew provisions "without measure or compare" from already famine-stricken provinces in the core.[37]

In the meantime, the throne passed from Murad III to his young son Mehmed III. Despite his inexperience, the new sultan sought to revive traditional Ottoman practice by leading his army in person to the front. Although the campaign that followed produced a remarkable victory at the Battle of Mezőkeresztes in October 1596, it failed to turn the tide of the war. Meanwhile, intense drought in the southern Balkans left the army suffering from hunger, thirst, and dysentery,[38] and disease began to spread through the fleet, leaving the navy "almost destroyed by plague" that autumn.[39] Worse still, the royal campaign created tremendous new demands on food and matériel, which proved the breaking point for already overstressed provisioning systems and the tipping point for discontent that had been simmering since the onset of the drought.

The Breakdown of Provisioning Systems

As the effects of the drought rippled across the empire, imperial provisioning systems began coming apart under the combined strains of

30 *Topçular Kâtibi 'Abdülkâdir Efendi Tarihi*, ed. Ziya Yılmazer (Ankara: TTK, 2003), 51 and 60.

31 *Tarih-i Selânikî*, 475–6.

32 *Topçular Kâtibi 'Abdülkâdir Efendi Tarihi*, 70. Rácz, "Price of Survival," 27–8, argues that war and depopulation contributed to flooding and the spread of marshlands in Hungary as water controls collapsed.

33 *Tarih-i Selânikî*, 556.

34 Ibid., 532–5.

35 Ibid., 572–3 and 601–2. See also Âlî, *Künhü'l-Ahbâr*, 559.

36 *A.S.V. Dispacci-Costantinopoli* 43 (2 June 1596).

37 *Tarih-i Selânikî*, 597–8.

38 *A.S.V. Dispacci-Costantinopoli* 43 (6 June 1596) and (20 July 1596).

39 *A.S.V. Dispacci-Costantinopoli* 43 (3 Aug 1596); and 44 (18 Sept. 1596) and (20 Oct. 1596).

famine and war. In the brief interval of peace after the Persian campaigns of the 1580s, the state had been so confident of supplies it had even authorized new grain exports to Venice.[40] As soon as the first spring of drought came in 1591, however, the imperial government started complaining once more of shortages, particularly of sheep and grapes.[41] That winter, imperial deficits grew deeper and its demands more persistent. Istanbul faced a severe shortfall of meat[42] and began to run low on grain and fats as well,[43] forcing the imperial government to call for extra requisitions through 1592.[44] By early the following year, the situation started to turn desperate.

With the demands of campaigning added to the effects of drought, Ottoman provisioning descended into a downward spiral. In each subsequent season, we find more and more complaints of shortages and requests for supplemental supplies – many times more than in similar crises of decades past.[45] From 1593 onward, we also find more urgent orders regarding "great shortages" (*hayli müzayaka*),[46] "severe shortages" (*ziyade müzayaka*),[47] or even "total shortages" (*külli müzayaka*)[48] and "permanent shortages" (*daima müzayaka*)[49] of necessities as diverse as wheat, honey, fruits, and above all sheep. Luxuries such as sugar from Egypt and Cyprus were smuggled away,[50] and even the cheapest necessities like barley ran low as the war and drought devoured available stocks.[51] The capital called on regions as far apart as Egypt, Bulgaria, and eastern Anatolia for goods, but without evident success. Even as another order arrived and another shortage was averted, the demands of the capital and the war always outpaced supply.

In typical fashion, Sultans Murad III and Mehmed III laid the blame on speculators and smugglers. In a series of increasingly frequent and vituperative threats and denunciations over the 1590s, we find constant

40 MD 67/114.
41 E.g., MD 67/414 and MD 67/446.
42 MD 69/435.
43 MD 69/467 and MD 69/75.
44 E.g., MD 69/479 and MD 69/516.
45 The relevant documents are found throughout MD 71–MD 74.
46 MD 71/489.
47 MD 71/552.
48 MD 71/413.
49 MD 71/440.
50 MD 71/565 and MD 73/61.
51 E.g., MD 71/749.

reports of stockpiled or diverted supplies.[52] Incidents of hoarding and price-gouging began as early as the spring of 1591,[53] spreading across the Black Sea and the Aegean by the following summer.[54] By then, all the major points of supply, including Rodosçuk,[55] the Mediterranean coast,[56] Egypt,[57] and the Crimea,[58] had begun diverting goods to more profitable illegal markets. İzmir, hitherto a modest Aegean port, also became a major source of black-market fruits, honey, and wax both within and without the empire.[59] Meanwhile, for reasons that become clear later in this chapter, sheep driven overland from the Balkans and Anatolia rarely reached their intended destinations.[60]

Rampant inflation fueled the diversion of supplies and widespread profiteering. On top of the ongoing "price revolution" driven by silver inflows and population pressure, the demands of war and the shortages of the Great Drought sent costs soaring. Taking the year 1489/90 as a baseline, Barkan calculated that the price index of basic foodstuffs in *akçes* had already risen to 365.52 by 1588/9, then jumped to 441.58 by the Battle of Mezőkeresztes, before climbing suddenly to 532.07 just one year later.[61] In Konya, in particular, *vakıf* records reveal sharp spikes in the real price of grains starting in 1594/5, giving a sense of the problems in Karaman, where full-scale rebellion was about to erupt.[62] Rapid debasement of the coinage only exacerbated the price swings,

52 E.g., MD 69/453, MD 71/128, MD 71/277, MD 71/418, etc. Venetian records apparently confirm this growing trade in contraband, at least until the worst of the famine in 1596, by which time supplies must have dried up altogether. See Aymard, *Venise, Raguse et la commerce de blé,* 165–6.

53 E.g., MD 67/285 and MD 68/130.

54 MD 5z/289

55 E.g., MD 71/97 and MD 71/191.

56 MD 71/418.

57 MD 71/440.

58 E.g., MD 71/637 and MD 72/781.

59 E.g., MD 71/290. See also Refik, *Hicrî On Birinci Asırda İstanbul Hayatı,* document 23.

60 E.g., MD 73/1154.

61 Barkan, "Price Revolution." According to Pamuk, "Prices in the Ottoman Empire" price levels reached 335 in the 1580s, 445 in the 1590s, and 543 in the 1600s, using a similar baseline. I have used Barkan's figures here rather than Pamuk's because the latter's are smoothed out so as to minimize short-term fluctuations from harvest conditions. Furthermore, Pamuk often relies on accounts of larger, more well-connected institutions less likely to suffer from the sudden price hikes that most consumers would have faced in times of famine.

62 Faroqhi, *Towns and Townsmen,* 209.

particularly for urban wage earners.[63] Yet even when expressed in terms of real silver, the inflation of the drought years was considerable.

As during past breakdowns in supply, the imperial response probably aggravated the crisis. Rather than adjust the *narh* in line with rising market values, the imperial government tried to clamp down on prices to control the spiralling costs of war. As the gap between real and official values continued to widen, those who could turned to hoarding and black-market profiteering. Worse still, the general inflation meant that the state's forced purchases for the war effort offered less and less real compensation for suppliers, often amounting to little more than extortion. On several occasions, the state sent out inquiries and tried to coordinate price levels throughout the empire in order to keep the *narhs* in line and preserve the flow of goods to the capital and the army.[64] Nevertheless, the very repetition of these orders serves as an indication of their failure. A number of documents have left us examples of the yawning gap between market and official prices for goods, often 100 percent or more. As early as 1592, for example, grapes were selling at İzmit for 120 *akçe* per *kantar* (around 50 kilograms) while the official price was only fifty to sixty.[65]

Shopkeepers and suppliers sought new ways to get around price restrictions. Some simply stockpiled in hopes of fetching a better price later. Others diluted goods or sold shorter measures, while others sought still more ingenious methods of evading the laws. In one case, we even find a complaint that grocers had gotten around the *narh* by selling their wares in marked-up fruit baskets.[66] At the same time, the Janissaries abused their privileges to buy up goods at a discount and sell at higher prices;[67] and the chronicler Selaniki, in particular, heaped much of the blame for famine and shortages on Janissary profiteering.[68]

To bridge gaps in supply and overcome breakdowns in provisioning, the state turned first to more taxation. On top of regular tithes and land dues, whose real value often declined as inflation set in, the sultans renewed irregular wartime contributions. These began with forced purchases of goods (*sürsat*), which had become little more than requisitions as the official price dropped far below market value; and once the war

[63] E.g., *Tarih-i Selaniki*, 784–85 *et passim*.
[64] E.g., MD 69/3, MD 69/523, and MD 69/556.
[65] MD 6z/236.
[66] Refik, *Hicrî On Birinci Asırda İstanbul Hayatı*, documents 32 and 37.
[67] E.g., MD 68/130 and MD 73/295.
[68] *Tarih-i Selânikî*, 594–5 and 608.

began, the state ordered new *avarız* assessments, or extraordinary cash levies on groups of households.[69] In short order, these new contributions became, in effect, another ordinary tax levied each year. Worse still, the state often farmed out collection of the same tax revenues to multiple collectors at once in order to pay off more supporters, encouraging abuse and extortion.[70] Imperial orders also required certain *sipahis* to contribute supplies in place of military service, as in previous wartime shortages.[71]

As even these new levies failed to meet the army's needs, the state tried to restrict consumption in order to free up more commodities. Starting in the winter of 1593–4, orders went out banning the slaughter of sheep over large parts of the Balkans and Anatolia.[72] In 1595, as animal products including lard and butter ran out, the imperial government prohibited private owners from oiling their ships, to save oil for imperial vessels.[73] A few months later, apparently concerned over the supply of flour, the sultan restricted the making of *simits* (round pastries) in the capital[74] – roughly the equivalent of restricting bagels in New York.

Historians and economists of famine continue to debate the effectiveness of such measures. Many have recently turned to a model "entitlement deficits" rather than "food availability deficits," implying that anti-hoarding and anti-speculation measures could help overcome market failures during famine.[75] Nevertheless, in conditions of segmented markets and extreme poverty, food availability itself can become a serious threat. Price controls can only aggravate the problem, when what are really needed are direct distributions of food.[76] In the Ottoman Empire of the 1590s, the scale of shortages and the demands of war precluded normal relief measures, especially in the landlocked provinces most affected by drought and famine. Furthermore, despite their often moralizing tone, imperial price control measures were less concerned with helping the Ottoman poor than securing cheap goods for the army from an already strapped treasury. Throughout the 1590s, official efforts

69 E.g., MD 72/281.
70 Tezcan, "Searching for Osman," 254–5.
71 E.g., MD 73/325 and MD 73/1125.
72 MD 71/150 and MD 72/340. See also Greenwood, "Istanbul's Meat Provisioning," 29.
73 MD 73/460.
74 MD 73/1205.
75 E.g., Amartya Sen, *Poverty and Famines* (Oxford: Clarendon Press, 1981).
76 See Cormac Ó Gráda, *Famine: A Short History* (Princeton: Princeton University Press, 2009), chapters 5 and 6.

had a mixed impact. On the one hand, despite periodic shortfalls of money and matériel, the Ottomans continued to supply an imposing army on the Balkan frontier without yet going bankrupt. On the other hand, imperial demands were fueling discontent at home that would threaten to undermine the empire from within.

The Rise of Banditry

Famine, war, and requisitions drove an unprecedented wave of banditry and disorder in the core provinces. After an apparent lull in rural violence from 1587 to 1591, the situation deteriorated again in the Great Drought. Looking over the hundreds of incidents of banditry in the imperial orders from this period,[77] a certain pattern emerges. Around 1590, reports remained fairly few and scattered, and early 1591 did not fare much worse. In late 1591, after the first season of drought, incidents of banditry multiplied rapidly, accelerating every year through early 1596, by which time we run into a gap in the surviving records[78] and the real Celali Rebellion had already begun. As the number of incidents rose, so they also tended to concentrate more and more around central Anatolia, and especially the province of Karaman. Furthermore, the scale of attacks grew worse, particularly raids by dozens or even hundreds of men on horseback plundering from village to village.

The initial rise in banditry probably reflected the impacts of the drought and its attendant hardships. After 1593, the demands of war must have played a significant role as well. The Venetian dispatches in particular recorded a rise in banditry starting in the later part of 1594, after the war effort in Hungary had run into trouble.[79] The provisioning of the campaigns drove up taxes and requisitions, pushing some *reaya* to evasion or resistance. The drain of grain and sheep from the countryside to the cities and the army left less and less for basic subsistence, prompting widespread theft of food and money. As in previous conflicts, the departure of soldiers also gave bandits license to attack with impunity.

Amid the inflation and shortages, the *sipahis* of Anatolia struggled to outfit their contingents for military service.[80] Out of exasperation, many

77 That is to say, *mühimme defters* 63 through 74. I have managed to catalogue over 500 orders regarding banditry in these years.

78 Very few *mühimmes* survive from between 1597 and 1602.

79 E.g., *A.S.V. Dispacci-Costantinopoli* 40 (6 Nov. 1594).

80 See the attached letter in *A.S.V. Dispacci-Costantinopoli* 46 (Nov. 1597). Also Griswold, *Great Anatolian Rebellion*, 12–14.

simply plundered or extorted from villagers. Under relentless pressure for money and supplies, tax collection began to collapse into indiscriminate pillaging of the provinces. In the records from 1593 onward, scores of reports flooded the capital complaining of officials, *sipahis*, and Janissaries using wartime requisitions as an excuse to gather gangs of men and ride from to village to village demanding goods and cash.[81] Just as often, bandits merely pretended to be soldiers or officials and took advantage of the confusion to loot the countryside.[82] The *reaya*, of course, had no way to tell these groups apart. And so, for every legitimate if burdensome tax, the peasants found themselves paying out as much or more to bandits.

In another troubling development, officials sent to contain the disorder sometimes joined in instead, using their "tours of inspection" (*devir, devriyye*, or *teftiş*) as a license to plunder the peasantry. By 1595, a few of these officials had gathered private armies of hundreds of bandits and irregular soldiers, sometimes armed with guns.[83] In response to their depredations, Sultans Murad III and then Mehmed III issued successive "imperial justice decrees" (*adalet fermanı*) affirming the *reaya's* right to self-defense.[84] Whether in response to these decrees, or simply out of desperation, the peasantry increasingly took up arms and organized resistance.[85]

In his original study of the Celali Rebellion, Mustafa Akdağ placed particular emphasis on the conflict between these two groups – *askeri* private armies and *reaya* militias – in the growing violence of the 1590s.[86] Others since have stressed the importance of irregular soldiers (the so-called *sekbans*) and the spread of firearms.[87] This book analyzes both theories in-depth in the following chapter. For now, suffice it to say that the evidence of these years lends only modest support to either theory, at least until the full-scale eruption of rebellion in 1596. Only a minority of the reports dealt with private armies and even fewer mentioned irregular soldiers or firearms. Overwhelmingly, petitions from *kadıs* and representatives of the *reaya* complained just of general outbreaks of lawlessness or

81 E.g., MD 72/186 and MD 72/208. See also Akdağ, *Celâlî İsyanları*, chapter 3F.

82 E.g., MD 72/721, MD 72/312, and MD 73/232.

83 Akdağ, *Celâlî İsyanları*, 133–4, 165–70.

84 Halil İnalcık, "Adâletnâmeler," *Belgeler* 2 (1965): 49–145.

85 Akdağ, *Celâlî İsyanları*, 150–2, 160–1.

86 Ibid., 171–6 *et passim*.

87 E.g., Halil İnalcık, "Military and Fiscal Transformation in the Ottoman Empire, 1600–1700," *Archivum Ottomanicum* 6 (1980): 283–337; İnalcık, "Socio-Political Effects of the Diffusion of Firearms"; and Barkey, *Bandits and Bureaucrats*.

assorted groups of bandits. Furthermore, we should hesitate to place too much distinction among the various types of lawlessness in the provinces at the time. In 1595, all the groups – whether "bandits" or "*sekbans*" or "*sohtas*" – were essentially the same men after the same things and ready to use the same violence. Desperation provided the motive and disorder the opportunity for gangs to plunder at will; or, as one author has put it, "tax collection and banditry collapsed into the same undifferentiated activity of living off the land."[88] Hitherto unaware of climatic and ecological pressures driving unrest, Ottomanists have focused on internal social and political factors for the outbreak of violence. However, as we have seen, the unprecedented drought and famine and the distraction of war could explain the worst disorders. Moreover, the timing fits perfectly, and the parallels with less dramatic incidents in the 1570s and 1580s tend to support this explanation.

Flight, Plague, and Famine

The famine and violence of the Great Drought drove an exodus of refugees from the countryside. The flight had already begun by 1592, when a report on banditry in Rum (east-central Anatolia) stated that the people of some villages were "scattered" (*perakende*).[89] The next year, the records turn up another report of abandoned fields and gardens around Tripoli (Lebanon),[90] perhaps in response to shortages around Syria. Once the war broke out and banditry spread, the movement gained momentum. Over the following years, reports came in from across Anatolia that peasants were fleeing or that they were "all decided upon flight" (*cümlemüz cıla-yı vatan itmek mükarrerdür*).[91] In some instances, they reported running from the exactions of soldiers and officials, and in others, from the abuses of bandits. Others in the Balkans fled the violence and famine of the war itself. By the spring of 1595, Venetian ambassador Marco Vernier lamented "the difficulty of provisions" and the "extreme scarcity" (*grandissima carestia*), writing that "each day with the winds from the north there arrive various ships from the Black Sea of people fleeing from there and coming here to add to the famine . . . "[92]

88 Cook, *Population Pressure*, 40.
89 MD 6z/144.
90 MD 71/700.
91 E.g., MD 72/706 and MD 73/1155.
92 *A.S.V. Dispacci-Costantinopoli* 41 (18 May 1595).

Given the influx of refugees, Istanbul faced two severe epidemics, in 1592 and again in 1595.[93] The former may or may not have been related to contagions reported in Antalya (southwest Anatolia) that year[94] and Palestine the next.[95] One contemporary called it a "*taun-ı veba*," and his description suggests it may actually have been bubonic plague. That summer it reached such a pitch that the sultan himself led desperate inhabitants of the capital in public prayer to ward off the infection.[96] The epidemic of 1595, described by the same author as a "*maraz-ı taun*"[97] ("sickness of plague"), was probably something altogether different. In this case, we have a detailed description from the Venetian ambassador, who saw the disease infect his own household.[98] By his account, it was a "most severe plague, and deadly" (*peste acutissima, et mortifera*). He described one of its victims as "half-dead with many swellings and with black marks all over his body. And once the plague took him by the throat, finally, in little more than a day, it suffocated him with great violence and killed him by a cruel death . . . " This he contrasted with past "plagues" that were treatable and not always fatal (that is, not really plague at all). Some of the symptoms would suggest anthrax, and the diagnosis is supported by another chronicler who referred to the disease with the Persian expression "*şir-pençe*," meaning anthrax, or literally "lion's paw," presumably for the characteristic black marks.[99]

By that time famine conditions engulfed the Eastern Mediterranean, afflicting even Constantinople. The turning point came in the dry winter of 1594–5. By that February, Ambassador Vernier wrote that "the scarcity here is tremendous," clarifying it was a "scarcity born of the evil of the weather," and adding that "given the contrary weather" ships could not enter to deliver grain, forcing the state to requisition provisions from overland by pack animals. Finally, he concluded, there was "always another reason that has been assigned to the shortage of bread and to the extreme want of meat and of many other things, that is the

93 See Chapter 9 for more on urban diseases and mortality in Ottoman lands. The role of refugees in spreading disease will also be treated in Chapters 9 and 10.

94 MD 69/125. See also Kılıç, *Genel Hatlarıyla Dünya'da ve Osmanlı Devleti'nde Salgın Hastalıklar*, 55.

95 Klein, "Fluctuations of the Level of the Dead Sea," 89.

96 *Tarih-i Selânikî*, 282–7.

97 Ibid., 545.

98 *A.S.V. Dispacci-Costantinopoli* 41 (Aug. 1595).

99 *Künhü'l-Ahbâr*, 693–4. Anthrax outbreaks in both animal and human populations were of ancient provenance in the Mediterranean: See Sallares, *Ecology of the Ancient Greek World*, 288.

war in Walachia, which takes a great part of the provisions belonging to this numerous people, while the immense army this year in Hungary has taken provisions from every region in the greatest quantity."[100] The ambassador made further reference to shortage in his letters of May and October of the same year, and again in April and May of 1596. In the last dispatch, he blamed the scarcity of provisions directly upon "the shortage or delay of the harvest caused by the continuing droughts."[101]

That spring, the famine reached a climax. The most dramatic descriptions come from the chronicler Selaniki, an eyewitness to developments in the capital. By March of 1596, he wrote, "everyone was stricken with famine" (*halk-ı alem kaht u gala ile müztaribler*).[102] Basic foodstuffs had soared in price.[103] In May, even the wealthy were ordered to stop giving banquets because food was running short.[104] Later that same month, out of desperation, the sultan had the leading men of state pray for an end to their affliction:

> And in the last days of Ramadan the great ulema and sheikhs – God preserve them – with all the leading men of state made a great congregation at the noble Mosque of Sultan Mehmed Han. With moans and supplications at the altar of God, they made their prayers, repenting and begging forgiveness, rubbing their faces in the dirt. They begged for the boundless mercy of rain from God, the Compassionate and the Merciful. Sheikh Hızır Efendi – God bless him – mounted the pulpit, and in words ringing with truth he ordered the people to beware of evil. In particular, he fired up the people with burning sermons against the crowd of speculators and usurers who brought famine. However, the tears trickling to the ground did not draw a drop of water from the heavens . . . [105]

The sultan's Mezőkeresztes campaign that June drained yet more goods from the markets. Departing Janissaries extorted grain, forcing shops to close and driving up the price of barley to over fifty *akçe* per *kile*.[106]

In July, a comet appeared in the sky, which the people took as a sign of impending doom. The Venetian ambassador described the confusion that followed:

[100] *A.S.V. Dispacci-Costantinopoli* 40 (11 Feb. 1595).
[101] *A.S.V. Dispacci-Costantinopoli* 43 (19 May 1596).
[102] *Tarih-i Selânikî*, 579.
[103] Ibid., 592–3.
[104] Ibid., 596.
[105] Ibid., 600.
[106] Ibid., 608, 615.

> ...So it goes, passing from one disorder to the next. Here there appeared a comet sent from the Lord with its tail turned towards the east, and according to the judgment of these fortune-tellers it means great ruin, great death, and great spilling of blood for these parts. And so this apparition has filled the city with fright, with terror, and still more with religion, [the people] having turned now to continuous prayers to God...[107]

The chronicler Selaniki summed up the state of affairs that August as follows:

> This blessed year, by the wisdom of God the Great and the Beautiful, there was a shortage of rain. The waters drew back, the wells dried up, and the signs of famine appeared and grew unmistakable. The cursed speculators of Istanbul began to hide provisions first in one place then another. In this way, food grew scarce, and there was nothing left to sow. Once the royal campaign began, fodder and barley became dear. Everyone fell into a panic that winter provisions would go short once the army returned from campaign...
>
> May God on high be merciful to his people's ways, and may they repent, show remorse, and beg forgiveness![108]

The rains returned at last that November, but by then the drought and war had already triggered a chain of events leading to rebellion and crisis.

Let Them Eat Goat

To the same entry in his chronicle on August 1596, Selaniki appended the following complaint: "In Istanbul, there were no sheep left for the Janissaries, and no suitable meat was provided for the palaces, nor even the imarets. It could not be found for even fifteen *akçe* per *vukiye*."[109] In almost every description of famine and shortage at the time, the want of cattle and sheep drew particular attention. Starting in 1591, the imperial orders began to record scores if not hundreds of complaints first of "shortages" then of "severe shortages" and even "total shortages" of meat, butter, and lard.[110] Smuggling, speculation, and shortfalls became an acute concern as heavy military demands went unmet.

[107] *A.S.V. Dispacci-Costantinopoli* 43 (20 July 1596).
[108] *Tarih-i Selânikî*, 624.
[109] Ibid.
[110] E.g., MD 70/452 and MD 71/624.

As explained in Chapter 3, the sheep provisioning system had steadily deteriorated in each conflict and shortage since the 1570s. By placing the burden of supply on individuals, the peculiar *celep-keşan* system proved vulnerable to supply shocks and price fluctuations. As market values diverged from the *narh*, suppliers faced serious losses and even bankruptcy. Moreover, the ecology of animal supplies differed from that of grain. Serious disasters could cut into breeding stock for years to come, especially if suppliers or taxpayers began butchering ewes in desperation to meet their quotas.

As with other commodities, the imperial government exacerbated the supply problem by refusing to revise official prices in line with market realities. As early as 1591, it appears the sultan had actually lowered the *narh* for sheep from forty to thirty *akçe*, while the market value had jumped to perhaps 100.[111] Then over the following years of drought, the sultan barely raised official prices even as the black market values soared. In early 1592, for example, the sultan chastised the *kadı* of Edirne for letting meat sell at seven or eight *akçe* per *vukiye* while the *narh* was set at only three;[112] and by the end of that year, the official price had risen to only four *akçe* in Bursa[113] and six in Istanbul.[114] Yet by 1596, as we have seen from the descriptions in Selaniki, meat could scarcely be had for fifteen *akçe* in the capital.

Time and again, imperial orders railed against speculators and smugglers of animals and animal products,[115] but to no avail. From the Danube sheep were smuggled into Poland,[116] and from the Kurdish and Türkmen regions they were diverted to markets in central and western Anatolia.[117] Given the circumstances, even wealthy *celeps* started going bankrupt all across the empire. Forced to buy thousands of sheep at high market prices and sell for only a fraction of their costs, even the richest of usurers must have seen their capital vanish.[118] As a consequence, the rolls of sheep suppliers fell quickly out of date, holding up provisions from critical areas. As early as the winter of 1591–2, the state sent out orders to the

111 MD 5z/167 and Greenwood, "Istanbul's Meat Provisioning," 142.
112 MD 69/89.
113 MD 69/556.
114 MD 71/636.
115 E.g., MD 72/291, MD 72/303, MD 72/335, and MD 5z/362.
116 MD 68/120.
117 MD 71/698.
118 For a further discussion of the problem, see Greenwood, "Istanbul's Meat Provisioning," 145–50.

kadıs of the Balkans to complain of dead and bankrupt *celeps* on the rolls and to demand replacements;[119] and by late 1593, the *kassaps* of Istanbul were going bankrupt as well.[120] By early 1595, according to another investigation, most of the sheep suppliers across the empire had either "perished or absconded" (*mürde ve gerühte*).[121]

As the *celep-keşan* system disintegrated, the imperial government turned to more desperate measures. The most ambitious plan consisted of a giant cash fund to purchase supplies, the so-called *sermaye-i kassap*.[122] Starting in the winter of 1592–3, the Porte raised millions of *akçes*, extorting heavy sums from Jews and Armenians in particular, to set up a permanent endowment to purchase sheep.[123] As even this fund failed to meet demand, however, sultans Murad III then Mehmed III turned to ever larger and more arbitrary requisitions from the core Ottoman provinces and nomadic tribes. Then in 1593, as previously described, the imperial government simply banned the slaughter of sheep over wide regions of the Balkans and Anatolia and ordered the people to eat goat instead.

However, the problem by this time was not just a breakdown in supply but an absolute shortage of the animals themselves. In desperation, suppliers started delivering ewes again, suggesting they had run out of lambs.[124] Meanwhile, sheep and other animals also became a major target of the theft and banditry in Anatolia. In dozens of cases, reports not only mentioned "plunder of goods and food" (*emval u erzak garet*), but particularly emphasized the theft of sheep and lambs and other animals.[125] In other cases, real or pretended officials used wartime taxes as an excuse to extort sheep from the peasantry.[126]

These animals, too, had fallen victim to the Little Ice Age. In part, the harsh winters and the turmoil of war cut into Ottoman flocks. For

[119] MD 67/486.

[120] MD 71/555.

[121] MD 73/489.

[122] Greenwood, "Istanbul's Meat Provisioning," 151–2 and chapter 4 *passim*.

[123] There are signs that some groups blamed the Jews of Istanbul for the famine, and preyed upon them as an easy target. See, for instance, *A.S.V. Dispacci-Costantinopoli* 51 (4 Aug. 1600). The imperial government later added an extra 1% customs tax to supplement these cash demands (Greenwood, "Istanbul's Meat Provisioning," 245–6). For more descriptions of the fund, see Refik, *Hicrî On Birinci Asırda İstanbul Hayatı*, documents 5, 7, and 22. On resistance to the cash levies, see especially *Tarih-i Selânikî*, 575.

[124] MD 72/85 and MD 72/907. MD 71/150 also specifically bans the slaughter of female and adult male sheep.

[125] E.g., MD 71/537.

[126] E.g., MD 72/457.

example, a report of 1595 on the failure of the Bursa sheep supply pleaded that "not only are Moldovia and Wallachia in turmoil, but many thousands of sheep have died from the freezing weather."[127] Likewise, eyewitness accounts of war on the Hungarian front placed emphasis on the shortage of horses and draft animals, who were dying off in the cold and snow.[128]

However, the worst mortality came from animal diseases that preyed upon the exposed and starving herds. As we find in the *Künhu'l-Ahbar* of the contemporary chronicler Mustafa Ali, a great plague among livestock had begun in 1591 or 1592 and then swept across the empire. Blending rumor and personal observation, Mustafa Ali left the following description:

> In the year 1000 (1591/2)... near the border with Iran a cow gave birth to a boy... Some say that a man must have [had intercourse with] the cow so that from his sperm a boy was born, and some say that such a birth could not be. At any rate, God on high, out of anger to his servants, revealed his warning. He must have created this lesson so that it might serve as a warning, and they might repent of their sins... Thus the people executed both the boy and the cow who bore him.[129] Moreover, one by one the cattle and sheep and other breeds died. Their corpses became one with the black earth. Indeed, in the capital Constantinople in the years 1001 and 1002 (1592–4) clarified butter stopped coming. When they enquired for the reason of this shortage and famine, they found proof that in those provinces there was an animal plague (*kırgun*) and no oxen or cattle remained. Afterwards, it apparently came from these parts spreading into Persia, and in the fourth year it appeared from Iraq. It reached first Diyarbakır (southeast Anatolia), then Zülkadriyye and the land of Rum (east-central Anatolia). In Muharrem 1004 (September 1595), this poor man – that is, the writer of this history – was appointed to the two offices of secretary (*defterdar*) to the treasury of Rum and general (*mirliva*) of Amasya... Among the towns and cities I visited... it so happened there were neighborhoods where not a single cow remained, and villages where the inhabitants were relieved that one or two cows were left from four or five hundred.

127 MD 73/789.

128 E.g., *Topçular Kâtibi 'Abdülkâdir Effendi Tarihi*, 169.

129 As bizarre as this episode seems, early modern Europe and colonial America often displayed a similar hysteria over bestiality, including execution of both animal and human perpetrators. See John Murrin, "Things Fearful to Name: Bestiality in Early America," in *The Human/Animal Boundary: Historical Perspectives*, ed. A. Creager and W. Jordan (Rochester, NY: University of Rochester Press, 2002).

And then in verse he added:

> So the corpses lay, so the animals perished
>
> That in the hearts of the *reaya* there was no hope . . .

Mustafa Ali continued this passage with a description of the suffering caused by the death of livestock:

> And so this general calamity spread to the great and learned. It was the curse of the peasants and the poor and hurt the interests of the *tımar*-holders. It was the cause of poverty and the distress of merchants and other inhabitants of the country . . . Moreover, God brought famine to his servants. With the cattle plague not only was there a shortage of cheese and yoghurt, but of the basic sustenance – barley and wheat. As the cattle died, they went without. Now in these circumstances in the province of Rum I saw that some *reaya* were hitched up and made to plow in place of oxen, and some of them even planted wheat and barley seeds and tilled the land with a hoe.

To the chronicler, this was a simple judgment from God: "The *reaya*, the *sipahis*, and merchants were all sinners . . . For that reason the famine and shortage spread. Some of the *reaya* gave no heed to justice or religion [and] the merchants and shopkeepers did not respect the *narh*."[130]

Barring divine punishment as an explanation, it seems the sheep and cattle were another casualty of extreme cold and drought. Anatolian sheep farmers whom I spoke with during my travels in the region generally agreed that severe winters and especially poor pasture during droughts still tend to spread infection, at least in the absence of antibiotics. Moreover, the episode displays some striking parallels with other historical famines, both in Ottoman lands and beyond. During the Great Anatolian Famine of the 1870s, a similar spell of cold and drought killed off over 80 percent of the cattle and 90 percent of the sheep in central Turkey, and the death of livestock caused even more famine and suffering than the actual loss of crops.[131] To take a contemporary example, the pastoral lands of the sixteenth-century Kingdom of Naples – similarly situated from an environmental perspective – also suffered regular murrains

[130] Âlî, *Künhü'l-Ahbâr*, 675–7.

[131] Erler, *Osmanlı Devleti'nde Kuraklık*, 132 and chapter 2 *passim*, and *The Famine in Asia Minor* (Istanbul: Isis, 1989), 41 *et passim*. For a similar episode in Syria in 1958–61, see Norman Lewis, *Nomads and Settlers in Syria and Jordan, 1800–1980* (New York: Cambridge University Press, 1987), 170.

in these years of bad weather.[132] Perhaps no other episode captures the suffering so well as the Great Famine of 1315–20 in Northern Europe, when a similar succesion of severe winter frosts helped spread animal infections that wiped out half or more of the livestock, contributing to the widespread starvation and disorder of those years.[133]

Mustafa Ali's account of the epizootic remains the most detailed we have, but there is additional evidence to emphasize the scale and scope of the loss. During the Great Drought, imperial orders made frequent reference to "wasting" (*telef*) and "perishing" (*zayi*) sheep.[134] Other documents described serious epizootics in Anatolia and even the Crimea. Sometime in late 1594 or 1595, for example, the provincial governor of Caffa wrote the capital to warn that: "In these parts a plague has befallen the sheep, and those who had flocks of four or five hundred have only ten or twenty left." At first, he claimed, there remained some surplus fats for export, but then apparently the sickness passed through a second time, "and the remaining cattle and sheep perished" leaving none at all to meet the sultan's demands.[135] As late as June of 1598, the Venetian ambassador wrote a dispatch mentioning "the famine of everything but principally of meat, since the animals that are usually brought here in other times for the use of the city in this season come from Anatolia, which has been almost emptied of every sort of animal by a mortality that came through the year before."[136] Given the high death rate, the animals may have been infected by an outbreak of anthrax like that which struck Istanbul in 1595. Rinderpest, a scourge of early modern European livestock, offers another possible explanation. However, the evidence remains too limited for a confident diagnosis.[137]

Whatever it was, news of the epizootic must have reached the capital quickly. As early as October 1593, an imperial order for fats informed the governor of Caffa that "in this blessed year, an animal sickness has appeared and most have died."[138] That was why one year later, as quoted the previous paragraph, the provincial governor had to emphasize the

[132] John Marino, *Pastoral Economics in the Kingdom of Naples* (Baltimore: Johns Hopkins University Press, 1988), 56–7.

[133] William Chester Jordan, *The Great Famine* (Princeton: Princeton University Press, 1996).

[134] E.g., MD 72/335, MD 72/905, and MD 74/181.

[135] MD 72/6.

[136] *A.S.V. Dispacci-Costantinopoli* 47 (13 June 1598).

[137] On the challenges of diagnosing historical epizootics, see Tim Newfield, "A Cattle Panzootic in Early Fourteenth-Century Europe," *Agricultural History Review* 57 (2009): 155–90.

[138] MD 71/214.

losses in his own domains as well. Yet the imperial government refused to change course, and the following years saw ever larger orders for sheep and animal products. Above all, the Porte made new requests for tens of thousands more sheep each year from eastern and central Anatolia, even though that was precisely where the plague originated.[139] In some orders, the sultan simply included warnings such as "do not let the animals waste or perish" (*zayi ü telef itdürmeyesin*), as though the owners or suppliers had a choice.[140] Not surprisingly, deliveries kept falling short, the sheep sickened, and animals were stolen or sold off during their long trek across the peninsula.[141]

Imperial orders were especially prone to blaming the people and officials of central Anatolia for disrupting supply.[142] This may have been the reason why Mehmed III chose to pick on the province of Karaman as he planned his imperial campaign in late 1595, issuing the following extraordinary demand:

> To the *kadı* of Konya and the Karaman provincial governor's lieutenant (*Karaman beylerbeğisinün kaymakamı*):
>
> Since sheep are vital to the provisions of Istanbul, it is ordered that you procure 200,000 sheep from your district and send them along with their owners or representatives.
>
> *So ordered*:
>
> Upon receipt, take full responsibility. Urgently send 200,000 sheep along with their owners or representatives to my capital so they may be sold for the sustenance of the people... [143]

Even in an ordinary year, 200,000 sheep would have represented an extraordinary number. It is true that during the Hungarian campaigns of the 1560s, Sultan Süleyman had placed orders for the forced purchase of up to 228,000 sheep at once. However, orders on such a scale had always come from the richer pastures of the Danubian provinces and principalities.[144] The Anatolian supply had always been a distant second; and even then, the largest orders for up to 100,000 at a time had always come from eastern Anatolia, and especially from the Türkmen. Single

[139] E.g., MD 69/611, MD 70/452, MD 71/698.
[140] E.g., MD 74/181.
[141] E.g., MD 72/12.
[142] E.g., MD 74/695.
[143] MD 73/964.
[144] Veinstein, "Some Views on Provisioning in the Hungarian Campaigns" and Greenwood, "Istanbul's Meat Provisioning," 20.

orders from Karaman had rarely come close to six digits, let alone the 200,000 demanded all at once in 1595.

Moreover, 1595 was no ordinary year. With the drought, famine, and animal plague already cutting into supplies, 200,000 sheep was a crushing requisition. As described in Chapter 2, livestock were often the only assets of the poor and their only safety net in times of want. Furthermore, with the breakdown of the supply system, the sultan's invitation to "sell" sheep in the capital was deceptive. The fixed price of meat, even in Istanbul, had drifted so far from the market value that even if the rightful owners had legally gone to "sell" their own animals the compensation would have been pitiful. Moreover, we can assume that this is not what happened anyway. Given the chaos in the countryside – and particularly in Karaman – such a requisition must surely have broken down into extortion and plundering.[145]

In any event, the demand proved to be a turning point for Karaman and for the empire as a while. The order marked not only the breakdown of the provisioning system, but also a break in that implicit circle of justice that bound the *reaya* to the imperial government. Without security against lawlessness and unjust demands, the *reaya* had no cause to serve the sultan any longer as peaceful taxpayers. I do not mean to suggest that peasants staged an organized revolution across Anatolia – far from it. However, the sultan's demand and the *reaya*'s resistance brought the general lawlessness to a critical mass, where instead of splintering into criminal gangs it snowballed into bandit armies. With that transformation, the Celali Rebellion had begun.

[145] Cf. Akdağ, *Celâlî İsyanları*, 171–2.

7

THE CELALI REBELLION

Even as the drought lifted in late 1596, conditions in the empire went from bad to worse. Bandit gangs grew larger and more brazen in their attacks, taking a mounting toll on provincial towns and villages. In time, these groups coalesced into rebel armies called Celalis, led by a motley succession of commanders. Meanwhile, wars in Hungary and then Persia along with a new rebellion in Syria left Ottoman forces incapable of handling the revolt. The violence unleashed a flood of refugees, driving a vicious cycle of desperation, lawlessness, and flight. Persistent Little Ice Age weather fueled the crisis, bringing famine even worse than that of the Great Drought. Only after peace with the Habsburgs in 1606 could the empire even begin to deal with the Celalis and bring a semblance of order to Anatolia. Even then the Ottomans had to pass through several more winters of extreme cold and privation, leaving parts of the empire depopulated for decades, even centuries to come.

"Karaman'ın Koyunu, Sonra Çıkar Oyunu"

("If it's a sheep of Karaman, there's going to be trouble" – Turkish proverb)

When the officials came to make the great requisition of sheep from Karaman province, they met outright rebellion for the first time. The contemporary chronicler Selaniki has given us the following account:

> His Majesty the Sultan took it upon himself to set out from these parts and embark upon a campaign. When men were sent out around and about to procure sheep from the provinces of Anadolu and Karaman for the campaign provisions of the men of state, some disgraceful profaner from among the Davud group in the district of Turgud (near Konya) in the province of Karaman stirred up the rabble and the traitors to his cause. "I am from the line of Alaeddin Feramurz, the last of the house of

> Seljuk,"[1] he claimed, rambling on about how he supposedly came from a line that had ended three hundred years ago. Claiming, "the house of Osman (i.e., the Ottoman dynasty) has gone the way of injustice and oppression, and I shall bring truth and justice," he took the sheep back from the hands of those gathering them for the campaign.[2]

This was hardly the first time since the Ottoman conquest of the late fourteenth century that the rebellious inhabitants of Karaman had rallied around an imperial pretender. With their memories of the independent Karamanid dynasty, the notables and peasants of the region had resisted imperial demands before, and often drove a hard bargain with the Ottoman state.[3] Nevertheless, nothing quite like this had been recorded since the sectarian wars with Shiite Persian sympathizers almost eighty years before. That is to say, no one in more than two generations had led a serious revolt that actually accused the Ottomans of oppression (*zulm*) and rejected the authority of their dynasty altogether.

Significantly, the chronicler also explained that the rebel leader aimed to become a "*celali*." This term, from which the Celali Rebellion received its name, had its origins in a small religious uprising of the early sixteenth century in Amasya, led by a certain Sheikh Celal.[4] The precise significance remains unclear, but the word appears in Ottoman documents as early as 1571, as in the following example of a major *sohta* uprising in the region southwest of Konya:

> To the *kadıs* of Manavgad, Ala'iyye, Duşenbe, and Teke Karahisar:
>
> [You] sent a sealed letter to my palace: "The *sohtas* of the Teke district have rebelled ... More than one thousand have joined the *levends* and broken into the Köprı market. They have broken into the houses of the nearby village of Uğraşır, plundered their goods, and ... killed two boys. They claimed, 'We have become *celalis* (*Biz celali olduk*). You do not go to market,' and they cut the beards of many men and executed them."[5]

To judge from the silence in later documents, this particular uprising of 1571 went nowhere, although it may have set some precedent for what was about to follow in Larende. It is interesting here that the *sohtas* actually claimed the title "*celali*" for themselves, as though it conferred

[1] This is presumably Alaeddin Keykubad III b. Feramurz, Seljuk shah for the last time in 1301–3.
[2] *Tarih-i Selânikî*, 581.
[3] İnalcık, "Ottoman Methods of Conquest."
[4] William Griswold, "Djalali," in *Encyclopedia of Islam Online*, ed. P. Bearman, http://www.brillonline.nl/.
[5] MD 12/676.

some legitimacy. It may also be significant that the "*celalis*" in this case are not ordinary bandits, but a large gang of *sohtas* and *levends.*[6] It is hard to pin down its precise significance, however, since the term remained very rare until the end of the 1590s. Among the hundreds of incidents of banditry from 1591–6, only a handful use the expression *celali.* By the time it came into common use, sometime around 1600, it had apparently turned into a term of abuse.

In any event, the immediate outcome of the 1596 rebellion over sheep in Karaman remains unclear. Selaniki claimed that "pronouncements were issued to console the people of the country" and the sultan apparently offered rewards to those who could capture the rebels.[7] However, the resistance by no means died away. In fact, the documents attest that in Turgud itself banditry persisted through the summer of 1596.[8] Mustafa Akdağ – who wrote his history of the Celalis apparently unaware of the Great Drought, the murrain, or the order for so many sheep – still considered the Turgud uprising a significant development in the rebellion;[9] and he cited several examples of growing peasant resistance and rising violence in the province over the following year.[10]

After the uprising against the sheep collectors, the general lawlessness in and around Karaman reached new levels. The Kırşehir region was perhaps the worst affected, as hundreds of bandits descended like locusts, stealing food and animals, provoking panic and flight.[11] The Konya region suffered from similar raids;[12] and other gangs of horsemen totaling in the thousands plundered the remainder of the province.[13] As in previous years, the distinctions blurred between legitimate tax collection and simple theft, and between bands of soldiers and criminal gangs. For every instance of some official's private army, the documents record at least another instance of ordinary local banditry or gangs of horsemen plundering from village to village.

Within this confusion, one crucial development stands out. Starting in late 1595, a movement of *sohtas* spread from the Taurus Mountains

[6] Mustafa Ali's *Counsel for Sultans* (1581) also referred to zealous preachers as "*celalis,*" again suggesting some connection with religious extremism. See Tezcan, *Second Ottoman Empire,* 124.

[7] "Tarih-i Selânikî," 581.

[8] MD 74/395.

[9] Akdağ, *Celâlî İsyanları,* 162–3, 172–3.

[10] Ibid., 164–5, 174–6.

[11] MD 74/119, MD 74/461, and Akdağ, *Celâlî İsyanları,* 180–1.

[12] MD 74/319.

[13] E.g., MD 74/311.

into the province of Karaman.[14] By 1596, these bandits had evolved into a serious threat, attacking throughout the region.[15] Over the following year, it seems they banded together in the district of Larende itself, from where they began to plunder the surrounding countryside.[16] By the spring of 1598, Larende had been completely overrun with thousands of bandits, *sohtas*, and *sekbans*. It appears to be the first instance where part of the empire had fallen completely into the hands of rebels. Selaniki gave the following account:

> In the province of Karaman in the city of Larende all the bandits – the dismissed district governors and provincial governors and the left-over *sekbans* – joined with the *sohtas*. They exceeded three thousand men. They wickedly plundered the people of the country. When the emissaries (*çavuş*) appointed to their protection were defeated and perished, they sent forth the soldiers of the province. Having assembled, there was a great battle with severe losses on both sides.[17]

Once again, the chronicler claimed the rebels were defeated, but the evidence suggests otherwise. The *sohtas* continued to use İçel and Larende as a base from which to raid the countryside.[18] Moreover, the disturbance led to a new imperial appointment to secure the province. Within a year, a corrupt former governor, Hüseyin Paşa, bribed his way into the office. Hüseyin abused his position to take his revenge on local officials for his previous dismissal, and to gather a private army of bandits and plunder throughout the province.[19] At this point, according to Selaniki, he and his men "became known as *celalis*" (*namı celali oldu*).[20]

In the same description, the chronicler mentioned for the first time another character plundering the province of Karaman: one Abdülhalim, better known by his nickname Karayazıcı ("Black Scribe"). Though past authors attributed various origins to this bandit leader, it appears he got his start in Syria in the 1580s as a sort of *condottiere*.[21] One description places him in the Tarsus-Silifke region (the mountainous region opposite Larende) as a *bölük-başı*, or mercenary commander, just as the

[14] MD 73/783.
[15] MD 74/127.
[16] *Târîh-i Naîmâ*, 197.
[17] *Tarih-i Selânikî*, 751.
[18] Akdağ, *Celâlî İsyanları*, 185, 226–7, 234.
[19] *A.S.V. Dispacci-Costantinopoli* 48 (25 July 1599).
[20] *Tarih-i Selânikî*, 816.
[21] Mustafa Akdağ, "Kara-Yazıcı," in *İslam Ansiklopedisi*, ed. M. Houtsma (Istanbul: Maarif Matbaası, 1940–88); Griswold, *Great Anatolian Rebellion*, 24–6; and Tezcan, "Searching for Osman," 207–8.

disturbances there spread into Karaman province.[22] Although Selaniki's first mention dates back 1007 AH (that is 1598/9 AD), a petition in the Ottoman archives sent by Karayazıcı himself from near the Syrian border reveals that he had already launched his rebellion by 1598.[23] Quite likely, Karayazıcı was one of the *sekban* leaders joining the banditry in Larende during the *sohta* takeover, given that he moved into Karaman from the same region at much the same time. Another strange possibility – because Selaniki described him as a *serdar-ı sohta* – is that Karayazıcı had actually been called on to put down the *sohtas* in Larende since he happened to command a force nearby.[24] If so, instead of suppressing the violence, he turned it to his own ends, placing himself at the head of the uprising.

Whatever his origins, Karayazıcı assembled a sufficient army in Karaman to establish leadership over the nascent rebellion. Taking over the forces of Hüseyin Paşa as well, Karayazıcı and his men managed to plunder the countryside and defy imperial forces for the next four years, until his death in the winter of 1601–2. His troops, by then swelled with the ranks of bandits, mercenaries, and disaffected soldiers, laid the foundation for each successive rebel army down to the Celalis' defeat in 1608.[25] Karayazıcı was hardly the only rebel leader at the time: Dozens of minor characters with colorful *noms de guerre* turn up in various reports throughout Anatolia in the late 1590s.[26] However, it was his leadership that transformed the chaotic uprisings of thousands of bandits into an organized rebel campaign.

The Celalis

The rebels of the 1590s and 1600s have left us no declaration of purpose or ideology. Some historians have argued for religious motives, and in fact there are a few scattered suggestions in the documents to support

22 Akdağ, *Celâlî İsyanları*, 190–2.

23 See Günhan Börekçi, "Factions and Favorites at the Courts of Sultan Ahmed I (r.1603–1617) and His Immediate Predecessors" (PhD diss., Ohio State University, 2010), 34. This date also accords with descriptions in Armenian chronicles: See Hrand Andreasyan, "Bir Ermeni Kaynağına Göre Celâlî İsyanları," *İstanbul Üniversitesi Edebiyat Fakültesi Tarih Dergisi* 13 (1963): 27–42 and *The History of Vardapet Arak'el of Tabriz*, ed. George Bournoutian (Costa Mesa, CA: Mazda, 2005), 69.

24 *Tarih-i Selâniki*, 818. Cf. Akdağ, *Celâlî İsyanları*, 194–5.

25 For a complete narrative, see Griswold, *Great Anatolian Rebellion* chapter 2 *et passim*.

26 Akdağ, *Celâlî İsyanları* covers these other uprisings in some detail.

their case.[27] However, if the Celalis were really Shiite sympathizers or some new sect, then imperial writings should have flaunted the fact to whip up hatred against the infidel, not buried it in a few obscure reports. Beyond Selaniki's description of Seljuk pretenders leading the initial uprising in Turgud, we find no trace of political persuasion either. This lack of evidence, as well as the rebels' later cynical bargains with the state, led their last historian to conclude the Celalis were motivated by sheer ambition and opportunism.[28]

Nevertheless, many Ottomanists have continued to interpret the Celali Rebellion as the product of underlying technological and social transformations. In particular, following the seminal work of Halil İnalcık, some have argued that the uprising represented a movement of "*sekbans*" – a difficult term that may obscure more than it clarifies. In İnalcık's account these *sekbans* were thought to be irregular soldiers dismissed from the front who turned to banditry. As gunpowder infantry rose in importance during the sixteenth and seventeenth centuries, poverty and landlessness drove more men to volunteer with the army, swelling the ranks of these *sekbans*. Following the dismissal of tens of thousands of soldiers after the Battle of Mezőkeresztes, these men supposedly formed a rebel army to plunder the countryside and extort concessions from the imperial government.[29]

New evidence and new studies of the Celali Rebellion now call this theory into question. First, there is little sign that Anatolian *sekbans* played any prominent role in the early years of the Long War. A detailed study of Ottoman logistics in the period has found that such units "were not of tremendous importance" and were mostly recruited from Bosnia and Albania anyway.[30] As late as 1602, the grand vizier would still lament: "The greater part of the enemy forces are infantry armed with muskets, while the majority of our forces are horsemen, and we have very few specialists skilled in the musket."[31] Furthermore, the timing of the dismissal from

27 For the original case for religious motives in the rebellion, see the entry for "Jelali" in the first edition of the *Encyclopedia of Islam* and also Mustafa Cezar, *Osmanlı Tarihinde Levendler* (Istanbul: Çelikcilt Matbaası, 1965), 86–98. Further references to Shiite and Persian sympathizers among the rebels may be found in MD 71/234 and MD 71/239.

28 Griswold, *Great Anatolian Rebellion*, chapter 6.

29 İnalcık, "Socio-Political Effects of the Diffusion of Firearms"; Barkey, *Bandits and Bureaucrats*; Griswold, *Great Anatolian Rebellion*, 17–21. This theory actually goes all the way back to the early nineteenth century (Hammer, *Histoire de l'Empire ottoman* vol. 7, 331).

30 See Finkel, *Administration of Warfare*, 39–48.

31 Cengiz Orhonlu, *Telhisler (1597–1607)* (Istanbul: Edebiyat Fakültesi Basımevi, 1970), document 81. This passage is quoted in both İnalcık, "Socio-Political Effects of the

Mezőkeresztes does not quite seem to match the outbreak of rebellion, nor would there have been any reason for all these ex-soldiers to gather in south-central Anatolia, if not to join a movement already well underway.[32]

Second, rather than trying to send these *sekbans* and other soldiers away to keep peace at home, the imperial government was actually calling men back from the front to restore order. Far from blaming military-civilian conflict for the violence, many petitions to the capital specifically cited the *absence* of soldiers for the disorder in the provinces. We hear in perhaps dozens of cases how "with the soldiers on campaign bandits and criminals have increased their activities,"[33] or how "with the soldiers gone . . . the bandits are raising their heads,"[34] or how once the soldiers left the bandits "found license" (*ruhsat bulup*) for their crimes.[35] Citing the general lawlessness, orders continued to go out calling on *sipahis* to stay in the provinces and put down the unrest.[36]

Third, the hundreds of reports of banditry leading up to the rebellion make relatively few mentions of firearms or dismissed soldiers. The great majority of cases refer indifferently to "criminals" (*ehl-i fesad*) and "bandits" (*eşkiya*) and occasionally to *sohtas*, usually leading assorted small gangs engaged in the plunder of goods and food, especially sheep. Armies of *sekbans* may have played some part in the violence, but in sheer volume they were dwarfed by the alarming numbers of ordinary unspecified pillaging bands. Some reports do mention bandit groups that combined

Diffusion of Firearms" and Barkey, *Bandits and Bureaucrats* as evidence that the Ottomans were trying to build a gunpowder army. However, if they had still failed to do so by 1602, then the formation of such a force could hardly be cited as a reason for the outbreak of the Celali Rebellion six years earlier.

32 Cf. Mustafa Akdağ, "Celâlî Fetreti," *Ankara Üniversitesi Dil ve Coğrafya Fakültesi Dergisi* 16 (1958): 53–107.

33 E.g., MD 73/485.

34 E.g., MD 72/318.

35 E.g., MD 73/205.

36 E.g. MD 73/1142. The situation parallels that of the campaigns of the 1580s (see Chapter 3). In a series of orders dating from late 1593, lower-ranked *tımar*-holders – usually those with less than 3,000 *akces* in income – were commanded to stay behind from the campaign and preserve domestic peace. There is no evidence that the abuses of some of these *sipahis* discouraged the sultans, since the orders carried on through at least 1595 (e.g., MD 73/404). In fact, as the situation grew even more desperate by early 1596, the new sultan Mehmed III continued appointing officials for the protection of the provinces (see orders in MD 74 *passim*; also Akdağ, *Celâlî İsyanları*, 159–60). As the imperial justice decree of that year makes clear, the sultan was well aware of *askeri* abuses in the countryside and clearly sided with the *reaya*. The most reasonable conclusion is that he simply considered the surge in general banditry to be a more pressing issue at the time.

sekbans and horsemen, but in almost every case the latter outnumbered the former, usually by a factor of four or five to one.[37]

Fourth, the focus on guns may overstate the effectiveness of the weapons, at least in the hands of undisciplined bandits. It is important to bear in mind that these were not modern rifles, nor even smoothbore muskets, but clumsy matchlock arquebuses often filled with powder and shot of indifferent quality. Their effectiveness arose not from any special accuracy or strength but from their massed impact when fired by a unit in formation.[38] Moreover, gunpowder itself was neither easy to come by nor to transport and store. Even for well-equipped armies, it was often difficult to realize the potential superiority of firearms over traditional weapons.[39]

Finally, the term *sekban* itself turns out to be more complicated and flexible than İnalcık's interpretation would suggest. Originally, the word probably had nothing to do with guns or infantry but simply referred to irregular military units, particularly to men *without* firearms.[40] There is little reason to assume that every mention of *sekbans* referred to dismissed footsoldiers. In fact, by the time of the rebellion, chroniclers apparently employed the term *sekban* for both Celali infantry and cavalry, and even for private armies formed for defense against Celalis.[41] Such usage implies that *sekban* had become a general word for any army outside the regular military; and in this sense, to say that the Celalis were a *sekban* movement is almost a tautology.

Nevertheless, the discussion of *sekbans* does raise one important element in the outbreak of rebellion. Over the late sixteenth century, the empire witnessed a rising use of mercenary bands in the provinces. The monetarization of the rural economy had encouraged the use of paid soldiers, poverty and landlessness had made more men available, and powerful regional factions had begun using private armies in struggles over local dominance.[42] These groups probably had little or nothing to do with changes in the imperial army, and before the Celali Rebellion

37 E.g., MD 74/461, MD 74/607, and MD 74/592. Note that it was impossible to load and fire the clumsy arquebuses of the time from horseback, so horsemen almost by definition did not use gunpowder weapons: See Barkey, *Bandits and Bureaucrats*, 68–9.

38 Grant, "Rethinking Ottoman Decline" and Börekçi, "Contribution to the Military Revolution Debate."

39 Murphey, *Ottoman Warfare*, 13–16.

40 Cezar, *Osmanlı Tarihinde Levendler*, 21–2.

41 E.g., *Topçular Kâtibi 'Abdülkâdir Efendi Tarihi*, 458.

42 Tezcan, *Second Ottoman Empire*, 141–5.

they had not posed a particular threat to imperial authority. However, once the Great Drought and Long War led to outbreaks of banditry and unrest, mercenaries took advantage of the situation to join the plunder. In particular, commanders of these private armies provided a kernel of leadership and organization, first for bandits and later for rebel armies. As mentioned in the previous chapter, incidents of violence grew not only in number but in scale after 1591, as bandits gangs swelled from handfuls to scores, hundreds, or even thousands of men. Reports quoted in the imperial orders described this pattern of consolidation in oft-repeated expressions of leaders "taking in" (*yanına cem' idüp*) or "becoming the head of" (*baş u buğ olup*) scattered bands; and commanders of *sekbans* played a prominent role.[43]

Thus Karayazıcı's revolt probably represented something like an avalanche from the snowballing of bandit gangs around the leadership of mercenary captains. As Karayazıcı moved into Karaman around 1598, he employed his modest corps of mercenaries to stir up disorder and take control of a large rebel army of thousands of disaffected provincials. We have already seen in Selaniki's description of the Larende uprising how various mercenaries combined with an already powerful *sohta* movement to take over the district. The description of another contemporary chronicler, Topçular Katibi, clarifies how all of these men, now organized under Karayazıcı's leadership, came to be known collectively as *sekbans* regardless of their origins:

> Hüseyin Paşa was the governor of Çemişgezek. Then he was transferred and he resided in the Adalya judgeship in the İçel district of Karaman province. And from the Tarsus district he recruited Karayazıcı from the *sekban* captains and a thousand *sekbans* from the *sohta* bandits... And he recruited some criminals from the Kilis and the 'Azâz Türkmen and Çûm Kurds. Once he appointed Karayazıcı *bölük-başı*, four thousand *sekbans* had appeared.[44]

The mercenaries, therefore, provided the core of expertise for what remained a much broader, perhaps even popular, rebel movement. Reports from the Venetian embassy also reveal that even as the original corps of (gun-toting) mercenaries dwindled, the Celalis continued to attract (horse-riding) bandits. In the summer of 1599, the Venetian ambassador described his forces as "two thousand archebusiers and one

[43] E.g., MD 70/353, MD 71/674, MD 71/712, MD 72/701, MD 73/458, and MD 73/650. Akdağ, *Celali İsyanları*, 121–5, describes the origins of this process in the 1580s.

[44] *Topçular Kâtibi 'Abdülkâdir Efendi Tarihi*, 321.

thousand five hundred horsemen";[45] but then in early 1602, he reported a band of some three thousand horsemen but only fifteen hundred infantry.[46] These numbers confirm the account of a slightly later Armenian chronicler who described Karayazıcı as one who, "with many horsemen, rebelled against the king."[47]

Only around the middle of the first decade of the seventeenth century did actual gun-toting foot soldiers come to play a leading role among the rebels. As the broken series of *mühimme* reports resumed around 1605, many began to mention bands containing as many or more gunmen than horsemen for the first time.[48] However, this must have been a gradual transformation. It would have taken years for the Celalis to plunder enough guns and other matériel and to train disciplined infantrymen. As late as the siege of Urfa in 1600, for instance, Karayazıcı's men went so short of bullets they supposedly had to melt down silver coins for shot.[49] In fact, despite some alarming pronouncements to the contrary, most bandits and criminals never managed to acquire firearms at all.[50] Renegade soldiers may have helped transform the Celalis' tactics and equipment, but such a change came too late to explain the outbreak of the rebellion itself.

The best explanation for the rebellion remains the desperation and disaffection among the people of Karaman. Ecological and economic pressures had been building for over a generation, and with the onset of the drought the *reaya* were left literally starving. Requisitions, oppressive taxation, and the arbitrary exactions of real and pretended *askeri* channeled this desperation into actual rebellion. Moreover, there is strong circumstantial evidence that by the 1590s many *reaya* would have been ready to support or join the Celalis. As Suraiya Faroqhi has shown in a number of articles,[51] political activity among the common people of

45 *A.S.V. Dispacci-Costantinopoli* 49 (7 Aug. 1599).

46 *A.S.V. Dispacci-Costantinopoli* 54 (28 Jan. 1602).

47 *History of Vardapet Arak'el*, 69.

48 See especially the reports on Anatolia in MD 8z.

49 Griswold, *Great Anatolian Rebellion*, 31.

50 Ronald Jennings, "Firearms, Bandits, and Gun Control: Some Evidence on Ottoman Policy toward Firearms in the Possession of *Reaya*, from the Judicial Records of Kayseri, 1600–27," *Archivum Ottomanicum* 6 (1980): 339–80.

51 Suraiya Faroqhi, "Political Tensions in the Anatolian Countryside around 1600: An Attempt at Interpretation," in *Türkische Miszellen*, ed. J. Bacqué-Grammont et al. (Istanbul: Editions Divit, 1987); "Seeking Wisdom in China: An Attempt to Make Sense of the Celali Rebellions," in *Zafarname: Memorial Volume of Felix Tauer*, ed. R. Vesely and E. Gombar (Prague: Enigma, 1996); and "Political Activity among Ottoman Taxpayers and the Problem of Sultanic Legitimation," *Journal of the Economic and Social History of the Orient* 35 (1992): 1–39.

Anatolian towns and villages had risen over the later decades of the sixteenth century, especially complaints against the demands of the elites. Then the imperial justice decrees of the 1590s gave even more force to these complaints, as the *reaya* could point to the specific abuses from which the state was supposed to protect them.

Furthermore, Karayazıcı found himself in just the right place at the right time to harness this popular discontent to his mercenary army and mercenary ambitions. As we saw in Chapter 4, Larende epitomized the worst of the empire's ecological stress, even before the drought of the 1590s. Rapid population growth, limited agricultural possibilities, and immigration from the lawless district of İçel had put this region on the brink of crisis for decades. During the drought and famine of the years leading up to rebellion, conditions must have been appalling, and wartime requisitions would only have made matters worse. The sultan's exorbitant demand for sheep gave particular momentum to the lawlessness in Karaman province, until resistance in Larende reached a critical mass. It should come as no surprise then that Larende saw the first concentrated, sustained rebellion. It should also come as no surprise that the violence attracted desperate men of all sorts, and not just the irregular infantry units whom most Ottomanists have blamed for the outbreak of rebellion.

Evidence from the Venetian dispatches confirms this interpretation. Throughout the late 1590s, reports from the ambassador at Constantinople emphasized the way that the emerging Celalis played upon popular discontent. In the summer of 1599, for example, Ambassador Girolamo Capello characterized them as "an uprising of those peoples" (*sollevatione di quei popoli*); and in the same letter, he mentioned a bandit in Anadolu province, who had "made himself master of these lands by employing great charity towards the common man (*la plebe*) but great tyranny towards the rich and powerful."[52] The following month, the ambassador sent another dispatch laying out the situation in more detail:

> The uprisings and rebellions of Karaman and Anadolu make themselves felt more every day, to judge by the continuous lamentations of the many people who have come from those parts, who cry out in the Divan over the cruelty done them by that Hüseyin, who appears to have no other aim but to destroy those provinces altogether, putting all the country to fire and the sword and wiping out those who fail to show themselves ready to obey him, and principally the powerful . . . and the literate . . .

[52] *A.S.V. Dispacci-Costantinopoli* 48 (25 July 1599).

> To that destruction and suffering is added the uprising of that other, the Scribe (i.e., Karayazıcı), who, accompanied by two thousand archebusiers and one thousand five hundred horsemen – all select men (*gente elletta*) – searches for a way to acquire the spirit of the people, affording them every kindness and granting them liberty to take the goods and treat as they please the great and powerful who depend upon the Sultan, such that the behavior of the latter are more to be feared than the cruelty of the former.[53]

None of this is to say that the Celalis were "social bandits" in any Marxist sense. It was ultimately the peasantry that suffered most from the violence. Nor is there evidence of plans to redistribute land or otherwise overturn the social order. Nevertheless, these descriptions illustrate that the groundswell of desperation in the wake of the famine, in conditions of ecological and economic pressure, provided fuel for the flames of rebellion. Without this fuel, it seems fair to say, the fire would never have spread or consumed the countryside as it did over the following decade.

Nor should it have made much difference that the principal cause of suffering was ecological and climatic. If the European experience of the Little Ice Age serves as any guide, then we should imagine that the peasantry saw the natural disasters that afflicted them as a sign of divine punishment and a judgment on the moral failings of the sultan and empire.[54] In fact, reports from the Venetian ambassador emphasized how much the people of Istanbul viewed the drought and disorder as an act of God and how they turned to fervent prayers and processions as the famine spread apace.[55] The frenzy may have inspired the hungry and discontent to join the ranks of outlaws or *sohtas*, like those that overran Larende in 1597. By that time, even as the rains finally returned, the Little Ice Age was bringing a new phase of extreme weather to Ottoman lands just as destructive as the last.

The Little Ice Age Continued

Even as the drought lifted in late 1596, Little Ice Age weather continued to afflict the empire. As a series of volcanic eruptions intensified the

53 *A.S.V. Dispacci-Costantinopoli* 49 (7 Aug. 1599).

54 E.g., Peter Becker, "Zur Theorie und Praxis von Regierung und Verwaltung in Zeiten der Krise," in *Kulturelle Konsequenzen der "Kleinen Eiszeit"* ed. W. Behringer et al. (Göttingen: Vandenhoeck and Ruprecht, 2005). Cf. Ülgener, *Darlık Buhranları*, 50–1.

55 *A.S.V. Dispacci-Costantinopoli* 43 (20 Oct. 1596) and 59 (28 Aug 1604).

general cold from 1597 onward,[56] Ottoman lands entered into their longest run of wet years in the past six centuries.[57] The harsh snowy winters and springs that followed were particularly severe on the Habsburg front, as described in a memorandum from the grand vizier:

> Your humble servant reports the following: Your Majesty, while the troops were in Belgrade, by the will of God on high there was a severe winter, and . . . such rain and such snow fell that the border people are at one in saying there has not been a winter like it in fifty or sixty years. With such a winter, the enemy cannot even draw their cannon . . . By the wisdom of God, while it goes on this way, the army of Islam cannot budge a foot either. With the mist and snow, you can hardly see. The animals, too, are getting weak, and can barely get up. There is such cold and flooding, it is beyond compare . . . [58]

Once again, the Danube froze over in successive winters: In January of 1597 and March of 1599, soldiers marched over the ice;[59] and in the winters of 1600–1[60] and 1602–3,[61] armies drew wagons and cannons over Hungary's frozen rivers.[62] In 1603–4, in another bitter winter in Serbia, the rivers iced over around Belgrade.[63] When not frozen, they flooded instead: In the autumn of 1597, driven by the heavy rains, a roaring Danube destroyed bridges,[64] and late 1598 and early 1599 witnessed more inundations along the front.[65] Throughout this entire period from 1596 to 1606, Ottoman chroniclers described nearly every winter as

56 See the dust veil indices in Lamb, "Volcanic Dust in the Atmosphere" and Atwell, "Volcanism and Short-term Climatic Impacts."

57 Touchan et al., "Reconstructions of Spring/Summer Precipitation."

58 Orhonlu, *Telhisler*, document 52. Unfortunately, in this and other such memoranda, it can be almost impossible to tell which vizier was writing and in which year. The dates given by the compiler Cengiz Orhonlu are sometimes mistaken. See Pal Fodor, "The Grand Vizieral *Telhis*: A Study in the Ottoman Central Administration 1566–1656," *Archivum Ottomanicum* 15 (1997): 137–88. In this case, our best clue is a Venetian dispatch of early 1601 mentioning a report from an Ottoman general trapped in heavy snows (*A.S.V. Dispacci-Costantinopoli* 52 (21 Jan. 1601)).

59 *Topçular Kâtibi 'Abdülkâdir Efendi Tarihi*, 205; *Tarih-i Selânikî*, 796–8; *A.S.V. Dispacci-Costantinopoli* 48 (23 March 1599).

60 *Topçular Kâtibi 'Abdülkâdir Efendi Tarihi*, 300. Cf. Rácz, *Climate of Hungary*, 94.

61 R. Knolles and P. Rycaut, *The Turkish History from the Original of That Nation, to the Growth of the Ottoman Empire* (London: Charles Brome, 1687–1700), 804.

62 *Peçevî Tarihi*, 397–8.

63 *Topçular Kâtibi 'Abdülkâdir Efendi Tarihi*, 347. For more documents on the freezing of rivers and raids across the ice, see Orhonlu, *Telhisler*, documents 62 and 65.

64 *Topçular Kâtibi 'Abdülkâdir Efendi Tarihi*, 220–1. Cf. Rácz, *Climate of Hungary*, 84.

65 Solakzade Mehmed Hemdemî Çelebi, *Solakzâde Tarihi*, ed. Vahid Çabuk (Istanbul: Kültür Bakanlığı, 1989), 398–9.

remarkably cold and wet, with the winters of 1597–8 and 1601–2 perhaps the most extreme.[66] The Venetian ambassador also mentioned reports from early 1598 that the Ottoman soldiers faced "very great snows" and "a great tempest of snow and rain."[67] Hungarian sources have left us with similar evidence as well.[68]

In this weather, the Ottoman soldiers suffered from constant breakdowns in supply and ever-present threats of famine and disease. Although many of the relevant documents no longer survive, we can imagine that the disturbances of the Celali Rebellion and the ongoing death of livestock only created new hardships for military provisioning. The difficult situation of the Great Drought failed to improve as Ottoman armies faced more shortages and illnesses in the wake of heavy snows, flooding, and military setbacks.[69] Soldiers often went months without pay or basic supplies on the front, stirring up discontent, especially among the restive Janissaries.[70] Reports reached the Venetian ambassador that among the armies "the famine was extreme and excessive"; and he began to doubt the *sipahis* would obey new orders to mobilize.[71] The contemporary English chronicler Richard Knolles also noted how "[the] Army, which beside the cold season of the year, suffered great want of Bread, the Plague also then raging therein; with the death of many of [the sultan's] best Souldiers, both Horse and Foot, beside the wonderful Mortality of their Cattel also; in such sort that the Souldiers, not able longer to endure, the famine and wants increasing, fell to robbing one another, and so at length into mutiny..."[72] He added that during the winter of 1601–2, some 2,000 Ottoman soldiers froze or starved to death.[73] Following the peace of 1606, the remaining troops would finally return home; but meanwhile, the Persian Shah took advantage of the confusion to invade

[66] E.g., *Târîh-i Naîmâ*, 201–6, 291–2, 416; *Peçevî Tarihi*, 402; *Hasan Bey-Zâde Târîhi*, 590; *Topçular Kâtibi 'Abdülkâdir Efendi Tarihi*, 319–21. Note that latter date would correspond to the effects of the dust veil cast by Huaynaputina (see Chapter 5).

[67] *A.S.V. Dispacci-Costantinopoli* 46 (17 Feb. 1598).

[68] Rácz, "Variations of Climate in Hungary."

[69] E.g., *Peçevî Tarihi*, 386–7 and *Hasan Bey-Zâde Târîhi*, 590–1.

[70] E.g., *Tarih-i Selânikî*, 692–3, 704–5.

[71] *A.S.V. Dispacci-Costantinopoli* 48 (31 Mar. 1599) and 50 (4 Sept. 1599).

[72] Knolles and Rycaut, *The Turkish History from the Original of that Nation*, 779. This passage is the clearest indications that epizootics had reached the Balkans. According to data compiled by Lajos Rácz, many parts of Hungary were also infected by a cattle pestilence in the summer of 1598 (personal communication).

[73] Ibid., 795.

from the east in 1603, and a rebellious pasha named Canbuladoğlu set up a rebel kingdom in Syria.

Constantinople faced the same severe winters as the northern Balkans. In December of 1597, Venetian dispatches complained that the weather was "very bitter with cold and snows" that did not let up all that month.[74] The ambassador also described the next winter as "horrid" with frosts persisting through the end of April.[75] The following years proved even worse:[76] By April 1604, the ambassador reported fish actually freezing in the Bosphorus or jumping onto land.[77] That winter, roofs in Istanbul caved in from the snow.[78] Meanwhile, reports came back of equally bad weather on the Persian front.[79]

The situation was worst of all in Anatolia. Even after the death of Karayazıcı in early 1602, the Venetian ambassador described Asia Minor as "more troubled than ever."[80] The rebellion surged as the war and famine dragged on, and as banditry and unrest spread across Turkey and Greece.[81] By 1605, the Celalis reputedly numbered over 30,000 and they had made life in Anatolia impossible "robbing, plundering, and killing everyone."[82] Venetian dispatches described Anadolu and Karaman – at the center of the disturbances – as "completely destroyed" and "almost reduced to desolation."[83] Apart from the main Celali armies, scores of smaller bandit gangs continued to prey upon the hapless villagers. In one case from 1605, a *kadı* reported that five or six hundred men had attacked a village near Eskiil, in Karaman. According to the people's petition, "They broke into the village and killed thirty people and wounded twenty with their weapons. They imprisoned and tortured many in the freezing weather, and twenty of the women lost their hands and feet in the cold . . . "[84]

74 *A.S.V. Dispacci-Costantinopoli* 46 (16 Dec. 1597) and (30 Dec. 1597).
75 *A.S.V. Dispacci-Costantinopoli* 48 (28 Apr. 1599).
76 E.g., *A.S.V. Dispacci-Costantinopoli* 50 (22 Feb. 1600), 51 (22 Mar. 1600), and 52 (3 Mar. 1601).
77 *A.S.V. Dispacci-Costantinopoli* 57 (5 Apr. 1603). There is a somewhat similar story told of the freezing of the Golden Horn in 1699: See Defterdar Sarı Mehmed, *Zübde-i Vekayiât*, ed. Abdülkadir Özcan (Ankara: TTK, 1995), 635–6.
78 *A.S.V. Dispacci-Costantinopoli* 61 (23 July 1605).
79 E.g., *A.S.V. Dispacci-Costantinopoli* 62 (1 Feb. 1606).
80 *A.S.V. Dispacci-Costantinopoli* 57 (28 June 1603).
81 *A.S.V. Dispacci-Costantinopoli* 58 (23 Sept. 1603).
82 *A.S.V. Dispacci-Costantinopoli* 61 (30 Apr. 1605).
83 *A.S.V. Dispacci-Costantinopoli* 59 (18 May 1604) and 62 (1 Feb. 1606).
84 Akdağ, *Celâlî İsyanları*, document 21.

Between the violence and the weather, famine consumed the provinces. Even as the constant demands of war put more strain on provisions, chaos in the countryside disrupted the normal business of farming and bringing grain to market. Exacerbating the shortfalls, the Nile flood fell seriously short again in both 1600 and 1604;[85] and in those years the famine in Egypt, aggravated by a serious plague, grew so extreme that there were reports of cannibalism.[86] Basic food prices in Anatolia roughly tripled from 1595 to 1604, and the cost of wheat and sheep rose fivefold by 1608.[87] In the meantime, a sharp debasement of the coinage and further attempts to regulate prices only brought more uncertainty to the markets and encouraged even more frantic hoarding and speculation.[88] As one chronicler put it, "no one bothered with the official price anymore."[89] Even in Istanbul, according to the Venetian ambassador, there was "extreme dearth" (*grandissima carestia*), and bread quadrupled in cost.[90] Eventually, the situation in the provinces grew so awful that he simply ran out adjectives to describe it: "In conclusion, I cannot represent the barrenness of the country to Your Serenity except to say that the rebels have so mistreated the provinces that of the poor common people who live there not ten percent have bread to eat," he wrote in 1606.[91] Throughout those years, petitions complaining of famine filtered into the capital from regions across Anatolia and the Balkans – some citing the weather, others the bandits, and others just pleading for relief.[92]

In this time of desperation, peasants began to flee the countryside in droves in a movement known as the "Great Flight" (*büyük kaçgunluk*).[93] Although Akdağ originally dated the development from 1603, the previous chapter discussed how the movement of refugees from famine and violence had started during the early years of the Great Drought. With the

85 Popper, *Cairo Nilometer*, 177. Egypt, too, witnessed a number of mutinies and minor revolts in this period: See Finkel, *Osman's Dream*, 180.

86 André Raymond, "Les grandes épidémies de peste au Caire aux XVIIe et XVIIIe siècles," *Bulletin d'études orientales* 25 (1973): 203–10, at 204.

87 Mustafa Akdağ, "Celâli İsyanlarından Büyük Kaçgunluk," *Tarih Araştırmaları Dergisi* 2 (1964): 1–49, at 1–10.

88 *A.S.V. Dispacci-Costantinopoli* 52 (12 Sept. 1600; 30 Sept. 1600; and 10 Oct. 1600); *Tarih-i Selânikî*, 738–9, 784–5.

89 Ibid., 732–3.

90 *A.S.V. Dispacci-Costantinopoli* 52 (22 Sept. 1600) and (13 Nov. 1600).

91 *A.S.V. Dispacci-Costantinopoli* 63 (20 May 1606).

92 E.g., MD 75/111, MD 75/132, MD 75/307, MD 75/309, MD 75/885, MD 78/281, MD 78/883, and MD 7z/36.

93 For the original study of this event, see Akdağ, "Celâli İsyanlarından Büyük Kaçgunluk."

outbreak of the Celali Rebellion the Great Flight snowballed, bringing an avalanche of refugees to fortresses, towns, and cities. Others simply scattered or took to the hills. This book returns to the question of population movements in later chapters. Suffice it to say, by the time the war in Hungary ended in 1606, some documents already described parts of Anatolia as "empty" and "ruined."[94]

The situation in the empire was summed up in a petition to the sultan from the leading men of state in 1603:

> In the provinces the Celalis have appeared, and the country has come under the control of the enemy *sekbans*. The governors do not interfere. The Celalis have entirely taken over the provinces of Anadolu, Karaman, Sivas, Mar'aş, Adana, Haleb, Erzurum, and Rakka. The leading men of the provinces have fled. The poor and the *reaya* have become separated from their families in the mountains. They have left their wives and children, limping away in flight. No cattle remain. The world is in confusion. Those who can use a gun have become *sekbans*. If no relief is sent, it will be cause for regret.[95]

Yet by then, the imperial government had already tried to send relief and crush the banditry in Anatolia several times, to no avail. With the distraction of war the efforts had been halfhearted, and the problem had simply spiraled out of control. Now the situation would only get worse until the Ottomans could find a competent commander capable of restoring order.

The Great Celali Campaigns

The campaigns of the Celalis and the Ottoman armies sent to oppose them have been described at length in other works, so this book covers only the outlines.[96] After Karayazıcı and Hüseyin Paşa united their forces in Karaman, they marched east to Maraş in 1599, where they defeated a small Ottoman detachment sent to oppose them. A larger Ottoman force put the rebel army to siege in Urfa (ancient Edessa) that winter, but cold weather cut short the effort before Karayazıcı could be forced into surrender. Instead, the Celali leader managed to bargain his way into an appointment as a military commander, first of Amasya and then of nearby Çorum. When he began to disobey imperial orders the following

94 E.g., MD 75/281.
95 *Topçular Kâtibi 'Abdülkâdir Efendi Tarihi*, 344–5.
96 In the following paragraphs, I have mostly followed Griswold, *Great Anatolian Rebellion*.

year, the grand vizier sent two more armies after his rebels. The first got caught in the heavy snows that winter of 1600–1; but when the second arrived the following summer, it delivered a serious defeat to Karayazıcı's army, the remainders of which fled to the mountains of northeastern Anatolia. In the freezing winter that followed, provisions fell short in the Celali camp, which lost men to desertion before losing its leader, Karayazıcı, to natural causes.[97]

At that point, Karayazıcı's brother, known as Deli ("Crazy") Hasan, took over his rebel band and marched south to Amasya and Tokat. There, he gathered new recruits and defeated two new imperial armies sent after him. After pillaging the Anatolian countryside through 1602, the new Celali chief sent negotiators to Istanbul that winter to bargain for the same official recognition previously given to his brother. Distracted by an uprising of *sipahis* in the capital, the state granted Deli Hasan the post of provincial governor of Bosnia, where he served as a commander on the Hungarian front for three years before his execution for treason in the war.

Buying off Deli Hasan, however, did little to diminish the disorder in Anatolia. New Celali leaders sprang up throughout the peninsula, leading bands of hundreds or thousands of men.[98] A new imperial force sent to restore order in early 1605 lost more than half its men to cold, starvation, and desertion, before suffering defeat at the hands of yet another old lieutenant of Karayazıcı,[99] whom the Ottomans had to buy off with the provincial governorship of Baghdad and twelve district governorships for his followers. In the meantime, the throne had passed to an inexperienced youth, Sultan Ahmed I (1603–17), and the new war with Persia was going badly as Ottoman forces struggled through freezing winters in the mountains of eastern Anatolia.[100] Taking advantage of some modest victories in Hungary, the Ottomans finally brokered a peace with the Habsburgs in 1606, in order to focus their attention on the home front.

First, however, the empire had to face a new threat to the south, where the rebel Canbuladoğlu Ali Paşa was trying to forge an independent kingdom in Syria. The general appointed to put down this rebellion – the old veteran Kuyucu ("Well-digger") Murad Paşa – turned out to

97 *A.S.V. Dispacci-Costantinopoli* 54 (28 Jan 1602).

98 Although there are not many *mühimmes* surviving from these years, the appendix to Akdağ, *Celâlî İsyanları* reproduces a number of reports on banditry from court records and other series of Ottoman records.

99 *A.S.V. Dispacci-Costantinopoli* 61 (30 Mar. 1605; 15 Apr. 1605; and 23 Aug. 1605).

100 Griswold, *Great Anatolian Rebellion*, 102–3. This weather continued throughout the war: See *Topçular Kâtibi 'Abdülkâdir Efendi Tarihi*, 573–5.

be one of the most effective commanders in Ottoman history. Leading experienced soldiers released from the long war on the Danube, Murad moved swiftly to Konya then Larende, dealing harshly with Celali rebels along the way. From there, his forces pressed on into Syria in 1607, defeating the allies of Canbuladoğlu on the way to the usurper's capital in Aleppo. That October, the Ottoman troops dealt the Syrian rebel army a decisive defeat, and two months later Ali surrendered.

In the meantime, campaigns against the Anatolian Celalis continued to go badly, as the imperial army once again faced adverse weather and the constant threat of starvation.[101] The rebels, now numbering as many as 70,000,[102] had managed to regroup under a new commander called Kalenderoğlu Mehmed. Under his bold leadership, the Celali army first attempted to besiege Ankara and then staged a successful raid on Bursa, the old Ottoman capital, in December 1607. The news of the sack – the Celalis' most daring yet – apparently reached Istanbul just as reports came back of Kuyucu Murad's victory in Aleppo.[103]

The Climax and Conclusion of Rebellion

That winter of 1607–8, the Little Ice Age entered its worst phase yet. After nearly a decade of terrible snow and rain, drought struck once again. While not as long as the dry spell of the 1590s, this drought proved far more severe.[104] According to some reconstructions, the following winter of 1608–9 was the driest of the last five centuries for the Mediterranean as a whole, from Italy all the way to Syria and Jordan.[105] The cold, too, struck with a vengeance. Even as the effects of the Huaynaputina explosion wore

[101] *Topçular Kâtibi 'Abdülkâdir Efendi Tarihi*, 472, and *A.S.V. Dispacci-Costantinopoli* 63 (2 May 1606).

[102] This figure comes from *Topçular Kâtibi 'Abdülkâdir Efendi Tarihi*, 458. However, other estimates vary widely. A contemporary Persian account puts the number at only 30,000: See Hirotake Maeda, "The Forced Migrations and Reorganization of the Regional Order in the Caucasus by Safavid Iran: Preconditions and Developments Described by Fazli Khuzani" (paper presented at the conference "Reconstruction and Interaction of Slavic Eurasia and Its Neighboring Worlds" Slavic Research Center, Hokkaido University, Sapporo, 2004). Venetian dispatches give figures ranging from over 30,000 (1 Jan 1607) to as high as 80,000 (12 May 1607).

[103] *A.S.V. Dispacci-Costantinopoli* 65 (23 Dec. 1607). See also Baron de Salignac, *Ambassade en Turquie* (Paris: H. Champion, 1888–9), vol. 2, 185.

[104] Touchan et al., "Standardized Precipitation Index" and "Reconstructions of Spring/Summer Precipitation."

[105] Luterbacher et al., "500-Year Winter Temperature and Precipitation Variability." Touchan and Hughes, "Dendrochronology in Jordan" also reveals an extended period of recurring drought in these years.

off, a new series of eruptions from Mt. Etna peaked in 1606–7, casting another dust veil across the globe for the next three years.[106] Venetian dispatches from Crete described another severe winter in 1607–8,[107] and Greek monastery records noted freezing lakes and rivers.[108] Indeed, the period from 1606 to 1610 proved perhaps one of the two or three coldest spells for Europe as a whole over the past 500 years;[109] and these Little Ice Age weather events stretched around the globe. London opened an ice fair on the Thames, Russians froze and starved in the "Time of Troubles," and on America's distant shores the first settlers at Jamestown struggled through two cruel winters as they fought to keep their new colony alive.

Back in Istanbul, the drought grew so bad that the grand vizier requested a recess from the imperial divan so the men of state could lead another prayer for rain.[110] Yet the situation proved still worse in the provinces. Throughout 1606, even as Ottoman soldiers returned from the Long War, the situation deteriorated. That year, according to one contemporary:

> The Celali bandits flooded the Anatolian provinces. Among the people of the provinces not one individual remained. From terror of the Celalis they took to the hills. The towns and cities lay in ruins. Most of the *reaya* came to the capital in panic. The imperial officers (*kapu kullari*) living in the province of Anadolu, from fear of the Celalis, constructed fortresses for the inhabitants of the villages, and they had gun-carrying *sekbans* protect their people.[111]

By the following winter, the same chronicler recorded, "By the will of God, so many men had been killed, there was no strength left among the people. The oppressors, who had appeared ten years ago, forced the *reaya* to flee their families. Their wives and children were wretched. Some suffered in the hills, and most were in flight. Their days were numbered, and they were perishing."[112] Meanwhile, reports began coming back of serious famine and banditry in Greece as well.[113]

106 See dust veil indices in Lamb, "Volcanic Dust in the Atmosphere" and Atwell, "Volcanism and Short-Term Climatic Change."
107 Grove and Conterio, "Climate of Crete."
108 Repapis et al., "Note on the Frequency of Occurrence of Severe Winters."
109 Luterbacher et al., "European Seasonal and Annual Temperature Variability."
110 Orhonlu, *Telhisler*, document 129.
111 *Topçular Kâtibi 'Abdülkâdir Efendi Tarihi*, 458.
112 Ibid., 503. See also Salignac, *Ambassade en Turquie*, vol. 2, 181–2.
113 MD 7z/36 and MD 8z/9.

As Ottoman soldiers marched through west and central Anatolia on their way to Syria in 1607, they found it impossible to gather provisions.[114] Bandits were everywhere pillaging food and goods and stealing livestock. (Writing a few years after the events, the Armenian traveler Simeon of Poland would remark of the Konya plains that "once there were great flocks . . . but the Celalis destroyed some animals and chased away some and took and led off those that remained."[115]) Reports came in from across Anadolu and Karaman that the peasants had fled: The people of Eskişehir were "scattered."[116] Karasu, Kayseri, and Alaiyye were "deserted."[117] In Akşehir the *reaya* had taken to the hills, leaving no one left to harvest.[118] When the soldiers came to collect grain from Karahisar-ı Sahib (modern Afyon), the people begged for a reprieve: "Not only have the rebels and other bandits been pillaging for several years, but by the will of God this blessed year, the grain has dried up and cannot be harvested. The condition of the poor is wretched, and they have no means to provide their provisions." The sultan, however, only ordered his army to press on with requisitions and avoid delay.[119]

Further east, the situation reached grim proportions. The most graphic description comes from the Armenian chronicler Arak'el, who witnessed the famine and suffering from near Erevan (Armenia).[120] His account of these years started with a description of the Celalis, who came and pillaged everything and tortured the peasants and priests to reveal caches of food and money. Nevertheless, the real famine began when the people took to flight in the fierce winter of 1607–8, as refugees died of starvation and frostbite on the roads. During the following year, violence and disorder rendered all the usual work of farming impossible, leaving nothing to sow or harvest. As the price of basic necessities skyrocketed, the hapless peasantry turned to the remaining livestock and then to famine foods, consuming anything and everything that could be eaten. Reports of cannibalism spread, reaching even the Venetian ambassador in Istanbul, as starvation and anarchy took hold in the provinces of

[114] The relevant documents from the campaign (originally from MD 8z) have been compiled in Mehmet Şahin, "Kuyucu Murad Paşa'nın Celâlî Seferi Mühimmesi (1607)" (Yüksek Lisans Tezi, İstanbul Üniversitesi, 2002).

[115] *Polonyalı Simeon'un Seyahatnamesi, 1608–1619* (Istanbul: Baha Matbaası, 1964), 163.

[116] MD 8z/479.

[117] MD 8z/434, MD 8z/438, and MD 8z/442.

[118] MD 8z/73.

[119] MD 8z/286.

[120] *History of Vardapet Arak'el*, 65–75. I would like to thank Günhan Börekçi for directing me to this passage.

Anatolia and northern Syria.[121] Concluding his description, Arak'el gave the following dates for the crisis:

> The famine spread between the two great seas, that is the White Sea and Black Sea . . . The famine began in the year 1606. The famine was not strong and cruel that year; it became much stronger at the beginning of the year 1607 and during the year 1608. It subsided once the year 1609 began and during the year 1610 it ended.

Over those same years of famine, Kuyucu Murad and his army finally managed to route the Celalis and bring a semblance of order to the empire. In the meantime, both sides in the conflict faced more hardships and setbacks. In the decisive winter of 1607–8, as Kalenderoğlu was poised to attack the capital itself, both armies were forced into winter quarters by the extreme cold and famine. Even Murad Paşa's soldiers around Aleppo were in such dire straits that there were rumors of cannibalism, and Anatolia suffered from such widespread disease and shortages that the army was forced to wait months for supplies from Egypt, now recovering from its famine of 1604.[122] The Venetian ambassador reported rumors of an impending revolt among the soldiers "given the great dearth of everything in the army, the lack of money, and the arrogance and strength of the rebels."[123] Meanwhile, new epidemics broke out in Istanbul.[124]

As Kuyucu Murad led his armies up from Syria, the Celali forces came at him from the northwest. The Ottoman general maneuvered into the Göksün plain (between Kayseri and Malatya in east-central Anatolia) behind the mountain pass that controlled the enemy's path. Arriving ahead of the Celalis, Murad's forces occupied the high ground and met the rebels as they passed through the defile, in mid-June 1608. In the battle that followed, the imperial forces inflicted a decisive defeat on Kalenderoğlu and his army.[125] As Kuyucu Murad returned to Istanbul for a hero's welcome, the Celalis fled to Persia, where they joined forces with the shah. Their alliance, uneasy from the start, fell apart over the next two years as the Celalis deserted en masse back into Anatolia. In 1610, Kalenderoğlu died in exile, bringing an end to the succession of

[121] *A.S.V. Dispacci-Costantinopoli* 66 (26 Apr. 1608 and 27 May 1608).

[122] Griswold, *Great Anatolian Rebellion*, 182–91. See also *Târîh-i Naîmâ*, 552, and Salignac, *Ambassade en Turquie*, vol. 2, 204–5, 214, and 219.

[123] *A.S.V. Dispacci-Costantinopoli* 65 (4 Nov. 1607).

[124] *A.S.V. Dispacci-Costantinopoli* 65 (8 and 29 Jan. 1608) and Salignac, *Ambassade en Turquie*, vol. 2, 162, 176, and 179.

[125] For a description, see Salignac, *Ambassade en Turquie*, vol. 2, 231.

Celali leaders who had challenged the empire and pillaged the provinces for over a decade.

In the meantime, the war with Safavid Persia continued to go poorly for the Ottomans. Having finally defeated the Celalis, Kuyucu Murad – by now in his eighties – set out east for one last campaign in 1610. Although the famine had lifted, the winter that year was still severe. According to one eyewitness:

> At Erzurum forty-five days before the start of winter (i.e., in late September)[126] a serious violent cold began. On the third Thursday of Receb (October 8), there was rain and snow. By the will of God, that night the weather brought a violent storm of cold and snow over the tents. The tent-ropes could not withstand the violent wind, and many collapsed, which was the cause of much hardship... It was excessively cold and icy, the horses were in wretched shape, and the tents froze.[127]

Over the following months as the cold persisted, the army suffered a shortage of provisions and fodder;[128] or as the Venetian ambassador Simon Contarini would report, troops "battled not only the enemy, but the sky, the winter, and hunger."[129] Ottoman forces never managed to force the Shah into a decisive battle, and Kuyucu Murad passed away in August 1611. The next year the sultan agreed to a treaty with Persia, conceding Tabriz and other lands held by the Ottomans since the time of Süleyman, but bringing a much needed respite to war-torn Ottoman lands.

Conclusion: The Rebellion in Perspective

The Celali Rebellion, from 1596 to 1610, was arguably the worst crisis in Ottoman history from the invasion of Tamerlane to World War I. Riding a wave of popular desperation and discontent, mercenary leaders gathered rebel armies that plundered the provinces and defied the imperial government for more than a decade, laying waste to wide stretches of the empire. At the same time, ongoing Little Ice Age weather events brought unprecedented flight, famine, and mortality.

126 "*rûz-ı Kasım*": In the traditional reckoning, the first stage of winter began on the 8th of November (Redhouse).

127 *Topçular Kâtibi 'Abdülkâdir Efendi Tarihi*, 573.

128 Ibid., 573–4, 580–3.

129 N. Barozzi and G. Berchet, ed. *Le relazioni degli stati Europei lette al Senato dagli ambasciatori veneziani nel secolo decimosettimo, vol. V – Turchia* (Venice: P. Naratovich, 1866), 137.

As examined in Part I, the forces of population pressure and economic dislocation had been building in the empire throughout the late sixteenth century. In each successive war and natural disaster from the 1560s to the 1580s, the Ottomans had faced more shortages and unrest. This catalogue of troubles has led some Ottomanists to imagine the Celali movement as a generalized development of the late 1500s, and the crisis as a gradual, if painful, transformation in imperial politics and society. Many Ottomanists continue to write of "Celali rebellions" in the plural, implying that the rebel campaigns of the 1590s and 1600s were just the worst example of an ongoing phenomenon.

However, the disorders of the 1570s and 1580s had been short-lived affairs, where the workings of provisioning systems and the forces of public order had been stretched, but not altogether broken. Violence and unrest had become real problems in Ottoman lands, but the empire remained resilient and its population continued to expand. By contrast, the 1590s and 1600s marked a turning point. Extreme cold and drought, dearth, and an expensive military stalemate combined to wreck imperial provisioning systems. Instead of scores or hundreds of bandits, rebel armies in the tens of thousands ravaged the provinces. Starvation and disease led to a contraction of population and agriculture in the core provinces that would take more than two centuries to reverse. And as the following chapter explains, similar climate-related disasters would continue to afflict the empire for generations to come.

8

IN THE WAKE OF THE CELALIS

CLIMATE AND CRISIS IN THE SEVENTEENTH CENTURY

Following the Celali Rebellion, another century of natural and human disasters prolonged Ottoman troubles and derailed the empire's recovery. Little Ice Age climate fluctuations brought recurring extremes of temperature and precipitation through the mid-1600s, playing a major role in the empire's chronic political instability and rural disorder. Then in the last decades of the seventeenth century, the Ottoman Empire underwent another conjuncture of severe weather, military setbacks, and internal disorder. By around 1710, once the worst of the Little Ice Age had passed, Istanbul had witnessed the deposition of five sultans, and many of the core provinces were left in much the same poor condition as a century before, in the wake of the Celali Rebellion.

This chapter provides an overview of these crises in the Ottoman Empire from the 1620s to the early 1700s. This troubled period has yet to receive the same scholarly treatment as the Ottoman "classical age" or the critical turning point of the 1590s. Climatologists, however, have compiled yet more precise and comprehensive data on weather, which this chapter employs for the first time. The case studies in this chapter suggest that ongoing climate fluctuations and other natural disasters produced severe periodic shortfalls in imperial resources, prompting many of the military mutinies and political uprisings of the era, from the regicide of Osman II in 1622 to the fall of Mehmed IV in 1687. These results place Ottoman troubles in the wider context of crises across the seventeenth-century world caused by ecological pressures and the Little Ice Age.

The Ottoman Crisis in Context

Traditionally, historians of the Ottoman Empire tended to write off the seventeenth century as an age of stagnation and corruption. Authors focused on the decline of royal authority and mocked the "sultanate of women" that emerged as palace factions quarreled over imperial power. More recently, revisionist historians have emphasized the adaptability and resilience of the empire instead, often playing down the disorders of the era. They have recast the 1600s as an era of transformation: an important if contested transition from top-down patrimonial rule to an institutionalized, negotiated state.[1] One Ottomanist has even called for analyzing the seventeenth and eighteenth centuries as a "second empire," in many respects more modern and democratic than either the classical age that preceded it or the age of centralizing reforms that followed.[2]

Often missing from this discussion is the context of crises across seventeenth-century Eurasia. As discussed in the introduction, the Ottoman Empire was hardly the only state to face serious disturbances during the 1600s. The crisis of the 1590s reached across the Mediterranean; Russia's "Time of Troubles" began the following decade, and the generation from the 1630s to the 1660s has been dubbed a "general crisis" for the near simultaneous wave of famines and uprisings that reached from England to Indonesia. Underlying much of this turmoil were similar forces of population pressure, rising costs, and climate fluctuations. As described in Chapter 5, the atmospheric phenomena that brought severe winters and droughts to the Eastern Mediterranean brought similarly destructive weather conditions to most of the globe, from cold wet summers in Northern Europe to monsoon failures in South and East Asia. Therefore, the Little Ice Age crisis in the Ottoman Empire represents only one extreme example of a general phenomenon.

The question remains, however, why the troubles of Ottoman lands did prove so extreme and so prolonged, even relative to other victims of the seventeenth-century global crisis. Paradoxically, the comparison with other early modern states suggests that Ottoman lands may have also suffered more precisely because the Ottoman Empire adopted the expedients it needed to survive. Ottomanists are fond of pointing to the empire's adaptability and endurance; but the persistence of the Ottoman dynasty itself was no protection against natural disaster and widespread disorder. As destructive as invasion and conquest could be, as in the case of the Ming-Qing transition in China, the change of regime nevertheless brought a cancellation of debts, a windfall of plunder and power, and

[1] See, e.g., Barkey, *Empire of Difference.*

[2] Baki Tezcan, "The Second Ottoman Empire: The Transformation of the Ottoman Polity in the Early Modern Era," *Comparative Studies in South Asia, Africa, and the Middle East* 29 (2009): 556–83, at 567–72.

new institutions. The "barbarians" really could be "a kind of solution." As Victor Liberman has observed in his vast survey of Eurasian history, interregna of the seventeenth-century global crisis were typically short and frequently brought in new regimes that hastened political consolidation and social integration.[3] Political revolutions, as in the Netherlands and England, also ushered in fiscal innovations that helped overcome problems of acute wartime shortages and deficits that still plagued the Porte.[4] The Ottoman Empire, despite or perhaps because of its dynastic continuity, underwent a long and tumultuous period of transition marked by ongoing financial turmoil, military setbacks, mutiny, and rebellion.

More importantly, recurring Little Ice Age episodes continued to expose the empire's persistent vulnerabilities to climatic extremes. Ottoman agriculture remained especially sensitive to adverse weather, as crop choices and land use patterns took some generations to adapt to new environmental conditions and new plants from the Columbian Exchange (see Chapter 11). Rural famine, flight, and disease remained a serious drain on population and provisions throughout the century. Imperial attempts to make up resulting deficits in resources and revenues through new taxes and tax farming sometimes proved shortsighted and counterproductive in the long term. Moreover, this fiscal transformation abetted the rise of powerful new factions in the capital, army, and provinces, leaving the imperial government subject to new political constraints and pressures. Often matters came to a head when extreme weather or natural disasters led to sudden shortfalls in military supplies or serious famines in the countryside. These events incited the military mutinies and rural rebellions that opportunistic factions could use to press for more power or raise rebellion.

Finally, any assessment of the Ottoman crisis must also make room for accidents of politics and personalities and chance events of weather and war. While past historians certainly made too much of the era's weak sultans and corrupt imperial relatives and advisors, there remains an important human component to this story. As in the foregoing account of the Celali Rebellion, ill-advised policies and untimely military ventures had a hand in some of the seventeenth century's worst troubles. In some cases, the Ottomans appear as victims of simple bad luck, faced with

3 Lieberman, *Strange Parallels*, vol. 2, 60 *et passim*.

4 Wantje Fritschy, "State Formation and Urbanization Trajectories: State Finance in the Ottoman Empire before 1800, as Seen from a Dutch Perspective," *Journal of Global History* 4 (2009): 405–28.

unforeseeable conjunctures of natural disaster, shortages, and military setbacks.

The Fall of Sultan Osman II

The first serious Ottoman crisis of this period, the overthrow of Osman II in 1622, had its roots in the troubled years of the Great Drought and the Celali Rebellion. As past historians have analyzed, the final decade of the sixteenth century saw a shift in the structure of imperial power.[5] The tradition of strong personal sultanic authority started to fade. During the reign of the young Ahmed I (1603–17), new factions gained power within the palace, among the mothers and in-laws of the sultans and the increasingly influential chief eunuchs.[6] Moreover, the practice of putting the sultan's sons in provincial roles and leaving them to fight out the imperial succession fell into disuse. As a series of short-lived sultans put the dynasty's survival in doubt, princes were held in the palace instead, and new rulers no longer executed their brothers as rivals for the throne. Following the death of Sultan Ahmed, rule passed to a sibling rather than a son for the first time. However, the new Sultan Mustafa proved mentally unbalanced and was deposed the following year, further diminishing royal authority. Increasingly, the state acquired a less personal and more institutional bureaucratic character.[7]

Furthermore, during the Long War and the Celali Rebellion the empire had witnessed a shift in fiscal-administrative power. In the centuries of Ottoman expansion, tax collection, administrative authority, and military power had been closely intertwined within the *tımar* system and were largely based on the value of village land and agriculture. Conversely, during the years of crisis, rapid inflation diminished the real value of traditional taxes, and farms lost much of their worth as peasants died or abandoned their land by the millions, creating a shortage of farmers to work the fields, as described later in this chapter. "Emergency"

[5] See, e.g., Halil İnalcık, "Military and Fiscal Transformation in the Ottoman Empire, 1600–1700," *Archivum Ottomanicum* 6: 283–337.

[6] For detailed analyses of this development, see Leslie Peirce, *The Imperial Harem* (New York: Oxford University Press, 1993), and Börekçi, "Factions and Favorites."

[7] This shift in power has also transformed the nature of Ottoman archival evidence in this period. The *mühimme defters* declined in importance as the imperial divan lost power. Instead, the various series of bureaucratic records in the *Maliyyeden Müdevver* (MAD) expanded, providing more accounting of various state functions but fewer reports on major developments in the provinces.

cash taxes became annual levies, and the imperial government turned to short-term tax farming of agriculture, customs, and other revenue as an expedient for ready money. Likewise, many provincial functions were transformed into venal offices to distribute pensions (so-called *arpalıks*), gradually diminishing direct central control over the provinces.[8] In the eighteenth century, these processes gradually privatized and commercialized Ottoman landholding and agriculture, as discussed in Chapter 11. However, in the short term, they brought more confusion to the countryside and the rise of a new class of fiscal agents, many from the provinces, whose power often came at the expense of the *sipahis*, whose *tımars* they bought and sold for investments.[9]

This shift in fiscal-administrative power accelerated a corresponding transformation of the Janissary corps. Although their numbers had swelled from around fifteen thousand to some forty thousand men, the Janissaries had ceased to be a slave army in more than name.[10] While they were still called up for war, their military role increasingly came second to their position as a hereditary privileged class and a political pressure group. Infiltrated by powerful factions, their payrolls and their threats of mutiny leveraged the political power of provincial and palace grandees. By the end of Ahmed's reign, the Janissaries had staged at least six uprisings, mostly over issues of pay or viziers who threatened their influence. Consequently, military payrolls and donatives demanded by elite soldiers helped drive the imperial treasury into chronic deficit over the early seventeenth century.[11]

8 On the transformation of provincial authority in the seventeenth century, see especially Kunt, *Sultan's Servants*, chapters 4 and 5.

9 Tezcan, "Searching for Osman," 140–1.

10 For various estimates, see Inalcık, *Ottoman Empire*, 48; Murphey, *Ottoman Warfare*, 16–17; and Sir Thomas Roe, *A True and Faithfull Relation* (London: B. Downes, 1622), 23. It also seems unlikely that this expansion came as a deliberate response to the rising firepower of European troops, as some authors have argued, all the more so as the ranks of elite cavalry forces expanded in equal measure: See Cezar, *Osmanlı Tarihinde Levendler*, 167, and Tezcan, *Second Ottoman Empire*, 177–9. According to the Venetian ambassador Alvise Foscarini, few Janissaries even knew how to use an arquebus: See Firpo, *Relazioni*, 756. For more on the transformation of the Janissary corps, see Cemal Kafadar, "Janissaries and Other Riffraff of Ottoman Istanbul: Rebels without a Cause?" in *Identity and Identity Formation in the Ottoman World*, ed. B. Tezcan and K. Barbir (Madison: University of Wisconsin Press, 2007).

11 Recent work on Ottoman budgets under the direction of Mehmet Genç has cleared up a once confused picture of the imperial fiscal situation. See Baki Çakır, "Geleneksel Dönem (Tanzimat Öncesi) Osmanlı Bütçe Gelirleri," and Erol Özvar, "Osmanlı Devletinin Bütçe Harcamaları (1509–1788)," in *Osmalı Maliyesi Kurumlar ve Bütçeler*, ed. M. Genç and E. Özvar (Istanbul: Osmanlı Bankası Arşiv ve Araştırma Merkezi, 2006).

Therefore, the new emperor Osman II faced a different set of realities as he took over from his deposed uncle Mustafa in 1618. Powerful factions had arisen with no stomach for a strong sultan bent on personal rule. Yet by all accounts, the young monarch proved headstrong, surrounded by favorites who abetted his ambitions to grasp the reins of state and restore sultanic authority. Consequently, whether they have championed him as a "reformer" or dismissed him as an "absolutist," historians of Osman II have portrayed his deposition in early 1622 as an inevitable clash between two visions of government.[12]

However, as the following narrative makes clear, this vision of the rebellion may read too much into the event, overemphasizing political changes and overlooking the role of climate and accident in the timing and repercussions of the rebellion. Just as it was no coincidence that the Celali Rebellion broke out at the culmination of the worst drought in the last six centuries, so there was also a strong connection between the extreme cold that froze the Bosphorus in 1621 and the fall of Osman II one year later.[13]

In the wake of the Celali Rebellion, there are indications in Ottoman chronicles that the extreme weather of the Little Ice Age had not entirely let up. The 1611 cease-fire with Persia barely had time to take effect before the Ottomans found themselves back at war over their border around Georgia; and in the campaigns that followed, soldiers continued to face harsh winters and shortages of provisions.[14] At the same time, the chronicler Topçular Katibi left descriptions of freezing weather and floods around Edirne and along the Danube.[15] In 1618, as Osman II

[12] Baki Tezcan, "The 1622 Military Rebellion in Istanbul: A Historiographical Journey," in *Mutiny and Rebellion in the Ottoman Empire*, ed. J. Hathaway (Madison: University of Wisconsin Press, 2003). By Ottoman standards, Osman II has received an unusual amount of recent critical analysis. See Tezcan, "Searching for Osman"; Gabriel Piterberg, *An Ottoman Tragedy* (Berkeley: University of California Press, 2003); and N. Vatin and G. Veinstein, *Le sérail ébranlé* (Paris: Fayard, 2003).

[13] In part, this connection has been missed because most authors have overlooked the chronicle of Bostanzade Yahya Efendi, which provides some key details of the event. Moreover, Ottomanists have tended to misconstrue the unusual natural occurrences described in the chronicles of 1621–22 as some sort of rhetorical or symbolic device, because such similar incidents are found in the descriptions of Sultan Ibrahim's and Sultan Mehmed IV's downfall as well (see, e.g., Piterberg, *Ottoman Tragedy*, 124, and Vatin, *Le serail ébranlé*, 23–5). However, since there is independent confirmation of these extreme events from other observers and from climate proxies, this goes to show that the "coincidence" does not represent some rhetorical device but rather that climate and natural disasters actually played a major role in several Ottoman political crises.

[14] E.g., *Târîh-i Naîmâ*, 685, and *Topçular Kâtibi 'Abdülkâdir Efendi Tarihi*, 645–56.

[15] *Topçular Kâtibi 'Abdülkâdir Efendi Tarihi*, 627–8, 631–2.

acceded to the throne, and as the defenestration of Prague brought Europe into the Thirty Years War, Istanbul suffered a major spring flood followed by a severe plague that summer.[16] The new sultan's short reign was also marked by one of the strongest clusters of El Niño activity in the last five hundred years, which may have contributed to the erratic precipitation of the period, including a destructive Nile flood of 1622. Egypt suffered serious famines and epidemics in 1619 and 1621–22,[17] which probably cut shipments of provisions – as it turns out, just when the capital and the army needed them most.

As described in the introduction to Part II, Anatolia and the Balkans suffered extreme winter conditions, culminating in the freezing of the Bosphorus in early 1621. Aside from the starvation in the capital as ice blocked incoming ships, the icy weather unleashed a general famine in the region that persisted over the following year, presumably as the deep freeze spoiled the harvest. An eyewitness, Bostanzade Yahya, recounted how during the winter of 1621–22:

> At this time, by the will of God, famine and high prices too added to the suffering. God is great! Among the people such hardship and misery appeared that it was though the Day of Judgement had arrived or that it meant death for the entire people.[18]

While the chronicler may have embellished his description, his account is confirmed by an anonymous English pamphlet of 1622, which described the natural disasters during Osman's reign, concluding:

> Last of all, and worst of all, by reason of the great concourse of people, and resort of strangers, such a famine happened in the city, and dearth in the country, that everyone complained, and though it was remedilesse by the pollicy of man, yet was the fault layed upon Superiors, and the Emperor himselfe did not escape scandall and calumniation.[19]

[16] Fahir İz, "XVII. Yüzyılda Halk Dili ile Yazılmış bir Tarih Kitabı: Hüseyin Tuği "Vak'a-i Sultan Osman Han."" *Türk Dili Araştırmaları Yıllığı Belleten* (1967): 119–55 (hereafter, "Tuği/İz"), at 142–3.

[17] See Fekri Hassan, "Environmental Perception and Human Response in History and Prehistory," in *The Way the Wind Blows*, ed. R. McIntosh et al. (New York: Columbia University Press, 2000), 131, and Raymond, "Grandes épidémies."

[18] Orhan Gökyay, "II. Sultan Osman'ın Şehadeti," *Atsız Armağanı* (Istanbul: Ötüken Yayınevi, 1976), 198 (hereafter, "Gökyay/Yahya").

[19] "The Strangling and Death of the Great Turke . . ." (London: I. Dawson, 1622). Although the author's sources are unclear, and although he misconstrues some of the developments of 1622, some details of the account suggest that it was written by an eyewitness or based on eyewitness reports. It may be particularly telling, therefore, that from an outsider's perspective, the general discontent caused by famine was assumed

Nevertheless, Osman II decided to lead a campaign in person against the Polish-Lithuanian Commonwealth that spring of 1621. His motives remain unclear, but it appears he intended to encircle the Habsburgs and strike a blow against one of their key allies in the Thirty Years War. Perhaps more important, the campaign served the young emperor's personal ambitions to enhance his prestige and power as a warrior sultan at the head of his troops. In the meantime, it provided an excuse to absent himself from Istanbul while his ministers abolished certain lucrative venal offices and strangled his brother Mehmed, a potential source of factional rivalry.[20]

Osman's plans backfired from the start. Setting out with a reported three hundred thousand men[21] at a time of general famine, the campaign soon faced serious shortfalls of money and provisions. As they marched to the front, Osman II found excuses to shortchange his Janissaries and other elite troops their usual donative, fueling their discontent.[22] Meanwhile, the sultan personally antagonized the soldiers on the march with impromptu inspections and arbitrary punishments.[23] However, the real troubles began as the army reached Poland. What had started as a major campaign with far-reaching ambitions quickly degenerated into a single failed siege of the fortress of Khotin. By autumn, Ottoman forces were forced to withdraw without any notable gains, at a tremendous cost to the imperial treasury, to the granaries, and to the sultan's prestige.

The Polish troops at Khotin doubtless deserve credit for a tenacious defense. Yet what really turned the course of the war – and with it, perhaps, the course of Ottoman history – was the horrendous weather of 1621. Bogged down by severe cold and heavy rains, morale already low, the Ottoman army faced unsustainable casualties and was compelled to cut its losses quickly before the ranks disintegrated. As Thomas Roe described in a dispatch:

> By relations of divers present in this warre, it is reported, that there dyed in the Turks camp, by the sword, famine, sickness, and cold,

to be the chief cause of Osman's downfall. Hammer, *Histoire de l'Empire ottoman* vol. 8, 287, also states: "A great shortage of provisions was announced at Constantinople. The people, discontent, attributed it to the avarice of the Sultan." It is unclear whether he has drawn on the same or a different source.

20 Baki Tezcan, "Khotin 1621, or How the Poles Changed the Course of History," *Acta Orientalia* 62 (2009): 185–98.

21 *Negotiations of Sir Thomas Roe* (London: 1740), 13 (possibly an exaggeration).

22 See especially the account of the Venetian ambassador Giorgio Giustiniani in Pedani-Fabris, *Relazioni*, 550 *et passim*.

23 Roe, "True and Faithfull Relation," 22.

> about 80,000 men, and above 100,000 horse; and the remayne, at their retorne, appearing so naked, poore, and sickly, made evident demonstration of the great losse and misery susteyned.

Therefore, the sultan "for divers reasons... was enforced to treat a cessation of armes":

> The first was, that considering he had spent so much time without any advantage, and the winter approaching, wherby his army suffered great extremities of cold, and their miseries, by reason of the terrible raynes with had carried away divers tents, horses, and other cattell, and sunk part of his cannons. Secondly, the provision of fodder was become so deare, that divers forsook their horses for want of means to feed them; besides, the great mortality of men of fluxes, feavers and colds, and the horses of Asia not used to such weather, that men of quality that came out with 10 and 12, were compelled to return on foote. Thirdly, the army, either for wearinesse or for discontent, received from the emperour himself, for his narrowness and avarice showed to the soldiour, contrary to the glorious example of his ancestors in like enterprises, not only refused to fight, but were little lesse then mutinied.[24]

Osman tried to winter his army at Edirne that year in order to set out for another campaign the following spring. However, facing mounting discontent, he found himself forced to abandon the idea and return to the capital that December.

By early 1622, it appears Osman II had already hatched a new plan: to cross the Bosphorus and travel into Asia in the guise of a hajj to Mecca.[25] His motives once again remain unclear. Certainly, it was an unusual step for any sultan to take, and it was suspicious under the circumstances. The French and English ambassadors reported he was planning to move against a rebellion in Lebanon and "to amuse and raise suspicion in the Persian."[26] Later, a report would circulate that his real intention was to raise a *sekban* army in Anatolia to confront the Janissaries in the capital and reestablish absolute sultanic rule. While some contemporaries dismissed the plot as a calumny of disaffected ulema,[27] circumstantial

[24] *Negotaions of Sir Thomas Roe,* 12. For Ottoman evidence of the cold and rain on the campaign, see *Topçular Kâtibi 'Abdülkâdir Efendi Tarihi,* 728, 753, and 755. *Hasan Beyzâde Târîhi,* 936–7, and *Solakzâde Tarihi,* 470, also describe how severe rains forced Osman II to retreat.

[25] According to Tezcan, "Khotin 1622," the French ambassador reported these plans in January. Roe makes the first mention in late February: See *Negotiations of Sir Thomas Roe,* 18.

[26] Tezcan, "Khotin 1622," and *Negotiations of Sir Thomas Roe,* 18.

[27] See, e.g., Giustiniani in Pedani-Fabris, *Relazioni,* 553–4.

evidence indicates that Osman may have already had agents recruiting men in Anatolia that spring.[28] After the fact, if not before, some observers would seize on the plan as the principal reason for his murder that May.[29] Nevertheless, this rumor does not seem to have surfaced until the uprising was already under way.

In fact, the immediate trigger for the disorders was not so much the threat of a sultanic coup d'état as the threat of starvation and disorder as the sultan prepared to depart along with his treasury. In these times of famine, the Polish campaign had already required extraordinary requisitions from the countryside just to provide the army enough food to get to the front;[30] and yet the soldiers had still faced severe shortages at Khotin. As the contemporary chronicler Beyzade observed following the freezing of the Bosphorus,

> So that winter, the people of Istanbul lived with famine. At harvest time in 1030 (i.e., May 1621) the army went on campaign to Khotin. The soldiers' provisions were delivered first, and from everywhere, even the Tatar soldiers carried off measureless quantities of grain to bring to the army. The soldiers did not face want on the campaign, and arrived with plenty. However, on the other side, even the soldiers were terrified that the extreme cold and famine would persist. They feared going on campaign in that direction (i.e., into Asia). That year, they made every effort to keep peace and stability and not to go on campaign.[31]

Venetian intelligence of early 1621 confirms that the famine had nearly sparked a mutiny among *siphahis* in Istanbul over pay and provisions.[32]

Therefore, as word spread of the sultan's "pilgrimage" in winter 1622, not only the soldiers but also the people of the capital were sent into a panic. As Bostanzade Yahya described,

> Talk spread: "What sort of campaign would this be without food or drink, when everywhere the country is dust and smoke from the disorders born of these troubles! What an unwelcome task is this!" Scholars, sheikhs, and good men sent letters and tried to inform the sultan that this was

[28] Tezcan, "Searching for Osman," 221–8.

[29] Roe, for instance, mentions nothing about it in his first dispatch on the rebellion on May 20, only including it for the first time in his dispatch of the 26th: See *Negotiations of Sir Thomas Roe*, 124–7.

[30] See *Topçular Kâtibi 'Abdülkâdir Efendi Tarihi*, 705–15 *et passim*.

[31] *Hasan Bey-zâde Târîhi*, 929. The Venetian ambassador Cristofo Valier also noted back in 1616 that given the devastation of Anatolia and the resulting lack of provisions there, the Ottoman army was adamantly opposed to any Persian campaign: See Firpo, *Relazioni*, 635–6.

[32] Cited in Hammer, *Histoire de l'Empire ottoman*, vol. 8, 271–2.

> not the time to set out. Pleading, they tried to get him to change his mind, saying "The Polish campaign still hinders the soldiers. With so many men lost, to set out on campaign again will bring suffering to everyone."[33]

As preparations got under way, "the shortage of food raised the people's alarm. Word spread that patience was running out and the matter could go no further. There was such a hue and cry that even pictures on the wall went white."[34] By May 9, the English ambassador reported "the present Grand Signor [i.e., sultan] following dreams and visions, and having phantasticque designes, that they say here are ominous; and all sorts of people discontent, even to a proneness to rebellion."[35]

It was in this context that the Janissaries engaged in a violent uprising just nine days later. Most likely, some among the corps had been plotting an insurrection ever since Osman failed to pay their donative in the summer of 1621.[36] Now the sultan's imminent departure forced their hand. Gathering at the Hippodrome and then at the Sultan Ahmed mosque, the soldiers complained of the sultan's conduct, supposedly blaming everything on wicked ministers and court favorites.[37] One of them purportedly declared, "What we want, what we gathered for, was to get rid of a couple of despoilers. But now our movement, joined by the tumult of the people rushes forward uncontrollably."[38] It was apparently around this time that the ulema began warning of Osman's plans to raise a *sekban* force across the Bosphorus. However, according to Bostanzade, the soldiers decried *any* plans for the sultan to leave for Asia. "What sort of sultan goes wandering around every part of the country . . . ? And is this any time for a campaign? Or for a hajj? After the Polish campaign,

33 Gökyay/Yahya, 198. *Negotiations of Sir Thomas Roe*, 18, and *Hasan Bey-zâde Târîhi*, 938–9, offer similar accounts.

34 Gökyay/Yahya, 199.

35 *Negotiations of Sir Thomas Roe*, 35–6.

36 See, e.g., Giustiniani in Pedani-Fabris, *Relazioni*, 550. Tezcan, "Searching for Osman," 238–9, concurs. The anonymous writer of "The Strangling and Death of the Great Turke," 13–14, has the sultan's viziers reply to mutinous soldiers that "you know the treasure is exhausted, & the dearth is so great, that we have not sufficient to buy us bread."

37 Tuği and Yahya's accounts are particularly critical of Osman's chief ministers in this episode, and the former's account would especially influence later Ottoman chroniclers. Nevertheless, the wicked minister and the corrupting palace favorite are common tropes in Ottoman chronicles, and they may have been used in this case to deflect blame from either the Janissaries and ulema or the Ottoman dynasty.

38 Gökyay/Yahya, 202.

what fool among the soldiers would go now?"[39] Later that morning the soldiers marched out to the palace gate to make their demands heard. At that point, common people joined the mob, adding to the tumult.[40]

The events that followed that day and the next have been narrated in detailed by others,[41] so a summary here will suffice. While the mob outside presented its demands, including the dismissal and death of some ministers, the sultan and his advisors inside remained indecisive. Stalling for time and trying to bargain down the Janissary ultimatum, they only further enraged the mob. Finally, sympathetic palace attendants opened the gates, letting in troops who managed to track down and rescue the deposed Mustafa, who had been locked in a tower and all but forgotten in the confusion. Osman debated fleeing, but ended up hiding in the palace grounds, as the Janissaries proclaimed his half-starved and barely comprehending uncle as the rightful sultan. The next morning, according to another eyewitness, the chronicler İbrahim Peçevi, "the streets were full of people, the world covered with rebellion and disorder."[42] At the palace, Osman's last offers were rejected, and their messenger hacked to pieces by the Janissaries. His hiding place betrayed, the sultan was dragged off to the Yedi Kule prison and executed that evening. Afterward, the Janissaries alleged excuse was that "everyone rose in revolt. It was a general insurrection (*guluv-i am*), it wasn't just us. What could we have done? I mean, how could we have stopped this brawl?"[43]

A Time of Troubles, 1620s–1630s

The murder of Osman II, while temporarily satisfying the Janissaries, only aggravated unrest in the capital and provinces over the following decade. Caught off guard by their own success and operating without an effective sultan, the perpetrators of the coup were left in disarray.[44] The Venetian ambassador would later relate, "it is impossible to represent the confusion

39 Ibid.

40 See especially Gökyay/Yahya, 208 ("Halk da askerlere katıldı, ansızın bir feryat koptu"). The chronicler also claims, "I found myself in the middle of it all, and saw the disaster unfold."

41 See, e.g., Piterberg, *Ottoman Tragedy*, 9–30, and Tezcan, *Second Ottoman Empire*, 156–75.

42 *Peçevî Tarihi*, 464.

43 Tuği/Sertoğlu, 505. However, this comment may be a later interpolation to deflect blame from the Janissaries. See Baki Tezcan, "The History of a 'Primary Source': The Making of Tughi's Chronicle on the Regicide of Osman II," *Bulletin of SOAS* 72 (2009): 41–62, for more on the background to this source.

44 For an eyewitness account of the political disorders of Mustafa's second reign, see especially Gökyay/Yahya, 233 *et passim*.

and disorders that took place in the ten months that Mustafa reigned, while the soldiers having committed their crime went unchecked, full of anger and pride, absolute masters of things."[45] Meanwhile, he described the markets closed, a chronic shortage of provisions, and "the plague at its peak."[46] Ultimately, the unstable ruler had to be deposed a second time, now in favor of the child Murad IV.

In the meantime, Istanbul and indeed the whole Black Sea region faced a new danger from the invasion of Cossack pirates. The unguarded Ottoman lake suddenly lay open to a series of daring attacks on the Balkan and north Anatolian coasts, where port towns were decimated by violence and the sudden disruption to trade.[47] In the summer of 1624, Cossack raids reached all the way into the Bosphorus, sacking a few seaside villages and sending the capital into a panic.[48] The attacks upset Black Sea provisioning as well, aggravating shortages of commodities in the capital.[49] In the summer of 1625, natural disasters combined to render the situation more desperate still: An earthquake was felt in May, followed by heavy storms in June and July. Plague broke out in the capital, and another disease afflicted sheep in the countryside. By August, thousands of people reportedly died each day in Constantinople "though multitudes have fled the city."[50]

Meanwhile in Anatolia and Syria, news of the Osman's death was received with alarm. By late summer, Ambassador Roe reported uprisings in the name of the murdered sultan breaking out in Baghdad, Damascus, and Erzurum, all feeding on widespread popular discontent.[51] The last of these insurrections swelled into a full-scale rebellion, whose leader Abaza Mehmed Paşa came to embody the cause of the sultan, *sipahis*, and *sekbans* against the rising power of the Janissaries. While Ottoman official accounts dismissed him as just another bandit, some contemporaries cast Abaza Mehmed in the role of a folk hero standing up to tyrannical Janissaries, or as a friend of the common people and the Armenian and Jewish minorities.[52] Further reports suggested that the rebel leader, like the early Celali captains, sought to win over the population of Anatolia

45 Pedani-Fabris, *Relazioni*, 557.

46 Ibid., 558.

47 Ostapchuk, "Human Landscape of the Ottoman Black Sea," 56–7, 70–4.

48 *Negotiations of Sir Thomas Roe*, 265.

49 Ibid., 159.

50 Ibid., 419–20, 427, 431.

51 *Negotiations of Sir Thomas Roe*, 125, 134, 175–6. See also Pedani-Fabris, *Relazioni*, 558–60.

52 See Hrand Andreasyan, "Abaza Mehmed Paşa," *Tarih Dergisi* 13 (1967): 131–42, and Aryeh Shmuelevitz, "MS Pococke No. 31 as a Source for the Events in Istanbul in the Years 1622–1624," *International Journal of Turkish Studies* 3 (1985–86): 107–21.

through conspicuous acts of charity to turn them against the ruling elites.[53] Abaza Mehmed's uprising would continue off and on for the next five years, at times controlling most of Anatolia. In late 1627, imperial troops finally drove the rebels back to their base in Erzurum and forced Abaza Mehmed to settle for the governorship of Bosnia.

In January 1624, in the wake of Osman's murder, officers in Baghdad betrayed that city to the Persians, setting off another decade and a half of war. Contemporary accounts of the long campaigns that followed have left us with some of the best descriptions of ongoing Little Ice Age weather extremes. In 1626, Egypt sent only half its usual tribute because of a major plague.[54] That same summer, harassed by the Safavid army, the Ottoman camp in Iraq fell into serious shortages of provisions and lost thousands of men from famine and disease.[55] (Later, the famous Ottoman scholar Katip Çelebi, who began his career as a soldier in the Iraq war, would recall how "I suffered hardships for nine months during the siege, from warring and fighting and from hopelessness, brought on by the dominance of drought and high prices and by the enemy's military superiority.")[56] The following winter turned particularly cold with deep snow across Anatolia, inflicting serious hardship on Ottoman soldiers camped at Erzurum or crossing to the front.[57] According to the later chronicler Gılmanî, some twelve thousand troops lost hands or feet from frostbite.[58] The next two winters proved almost as bad, as troops on the eastern Anatolian frontier, already beleaguered by Persian forces, continued to face extreme cold with heavy winds and rains, exacerbating a dearth of provisions and cutting short campaigns and sieges.[59]

The following decade witnessed further climatic extremes accompanied by more political unrest. In 1629–30, a strong El Niño year, Mecca was struck by a destructive flood,[60] and Venetian officials reported

[53] E.g., *Negotiations of Sir Thomas Roe*, 187–8, 197, 241.

[54] Hammer, *Histoire de l'Empire ottoman* vol. 9, 65, citing a Venetian dispatch.

[55] *Negotiations of Sir Thomas Roe*, 534, 550.

[56] Quoted in G. L. Lewis, ed., *The Balance of Truth* (London: Allen and Unwin, 1957), 7.

[57] *Negotiations of Sir Thomas Roe*, 585; *Topçular Kâtibi 'Abdülkâdir Efendi Tarihi*, 830, 846–8; and Orhan Gökyay, ed., *Kâtip Çelebi'den Seçmeler* (Istanbul: M.E.B., 1968), 71.

[58] Mehmed Halife, *Tarih-i Gılmanî*, ed. Kâmil Su (Ankara: Kültür Bakanlığı, 1984), 10–11.

[59] *Topçular Kâtibi 'Abdülkâdir Efendi Tarihi*, 879 and 906–54 *passim*, and *Solakzâde Tarihi*, 529. Hammer, *Histoire de l'Empire ottoman* vol. 9, 96 and 135–6, includes even more dramatic descriptions, including seventy straight days of rain and a total inundation between the Tigris and Euphrates late 1629 to early 1630, but his sources are unclear.

[60] Muhammad Abdulla, "Climatic Fluctuations and Natural Disasters in Arabia between Mid-17th and Early 20th Centuries," *GeoJournal* 37 (1995): 176–80.

drought in Crete.[61] Meanwhile, Istanbul suffered a "total shortage" of grain.[62] In early 1632, discontent over failures in Baghdad and the dismissal of a popular general led to another mutiny in the capital and a bloody purge of unpopular ministers. The same decade witnessed the rise of the puritanical Muslim Kadızadeli movement in the capital.[63]

Throughout this time of troubles, a renewed series of local petitions and imperial orders offer another glimpse of conditions in the provinces.[64] The evidence suggests that banditry in the countryside had diminished from its peak of 1595–1610 but prevailed for decades at levels well beyond those of the sixteenth century. Apart from the major uprisings already described, criminal gangs continued to take advantage of the prevailing lawlessness to plunder the *reaya.* A number of documents suggest that some were also lured by the spread of firearms in the countryside; and in one case we find a report of an entire village outside Kayseri which had supposedly abandoned agriculture and taken up weapons and banditry.[65] Some documents also refer to "leftover Celalis" still plaguing the peasants,[66] although others suggest that many of the former rebels had now started to settle down.[67]

Moreover, the disorder in the provinces and the waning of central authority had left local officials and strongmen at liberty to invent taxes and extort from the peasantry. Imperial orders from the 1620s onward are littered with similar complaints, usually forwarded by *kadıs* sympathetic to the plight of the *reaya.* One such petition from Larende, the erstwhile home of the Celalis, summed up the state of official abuse:

> The provincial governor of Karaman ... has demanded his "inspection money" (*devir akçesi namına*) of over one hundred thousand *kuruş* three times in one year, and he has quartered in the town of Larende with over one thousand horsemen for sixty to seventy days ... and has taken over thirty thousand *kuruş* from Larende and even more from the surrounding area. They have descended upon the Muslims' families and

61 Grove, "Climate of Crete."

62 MD 85/463.

63 Madeline Zilfi, "The Kadızadelis: Discordant Revivalism in Seventeenth-Century Istanbul," *Journal of Near Eastern Studies* 45 (1986): 251–69.

64 The *mühimme defters*, frustratingly absent during Osman II's reign, do cover the late 1610s and much of the late 1620s, as well as part of the 1630s and 1640s (MD 81–90). After that, while the series continues, it becomes less useful as a source on major developments.

65 MD 85/116. See also MD 89/3 and MD 89/38 for mention of firearms.

66 E.g., MD 85/151.

67 E.g., MD 82/350.

> brought ruin. Unable to endure, they have taken to flight, leaving their families in the hands of the *levends*... They report that "even in the time of the Celalis there was no one so oppressed."[68]

This violence and instability drove a constant stream of flight from the countryside that lasted well into the eighteenth century. Once again, the imperial orders record scores of examples: Sometimes whole villages departed at once,[69] and sometimes entire districts were "scattered."[70] In some cases, if some inhabitants of a village departed but the state had failed to lower taxes accordingly, the remaining population would be unable to meet demands and would flee ahead of the tax collector.[71] In other cases, the reassessment of taxes served as an excuse for extortion, forcing peasants into flight.[72] In other examples, the *reaya* sought to escape moneylenders or greedy landlords.[73] Just as often, they simply fled from the chronic dangers of lawlessness and banditry.[74]

In sharp contrast to conditions of the later sixteenth century, desertion and mortality during the Celali Rebellion now left an abundance of land relative to people.[75] Although flight meant the loss of home and property, it appears peasants were often willing to make the sacrifice rather than endure maltreatment. As Michael Adas has observed in Southeast Asian history, whereas situations of ecological pressure call for "strategies of confrontation," situations of abundant land and scarce labor may call instead for "strategies of avoidance."[76] Flight became almost a tool of bargaining with landlords and officials as labor became relatively scarce; peasants sometimes "scattered" over relatively minor exactions.[77] To keep

68 MD 85/622.

69 E.g., MD 85/116.

70 E.g., MD 92 s5/4, in Murat Yıldız, "92 Numaralı ve 1657–58 Tarihli Mühimme Defteri" (PhD diss., Fırat Üniversitesi, 2005).

71 E.g., MAD 14680 (26 R 1062). For an explanation of this problem, see Faroqhi, *Towns and Townsmen*, 203.

72 E.g., MD 89/146.

73 E.g., MD 82/246.

74 E.g., MD 85/528. For a microcosm of rural problems in this period, see also Suraiya Faroqhi, "Town Officials, *Timar*-Holders, and Taxation: The Late Sixteenth-Century Crisis as Seen from Çorum," *Turcica* 18 (1986): 53–82.

75 This impression can be confirmed by the relative abundance of land recorded without owners or heirs that escheated to the state. See Peter Sugar, "Major Changes in the Life of the Slav Peasantry under Ottoman Rule," *International Journal of Middle East Studies* 9 (1978): 297–305.

76 "From Avoidance to Confrontation: Peasant Protest in Precolonial and Colonial Southeast Asia," *Comparative Studies in Society and History* 23 (1981): 217–47.

77 See, e.g., MD 90/245 and MD 90/426.

peasants bound to the land, successive sultans raised the *çift-bozan akçesi* (the fee for abandoning farms) from 96 *akçes* up to 360 *akçes* over the early decades of the seventeenth century, but the measures evidently made no impression upon the restless peasantry.[78]

Over the same decades of crisis, imperial efforts to protect and regulate agricultural settlement broke down in the face of lawlessness and depopulation. The system of *derbends* (see Chapter 1) fell into disarray as greedy officials ignored their tax exemptions and as flight famine and disease left the colonies too weak to withstand assaults.[79] Attempts to revive the system in the eighteenth century using fortified towns and caravanserais met with only mixed success.[80] Rebellious villagers once again took to the hills and returned to plundering the peasantry;[81] corrupt officials and their private armies threw up forts (*palankas*) from where they raided the countryside;[82] and bandits gathered in now empty lands and villages, which once again became a haven for lawlessness.[83] An English traveler joining a caravan through Anatolia in 1638, noted how "in the way, wee passed by a *Palanga*, which is a Village fortified with mud walles against Theeves; where wee found a small *Caravan* to have beene assaulted the day before, and divers remaining fore wounded; for through all *Turkie*, especially in places *desert* there are many *Mountaineers*, or *Outlawes*, like the wild *Irish*, who live upon spoyle, and are not held members of the State, but enemies, and used accordingly."[84]

Official correspondence of the period indicates that local and imperial authorities understood this challenge and tried to take measures in response. Imperial orders continued to accommodate the resettlement of peasants and to promote the revival of agriculture when the occasion arose. Returning villagers could, for instance, negotiate special protections or an amnesty from back taxes.[85] In 1629, the sultan even ordered the *kadı* of Simav (near Kütahya in northwest Anatolia) to allow repenting *sohta* bandits to go unpunished and to resettle on the land, provided

78 Rhoads Murphey, "Population Movements and Labor Mobility in Balkan Contexts: A Glance at Post-1600 Ottoman Social Realities," in *Southeast Europe in History: The Past, the Present and the Problems of Balkanology* (Ankara: Ankara Üniversitesi, 1999).

79 Orhonlu, *Osmanlı İmparatorluğunda Derbend Teşkilâtı*, chapter 5.

80 Yusuf Halaçoğlu, *XVIII. Yüzyılda Osmanlı İmparatorluğu'nun İskân Siyaseti ve Aşiretlerin Yerleştirilmesi* (Ankara: TTK, 1988), 70–6, and chapter 3 *passim*.

81 E.g., MD 85/528.

82 E.g., MD 8z/122.

83 E.g., MD 79/76.

84 Henry Blount, *A Voyage into the Levant* (London: I. Legat, 1638), 13.

85 Faroqhi, "Political Activity among Ottoman Taxpayers."

they promised not to make any more trouble.[86] Other imperial orders annulled the forced sale of land by debtors, returning farms to their previous owners.[87]

Nevertheless, with some minor exceptions,[88] these rural resettlement initiatives found little success. State initiative alone could not organize new settlements or population movements without some corresponding initiative from the ground up. As Part III explores, imperial authorities were no longer working with, but rather against, the momentum of population movements and ecological change. Moreover, the state had lost one of its most powerful tools in the work of resettlement: its tax exemptions. Fiscal demands and official venality made it difficult to enact and impossible to enforce immunities from tithes and requisitions.[89] In fact, the general political instability and weakening central authority now made it a challenge to enact and carry through major policies in the provinces at all.

The Demographic Crisis

Ottoman documents from the 1630s have also left historians with another glimpse into the empire's demographic situation. After 1632, as Murad IV came of age and as the worst disorders of the Abaza Mehmed rebellion and Little Ice Age winters temporarily subsided, the sultan and his grand viziers initiated fiscal reforms and new cadastral surveys. Rather than revive the *tahrirs* of the classical age, the imperial government tried instead to formalize and regularize the system of *avarız* contributions. In effect, this policy recognized new ecological realities by shifting the burden of taxation from agricultural land, which was now plentiful, to settled populations, which now proved scarce. Furthermore, the system offered more flexibility as imperial and provincial authorities negotiated the number of *avarız* "households" and thus the level of taxes according to population movements and ability to pay.[90]

86 MD 82/350.

87 Faroqhi, *Towns and Townsmen*, 285.

88 E.g., MD 82/50.

89 This issue stands out when we compare the Ottoman case with the resettlement of China in the wake of the calamitous Ming-Qing transition and subsequent civil wars. Since China remained free from serious military threats for almost another two centuries, the state was able to sharply cut its fiscal demands and use tax exemptions generously to encourage a return to the land. See Perdue, *Exhausting the Earth*, chapter 4.

90 For more on fiscal transformation in this period and the development of the *avarız* system, see Darling, *Revenue-Raising and Legitimacy*.

The absence of regular *tahrirs* during the seventeenth and eighteenth centuries had once left Ottomanists in doubt over population trends. Despite overwhelming impressions of settlement desertion during and after the "great flight,"[91] some historians still debated whether losses had taken place at all.[92] Now recent research into the new surveys ordered under Murad IV, building on data from occasional *cizye* and *tahrir defters*, has settled the question.[93] By 1640, losses were widespread and very deep – often half or more in rural areas.

While much basic research remains to be done, studies from Anatolia already present a clear picture of the demographic disaster. According to the new evidence from the mid-seventeenth century, household numbers fell by up to 80 percent in some parts, with 30–40 percent of

[91] The key work in this regard has come from Wolf-Dieter Hütteroth and his collaborators as cited throughout this book. For an overview of this research and other earlier studies on settlement desertion, see Suraiya Faroqhi, "Anadolu İskânı ile Terkedilmiş Köyler Sorunu," in *Türkiye'de Toplumsal Bilim Araştırmalarda Yaklaşımlar ve Yöntemler Semineri*, ed. Y. Yeşilçay and S. Karabaş (Ankara: Baylan Matbaası, 1977).

[92] For instance, the Balkan historian Maria Todorova tried to counter that the Balkan figures, which are based on the fact that the non-Muslim head tax (*cizye*) only fell from 800,000 in 1530 to 636,000 in 1700 – a drop that might represent emigration or conversion to Islam ("Was There a Demographic Crisis in the Ottoman Empire in the Seventeenth Century?" *Etudes Balkaniques* 2 [1988]: 55–63). However, there are two problems with that argument. First, there is no evidence for conversion or emigration on quite such a large scale. Second, even by Todorova's own estimates, the population of the empire nearly doubled from 1530 to 1590, and the Christian population presumably shared in that growth. Therefore, the real drop in *cizye* numbers over the course of the seventeenth century may actually have been half or more.

[93] The breakthrough came with the study of *mufassal* ("detailed") *avarızhane defters*, which enumerated the number of real households per tax unit. For an explanation of these registers and their potential for demographic reconstruction, see Süleyman Demirci, *The Functioning of Ottoman Avarız Taxation: An Aspect of the Relationship between Center and Periphery* (Istanbul: Isis, 2009); Oktay Özel, "Avarız ve Cizye Defterleri," in *Osmanlı Devleti'nde Bilgi ve İstatik*, ed. Ş. Pamuk and H. İnalcık (Ankara: T. C. Başbakanlık Devlet İstatistik Enstitüsü, 2000); and Oktay Özel, "17. Yüzyıl Osmanlı Demografi ve İskan Tarihi İçin Önemli Bir Kaynak: 'Mufassal' *Avârız Defterleri*," in *XII. Türk Tarih Kongresi* (Ankara: TTK, 1994). For examples of published *mufassal avarız defters*, see Mehmet Öz, *Canik Sancağı Avârız Defterleri (1642)* (Ankara: Atatürk Kültür Dil ve Tarih Yüksek Kurumu Yayınları, 2008) and M. Öz and F. Acun, *Karahisar-ı Şarkî Sancağı Mufassal Avârız Defteri (1642–43 Tarihli)* (Ankara: Atatürk Kültür Dil ve Tarih Yüksek Kurumu Yayınları, 2008). For overviews of the findings and historiography, see Oktay Özel, "Nüfus Baskısından Krize: 16.–17. Yüzyıllarda Anadolu'nun Demografi Tarihine Bir Bakış," in *VIII. International Conference on the Economic and Social History of Turkey*, ed. Nurhan Abacı (Morrisville: Lulu Press, 2006); Özel, "Population Changes"; and Daniel Panzac, "La population de l'Empire ottoman et ses marges du XVe au XIXe siècle: Bibliographie (1941–1980) et bilan provisoire," *Revue de l'Occident musulman et de la Méditeranée* 31 (1981): 119–35.

villages left ruined and empty.[94] In Amasya (east-central Anatolia), for example, the number of rural households dropped by almost four-fifths between the 1580s and 1640s.[95] The population around Samsun (north-east Anatolia) collapsed from 3,597 households in the *tahrir* of 1576 to only 891 households in 1642;[96] and in nearby Canik and Bozok, the number of recorded households also fell by about two-thirds over the same period.[97] The Kayseri area lost about half its population.[98] Farther east, almost three-quarters of Harput's households disappeared,[99] and Şebkinkarahisar lost around 40 percent.[100] In the northeast, Trabzon's Christian population fell from some fifteen thousand taxpayers in the sixteenth century to only twenty-five hundred by 1610.[101] Even in the western part of Anatolia, Kocaeli for example fell significantly below population levels of the 1520s, let alone levels of the 1580s.[102]

Outside of Anatolia, while the numbers are not as firm, the situation was apparently little better. As much as two-thirds of the rural population of Mosul had fled or perished by the late seventeenth century.[103] In Boeotia (Greece), the number of households in 1688 had fallen to half the level of century before.[104] By one estimate, the Balkans as a whole may have lost more than half its population from the late sixteenth to the early eighteenth centuries, before recovering somewhat by 1800.[105] Hungary may have lost about a fifth of its population during the Long War, and by the end of Ottoman rule in 1699, the Hungarian Plain had been largely deserted.[106]

94 Özel, "Population Changes."

95 Özel, "17. Yüzyıl Osmanlı Demografi," and Jennings, "Urban Population in Anatolia." Note that all the figures in this paragraph refer to whole *kazas*, not the towns themselves.

96 Öz, "XVII. Yüzyıl Ortasına Doğru Canik Sancağı."

97 Mehmet Öz, "Population Fall in Seventeenth Century Anatolia: Some Findings for the Districts of Canik and Bozok," *Archivum Ottomanicum* 22 (2004): 159–71.

98 Ronald Jennings, "Zimmis in Early 17th Century Ottoman Judicial Records: The Sharia Court of Anatolia in Kayseri," *Journal of the Economic and Social History of the Orient* 21 (1978): 225–93.

99 Yücel Özkaya, "Osmanlı İmparatorluğunda XVIII. Göç Sorunu," *Tarih Araştırmaları Dergisi* 14 (1982): 171–203.

100 Erder, "Population Rise and Fall."

101 Faroqhi, *Towns and Townsmen*, 276.

102 Ibid. Note that the figures in this study actually come from rare examples of late *tahrirs* rather than the *mufassal avarızhane defters* described earlier. For more sources confirming such population losses, see Börekçi, "Factions and Factionalism," 28–9.

103 Khoury, *State and Provincial Society*, chapter 2.

104 Kiel, "Ottoman Imperial Registers."

105 Bruce McGowan, "Age of the Ayans, 1699–1812," in *An Economic and Social History of the Ottoman Empire*, ed. H. İnalcık and D. Quataert (New York: Cambridge University Press, 1994), 652.

106 Rácz, "Price of Survival," 28–9.

These numbers tend to confirm impressions of contemporary observers, who marveled at the depopulation of the countryside. Returning from Istanbul to Venice in 1609, the ambassador Ottavio Bon remarked to the Senate that "Anatolia and Karaman remain, for the most part, bereft of habitations, of inhabitants, and of animals" and that "the Turks will have a tough task to repopulate Anatolia with its own inhabitants, because endless numbers of them have died and those left alive have found themselves without any subsistence and have fled to the cities of Üsküdar, Pera, and Constantinople."[107] Ambassador Thomas Roe would add in 1622 that "all the territory of the Grand Signor is dispeopled for want of justice, or rather by violent oppressions, so much as in his best parts of Greece and Natolia, a man may ryde 3, and 4, and sometimes 6 daies, and not find a village able to feed him and his horse; whereby the revenue is so lessened, that there sufficeth not to pay for the soldiour and to mayteyne the court."[108]

Some of this description may be chalked up to Western and Christian contempt for an infidel enemy newly vulnerable after centuries of conquest. Yet even Ottoman documents lamented the losses incurred in these years of famine and rebellion. Perhaps the best comment on the state of the empire in the Celali aftermath actually comes from a tract (*risale*) issued by Sultan Murad IV:

> And previously in the year 1004 (1595/6) the Celali bandits appeared. They plundered and burned the towns and cities in the provinces of Anadolu, Karaman, Sivas, Meraş, Aleppo, Damascus, Urfa, Diyarbakır, Erzurum, Van, and Mosul, and many lands were ruined and empty. Even the ancient capital Bursa was plundered and many quarters burned in the flames. The Arab and Türkmen tribes, too, ceased to obey. When the poor *reaya* were oppressed beyond endurance, many villages in these parts, too, were emptied. Many oppressors from among us even burned the remaining lands. Such a calamity was this![109]

The traditional declensionist historiography assumed that these depictions of desolation reflected some peculiar decay within the Ottoman Empire, while revisionist accounts have tended to dismiss them as literary tropes or Orientalist rhetoric. Yet both these interpretations have missed

[107] Pedani-Fabris, *Relazioni*, 495.

[108] *Negotiations of Sir Thomas Roe*, 67. Similar descriptions can be found in subsequent Venetian reports as well: See, e.g., Luigi Firpo, ed., *Relazioni de ambasciatori veneti al senato XIII: Costantinopoli* (Turin: Bottega d'Erasmo, 1984), 503.

[109] Quoted in M. Ç. Uluçay, *XVII. Asırda Saruhan'da Eşkiyalık ve Halk Hareketleri* (Istanbul: Resimli Ay Matbaası, 1944), 145–6.

the clear parallels around the seventeenth-century world. By 1648, Germany would lose at least a quarter of its population in the Thirty Years War, and China would lose a third or more in the cold, famine, and violence that accompanied the Ming-Qing transition.[110] This level of devastation and population loss in Ottoman lands over the half-century since the Great Drought actually accords well with descriptions of seventeenth-century crisis across Eurasia.

Furthermore, by analyzing such better-documented cases from early modern Europe and comparing them to the Ottoman situation, we can understand why Ottoman lands proved so vulnerable to a sudden crisis of mortality. As explained in Chapters 2 and 3, much Ottoman agriculture occupied marginal land, and much of the Ottoman peasantry had already been on the margins of subsistence. Imperial measures dealing with famine and epidemics, while not inconsiderable, were nonetheless overwhelmed by population movements and disorder in the provinces, especially in inland areas cut off from easy communications by sea. Moreover, the Ottoman population proved particularly vulnerable to synergies among starvation, flight, and infection.

Therefore, the direct effects of Little Ice Age weather – terrible as they could be – were probably not to blame for most losses. While thousands of *reaya* might have frozen to death or perished of cold-related illnesses, their losses could not account for more than a small fraction of the millions who disappeared in the crisis. The only direct evidence of death from cold concerns refugees who died of exposure as they fled Celali violence. Furthermore, prevailing cold and drought could also benefit health in other ways. To judge from weather conditions and infections observed by Alexander Russell in Aleppo and those recorded in the Venetian dispatches from Istanbul, dry freezing weather often proved a powerful disinfectant for hot-weather illnesses such as gastrointestinal infections and bubonic plague.[111] The Venetian ambassador's

110 See Parker, "Crisis and Catastrophe" for global comparisons of these crises and their impacts.

111 See Chapter 10 for more on these observations. Note that observations of European bubonic plague outbreaks seem to confirm that the disease was more likely to flare up in hot, humid weather and die down in times of cold and drought: See Biraben, *Les hommes et la peste*, chapter 3, and H. H. Lamb, *Climate, History, and the Modern World*, 2nd ed. (London: Routledge, 1995), 312–13. Modern studies on rodent-borne bubonic plague also reveal a weak but statistically significant correlation between precipitation and plague cases, since drought tends to reduce overall rat populations: See R. Parmenter et al., "Incidence of Plague Associated with Increased Winter-Spring Precipitation in New Mexico," *American Journal of Tropical Medicine and Hygiene* 61 (1999): 814–21.

correspondence of the 1590s, in particular, established that most Ottomans had more to fear from the occasional mild winter than from spells of severe frost.[112]

Famine may have killed hundreds of thousands or even millions more. We have already witnessed the graphic depictions of starvation and even reports of cannibalism among the Anatolian *reaya* during the 1590s and 1600s. While we lack precise figures, circumstantial evidence and comparison with better-documented cases in early modern Europe emphasize just how vulnerable the Ottomans might have been once their initial reserves had run dry. The Mediterranean core of the empire relied almost entirely on a single annual harvest of winter wheat and barley, crops whose yield depended overwhelmingly on a mild temperature at germination and above all on an adequate spring rainfall.[113] A long spell of cold and drought would have decimated food output and left the population with little alternative subsistence. Furthermore, highly segmented markets and poor internal transportation hindered access to outside grain supplies, especially in inner Anatolia.[114] Finally, and perhaps most important, European historical examples indicate that famine struck most severely where landholdings were small or marginal and economic opportunities were few[115] – precisely the conditions which

[112] E.g., *A.S.V. Dispacci-Costantinopoli* 52 (12 Dec. 1600).

[113] B. Özkan and H. Akçaöz, "Impacts of Climate Factors on Yields for Selected Crops in Southern Turkey," *Mitigation and Adaptation Strategies for Global Change* 7 (2002): 367–80. The correlation of harvests and spring precipitation shows up even more clearly in early U.S. Department of Agriculture studies conducted before the introduction of modern fertilizers and improved varieties: See May, *Ecology of Malnutrition*, 620. Also note that given the very low yield ratios of the time, net yield would have risen and fallen much faster than gross yield, assuming that farmers preserved enough seed to plant the following year. Of course, if they ate the seed corn, then the situation would have been even worse, with no harvest at all the following year: See E. A. Wrigley, "Some Reflections on Corn Yield and Prices in Pre-industrial Economies," in *Famine, Disease and the Social Order in Early Modern Society*, ed. J. Walker and R. Schofield (Cambridge: Cambridge University Press, 1989).

[114] By contrast, the use of crop rotations and mixed winter and summer crops played a major role in relieving famine in parts of northern and western Europe with more developed grain markets. In fact, such differences in markets and continuity of supply were likely the principal reason that England and the Low Countries escaped famine in the eighteenth century while France and other parts of Europe did not. See Post, *Food Shortage, Climatic Variability, and Epidemic Disease*, chapter 5; David Weir, "Markets and Mortality in France 1600–1789," in *Famine, Disease, and the Social Order in Early Modern Society*, ed. J. Walker and R. Schofield (Cambridge: Cambridge University Press, 1989); and Jacques Dupâquier, "Subsistence Crises in France 1650–1725," in ibid.

[115] See especially the case studies of northwestern England in Andrew Appleby, *Famine in Tudor and Stuart England* (Stanford, CA: Stanford University Press, 1978).

prevailed in semiarid lands most vulnerable to drought. In other times, the poor might have fallen back on livestock to get through bad harvests, but the epizootic of the 1590s had robbed them of that safety net. Moreover, given the way the famine years stretched on, birthrates probably fell from malnutrition, exacerbating the ongoing population loss.[116] Taking these factors together, the Ottoman famine from 1590 to 1610 was probably much worse than any famine in contemporary France or England, for instance, and may have proved as devastating as the famines of the 1690s in Scotland and Finland, which lost around 11 percent and 25 percent of their populations, respectively.[117] Just as these northern lands lay at the margins of temperature, many Ottoman lands lay at the margins of aridity for viable agriculture.

However, in the Ottoman case, as in other Little Ice Age mortality crises, most deaths probably came from disease. First, peasants would have been exposed to opportunistic infections that prey on the weak and malnourished; and such infection would have made it difficult to carry on work and to grow more food.[118] Second, famine and violence would have driven refugee movements, which in turn gave rise to breakdowns in sanitation and the spread of infections from one region to the next. To judge from European examples, these diseases usually proved the leading cause of death in times of crisis, particularly where disorder prevailed in the countryside and where the prospect of relief and protection encouraged flight to towns and cities.[119] As we have seen, these were precisely the conditions found in Ottoman lands in the 1590s through the 1620s. Taken together, these factors and comparisons suggest that the declines of half or more in much of Anatolia were probably not exaggerations

116 Cf. Emmanuel Le Roy Ladurie, "L'aménorrhée de famine (XVIIe–XXe siècles)," *Annales* 24 (1969): 1589–1601, and Patrick Galloway, "Basic Patterns in Annual Variations in Fertility, Nuptiality, Mortality, and Prices in Pre-industrial Europe," *Population Studies* 42 (1988): 275–302.

117 Le Roy Ladurie, *Histoire humaine et comparée*, 491–3 and 495–501.

118 Synergies among starvation and contagion vary widely from one disease to the next. See Ann Carmichael, "Infection, Hidden Hunger, and History," in *Hunger and History*, ed. R. Rottberg and T. Rabb (Cambridge: Cambridge University Press, 1983); Thomas McKeown, "Food, Infection, and Population," in ibid.; Carl Taylor, "Synergy among Mass Infections, Famines, and Poverty," in ibid.; and especially Livi-Bacci, *Population and Nutrition*, 38–9 *et passim*.

119 The best evidence for such a phenomenon may be found in the comparative study of European mortality in the 1740s in Post, *Food Shortage, Climatic Variability, and Epidemic Disease*. Other studies based on early modern and modern evidence have reached similar conclusions: See, e.g., Appleby, "Epidemics and Famine in the Little Ice Age."

and, moreover, that the rest of the core provinces affected by famine and violence probably suffered significant population loss as well.

The Fall of Sultan Ibrahim and the Disasters of 1660

After an interval of relative calm, troubles began again in 1639 with the death of Murad IV and the accession of the only surviving adult male in the Ottoman line. The new sultan İbrahim, known as *Deli* ("the Mad"), turned out to be one of the more regrettable rulers in the empire's long history. In his short reign, İbrahim managed to let corrupt advisors into his confidence, to alienate powerful palace factions, and to drive the treasury almost into bankruptcy. By the time the Janissaries deposed him in a violent uprising of 1648, with the collusion of most of the ulema and the imperial family,[120] imperial revenues had fallen to barely half the levels of the sixteenth century, while expenditures nearly doubled income.[121] Meanwhile, in 1642, the sultan had launched an ill-fated war with the Venetians over the island of Crete that was to drag on for a quarter-century.

İbrahim also had the misfortune to reign over another series of significant natural disasters and rebellions in the provinces, which played some role in his turbulent reign and violent downfall. Even as the Ottoman army wrapped up the Iraqi war in 1638–1639, supposedly massacring tens of thousands of people in the reconquest of Baghdad,[122] the troops endured one last snowy winter on the front.[123] Facing exposure and starvation, soldiers returned home in tatters, spreading disease into the capital.[124] The following winter and spring of 1640–41 turned into one of the wettest on record,[125] causing major floods in Istanbul.[126] In Egypt,

[120] For a detailed original account of the uprising, see Ivan Dujcev, ed., *Avvisi di Ragusa* (Rome: 1935), 127–36.

[121] Özvar, "Osmanlı Devletinin Bütçe Harcamaları."

[122] Described in the *Vecihi Tarihi*, 11, reproduced in Bugra Atsız, *Das Osmanische Reich um die Mitte des 17. Jahrhunderts nach den Chroniken des Vecihi (1637–1660) und des Mehmed Halifa (1633–1660)* (Munich: Rudolf Trofenik, 1977). This episode, described in Hammer, *Histoire de l'Empire ottoman*, vol. 9, 344–5, leads the author to make a direct comparison between the violence in the Ottoman Empire and that in Europe during the Thirty Years War.

[123] Northwest Anatolian tree rings registered precipitation two standard deviations above normal for 1638 (Akkemik et al., "Preliminary Reconstruction").

[124] *Tarih-i Gılmanî*, 18–19.

[125] The spring–summer of 1641 also recorded two standard deviations above normal (Akkemik et al., "Preliminary Reconstruction").

[126] *Topçular Kâtibi 'Abdülkâdir Efendi Tarihi*, 1156.

however, the Nile flood fell short, driving up food prices and causing famine over the next two years.[127] By the following summer, the weak and starving peasantry had fallen prey to one of the worst plagues of the century, reputedly leaving hundreds of villages depopulated. Egypt's tribute fell to a fraction of normal levels.[128]

Widespread rural flight and disorder persisted throughout the decade.[129] From 1642 until 1648, another provincial uprising under the bandit leader Karahaydaroğlu Mehmed Paşa looted and burned Anatolian villages.[130] Rounding out İbrahim's troubled reign, in 1647 volcanic activity spread cold and dry fog across the Mediterranean,[131] and Cyprus suffered a severe attack of locusts that created a tremendous famine.[132] The next year, the Venetians succeeded in blockading the Dardenelles, cutting off supplies to Istanbul until 1649. Finally, in July 1648, just a month before İbrahim was deposed, a major earthquake struck the capital, reportedly killing some thirty thousand inhabitants and destroying the city's main aqueduct.[133] According to the chronicler Mehmed Halifa, when the people saw that the sultan's favorites still had water while the mosques and fountains went dry, they rose up and forced out the grand vezier, paving the way for the Janissary uprising that dethroned the sultan.[134]

In the meantime, the ongoing Cretan War demanded a sacrifice of revenue and resources far out of proportion to any gains from conquest. Although the Ottomans vastly outmatched the waning Venetian empire in men and matériel, they could no longer bring those advantages to bear in a decisive victory, as they had in centuries past. Without the smooth functioning of provisioning systems, war requisitions turned into

[127] Hassan, "Environmental Perception," 131, and Raymond, "Grandes épidémies."

[128] K. Yusoff, "Ottoman Egypt in the 17th Century according to the Unique Manuscript *Zubdah Ikhtisar Tarikh al-Mahsurah*," in *International Congress on Learning and Education in the Ottoman World*, ed. A. Çaksu (Istanbul: IRCICA, 2001), 353, and Hammer, *Histoire de l'Empire ottoman* vol. 10, 31.

[129] *Mühimme defters* 89 and 90, covering the early and mid-1640s, contain nearly as many reports of banditry and deserted villages as *mühimme defters* 84 and 85, covering the late 1620s and early 1630s.

[130] Evliya Çelebi, *Seyahatname*, ed. Y. Dağlı et al. (Istanbul: Yapı Kredi Yayınları, 2001–5), vol. 2, 252–3, describes the destruction in the aftermath of the rebellion.

[131] Camuffo, "Chronology of Dry Fogs."

[132] Jennings, "Locust Problem in Cyprus."

[133] Kenneth Setton, *Venice, Austria, and the Turks in the Sixteenth Century* (Philadelphia: American Philosophical Society, 1991), 150–1.

[134] See the chronicle of Mehmed Halifa, 15, reproduced in Atsız, *Das Osmanische Reich*.

little more than state-sanctioned extortion. The fixed price offered for goods had less and less to do with market forces, as a cash-strapped state demanded far more than it could really afford. While European wars may have been inflationary for the economy and ruinously expensive for the state, they did at least tend to encourage production. Ottoman requisitioning, by contrast, prompted producers to flee the market to escape forced purchases.[135]

Nevertheless, these renewed pressures of war and natural disaster also forced the Ottomans to undertake some serious measures of reform under a new line of leaders. In 1656, following several years of fiscal instability and another military mutiny that almost paralyzed the imperial government, the grand vizier Köprülü Mehmed Paşa took the reins of state and established a dynasty of powerful viziers that would endure throughout the long reign of İbrahim's successor Mehmed IV (1648–1687) and beyond. Although some historians have given the Köprülüs too much credit for restoring the empire, they did achieve a number of notable successes. In 1669, Köprülü Ahmed Paşa brought the Cretan War to a victorious conclusion and absorbed the island as an Ottoman province. The ministers managed to improve and centralize revenue as well; and during the 1670s, Ottoman budgets achieved a surplus for the first time in nearly a century. Moreover, it was these new viziers who undertook most of the major resettlement initiatives to be described in Part III. By most accounts, the Köprülüs brought an important measure of stability and strength to Ottoman rule over the mid-seventeenth century – and with a little more luck, the fortunes of empire might have recovered further.

In the short term, however, Köprülü Mehmed's rise to power coincided with the empire's worst crisis since 1622. The unstable rule of İbrahim and the minority of Mehmed IV further entrenched the power of palace and provincial factions. While many accepted the need for a stronger guiding hand to turn the tide of the Cretan War, others fiercely resisted the grand vizier's centralizing tendencies and sometimes brutal confiscation of money and power. In 1658, opposition would coalesce around the rebellion of Abaza Hasan Paşa in Anatolia, in an uprising in many respects reminiscent of his compatriot Abaza Mehmed's a generation earlier, feeding on popular discontent as well as factional

[135] Mehmet Genç, "18. Yüzyılda Osmanlı Ekonomisi ve Savaş," in *Osmanlı İmparatorluğunda Devlet ve Ekonomi*.

interest.[136] By that autumn, the rebels had come within reach of Bursa and İznik.

As in the 1620s, the rebellion coincided with a period of major Little Ice Age weather events, fueling discontent and amplifying devastation in the countryside. Starting in 1657–58, a spell of freezing snowy weather struck Anatolia and parts of the Balkans, blocking roads and leaving towns and villages stranded without food or fuel.[137] Around Edirne, the winter was so extreme that villagers reportedly burned down orchards and houses for warmth.[138] The next year famine spread across western Anatolia, and ultimately the cold turned so severe that Abaza Hasan's exposed and starving army started to melt away. As another hard winter set in, freezing weather forced the remaining rebels south, first to Ayntab (Gaziantep) and then Aleppo, where men continued to desert and defect, and where Abaza Mehmed was finally captured by a ruse in February 1659.[139]

The following winter, the Aegean region entered perhaps its deepest drought of the last millennium, as revealed in the dendrochronology.[140] According to the chronicler Gılmanî,

> by the will of God, that year in the Edirne region it did not snow. It was cold and dry. Moreover, from April to July 15 it did not rain at all. It was so dry that from around Edirne to Sofia, in all of Silistre province, around Üsküdar and parts of Anatolia, while the seedlings were sprouting they were scorched by the sun. According to what everyone says an *okka* of water in Dobruca went for seven *akçe*... Most of the animals perished from hunger and thirst.[141]

In the drought, the ramshackle wooden buildings of Constantinople became a tinderbox. On July 24, 1660, a fire tore through the city unlike

[136] Finkel, *Osman's Dream*, 258; see also *Tarih-i Gılmanî*, 69–70. The chronicle of Mehmed Halifa, 93, claims that at the height of the rebellion "the preference and inclination of all the people was on the side of Hasan Paşa." For the most complete contemporary account of the rebellion, see Silahdar Fındıklı Mehmed Ağa, *Silahdar Tarihi* (Istanbul: Devlet Matbaası, 1928), vol. 1, 133–9.

[137] *Târîh-i Naîmâ*, 2866.

[138] Adurrahman Abdi Paşa, *Vekayi'nâme*, ed. Fahri Derin (PhD diss., İstanbul Üniversitesi, 1993), 98; *Târîh-i Naîmâ*, 2866, 2808; and *Tarih-i Gılmanî*, 69.

[139] *Vekayi'nâme*, 111–12.

[140] According to Griggs et al., "Regional High-Frequency Reconstruction," the spring–summer of 1660 was easily the driest in the last 900 years. (See the article's supporting online material for annual data.)

[141] *Tarih-i Gılmanî*, 100. According to *Silahdar Tarihi*, 214–16, there was also a famine in Syria at this time.

any before or since. One recent study concludes that "two-thirds of Istanbul was destroyed in the conflagration, and as many as 40,000 people lost their lives."[142] In the aftermath of the fire, famine spread, followed by one of the city's worst plagues of the century.[143] According to the English ambassador Paul Rycaut, the Janissaries kept a record of corpses carried out of the city's north gate, "which for some Weeks amounted (I speak moderately) to Twelve or thirteen hundred a Day."[144]

These catastrophes also stoked fundamentalist revivals underway among Muslims, Jews, and Christians alike. The disasters appear to have encouraged a resurgence of the Kadızadelis; and in the wake of the fire, the Valide Sultan (queen mother) cleared out the Jewish quarter in Eminönü to build a new mosque, fueling unrest among Ottoman Jews.[145] In 1664, moreover, a strange comet appeared, exciting revolutionary prophecies among all sects.[146] The next year, in 1665–66, Sabbatai Tzi launched a major millenarian Jewish movement that ultimately led to his and his followers' forced conversion to Islam.

The Late Maunder Minimum

Once these disorders subsided, until 1682, the Ottoman Empire enjoyed perhaps its most stable period for a century. Following the conquest of Crete in 1669, the ongoing regime of strong, long-serving grand viziers oversaw a short and successful war against Poland; and in 1672, the empire actually reached its largest extent by adding the province of Kamenets in Podolia. Nevertheless, as they went to war with the Habsburgs again a decade later, the Ottomans saw their fragile gains swept away. Just as the combination of extreme drought and military stalemate had set off the Celali Rebellion nearly a century before, so a new conjuncture of anomalous weather and prolonged warfare led to serious crisis in the 1680s and 1690s.

As described in Chapter 5, the 1670s marked the start of a new phase of Little Ice Age climate fluctuations known as the Late Maunder Minimum. This new period produced weather anomalies across the Mediterranean, characterized by "drought in winter, exceptionally severe winters, and

142 Marc Baer, "The Great Fire of 1660 and the Islamization of Christian and Jewish Space in Istanbul," *International Journal of Middle East Studies* 36 (2004): 159–81, at 159.

143 On the chain of related disasters, see *Tarih-i Gılmanî*, 94–100.

144 "Memoirs of Sir Paul Rycaut" in Knolles, *Generall Description*, vol. 2, 111.

145 Baer, "Great Fire."

146 Knolles, *Generall Description*, vol. 2, 162.

heavy rainfall in summer."[147] Hungary and much of the Balkans, meanwhile, suffered a period of extremely cold wet springs, chill autumns, harsh winters, and very hot summers.[148]

Combining proxy data such as tree rings with descriptions from historical sources, we can draw together the narrative of natural and human disasters that afflicted Ottoman lands starting in the late 1670s. In 1676, as temperatures cooled across Europe, the southern Balkans entered into a long series of extremely cold winters.[149] Over the following years, drought extended across Anatolia,[150] and famine and plague were reported in Egypt.[151] (In early 1681, however, Mecca witnessed another major flood.)[152] In 1682, Mount Etna erupted again, casting a dry fog over the Mediterranean;[153] İzmir suffered an invasion of locusts;[154] and Crete and Greece witnessed exceptionally cold winters marked by the death of livestock and loss of crops, followed by famine.[155]

In early 1683, Grand Vizier Merzifonlu Kara Mustafa Paşa made the unfortunate decision to invade Austria, turning a long-running border conflict into a full-scale war. The events that followed have been narrated before, especially the Ottomans' historic retreat from the gates of Vienna that summer, driven from the siege by the Polish troops of Jan Sobieski.[156] Historians have generally recognized the Ottoman defeat of the 1680s and 1690s as a turning point in the empire's history. Yet few have noticed the role of the Little Ice Age.

147 Grove, "Climate in the Eastern and Central Mediterranean." See also Camuffo and Enzi, "Climate of Italy"; Xoplaki, "Variability of Climate"; and Luterbacher et al., "Late Maunder Minimum" for more on the climatology of the LMM.

148 Rácz, "Climate of Hungary," and Xoplaki, "Variations of Climate."

149 Xoplaki, "Variability of Climate."

150 Akkemik et al., "Preliminary Reconstruction"; Touchan et al., "Standardized Precipitation Index"; and Touchan et al., "Preliminary Reconstructions." An Armenian chronicler also records a severe summer drought from Erzurum to Isfahan in the summer of 1677: See "The Journal of Zak'aria of Agulis," ed. George Bournoutian (Costa Mesa, CA: Mazda, 2003), 137.

151 Hammer, *Histoire de l'Empire ottoman* vol. 11, 429–30.

152 *Zübde-i Vekayiât,* 117–18.

153 Ibid. See also Camuffo, "Chronology of Dry Fogs."

154 *The Chronicle of Deacon Zak'aria of K'anak'er,* ed. George Bournoutian (Costa Mesa, CA: Mazda, 2004), 227.

155 Xoplaki, "Variability of Climate"; Repapis et al., "Note on the Frequency of Occurrence of Severe Winters"; Grove, "Climate of Crete"; and Grove and Conterio, "Climate in the Eastern and Central Mediterranean."

156 See, e.g., John Stoye, *The Siege of Vienna,* new ed. (New York: Pegasus, 2000).

As the Ottomans set out for Vienna in 1683, freezing weather and heavy spring rains plagued the soldiers' advance across the Balkans.[157] Weather on the Hungarian front turned extremely cold that winter and the next.[158] Following Venice's entry into the Holy Alliance in 1684, the European blockade and military requisitions brought shortages to cities along the Aegean[159] and even Istanbul itself.[160] However, the real crisis started in 1685, while Ottoman forces were being pushed back toward the Danube. By that time, the persistent cold and drought had brought serious famine to Greece and Anatolia.[161] As one contemporary chronicler recorded,

> with the start of the campaign and the absence of rain, the fields could not be planted, and even what was planted did not sprout. From the year 1096 (1685) on, a great famine appeared in all the lands of Islam. A *kile* of wheat reached two *kuruş*, and an *akçe* could not even buy thirty *dirhems* (about 90g) of bread... And it was reported that in parts of Anatolia many perished trying to eat gallnuts and grass roots and walnut shells.[162]

During the same years, a dismissed *sekban* leader Yeğen Osman Paşa led a wave of banditry in Anatolia, plundering towns and villages from Sivas to Bolu, until the Ottoman government bought him off with another military command and sent him and his forces to the Hungarian front.[163]

Following the loss of Buda in the autumn of 1686, the region witnessed one of the coldest winters since 1621. Lake Ioannina in Greece froze over for three months;[164] and in Istanbul, the Golden Horn was covered in ice.[165] According to one eyewitness, roofs in Istanbul caved in from the heavy snowfall, and the roads remained impassable for fifty days.[166] In

157 Grove and Conterio, "Climate in the Eastern and Central Mediterranean," and Finkel, *Osman's Dream*, 284.
158 Rácz, *Climate History of Hungary*, 30 and 37.
159 *Chronicle of Deacon Zak'aria of K'anak'er*, 227–8.
160 Andreasyan, "Eremya Çelebi'nin Yangınlar Tarihi."
161 For evidence of the drought, see especially Touchan et al., "Reconstructions of Spring/Summer Precipitation," and Touchan et al., "Preliminary Reconstructions."
162 *Silahdar Tarihi*, vol. 2, 243.
163 Ibid., vol. 2, 228, 269–72.
164 Xoplaki, "Variability of Climate," and Repapis et al., "Note on the Frequency of Occurence of Severe Winters."
165 *Silahdar Tarihi*, vol. 2, 262–4.
166 Ibid.

the winter and spring of 1687, the drought reached its climax. The Aegean and northern Anatolia were the worst affected, facing one of their driest years in the last millennium.[167] Further dendroclimatology reconstructions confirm that the dry weather stretched all across the Eastern Mediterranean, including parts of Anatolia, where it lasted into 1688.[168] By late summer of 1687, Istanbul had supposedly gone seven months without rain.[169]

As had happened before in the 1590s, 1620s, and 1640s, a combination of military defeat and natural disaster set off rebellion. By 1686, short of cash to pay the troops, the sultan decreed an extra "war contributions tax" over widespread opposition.[170] Yet given the general famine, the imperial government still failed to adequately provision its troops.[171] After a quick victory over Habsburg forces at Osijek in May, the situation in the army started to unravel. As the mutineers would later describe it:

> In the year 1096 (1686/87) Grand Vizier Süleyman Paşa was sent on campaign. When they descended to the Osijek plain, although it is the ancient Ottoman custom to give a general distribution of provisions (*umum zahiresi*) to the *sipahi* and *silahdar* (swordbearer) corps, on that occasion he invited these soldiers over and said that "this year there is a shortage of provisions, and not enough reached us to make a general distribution," and he promised that "however, instead of a general distribution, I shall give an advance of three *akçes* apiece to meet your needs." Afterwards, he chose to lie rather than carry out his promise.[172]

Over the following months, as the Ottoman army pursued the enemy north, the general continued to make more promises and announcements of provisions and payment, only to renege each time. That summer, Ottoman forces suffered major defeats in the Peloponnese; and

[167] According to Griggs et al., "Regional High-Frequently Reconstruction," it was the twelfth driest year in the north Aegean since 1089; while Akkemik et al., "Preliminary Reconstruction" records it as by far away the driest year since 1635. See their supporting online material.

[168] Touchan et al., "Reconstructions of Spring/Summer Precipitation" reveals a dry year generally over the whole Eastern Mediterranean, while D'Arrigo, "350-Year (AD 1628–1980) Reconstruction" shows central Anatolia at one standard deviation below normal in both 1687 and 1688. Accounts in Rácz, *Climate History of Hungary*, 69, 71, 84, suggest these summers were unusually hot and dry in Hungary as well.

[169] This is mentioned in Hammer, *Histoire de l'Empire ottoman* vol. 12, 213–14, but I have not been able to locate the original source.

[170] *Zübde-i Vekayiât*, 221–3.

[171] Setton, *Venice Austria and the Turks*, 281–2, quotes a Venetian intelligence report that despite the scale of the proposed campaign "non si vedevano provisione di vettovaglia."

[172] *Zübde-i Vekayiât*, 235.

on August 17, the main army lost the decisive Battle of Mohacs, forcing the Ottoman defensive line to fall back toward Belgrade in unusually wet summer weather.[173] Ten days later, spotting a chance to strike at the enemy, the grand vizier made another fateful miscalculation by sending a large contingent of his soldiers, including Yeğen Osman and his *sekbans*, lightly armed over a narrow bridge back across the Danube to attack enemy forces. Once again, the general reportedly shortchanged the soldiers their promised provisions and sent them on a longer mission than originally announced – a twelve days' march all the way up to Eğre Castle.[174] And then, just as at the siege of Khotin six decades before, Little Ice Age weather drove the army from disaffection to mutiny. As one contemporary chronicler described:

> By God's wisdom, there was a great storm and the rain did not let up at all those days or nights. As for the soldiers on the far bank, they had neither tents nor pavilions nor anything to protect themselves from the pouring rain. For two days and two nights, the rain went on without a pause. Everyone's horses and persons were soaked. Once the gate of the bridge they crossed over was shut, and they saw it was absolutely impossible to cross back to the other bank, and everyone was in a miserable state from these calamities, the *sipahis* and the *levends* joining together all decided and made a pact to return to the bridge and march through to the other side.[175]

As the mutineers later reported: "That night and day, by the will of God, with the endless rain we were all in a terrible state . . . In that unforgiving place we would surely have perished in the mud and rain."[176]

This refusal to obey orders became a tipping point for a general rebellion among the soldiers. The grand vizier panicked when he heard the news, supposedly declaring, "If they want provisions, let's give them! The salaries are ready too – let's pay them out immediately!"[177] By that point, however, the army was unwilling to hear any more promises. His offers rejected, Süleyman fled, and Yeğen Osman rose to the leadership of the mutinous army.

As word of events reached Istanbul, Mehmed IV ordered the army to winter in Belgrade and tried to placate the rebellion by dismissing a few generals. Nevertheless, the mutinous soldiers kept raising their demands.

[173] See Rácz, "Weather of Hungary," for seasonal precipitation indices.
[174] *Zübde-i Vekayiât*, 236–7.
[175] Ibid., 232–3.
[176] Ibid., 237.
[177] Ibid., 232–3.

Continuing their march south, they reached Edirne in late October. After some debate with the *sipahis*, the Janissaries persuaded the army to continue toward Istanbul and demanded the sultan's deposal. Finding himself without upport, and finally convinced that he would come to no harm, Mehmed IV ceded the throne to his brother Süleyman II that November.[178]

However, the substitution of one sultan for another did little to turn the tide of war. In the short reigns of Süleyman II (1687–91), Ahmed II (1691–95), and Mustafa II (1695–1703, deposed by another mutiny), Ottoman armies continued to suffer setbacks, their position salvaged only by the outbreak of the War of the League of Augsburg (1688–97), which distracted their cobelligerents. While Ottoman ministers continued to devise new taxes and reforms (discussed in Chapter 11), their benefits came too late to save the military effort. After another decade of conflict, the Ottomans finally concluded a humiliating treaty at Karlowitz in 1699. Ceding much of Hungary to the Habsburgs and the Peloponnese to Venice, the peace marked the empire's first major territorial retreat in almost three centuries.

Meanwhile, extreme Little Ice Age weather persisted through the final decade of the war and beyond. Starting in 1689, more volcanic activity drove down temperatures across Europe and the Near East and cast another dry fog over the Mediterranean.[179] Precipitation now fluctuated wildly from one year to the next. That year, Anatolia faced tremendous rains and flooding,[180] while Iraq suffered famines and epidemics thought to have killed more than one hundred thousand.[181] Starting 1690, historical records from Greece and Crete recorded the onset of prolonged recurring drought.[182] Likewise, in 1692 and 1693, tree rings in parts of

178 For a detailed account of the mutiny and the fall of Mehmed IV, see *Zübde-i Vekayiât*, 221–53.

179 Lamb, "Volcanic Dust in the Atmosphere," and Camuffo, "Chronology of Dry Fogs."

180 The extraordinarily wet spring shows up clearly in the dendroclimatology: two standard deviations above normal precipitation in the Aegean and northwest and central Anatolia, and one standard deviation in the south and southwest. See Griggs et al., "Regional High-Frequency Reconstruction"; D'Arrigo and Cullen, "350-Year (AD 1628–1980) Reconstruction"; Touchan et al., "Preliminary Reconstructions"; and Akkemik et al., "Reconstruction (1689–1994)." We also have a historical record of a serious flood in Edirne that year: See Suraiya Faroqhi, "A Natural Disaster as an Indicator of Agricultural Change," in *Natural Disasters in the Ottoman Empire*, ed. E. Zachariadou (Heraklion: Crete University Press, 1999).

181 Charles Issawi, *The Fertile Crescent 1800–1914: A Documentary Economic History* (New York: Oxford University Press, 1988), 99.

182 Xoplaki, "Variability of Climate."

Anatolia registered a couple of the driest springs in the last three and a half centuries,[183] and a contemporary chronicler noted further famine and plague in Iraq.[184]

In 1695, another El Niño year, an exceptionally low Nile flood set off a chain of disasters in Egypt. As the chronicler Al-Damurdashi described it, "the blessed Nile flood was low that year and the people left their villages for Cairo since they were unable to irrigate their fields." Over the following months,

> they entered Cairo and began stealing bread from the bakeries. As a result, the ovens and bakeries closed and rich people baked their bread in their houses. But the poor had only a fourth [of what they needed to survive], suffered greatly and took to eating cats and carcasses. In the *khamasin* period of the year 1105 (April and May 1695) the plague struck and the lanes and alleyways were filled with corpses. Every morning you saw ten corpses... The plague spread throughout the province and its dependencies.[185]

According to another contemporary, the famine reached its peak in late summer, with dead bodies strewn in the streets and people reduced to cannibalism.[186]

The following winter and into 1696, the drought moved north. From Jordan through central and western Anatolia and into the Aegean the tree rings record an exceptionally dry year.[187] In Greece, the harvest failed and church litanies were held to pray for rain.[188] The severe cold persisted as well: in the winter of 1699, the Golden Horn froze over once more as ice covered parts of the capital,[189] and Greece witnessed heavy snows, another bad harvest, and the death of livestock.[190] An even

[183] Akkemik et al., "Reconstruction (1689–1994)," and Akkemik et al., "Preliminary Reconstruction."

[184] *Zübde-i Vekayiât*, 454–5.

[185] *Al-Damurdashi's Chronicle of Egypt*, trans. D. Crecelius and ʻAbd al-Wahhab Bakr (Leiden: Brill, 1991), 42 and 61.

[186] Yusoff, "Ottoman Egypt in the 17th Century," 353–4. Raymond, "Grandes épidémies," drawing on different sources, states that the famine began in 1694 and that the plague took place in early 1696.

[187] Two standard deviations below normal precipitation in Akkemik et al., "Preliminary Reconstruction," and D'Arrigo and Cullen, "350-Year Reconstruction"; and one standard deviation below normal in Griggs et al., "High-Frequency Regional Reconstruction," and Akkemik et al., "Reconstruction (1689–1994)."

[188] Xoplaki, "Variability of Climate."

[189] *Zübde-i Vekayiât*, 635–6.

[190] Xoplaki, "Variability of Climate."

colder winter struck a decade later in 1708–9[191] followed by a spring of torrential rains in Anatolia, famine in Egypt,[192] and freezing weather famine and plague in Serbia.[193]

Thus the surrender at Karlowitz and the droughts, floods, and famines of the Late Maunder Minimum rounded out another century of calamities associated with the Little Ice Age. Alone, none proved as significant as the crisis brought on by the Great Drought and the Celali Rebellion in 1595–1610. However, taken together, these recurring human and natural disasters postponed any chance of recovery in Ottoman lands. Whereas most of the regions affected by the "general crisis" witnessed one or two generations of serious turmoil and population loss, the Ottoman Empire had now endured a succession of significant cold, drought, flight, famine, and unrest lasting for more than a century. This environmental context remains crucial to understanding the major political events of the age, from the fall of Osman II to the fall of Mehmed IV. Moreover, this century of setbacks goes further than perhaps any other factor in explaining the relative weakness of the empire vis-à-vis its neighbors to the north during the eighteenth century, as the Little Ice Age and its attendant crises came to an end.

Conclusion: Climate, Crisis, and Transformation

As the foregoing narrative demonstrates, climate was a critical factor – perhaps *the* critical factor – in understanding Ottoman crises of the seventeenth century. It would be quite a coincidence, to say the least, if the most troubled period of Ottoman history just happened to overlap with the Little Ice Age, and if the era's worst political turmoil and outbreaks of violence just happened to coincide with its worst natural disasters. Moreover, we have seen specifically in several cases how an atmosphere of famine, flight, and unrest born of extreme climate events fueled both

[191] That winter has been cited as the coldest for Italy, for Hungary, and for Europe as a whole during the entire early modern period. See Camuffo and Enzi, "Climate of Italy"; Rácz, "Climate of Hungary"; and Luterbacher et al., "European Seasonal and Annual Temperature Variability." The same freezing weather in Russia would also contribute to the failed invasion of Charles XII, who then took refuge with the Ottomans. See Finkel, *Osman's Dream*, 333–6.

[192] Three Anatolian tree-ring studies record precipitation two standard deviations above normal for the spring of 1709. See Akkemik et al., "Reconstruction (1689–1994)"; Akkemik et al., "Preliminary Reconstruction"; and D'Arrigo and Cullen, "350-Year (AD 1628–1980) Reconstruction." See also Hammer, *Histoire d'Empire ottoman*, vol.13, 198–9, for mention of a major flood and famine in Egypt.

[193] Xoplaki, "Variability of Climate."

political violence in the capital and widespread rebellion and banditry in the provinces. Finally, the evidence points to the Little Ice Age as a major cause of the empire's severe population loss of the early 1600s, one of the most significant issues in the social and economic turmoil of the seventeenth century.

Taking these ecological factors into account forces us to seriously reconsider the meaning of Ottoman crisis and transformation. Above all, this perspective argues strongly against current forms of Ottoman exceptionalism, whether of a declensionist or revisionist variety. On the one hand, there is no need to blame the region's troubles on the decline of powerful sultans or decay of old institutions – developments which appear more as the consequence than the cause of the Ottoman crisis. On the other hand, it will not do to minimize the crisis as just a series of conflicts among political and economic interest groups or the inevitable by-product of a peculiar political and economic transition.

Instead, the experience of the Ottoman Empire needs to be analyzed in the wider context of the global "general crisis." While the specific forms and directions of the Ottoman crisis may have been unique to local circumstances, it nevertheless shared the same underlying causes as crises across the early modern world: ecological pressures and Little Ice Age climate events. Contrary to some historical tropes,[194] these worldwide revolutions and rebellions were *neither* signs of rising capitalism and modernity in Europe *nor* signs of stagnation and decay in Asia, but rather signs of the *common* vulnerabilities of precapitalist, preindustrial societies around the world to population pressure and climate change.[195] Given the empire's ecological vulnerabilities, the Little Ice Age crisis of Ottoman lands was more costly and protracted than most; yet it was not unique. If the Ottoman case proved exceptional, it was more in the empire's slow pace of recovery in the century and a half that followed – a development explored in Part III.

Conclusion to Part II: Climate and Causation in the Ottoman Crisis

From the 1570s onward, Ottoman lands underwent a period of unusually cold and variable climate. In the final decade of the sixteenth century,

194 Cf. the question posed recently by Tezcan, "Second Ottoman Empire," why early modern European revolutions are interpreted as progress and Ottoman rebellions as decline.

195 Cf. Goldstone, *Revolution and Rebellion*, 459–85.

these climatic fluctuations brought the longest drought in the last six hundred years to the Eastern Mediterranean. Given the conditions of ecological pressure which then prevailed in central Anatolia and especially in the province of Karaman, the cold and drought created severe famine and widespread death of livestock. At the same time, the Ottoman Empire launched a major military campaign in Hungary, draining vital resources and driving up taxes and requisitions. This combination of climate change, war, and an ill-timed epizootic broke down Ottoman provisioning systems, forcing the sultan to make unreasonable demands on the peasantry that turned their desperation into disaffection and violence. Once a leader emerged who could forge the discontent into an army, rebellion broke out, which the state proved helpless to contain until it could free soldiers from the wars along its borders. Through nearly two decades of fighting, a succession of freezing winters, alternating with droughts and heavy snows, fueled widespread famine, flight, and mortality.

Over the following century, the empire would see a succession of sultans deposed and armies defeated. Underlying these political disorders were serious natural and human disasters: Extreme cold or drought and famine presaged most of the major crises that marked the 1600s. And in the wake of each uprising in Istanbul, desperate conditions in the provinces aggravated outbreaks of rural banditry or rebellion. The 1680s and 1690s in particular witnessed a return to many of the same conditions of the 1590s, putting an end to a brief period of recovery. Once again, a combination of extreme Little Ice Age weather events and a protracted war bred serious famine, flight, and unrest, playing a significant role in the Ottomans' surrender of land to the Habsburgs and hence the empire's gradual retreat as a major European power.

Unaware of the magnitude and impact of these climate fluctuations, historians have focused on Ottoman social and political transformations to account for the empire's sudden turn of fortune. As discussed in the foregoing chapters, some of these explanations have more merit than others, and many could be useful in understanding the events of these decades. Nevertheless, none of these internal factors – either alone or in conjunction – could explain when or how the crisis actually occurred. None could account for the scale, suddenness, and timing of the catastrophe.

It was with this problem in mind that William Griswold first proposed the Little Ice Age as the trigger for the Celali Rebellion. As the author noted, climatic explanations tend to be dismissed as simplistic and monocausal. Historians opt instead for combinations of social and economic forces to explain large events because the latter appear more subtle and sophisticated. However, as Griswold concluded, "accepting that single cause explanations are shallow and inaccurate, the multi-cause explanations sometimes do not solve the problem either, and leave one with the feeling of equal inaccuracy. How does one explain, for example the movement of thousands of peasants in bloody social revolution for a period of years or even decades, where for centuries before these people had accepted their economic and social conditions?"[196]

Yet as this book demonstrates, climate-based explanations do not have to be simple and monocausal. Bringing together new historical and climatological evidence, we can forge stronger and more complex linkages among events. In Part I of this study, we explored the ecological pressures and shortcomings of the empire's provisioning systems which had made Ottoman lands vulnerable to such a disaster in the first place. In Chapters 6 and 7, we saw the role of accident and human error in triggering the initial Celali Rebellion. Climate, therefore, was not the only culprit for the crisis, but part of an important historical conjuncture.

This environmental approach offers the most coherent paradigm for Ottoman crisis and transformation and the one with the most explanatory power. Without resorting to vague concepts like "decline" or "decentralization," it actually addresses why and how the rapid growth of the sixteenth century came to an end in the 1590s and why the empire suffered such tremendous setbacks over the century that followed. It can draw on abundant evidence from a wide range of sources and on comparisons from around the seventeenth-century world. Furthermore, it puts the Ottoman crisis in its rightful context as part of a general crisis: a global conjuncture of ecological pressures and climate fluctuations.

Finally, an environmental approach to the crisis can also help us reinterpret Ottoman history over the *longue durée.* As we see in the next part of this book, the Little Ice Age marked a shift in the human ecology of the Near East, as the crisis and its aftermath left a profound impact on patterns of land use and settlement, which would persist into the eighteenth century and beyond.

[196] Griswold, "Climatic Change."

PART III

ECOLOGICAL TRANSFORMATION

Introduction to Part III: The Slow Recovery

To judge from accounts of the early eighteenth century, the level of population and agriculture in Ottoman lands had made little progress since the aftermath of the Celali Rebellion. In 1706, the returning Venetian ambassador could still report that "Asia is a country bereft of people with scarce revenue, full of brigands, breeding rebels, scattered with wandering tribes and people living in tents, governed by officers too far from the eye of the sovereign."[1] Over the following decades Ottoman lands became a trope for neglect and desertion in the literature of the Enlightenment.[2]

Yet what remains even more remarkable is how little the region's demography had recovered yet another century later, long after the worst of the Little Ice Age and "general crisis" had passed. Over the 1700s and early 1800s, in an era when populations from Britain to China doubled and in some cases redoubled, Ottoman numbers remained curiously flat. By the time of our next reasonably accurate estimates around the 1830s, the population of the empire had again reached only some 25 million to 32 million – still significantly below its peak of perhaps 35 million around 1590, even factoring in the loss of Hungary and parts of Greece.[3] Assuming that the empire lost a quarter or even a third of its population by 1640, and that the gains of the Köprülü years were wiped out by the disasters of the Late Maunder Minimum, it appears the eighteenth and early nineteenth centuries still brought only modest demographic recovery.

1 Pedani-Fabris, *Relazioni*, 777.

2 Thomson, "Perceptions des populations du Moyen-Orient."

3 McGowan, "Age of Ayans," 646. For a thorough study of nineteenth-century Ottoman censuses, see Kemal Karpat, *Ottoman Population 1830–1914* (Madison: University of Wisconsin Press, 1985).

Therefore, Part III of this book seeks to explain why Ottoman losses proved so steep and enduring, taking a historical ecology perspective. As described in the introduction, the Near East had witnessed a long pattern of environmental crisis and protracted recovery. Time and again, climate shifts had devastated agriculture and left inroads for pastoral nomads, shifting the balance between desert and sown. Movement to crowded cities had stirred up endemic and epidemic diseases, draining demographic recovery, while disorder and depopulation in the countryside had hindered the revival of agriculture.

The following chapters analyze how these factors played out once more over the course of the seventeenth and eighteenth centuries. In Chapter 9, we see how population movements and climatic disasters set off a widespread nomad invasion of farms and villages, leading to serious and enduring depopulation of semiarid lands. This shift in the basic ecology of land use at the core of the empire constituted the most serious obstacle to recovery over the centuries that followed, leaving some Ottoman farms of the late 1500s unplowed again until the coming of modern tractors. Chapter 10 examines how the prevailing insecurity of the seventeenth century drove a flood of people from the countryside into already dangerous and crowded urban areas, leading to a steady demographic drain. Finally, Chapter 11 considers broader changes in Ottoman landholding and commerce, exploring how the region's agriculture slowly shifted from subsistence and imperial provisioning to cash crop production for an expanding Europe-centered world economy.

9

DESERT AND SOWN

The aftermath of the Celali Rebellion witnessed a great nomad invasion into large parts of Anatolia, Syria, and northern Iraq. Tribes once restricted to mountainous or desert land in the eastern provinces poured almost to the western end of Turkey. The movement proved sudden, surprising, and – for over two hundred years – irreversible. As discussed in previous chapters, a combination of state policy and demographic expansion had gradually forced back the bounds of nomadic pastoralism since the early 1500s, paving the way for settled villages. Tribal resistance, though persistent, had been unable to stop the encroachment of farming into former grazing lands. The Little Ice Age crisis, however, offered the nomads a chance to push back. In the space of a few years, this pastoral movement virtually wiped out the settlement gains of a century. As in past disasters, both human and environmental factors played important roles.

The invasion illustrates for the last time that ebb and flow of the "desert and sown" in arid and semiarid lands described in the introduction. Like so many of their predecessors in the ancient and medieval Near East, the Ottomans saw large swaths of their settled territory revert to nomadic pastoralism in the wake of crisis. In spite of large and sophisticated resettlement schemes, the empire failed to recover the momentum of population and settlement expansion that marked the classical age. More than any other factor, this shift in land use underlay the demographic and economic contraction of the empire during the following two centuries, and it contributed greatly to the waning of Ottoman power with respect to the other major empires of Europe and Asia.

Ottomans and Nomads

The place of nomads in the origins and development of empire remains a contested issue in Ottoman historiography. It is generally accepted that the Ottomans were themselves distant successors of the nomadic Seljuk Turks, who invaded from Central Asia through Iran in the eleventh century, probably driven by a period of intense cold in the steppes.[4] After the Seljuks defeated the Byzantine Empire at the Battle of Manzikert in 1071, these Turkic warriors pushed into Anatolia to found the Rum Seljuk state. As succession disputes and the division of kingdoms among heirs fragmented the Seljuk domains, successor empires grew up across Asia Minor, with the Ottomans emerging as a distinct group by the end of the thirteenth century. However, the extent to which these early Ottomans were really "Turkish" or "tribal" nomads has been the subject of some contention.

The origins of the modern debate may be traced to the writings of Paul Wittek and M. Fuad Köprülü in the early twentieth century, who each set up opposing theories on what came to be known as the "gazi thesis." In Wittek's formulation, the Ottomans were not so much Turkic tribesmen as Islamic "holy warriors" (*gazi*); and the Ottoman state was not the work of nomadic invaders but of former Byzantine elements who regrouped around the new conquerors.[5] Köprülü, arguing from an emerging Turkish nationalist perspective, countered with the claim that the Ottomans were no different than other Turkic tribes, only more successful. Therefore, their empire reflected the native genius of the Turkic peoples, and their population was ethnically Turkish.[6]

In recent decades, the work of Rudi Lindner,[7] Cemal Kafadar,[8] and Heath Lowry[9] has further complicated this debate. Without entering into the details, which are not relevant to the present study, the current historiography modifies both the traditional "gazi thesis" and the more nationalist approaches to Ottoman origins. The emphasis has shifted to the fluidity of religion and identity in these formative years of empire, and to the complicated question of what constitutes a "tribe" or a "*gazi*." Although the evidence remains sparse and contested, it would appear

4 See Bulliet, *Cotton, Climate, and Camels.*

5 The classic formulation of this thesis may be found in Paul Wittek, "Le rôle des tribus turques dans l'Empire ottoman," in *Mélanges Georges Smets* (Brussels: Éditions de la Revue encyclopédique, 1952).

6 M. Fuad Köprülü, *The Origins of the Ottoman Empire*, trans. Gary Leiser (Binghamton: SUNY Press, 1992).

7 Rudi Lindner, *Nomads and Ottomans in Medieval Anatolia* (Bloomington: Indiana University Press, 1983) and "What Was a Nomadic Tribe?" *Comparative Studies in Society and History* 24 (1982): 689–711.

8 Kafadar, *Between Two Worlds.*

9 Heath Lowry, *The Nature of the Early Ottoman State* (Binghamton: SUNY Press, 2003).

that the early Ottoman state represented neither another tribal band nor a mere continuation of the Byzantine Empire under different rulers, but rather a genuinely new polity forged from diverse elements.

Whatever else the Ottomans may have been, they were certainly not the nomadic horde of popular imagination. The new ruling dynasty and its followers were evidently committed to state-building, agriculture, and regular taxation from a very early stage of their history.[10] Likewise, the people of modern Turkey are not physically the descendants of medieval Turkic tribes, regardless of national myth. Genetic studies of Anatolia suggest the makeup of populations has remained fairly steady for millennia, revealing few traces Inner Asian heritage.[11] The Turkish language and the pastoral lifestyle of the invaders spread far faster than their actual, biological population. Given the low demographic density of pastoralists vis-à-vis settled farmers, nomads probably remained a small minority even as their power and influence reached their peak in the waning years of the Byzantine Empire.

What gave the nomads such a presence in the first centuries of empire was not their numbers but their role in early Ottoman expansion. Nomadic forces constituted a crucial part of the early Ottoman military, especially its mobile frontier raiders. Furthermore, nomads continued to provide horses, camels, and animal products essential for imperial provisioning. Finally, an imagined tribal past written into Ottoman history in the fourteenth and fifteenth centuries conferred the legitimacy of Seljuk and even Mongol heritage on the upstart Ottoman dynasty.

Nevertheless, their role in forging the empire did not translate into any permanent gains in power or territory. By the mid-1500s, when imperial records began to record everyday dealings with nomad tribes, their place in the imperial order had begun to fade. First, and most importantly, the nomads' traditional military role had gone into decline. The army had become more professionalized, and the *sipahi* cavalry and Janissary infantry had come to replace the irregular nomad raiders who had spearheaded the first two centuries of Ottoman expansion. Meanwhile, as discussed in previous chapters, settled agriculture was expanding at

[10] According to Lindner, the Ottomans probably made the decisive turn from mobile pastoralism to settled agriculture as early as the 1330s. The fledgling dynasty was confronted at that time by the need for manpower and lured on by the rich agricultural lands of Bythinia (today's Bursa) where they first made their capital. See *Nomads and Ottomans*, 29–32.

[11] Luigi Cavalli-Sforza, *Genes, Peoples, and Languages* (Berkeley: University of California Press, 2000), 152 *et passim.*

the expense of mobile pastoralism, which forced back the territory and power of the tribes. The place of nomads in Ottoman society, always ambiguous, had turned increasingly precarious with the empire's success in promoting settled agriculture.

Settlement and Conflict

As formulated in the classic study of Frederik Barth,[12] the ecology of nomads in semiarid lands tended to follow a basic pattern: Populations, relatively free from the diseases of settled life, would gradually rise. Meanwhile, the carrying capacity of the land remained fixed, since the pastoral lifestyle favored mobility over intensification. Some nomads of each generation, usually young men, were forced to join agricultural life, and this settlement could take one of two paths. For the successful nomad, the wealth of his herd might allow him to buy his way in as a rentier landlord. For the unsuccessful nomad, his poverty would likely to force him into the life of a landless laborer or a settler on the margins of agriculture.

The net effect of Ottoman policy was to force nomads onto that second path – the path of marginalization – through taxes and restrictions on nomad freedom. Traditionally, the state subjected nomads to three different taxes: one on the size of herds, one on animal products, and one on manpower. Although wealthier nomads might pay more altogether than poorer nomads, the weight of the poll tax alone made the overall scheme regressive. According to Rudi Lindner's calculation, the profits of a successful herd in a good year might have been some 30 percent on the cost of this "capital." For an owner of a herd of 300, Ottoman taxes would run to only 6 percent of capital, or about 20 percent of profit. On the other hand, for a household with a herd of only thirty, the same taxes would almost wipe out the annual surplus, rendering it all but impossible to keep the herd going in lean years of drought or disease.[13] Thus the eventual result of Ottoman taxation was to drive the owners of smaller herds to abandon their way of life altogether and join the peasantry.

Furthermore, imperial policy began to cut into the flexibility and resiliency of nomadic ecology by the very fact of regulation. With the

[12] *Nomads of South Persia.*

[13] Lindner, *Nomads and Ottomans,* chapter 2, especially 59–61. See also Cengiz Orhonlu, *Osmanlı İmparatorluğunda Aşiretleri İskân Teşebbüsü* (Istanbul: İstanbul Üniversitesi, 1963), chapter 1, on tribes' difficulties meeting tax burdens.

growth of imperial power, as described in Chapter 1, officials defined particular routes for grazing and migration. Sometime by the sixteenth century, the empire added further cash taxes on nomad households and fines for straying from assigned winter and summer pastures. Although phrased within the language of tradition and traditional rights, these restrictions ignored the fact that whatever customary paths the nomads had taken, freedom of movement was a critical part of nomad land use. Particularly in times of drought or other adverse weather, pastoralists needed mobility to keep their herds alive. As with its scheme of regressive taxation, the empire's regulations fell hardest on nomadic groups already on the margins of viability, encouraging them to abandon their traditions in favor of farming.

Such restrictions became inevitable as permanent settlement encroached into once empty or thinly settled lands. As discussed in Chapters 1 and 2, the population of early Ottoman territories had been hard hit by the collapse of Byzantine rule and the Black Death, whose ravages reached well into the fifteenth century. In those circumstances, the conflict between desert and sown had been put on hold. While nomads may have raided settled communities from time to time, the abundance of land relative to people presumably left enough room for both groups to coexist without a basic struggle over territory or resources. Contention revived when demographic growth got underway again during the late fifteenth and early sixteenth centuries. Village populations now grew far faster than the nomadic tribes, as settled agriculture invaded pastoral land.[14] Throughout the 1500s, pastoralists had to accept rising restrictions on their movement, or else settle down themselves and join the villages that usurped their traditional pastures.

Squeezed by the expansion of agriculture, some tribes began to strike back, sparking clashes with villagers throughout the late sixteenth century. The province of Baghdad, for example, reported nomadic invasions on several occasions from the 1550s to the 1580s.[15] In the Balkans, Tatars strayed into the settled lands of Hungary.[16] Down in Syria, Bedouin

[14] According to Barkan's calculations, while the settled population of Anatolia grew by at least 60% from the 1520s to the 1570s, the nomadic population grew by only 38%. By 1580, therefore, nomads had fallen to about 16% of the total population on the peninsula and presumably a smaller share of the empire as a whole. See "Essai sur les données statistiques."

[15] E.g., MD 3/235 and MD 48/668.

[16] E.g., MD 6/452 and MD 6/463.

attacked the eastern edge of settlement.[17] Even in the relatively rich lands of Black Sea region, nomads invaded fields during the difficult years of the 1580s.[18] And as we see in the following section, the most intractable conflicts centered on central and eastern Anatolia.

Clearly, some of these tribal incursions were nothing more than opportunistic banditry. The Bedouin, in particular, were frequently blamed for theft and violence.[19] However, the majority of reports indicated that disputes over land and grazing rights lay at the heart of the conflict. Villagers accused nomads of invading farmland, and tribes accused villagers of plowing up their traditional pasture. As another indication of ecological stress, the conflicts turned especially severe in times of drought or famine. During the spring of 1571, for example, the treasurer (*defterdar*) of Aleppo advised that soldiers called away on campaign should stay behind instead for the protection of the province: "Since the rain has not rained this blessed year, the Arabs (i.e., Bedouin) and Türkmen are getting ready to come here at harvest time and there is a likelihood they will plunder."[20] In 1588 the provincial governor of Rakka (northeast Syria) also wrote the sultan to warn that "while there is famine around Aleppo and Damascus, it is certain that Arab bandits will move into Rakka," and he requested additional men to ward off the impending invasion.[21] Finally, in 1591, yet another drought and famine set off alarms around Tripoli (Libya), where officials warned that "there is a chance [the tribes] will start a *celali* movement" (*celali hareket itmek ihtimali olmağın*) – one of the rare uses of this term before the 1600s.[22]

As described in Chapter 1, the imperial government had interests in both settled agriculture and pastoral nomadism for the resources each could offer. Imperial orders tried to strike a delicate balance between the traditional rights of tribes and the prerogatives of settlement expansion. In the spring of 1571, for instance, the sultan issued an order weighing rival claims of *reaya* and tribesmen in Hınıs (near Erzurum).[23] The local *kadı* had written to warn that the nomads were "in rebellion," feeding their flocks on the grain and generally terrorizing the inhabitants.

17 E.g., MD 64/277, MD 30/721; and Ahmet Refik, *Anadolu'da Türk Aşiretleri (966–1200)*, 2nd ed. (Istanbul: Enderun Kitabevi, 1989), document 77.
18 Güçer, *Osmanlı İmparatorluğunda Hububat Meselesi*, 18.
19 E.g., MD 6/544 and MD 48/973.
20 MD 12/499.
21 MD 64/99.
22 MD 69/311–12.
23 MD 10/57.

However, in the same document, we find that the tribal groups in question had also petitioned the sultan claiming, "We have come here from ancient times for pasture, and the places where we wandered were previously empty lands. Now villages have been built." And in fact, according to previous law codes, the tribesmen were probably in the right.[24] The sultan tried to steer a middle path, ordering an investigation into the claims of both sides.

By the 1570s, however, it appears that settled farmers had generally gained the upper hand, pushing aside nomadic tribes in spite of imperial decrees. In 1564, for instance, the sultan had actually expelled *tımar*-holders who had illegally moved into tribal lands in Diyarbakır (eastern Anatolia).[25] Yet only a decade later, we find complaints that nomads in the region had been squeezed out of their traditional summer pastures once again by the renewed expansion of agriculture.[26] At about the same time, Diyarbakır tribes were reported encroaching into settled lands in nearby Bitlis[27] and farther afield in Baghdad,[28] probably due to their loss of land. Furthermore, similar conflicts emerged during these years in nearby Sivas[29] and Zülkadriyye,[30] suggesting that nomads throughout the semiarid steppes were being pushed aside from traditional grazing areas and forced to seek out new pastures.

Admittedly, this evidence runs counter to much of the recent historiography on nomads, which has tried to play down the historical conflict between "desert and sown" and to emphasize peaceful coexistence.[31] On the one hand, it is true that past scholarship all too often presented a paradigm of zero-sum conflict between nomads and settled peoples – a historical trope as old as the medieval writings of Ibn Khaldun, if not older. Scholars are right to be critical of one-sided official histories

[24] Imperial law had previously assigned Hınıs as a legal route for transhumance. See Güçer, *Osmanlı İmparatorluğunda Hububat Meselesi*, 15.

[25] MD 6/645–46.

[26] MD 24/601.

[27] MD 16/320.

[28] MD 48/668.

[29] MD 46/476.

[30] Refik, *Anadolu'da Türk Aşiretleri*, document 55.

[31] See Brian Spooner, "Desert and Sown: A New Look at an Old Relationship," in *Studies in 18th Century Islamic History*, ed. T. Naff and R. Owen (Carbondale: Southern Illinois University Press, 1977); Rhoads Murphey, "Reflections on Ottoman Tribal Policy as Recorded in the Eighteenth Century Law Court Records of Aleppo," in *IX. Türk Tarih Kongresi* (Ankara: TTK, 1981); and Kasaba, *Moveable Empire*, chapter 1, for an overview of the historiography.

and their outraged depictions of rampaging tribes. On the other hand, we cannot overlook the powerful ecological pressures of the period pitting each group against the other. As described in Part I, Ottoman agricultural techniques of the sixteenth century had fallen short of the demands imposed by rapid population growth and imperial provisioning. Although traditional practices might foster a certain coexistence between pastoralists and farmers on the same land, in the end this land was a limited resource and a bone of contention in hard times. Furthermore, the semiarid steppe was not like the desert, where nomads and settled populations occupied separate ecological niches. This was land that could shift to either farming or pastoralism in a tradeoff that was often, if not always, mutually exclusive. Finally, as we have seen, the sixteenth-century state actually tried to pursue an evenhanded policy of balancing claims by villagers and tribes, which makes official reports of destructive nomad invasions that much more credible.

The Invasion

The Celali Rebellion marked a crucial turning point in the balance between desert and sown. Although the nomad invasion did not follow right away, it apparently built up momentum in the years of fighting and disorder. Gaps in the surviving record and a scarcity of Ottomanist research on the tribes have left us without a clear picture of how nomads lived throughout these troubled times. Nevertheless, enough evidence remains to discern a trend of rising conflict and bolder nomad incursions leading up to the real invasion around 1613. Furthermore, the timing of that invasion – coming just on the heels of the Celalis and the great famine of 1607–10 – remains strongly suggestive. The overall impression is that nomadic tribes took advantage of Ottoman weakness to turn the tables on the settled population and retake what they had lost over the past century of settlement.

As explained in previous chapters, the Celali Rebellion that began in the 1590s was not primarily a tribal movement, but rather an uprising of bandits and *sohtas* led by mercenary commanders. However, tribal elements appeared among the bandits from a very early stage, evidently motivated by the same desperation and opportunism as the other rebels. The first such examples, from 1592–3, concern mostly Bedouin raids in the Arab provinces. The regions around Baghdad, Aleppo, and Diyarbakır – already suffering from the growing drought and famine – were probably the worst affected.[32] By 1594, the movement had spread among the Türkmen and Kurdish tribes, as revealed in reports from the east Anatolian districts of Malatya[33] and Kars.[34] In the latter it was reported that "Kurdish and Türkmen tribes and other criminals came and occupied the land [and] pillaged," leaving the *reaya* "scattered" and "many villages and farms empty." Parts of Erzurum met the same fate over the following year,[35] and meanwhile Türkmen tribes joined the Bedouin in their invasion of the province of Aleppo.[36]

By the time the drought and famine peaked in 1596, even more tribes were reported moving onto settled lands. Warnings from the provinces reveal that the nomads were not only drawn by plunder but also pushed by hunger and desperation. In late 1595, the provincial governor of Rakka wrote again to warn the sultan that "this blessed year, while there is famine in this region" the Bedouin tribes were attacking the peasantry and stealing grain.[37] Although the governor requested more men to defend the province, less than a year later we hear of nomads around Rakka "in rebellion" with a force of over a thousand tribal horsemen and foot soldiers, plundering the *reaya* for money and food.[38] Meanwhile, Türkmen further west, in the regions of Karaman and Maraş, were reported rustling the peasants' livestock.[39]

Unfortunately, the gap in surviving imperial orders from 1596 until the early 1600s has left little evidence regarding nomad activities during the following critical years. It would appear that once the drought had passed, nomad movements might have settled down, even amid the chaos of the great Celali campaigns. It may well be the case that the animal plague of those years so decimated nomad flocks that they had no cause to invade new land for pasture. On the other hand, it could equally be the case that with their mobile way of life, the tribes simply tried to avoid the chaos in Ottoman villages. In any event, nomads do not clearly reenter the historical picture until 1610, just after the worst period of starvation and violence.

32 MD 72/62, MD 72/498, and MD 73/165.
33 MD 73/217–18.
34 MD 73/606.
35 MD 74/429.
36 MD 74/511 and Refik, *Anadolu'da Türk Aşiretleri*, documents 110–11.
37 MD 73/1120.
38 MD 74/447.
39 MD 74/428.

That spring, the imperial orders contain several significant mentions of tribal activity. Around Karahisar-ı Şarki, in eastern Anatolia, nomads had invaded villages and started plundering the local *reaya*.[40] The Tatars of the Crimea, driven by famine, had wandered south into the Danube region forcing out farmers.[41] Near Kayseri, some Türkmen bandits had started extorting food and animals from the villagers;[42] and meanwhile, another tribe pillaged the area around Aleppo.[43] More reports of conflict came back to Istanbul that autumn and winter, especially tribal attacks on soldiers returning from the Persian front.[44] However, the real invasion gained momentum in the following two years, during another regrettable gap in the documentary record.

By 1613, it appears, this tide of nomad incursions had turned into a flood which engulfed much of the Ottoman countryside. The scant surviving evidence does not give a clear sense of how or when the movement began, but the few descriptions of events leave an impression of widespread devastation.[45] Across most of east and central Anatolia and northern Syria, nomads abandoned their traditional pastures and moved into new land, destroying villages and chewing up fields as they went. The scale of the movement was summed up in a single order recorded in January of 1614[46] and copied with addenda to numerous provincial governors. The original runs to several pages, but some of the key passages are as follows:

> To the provincial governor of Anadolu and the district governors and *kadıs* in the aforementioned province:
>
> Although [seven tribes] of the Bozulus confederation and the Yadlı and other Kurdish tribes and others have grazed in their summer and winter pastures in Diyarbakır from ancient times and passed through other territories without bothering anyone, now contrary to custom, they graze

[40] MD 79/45.

[41] Güçer, *Osmanlı İmparatorluğunda Hububat Meselesi*, 19.

[42] Refik, *Anadolu'da Türk Aşiretleri*, document 114.

[43] Ibid., document 116.

[44] Ibid., document 115.

[45] The relevant documents come from *Mühimme Defter* 80 (e.g., documents 204, 334, 352, and 391), some of which have been reproduced in Refik, *Anadolu'da Türk Aşiretleri*, documents 121–30. Güçer, *Osmanlı İmparatorluğunda Hububat Meselesi*, chapter 1, provides some additional references.

[46] Note that the surviving copies of these orders are recorded by the date the scribe took the copy, not the date of sending or receipt, but that these dates were typically within a couple months of each other. See the introduction in Heyd, *Ottoman Documents on Palestine*.

in your province. They feed their flocks on the grain the peasants have farmed and chew up the fields [and] it has been reported that they have been tyrannizing the people... The *reaya* lack the strength to endure their tyranny, and that is why they have scattered...

Appendix (*bir sureti*) – To the provincial governor of Karaman and the district governors and *kadıs* of the aforementioned province, let it be written:

The Türkmen of Aleppo and [eleven tribes] of Yeni İl Türkmen used to pasture during the summer in the province of Rum and during the winter around the province of Damascus. Now contrary to custom, they pasture winter and summer in your province. The peasants' [farmed grain they have fed to their animals, and chewed up the fields, and they are tyrannizing them...][47]

Appendix – To the provincial governor of Rum and the district governors and *kadıs* of the aforementioned province:

[Nine groups] from the Bozulus and other Türkmen tribes and others from ancient times pastured during the summer in Rum and when the cold season arrived they found winter pasture in the province of Damascus and they did not harass the peasants. For the last few years contrary to custom they find winter pasture in Rum as well. The peasants'[farmed grain they have fed to their animals, and chewed up the fields, and they are tyrannizing them...]

Appendix – To the provincial governor of Erzurum and the district governors and *kadıs* of the aforementioned province:

While tribes from the Ulus Türkmen and other Türkmen tribes from ancient times pastured winter and summer in the region of [...], now contrary to custom they come to your province for winter and summer pasture. The peasants' farmed grain they have fed to their animals, and chewed up the fields, and they are tyrannizing them...

Appendix – To the *kadı* and governor (*voyvoda*) of Yeni İl:

While the Türkmen tribes used to pasture winter and summer in the region of [...] now for a few years they have come and pastured in the provinces of Anadolu, Karaman, and Rum. They have fed on the crops of the Muslims and other *reaya* and chewed up their fields... [etc.][48]

In other parts of the order, the sultan included strong exhortations to send the nomads back to their accustomed grounds and make them obey orders – all apparently in vain.

47 See the third appendix to this order. It appears the order gave the same description for the destruction of peasants' fields in each case, and the scribe tried to save time by copying it only once.

48 MD 80/259 (also reproduced as Refik, *Anadolu'da Türk Aşiretleri*, document 124).

Other commands sent out that year emphasized the breadth and destruction of the nomad advance. In eastern Karaman for example, where nomads had the traditional right to pass for three days between winter and summer pastures, now two hundred nomad households (*oba*) reportedly plundered the countryside and assaulted the peasants "like Celalis."[49] In another case, Türkmen tribes invaded all the way to Kütahya, in northwest Anatolia, just a short distance from the capital. "Although from ancient times until the present they had never invaded the district and had pastured elsewhere," the order informed, "now they have come to the district and devoured the peasants' fields and crops and they oppress them."[50]

Reports of nomad invasions continued to reach the capital throughout the following years, reaching far across Ottoman lands. In 1615, for example, the governor of Şehrizor (in the Mosul area) reported a new migration of perhaps a dozen tribes who had left their old lands and resettled in the district, refusing imperial orders to return to their traditional homelands.[51] Even the Balkans were affected: Fifteen years later, a "foreign nomad tribe" invaded the lands of Niğbolu, Silistre, Kırkkilise, and Vize in what is now the European part of Turkey. Aside from the usual banditry, there they burned farms, presumably to clear wooded land for pasture.[52] Reports of ongoing nomad invasions also entered local court records over the following decades, such as a report of a Türkmen tribe encroaching on a village near Kayseri in 1645.[53]

Descriptions from travelers both foreign and Ottoman confirm these impressions of widespread incursions and abandoned farms. In some parts where nomads had invaded, particularly in east and central Anatolia, settled life had supposedly all but vanished. As early as the 1610s, when the Armenian traveler Simeon of Poland passed through the once cultivated region along the Kızılırmak between Kayseri and Ankara, he described it as inhabited entirely by nomad Türkmen and their flocks of fat-tailed sheep.[54] The famous Ottoman wanderer Evliya Çelebi made a similar observation about the region around Konya and Maraş a

49 Refik, *Anadolu'da Türk Aşiretleri*, document 127.
50 Ibid., document 123.
51 MD 81/317.
52 MD 85/363.
53 Sefure Deveci, "55/2 Numaralı Kayseri Şer'iyye Sicili (H.1055/M.1645) Transkripsiyon ve Değerlendirme" (PhD diss., Erciyes Üniversitesi, 2002), document 120 n.321.
54 *Polonyalı Simeon'un Seyahatnamesi*, 162.

generation later.[55] Over the following two centuries, observers passing through Anatolian lands in particular would continue to blame the nomads and their flocks and fires – whether fairly or not – for the apparent desolation and thin population of the countryside.[56]

Subsequent work by historical geographers has broadly confirmed these impressions. Unfortunately, the Ottoman system of cadastral surveys fell into disuse during these years of crisis, leaving Ottomanists without a definite picture of settlement changes. Nevertheless, studies relying on field work and extrapolating backward from nineteenth-century data have produced some fairly convincing results. From records of tribal names and toponyms, it would appear that Anatolia's tribes witnessed a major reshuffling in these years, with many groups migrating hundreds of miles from their previous homelands.[57] Furthermore, there are strong indications of widespread settlement desertion across the semi-arid regions where population growth had been most rapid the century before. To judge by the work of W. Hütteroth and his collaborators,[58] south-central Anatolia and the region at the border between today's Turkey, Syria, and Iraq were perhaps the worst affected. Palestine also suffered some serious reversals, particularly along its eastern edge of settlement.[59] By the 1830s, nomads and seminomads may have outnumbered peasants around Basra and Aleppo.[60] Agriculture underwent a serious retreat, and most of the land was not put back under the plow until the late 1800s. More than a century of settlement expansion came undone in the space of a generation.

The nomads themselves left no written records of their motives, and the official reports never concerned themselves with why the invasion had spread so far and so fast. Given the obscure place of nomads in the historiography, no modern Ottomanist has seriously considered the issue either. Therefore, we can only venture theories as to what drove such a large and sudden movement of peoples. From the evidence at hand, there appear to be three possible explanations.

55 *Seyahatname*, vol. 3, 102–4.

56 Planhol, "Les nomades, la steppe, et la foret en Anatolie."

57 Planhol, *Fondements géographiques*, 235–43. The original work on this subject comes from the research of Faruk Sümer.

58 For a summary, see Hütteroth, "Ecology of Ottoman Lands."

59 See also Lewis, *Nomads and Settlers*, 15–23.

60 Kasaba, *Moveable Empire*, 86 and 116, claims there were up to ten tribesmen for each villager in the latter.

This chapter has already raised the first and most likely possibility, namely that nomads smarting under Ottoman restrictions saw a chance to retake lost land during the crisis. As previously described, friction between nomadic tribes and settled communities had been building up for decades alongside the rise of population and the expansion of agriculture. When the empire was at its weakest, just in the wake of the Celali Rebellion and the famine of 1607–10, then various nomadic tribes may have decided to take advantage of the situation and push into settled land. As discussed in Chapter 7, widespread flight and mortality had begun as early as the 1590s, and the tribes may have been drawn into the vacuum. The army was also weak and demoralized after two unsuccessful wars on the Hungarian and Persian fronts; and tribal raids on returning soldiers highlight the willingness of nomads to capitalize on the crisis.

Second, climate fluctuations of the Little Ice Age may have forced the tribes to abandon traditional grazing lands and strike out into new territory. Climatologists and historians have discerned correlations among cold, drought, and nomadic movements in early modern China;[61] and it would make sense to find similar patterns in Ottoman lands. This chapter has already illustrated how droughts of the late sixteenth century sometimes drove pastoralists to invade settled lands for food and pasture. More serious droughts from the 1590s to the 1610s may have compelled them to shift their transhumance patterns altogether. Tree rings in southern Jordan have recorded a period of severe recurring drought from 1608 to 1621 – probably one of the region's worst dry spells in the past 400 years.[62] Quite possibly, extreme conditions in Arab lands forced some tribes west and north from the desert margins, setting off a chain reaction of migration.[63] Likewise, tree rings from southern Anatolia have recorded a sharp drought from 1612 to 1613,[64] which may have prompted movements into central and western Turkey at the time of the invasion. However, a comparable series of tree rings from northern

[61] E.g., Jin-Qi Fang and Guo Liu, "Relationship between Climatic Change and the Nomadic Southward Migrations in Eastern Asia during Historical Times," *Climatic Change* 22 (1992): 151–69.

[62] Touchan et al., "396-Year Reconstruction."

[63] Lewis, *Settlers and Nomads*, 3–8, has also suggested that the migrations of the period may have been climate induced, inferring from analogous instances in the eighteenth and nineteenth centuries.

[64] Touchan et al., "Preliminary Reconstructions."

Jordan shows less evidence for such droughts, which may cast this theory in some doubt.[65]

Third, tribes may have been driven west by developments in Persia. Under the reign of Shah Abbas (r.1588–1629), the Safavids embarked on a period of imperial expansion and centralization. Faced with threats on both his western and eastern frontiers, Abbas sought to strengthen his borders through a program of forced migrations, relocating tribes from the peripheries closer to the new imperial capital Isfahan.[66] Although the bulk of his transfers came from the Caucasus, the shah also relocated a number of Kurdish tribes from the Zagros Mountains. Furthermore, he directed a "systematic and savage depopulation"[67] of Azerbaijan during his scorched earth defense against Ottoman campaigns in the 1600s, even massacring a Kurdish tribe on the Ottoman frontier in 1610. It remains a strong possibility, therefore, that Safavid actions sparked a wave of flight among nomads in the border regions. If so, a chain reaction may have followed as one tribe pushed out another until Anatolian Türkmen and Syrian Bedouin poured west into settled Ottoman land. Unfortunately, no one has yet found direct evidence tying together developments on either side of the Persian-Ottoman frontier. Nevertheless, the timing between the massacres and nomad movements would match well, and the link would seem to offer a sensible explanation for the outbreak of the invasion.

None of these three theories is mutually exclusive of the others. On the contrary, it is likely a conjuncture of environmental and political factors that drove the tribal invasion of the 1610s. Similar to the outbreak of the Celali Rebellion, ecological pressures that had built up for decades burst apart just as the empire stumbled upon climatic disaster and the stress of war. Once again, both human and natural forces conspired to precipitate a major crisis.

Resettlement Efforts – Promise and Failure

Although it took generations for the empire to adjust and recover from these years of foreign and civil war, officials in Istanbul did not just stand

65 Touchan and Hughes, "Dendrochronology in Jordan."

66 John Perry, "Forced Migration in Iran during the Seventeenth and Eighteenth Centuries," *Iranian Studies* 8 (1975): 199–215. My thanks to Owen Miller for alerting me to this evidence.

67 Ibid., 206–7.

by idly as tribes overran large stretches of the empire. During the late 1600s, under the leadership of the Köprülü grand viziers, the state formulated ambitious programs for tribal control and resettlement surpassing in scale and sophistication even the work of the classical age. Fortunately for Ottomanists, these efforts left extensive documentation, which has been analyzed in a pair of Turkish monographs.[68] From these, we can gather a sense of why – despite some palpable successes – the Ottomans ultimately fell short in their ambitions to restore settled agriculture to the semiarid lands. As in the chain of events leading up to the invasion, the answer lies in both policy failures and accidents of climate.

Ottoman resettlement efforts offered nomads both sticks and carrots to encourage their transition from mobile pastoralism to sedentary farming. On the one hand, the policy was basically coercive. Tribes selected for settlement were forced to move onto allotted lands and abandon their nomadic way of life. Although they did not have to give up their flocks, the nomads had to sacrifice their traditional transhumance and designate certain shepherds to guide their animals while the rest of the population took up agriculture.[69] To secure compliance, the imperial government posted soldiers and took hostages from the tribes and meted out punishments for groups who tried to resist. On the other hand, the state also offered generous incentives to encourage voluntary compliance and foster the new colonies. Settling nomads received free land and sometimes horses, and what is more, a blanket exemption from extraordinary taxation. Istanbul also sent out soldiers to guard the new colonies against bandits and other tribes and appointed officials to oversee various aspects of the settlement effort, in some instances even experts to develop irrigation.

The resettlement efforts targeted primarily the regions from northern and eastern Syria through east and central Anatolia. The largest enterprise of all concerned the region of Rakka, already mentioned several times as one of the worst areas of conflict between nomads and settled

[68] Orhonlu, *Osmanlı İmparatorluğunda Aşiretleri İskân Teşebbüsü* and Yusuf Halaçoğlu, *XVIII. Yüzyılda Osmanlı İmparatorluğu'nun İskân Siyaseti ve Aşiretlerin Yerleştirilmesi* (Ankara: TTK, 1988). See also Stephan Winter, "Osmanische Sozialdisziplinierung am Bespeil der Nommadenstämme Nordsyriens im 17.–18. Jahrhundert," *Periplus* 13 (2003): 51–70; Stefan Winter, *The Shiites of Lebanon under Ottoman Rule, 1516–1788* (New York: Cambridge University Press, 2010), 112–14; and Kasaba, *Moveable Empire*, 66–79, for further descriptions and evaluations of the resettlement effort.

[69] This particular practice is described in Murphey, "Reflections on Ottoman Tribal Policy." The other details may be found in the two Turkish monographs already mentioned.

communities. Despite some earlier efforts, the first great settlement initiative did not get underway until about 1690. At that point, we find a considerable series of orders sent out to officials in Anatolia and Syria outlining some of the tribes and regions to be resettled.[70]

It would be an exaggeration to say that the policy failed completely. From the tribal names of some villages in Syria and Anatolia today, we may gather that quite a few groups really did settle down during the seventeenth and eighteenth centuries.[71] Nevertheless, the overall resettlement scheme fell far short of its intended effects. Most of the targeted tribes fled or rebelled after just a few years or decades in the new colonies. Many went back to their traditional ways of life at the first opportunity; and many others, although committed to agriculture, found the conditions of settlement impossible in the prevailing insecurity. As already described, most settled land that had been deserted in the seventeenth-century crisis remained largely uncultivated until well into the 1800s.

The reasons for the failure were several. To begin with, the whole policy was simply too ambitious. Rather than choose the most simple and manageable path to resettlement, the state tried to pursue three goals at once. First, the colonies were supposed to turn nomads into farmers; second, they had to reclaim abandoned territory in the east, often land at the margins of viable agriculture; and third, by virtue of location, the settlements had to serve as a buffer against the incursion of less tractable tribes to the east, and so protect the better agricultural lands to the west.[72] Had the plan worked as intended, the resettlement effort could have killed three birds with one stone and greatly hastened the repopulation of the empire. Instead, the results were often predictably disastrous. As inexperienced farmers, the tribes had trouble working the dry land and complained of chronic famine. Worse still, the new colonists had to contend with more aggressive tribes who raided from the mountains and desert, while guards posted to defend the new settlements often proved inadequate. In eastern Syria, above all, many colonists began to flee just a few years into settlement, terrorized by invading Bedouin.[73]

Furthermore, from a climatological point of view, the Ottomans picked one of the worst times to promote agriculture in semiarid lands. From 1664 to 1680, as officials planned the settlement initiative, south

[70] Refik, *Anadolu'da Türk Aşiretleri*, documents 141–9 *et passim*.

[71] Orhonlu, *Osmanlı İmparatorluğunda Aşiretleri İskân Teşebbüsü*, 34.

[72] Ibid., chapter 3, part A.

[73] Ibid., 88–91.

Jordanian tree ring sequences recorded the longest run of years without a drought over the past four centuries.[74] If this weather pattern generally held throughout eastern Palestine and Syria, as we might expect, then officials may have been lured into a false sense of optimism about the prospects for agriculture there. Unfortunately, by the time the settlement actually got underway, the picture had reversed completely. For the decade from 1688 to 1698, during the Late Maunder Minimum, tree ring data in both northern and southern Jordan reveal perhaps the second worst period of recurring drought in 400 years.[75] Thesse data give added emphasis to the settlers' complaints of crop failures and famine.[76] Considering the fragile nature of farming in the region, this accident of climate may well have proven the deciding factor in an already precarious enterprise that had promised to change the course of empire.

Finally, there remains a more general reason why the whole resettlement project may have been destined for failure. In Chapter 1, we saw how Ottoman settlement initiatives of the classical age had worked from the bottom up as well as the top down. The state enacted policies to direct population movements and overcome obstacles to colonization, but this planning from above still relied on initiative from below. Rulers did not create growth from scratch but guided the momentum of demographic expansion already present on the ground. In the 1600s, however, the momentum had been lost, perhaps even reversed. In place of that virtuous cycle of growth, Ottoman lands entered a downward spiral of contraction. Under these altered ecological circumstances, imperial policies could only accomplish so much.

The fate of subsequent initiatives during the eighteenth century illustrates this point more clearly. By that time, the worst decades of insecurity and Little Ice Age climate events had passed, and Ottoman officials took up comprehensive resettlement schemes once more, even reenacting the construction of large *derbends*.[77] Nevertheless, in spite of some modest successes, most settlement initiatives still failed to meet their goals. Newly settled pastoralists often fell victim to other more aggressive tribes, or else took the first opportunity to return to their old way of life. And even where the new colonies did take hold, they still failed to attract

74 Touchan et al., "396-Year Reconstruction."

75 Ibid. and Touchan and Hughes, "Dendrochronology in Jordan."

76 Orhonlu, *Osmanlı İmparatorluğunda Aşiretleri İskân Teşebbüsü*, 89–90.

77 These initiatives are discussed throughout Halaçoğlu, *XVIII. Yüzyılda Osmanlı İmparatorluğu'nun İskân Siyaseti*.

surrounding agricultural settlements as during the decades of rapid growth in the sixteenth century. For the Ottomans, the problem of nomad resettlement remained unresolved until the imposition of modern armies and the resumption of population growth in the later 1800s.

These failures and their consequences prove all the more striking when placed in global perspective. Over these same decades, the Ottomans' emerging adversary Russia began its long struggle to conquer the Siberian steppes, pushing aside nomadic tribes and opening vast new lands to hunting, logging, and agriculture.[78] Along their southern frontier as well, the Russians and Habsburgs successfully used military and ex-soldier colonies to hold the steppeland, in sharp contrast to the detrimental effects of an increasingly unruly Ottoman army on the other side of the border.[79] At the same time, Qing China finally put an end to the age-old problem of nomad incursions, defeating and forcibly settling Turkic and Mongol tribes on its western frontiers.[80] While other early modern empires resumed the process of colonization, conquest, and frontier expansion after the hiatus of the "general crisis," the Ottomans struggled just to regain what had already been lost.

Conclusion: The Sheep's Revenge?

If we could stand back in space and view the Ottoman expansion and crisis in fast motion, a striking spectacle would pass before our eyes. Three players would move about the Near Eastern landscape: the grass, the sheep, and the humans. In the opening frames, vast flocks would graze green grass up and down the plains, while the humans huddled about the margins – the coasts, hills, and caravan towns. Gradually the green grass would cede to brown cereals (just a more delicate and nutritious grass, after all) as humans spread from the margins back across the plains. Meanwhile, the sheep would be pushed out of the best valleys and retreat up the hills and mountains and into the more arid land, as farming edged out nomadic pastoralism. Then, in a flash, the sheep would be decimated by the great epizootics of the 1590s, and shortly afterward, swathes of humans would disappear in the chaos of the Little

78 See Willard Sunderland, *Taming the Wild Steppe: Colonization and Empire on the Russian Steppe* (Ithaca, NY: Cornell University Press, 2004) and Carol Stevens, *Russia's Wars of Emergence* (New York: Pearson Longman, 2007).

79 Virginia Aksan, "Locating the Ottomans among Early Modern Empires," *Journal of Early Modern History* 3 (1999): 103–35.

80 Perdue, *China Marches West.*

Ice Age crisis. Yet in the next instant, the sheep would pour back into the plains from the margins, and the cereals give way to green grass again as pastoralism displaced agriculture once more.

From this Olympian perspective, the conflict between desert and sown would appear not as a clash between settled villagers and nomads, but between humans and sheep. And in this contest, it appears the sheep ultimately held the upper hand. Ironically, the die-off of livestock paved the way for their eventual triumph. In the crisis that followed, the human ecology of agriculture proved the more fragile. After all, the region grows grass, and the ruminants could feed on the hardier natural vegetation – not the fragile yield of cereals. Worse still, the humans fell out among each other in the wake of the disaster, killing as many of their own perhaps as did the famine. The sheep, on the other hand, grazed on and recovered their numbers. Time was on their side: In the roughly fifteen years between the epizootic and the invasion, five sheep generations could have already passed.[81] It would take at least as many human generations for people to reach the same sort of recovery, and in the meantime it was the humans' turn to be pushed out of the semiarid plains and crowded onto the margins once again.

[81] For recovery times of early modern sheep herds, see Marino, *Pastoral Economics*, 57.

10

CITY AND COUNTRY

The next major long-term shift in the human ecology of Ottoman lands was the mass movement of rural populations into towns and cities. As bandits and nomadic tribes invaded the countryside during the Little Ice Age crisis, the inhabitants were, to use the Ottoman phrasing, "scattered" (*perakende*). Some took to the hills and some migrated to more distant provinces or foreign lands in search of safety. Others still, probably millions, perished in the famine and violence. Yet over the long run the greatest number migrated to urban centers in search of food and safety. Even as so much settlement in the countryside lay abandoned, populations in the major cities – and above all in Istanbul – continued to rise, in a movement that continued well after the worst of the Little Ice Age crisis had passed.

This population shift presented the empire with grave problems. Urban administration was ill-equipped to deal with a refugee crisis. Economic turmoil left many or most of the newcomers unemployed and dependent on the charity of religious foundations, which were themselves already suffering from lost revenue. The imbalance of rural and urban inhabitants exacerbated difficulties of provisioning. Rudimentary sanitation and poor municipal water supplies proved a recipe for endemic and epidemic disease. Consequently, like most premodern urban centers, Ottoman towns and cities were population sinks with mortality likely well in excess of birth rates. Until the mid-nineteenth century, when urban populations finally began to hold their own, this migration from country to city constituted a considerable drain on Ottoman resources and demography.

There has been some debate over this "urban graveyard" effect among historical demographers of early modern Europe, as several studies have shown examples of towns with higher birth rates and lower death rates than once thought possible.[1] Nevertheless, these studies do not detract from, but rather emphasize the gravity of the situation in Ottoman lands. The factors found to raise fertility or reduce mortality – such as clean water, sanitation, and economic growth – were wanting in Ottoman towns and cities. Instead urban areas such as Istanbul had the ingredients for a demographic disaster: crowding, disorder, garbage, disease, and streams of destitute rural migrants. While not all cities were equally troubled, living conditions in the seventeenth and eighteenth centuries remained poor on the whole. Many of the empire's urban problems predated the crisis, but the Little Ice Age gravely exacerbated an already difficult situation for Ottoman towns and cities.

Urban Growth before the Crisis

The issue of urban overcrowding in the Ottoman Empire emerged in the mid- to late 1500s. Previous Ottoman rulers had faced just the opposite problem. To take only the best-known example, when Mehmed the Conqueror captured Constantinople in 1453 he found it so empty of people that he had to offer subsidies and tax exemptions to anyone willing to reside in the new capital. As recurring epidemics wiped out the new settlers, the sultan resorted to forced population transfers from the Balkans. Only in the early sixteenth century, after several more decades of immigration, did the city grow into a metropolis befitting the center of a world empire.[2]

Subsequently, urban populations throughout Ottoman lands began to rise quickly, buoyed by the general demographic surge. Curiously, our figures from Istanbul itself are some of the least comprehensive, because the capital was excluded from the usual cadastral surveys. However, we do know that the city's tax records already included some 80,000 male taxpayers in the 1520s, reaching 104,000 around mid-century.[3] The other

[1] This notion, first discovered in seventeenth-century London by John Graunt, was a traditional mainstay of historical demography. Challenges to the thesis emerged in some work of the Cambridge School of demographic historians and spurred debates and revisions from the late 1970s to the early 1990s. See Allan Sharlin, "Natural Decrease in Early Modern Cities: A Reconsideration," *Past and Present* 79 (1978): 126–38; Roger Finlay, "Natural Decrease in Early Modern Cities," *Past and Present* 92 (1981): 169–74; Jan de Vries, *European Urbanization 1500–1800* (Cambridge, MA: Harvard University Press, 1984), 179–98; and Chris Galley, "A Model of Early Modern Urban Demography," *The Economic History Review* 48 (1995): 448–69.

[2] Lowry, "Pushing the Stone Uphill."

[3] Mantran, *Istanbul*, 44–7.

Table 10.1. *Sixteenth-Century Urban Populations*

	City	Population 1520s–1530s	Population 1570s–1580s
Balkans	Athens	12,633	17,616
	Edirne	22,335	30,140
	Monastir	4,647	5,918
	Sarajevo	5,632	23,485
	Skopje	4,631	9,867
	Sofia	3,899	7,848
Anatolia	Ankara	14,872	29,007
	Bursa	34,930	70,686
	Hamid	18,942	31,443
	Konya	6,127	15,356
	Sivas	5,560	16,846
	Tokat	8,354	13,282
Syria	Aleppo	56,881	45,331
	Damascus	57,326	42,779 (1595)

major cities of the empire – though far smaller to begin with – recorded equally rapid growth throughout the 1500s. Once again, Barkan's calculations based on the Ottoman *tahrirs* offer some useful indications:[4]

Although the figures in Table 10.1 may be misleadingly precise, there is no reason to doubt the general impression of growth, at least outside of Syria. Subsequent studies of local records have confirmed the overall accuracy of Barkan's numbers;[5] and even if his estimates of household size or the numbers of the unregistered are sometimes debatable, they do not call into the question the proportional changes from one assessment to the next. Furthermore, the figures are more or less what we would expect given the overall rate of growth in the empire, as described in Chapter 2. Both sets of numbers roughly doubled in the span of a century as the empire settled and expanded. Research on Anatolian tax records has also uncovered similar rates of growth in smaller market towns throughout the peninsula.[6]

4 See Chapter 2 for an explanation of Barkan's demographic statistics.

5 E.g., Ergenç Özer, *XVI. Yüzyılın Sonlarında Bursa* (Ankara: TTK, 2006) and Jean-Paul Pascual, *Damas à la fin du XVIe siècle* (Damascus: Institut franc¸ais de Damas, 1983). See Yunus Koç, "Osmanlı'da Kent İskânı ve Demografisi (XV.–XVIII. Yüzyıllar)," *Türkiye Araştırmaları Literatür Dergisi* 6 (2005): 161–210 for a comprehensive bibliography on urban demography.

6 The extensive work of Suraiya Faroqhi has been particularly useful in this regard – see "Taxation and Urban Activities," "Urban Development in Ottoman Anatolia," "Towns, Agriculture and the State," and *Towns and Townsmen.*

For much of the sixteenth century, the rise of Ottoman towns and cities probably represented a natural outgrowth of rural prosperity. Although work on the Balkans in this period has lagged somewhat behind, recent studies of Anatolian towns offer a detailed picture of economic activity during the 1500s.[7] Rising receipts from tax farms, customs, and agriculture all point to solid growth early in the century. Furthermore, the imperial government remained relatively permissive when it came to migration from the provincial hinterlands to the expanding market towns.[8] Perhaps as late as the 1550s or even the 1560s, "pull" rather than "push" factors still drove most rural to urban migration. Even where peasant life had not run up against Malthusian limits, towns and cities offered better economic opportunities than villages. Handicrafts such as leatherworking, silk-making, and wool and cotton textiles all grew up to meet burgeoning demand. Meanwhile, immigrants came over from the newly conquered populations in the Balkans and the Arab world.

Nevertheless, sometime before the second round of cadastral surveys in the 1570s and 1580s urban economic growth had fallen well behind population. As one study has concluded, at least in Anatolia urban demographic growth "was all too often not accompanied by a corresponding growth in commercial possibilities: If such opportunities had been greater, we would expect to find a clearer record of them in the tax registers."[9] Push factors replaced pull factors, driving peasants off their farms and into towns and cities. Even as economic prospects dimmed, the rising tide of landlessness, famine, and banditry in the countryside kept up the stream of migrants.

Even without the promise of employment or social mobility, towns and cities still offered certain advantages. To begin with, they were relatively safe. Although not without ordinary crime, most were fortified against raids by bandits and *sohtas.* Moreover, urban centers – particularly Bursa, Edirne, and the capital – received a higher priority in the chain of provisioning, as discussed in Chapter 1. Although costs may have been higher than in the villages, these elevated prices also helped guarantee bigger markets and more consistent supplies in times of scarcity.

Finally, major towns and cities housed the empire's charitable institutions. Although the Ottomans, like other early modern empires, made

7 E.g., Suraiya Faroqhi, "Sixteenth Century Periodic Markets in Various Anatolian "Sancaks": İçel, Hamid, Karahisar-ı Sahib, Kütahya, Aydin, and Menteşe," *Journal of the Economic and Social History of the Orient* 22 (1979): 32–80.

8 See Faroqhi, "Towns, Agriculture and the State."

9 Faroqhi, "Taxation and Urban Activities," 37.

little attempt at a welfare state, major pious endowments located in important urban centers provided many public services. Their capabilities were limited compared to the needs of a vast empire, but their resources were considerable nonetheless. They typically offered baths, fountains, and shelters. Most important of all, from the point of a view of a desperate peasantry, were no doubt the great soup kitchens usually attached to the imarets of major mosques and shrines. By the mid-sixteenth century, a soup kitchen endowed by the wife of Sultan Süleyman fed 400 of the poor each day in Jerusalem, and the Fatih and Süleymaniye imarets in Istanbul each served some 3,000 free meals daily – and these were only a few of many such institutions throughout the empire.[10]

Over the late sixteenth century, the state grew increasingly uneasy about the rising tide of immigrants. Part of this concern stemmed from growing problems of unemployment and crime in major cities. Landless migrants were often singled out in official reports of drinking, gambling, prostitution, and other offenses, particularly in Istanbul. Furthermore, the numbers of unemployed villagers reaching urban centers threatened to undermine the viability of Ottoman administration and provisioning. As rural populations drifted in, it became more and more difficult to keep the urban masses registered and regulated. As farmers abandoned their fields for the city, they threatened to upset the balance between rural production and urban provisioning.

In response, Ottoman authorities began to take stronger measures to control their restless subjects. As early as 1567, the sultan wrote the *kadı* of the imperial domains (*hassalar kadısı*) to warn that:

> Some *reaya* from the Balkans and Anatolia have left their farms and have each made their way to the region of Istanbul. They have settled along the waterfront, some in Istanbul and some in Eyüp and others in Kasımpaşa. Their lands remain empty; and not only is this bad for the *sipahis* or state lands, but it is also creating shortages in the provisions of the old inhabitants of [Istanbul].[11]

And so in the same dispatch, the sultan promulgated perhaps the first major order to control migration to the capital:

[10] See Amy Singer, "Serving up Charity: The Ottoman Public Kitchen," *Journal of Interdisciplinary History* 35 (2005): 481–500 and Oded Peri, "Waqf and Ottoman Welfare Policy: The Poor Kitchen of Hasseki Sultan in Eighteenth-Century Jerusalem," *Journal of the Economic and Social History of the Orient* 35 (1992): 167–86.

[11] Refik, *Onaltıncı Asırda İstanbul Hayatı*, chapter 10, document 5.

> Upon receipt, see to the matter personally. Inspect the neighborhoods along the waterfront in your district in Kasımpaşa and as far as Fener and report back. Make an account of houses, endowments, properties, and inhabitants and where they came from in every neighborhood. As for anyone who has come from the Balkans or Anatolia and settled in the past five years, whether he owns property or not, make an account of where he came from, when he came, and what kind of man he is. And from now on, warn the imam and the muezzin and the steward (*kethüda*) of every neighborhood that from this day forth they are not to let these outsiders settle on the waterfront. Inspect those who are criminals or who do not have a guarantor (*kefil*) and... prosecute them. Seal your account of those who have come in the last five years and send it on.

Yet given the geography of the expansive capital, the order proved unenforceable. Even if the walled city could hold its own, the sprawling suburbs along the Bosphorus and down the Asian shore escaped official control. Less than a year after the original command, for example, the sultan wrote again to complain of a growing band of aggressive Arab beggars who terrorized Istanbul's citizens and spread disease. Having been expelled just months earlier, they had already found their way back into the city.[12] Furthermore, the problems of Istanbul were only the most extreme case of an empire-wide phenomenon. As in many modern Middle East countries, perhaps the only way to prevent migration would have been to expand economic opportunities in the countryside. But far from improving, the situation in the provinces was about to get much worse.

The Flight to the Cities

In the 1590s and 1600s, the Great Drought and the Celali Rebellion unleashed a deluge of rural migrants to urban centers. Particularly in Anatolia, fortified towns and cities found themselves flooded with peasants fleeing starvation and violence.[13] While most came in search of temporary shelter, many ended up staying, compelled by the deteriorating situation in the countryside. The nomadic invasions and recurring famines and uprisings of the 1600s brought millions more, swelling urban populations even while much of the countryside lay abandoned.

Official records suggest that at first most of the refugees came from the immediate hinterland to protected urban areas in neighboring regions.

[12] Ibid., chapter 10, document 4.

[13] See Faroqhi, *Towns and Townsmen*, 272–5, and Akdağ, "Celâli İsyanlarından Büyük Kaçgunluk."

Tokat reported villagers fleeing to Erzurum,[14] for instance, and Kayseri reported immigration from surrounding villages.[15] Then over the following years, as conditions failed to improve, more and more peasants began the long trek to major cities in western Anatolia and beyond.[16] Seventeenth-century court records from Bursa, for example, mentioned refugees from the Celali Rebellion coming all the way from Karaman.[17] The movement may have been most pronounced among minority diaspora communities. The Armenian traveler Simeon of Poland, arriving in Istanbul in 1608, observed of his co-religionists that, "the native Armenians of Istanbul consist of scarcely 80 households. However, the number who have come to Istanbul, Galata, and Üsküdar from outside the city living as migrants surpasses 40,000 households. Since the Celalis have laid waste to the other shore, the people have entirely taken refuge in Istanbul."[18] Even as far away as Cairo he found "more than 200 Armenian families who had taken refuge on account of the Celalis."[19] Tens of thousands more Christians fled to towns and cities of the Balkans during these decades, some driven out by the rebellion and others by the Perso-Ottoman war of the same years.[20]

Although we lack comprehensive cadastral surveys for the seventeenth century, various local studies give an impression of rapid urban growth. Some smaller towns lost their inhabitants, but the larger cities tended to grow even as populations in their hinterlands shrank. Konya, for instance, which had held just over 15,000 residents in the late 1500s, had grown to about 20,000 by the mid-seventeenth century, fueled by flight from the countryside.[21] Tokat and Manisa also rose from about 13,000 to 21,000[22]

[14] MAD 1294/15615.

[15] Suraiya Faroqhi, *Men of Modest Substance* (New York: Cambridge University Press, 1987), 46.

[16] Akdağ, *Celâlî İsyanları*, 253, cites examples of people from Sivas, Maraş, and Karahisar-ı Şarki fleeing as far as Gurcistan, and people from Bozok and Amasya fleeing to Ankara and Kırşehir.

[17] Haim Gerber, *Economy and Society in an Ottoman City: Bursa 1600–1700* (Jerusalem: Hebrew University Press, 1988), 13.

[18] *Polonyalı Simeon'un Seyahatnamesi*, 4.

[19] Ibid., 106.

[20] Faroqhi, *Towns and Townsmen*, 275–8.

[21] Hüseyin Muşmal, "XVII. Yüzyılın İlk Yarısında Konya'da Sosyal ve Ekonomik Hayat (1640–50)" (PhD diss., Selçuk Üniversitesi, 2000), 66–8, and Yusuf Oğuzoğlu, "17. Yüzyılda Konya Şehrindeki İdari ve Sosyal Yapılar," in *Konya*, ed. F. Halıcı (Ankara: Konya Kültür ve Turizm Derneği 1984).

[22] Barkan, "Research on the Ottoman Fiscal Surveys."

and from 8,000 to 18,000 inhabitants,[23] respectively. Ankara, which protected refugees in its citadel during Celali attacks, continued to expand in the decades of crisis, growing from roughly 5,344 to 6,066 households between the 1570s the mid-1600s,[24] and from 85 to 91 neighborhoods (*mahalles*) over the course of the seventeenth century.[25] Bursa had lost a great deal of population in the Celali attacks of the early 1600s, but it then more than doubled its inhabitants from 1630 to 1670.[26] İzmir mushroomed from a mere village of about 3,000 in the 1570s to a major port of perhaps 90,000 by the late seventeenth century.[27]

However, these figures pale in comparison with the growth of Istanbul and the major Arab cities. The capital's 104,000 male taxpayers in the mid-1500s had given it a total of perhaps half a million, assuming some under-registration and a number of tax-exempt elite families. The next available figure comes from the *cizye* (non-Muslim head tax) of 1642, which recorded some 62,000 non-Muslim households. If the proportion of non-Muslims to total population in Istanbul remained around 42 percent, as it had been in 1550, then the overall population of the city would have risen to some 600,000 or more a century later. Taking into account the city's expanding periphery, where so many of the new migrants settled, the whole urban area may have reached 700,000 or even 800,000[28] – far and away the biggest city in Europe and easily among the largest in the world. Meanwhile, according to the research of André Raymond, almost all the major Arab cities of the Ottoman world grew significantly in size and population as well. Aleppo rose from 9,583 households in 1537 to 13,854 households (about 70,000 people)

[23] Behar, *Osmanlı İmparatorluğu'nun ve Türkiye'nin Nüfusu*, 16.

[24] Faroqhi, *Men of Modest Substance*, 32–3 (citing Evliya Çelebi).

[25] Hülya Taş, *XVIII. Yüzyılda Ankara* (Ankara: TTK, 2006), 111.

[26] Gerber, *Economy and Society in an Ottoman City*, chapter 1.

[27] Faroqhi, *Towns and Townsmen*, 120. Another traveler estimated that the population had reached about 80,000 by the time of the plague of 1679: See Cornelis de Bruyn, *A Voyage to the Levant: Or, Travels in the Principal Parts of Asia Minor, the Islands of Scio, Rhodes, Cyprus, &c.* (London: 1702).

[28] Robert Mantran, *Histoire d'Istanbul* (Paris: Maisonneuve, 1996), 253–4, and Mantran, *Istanbul*, 44–7. Confirming this figure, Lütfi Güçer calculated that the grain deliveries to Istanbul reached over six and a half million *kiles* (perhaps 237,000 tons) in 1758, or easily enough to supply 700,000–800,000 people and a number of animals: See "XVIII. Yüzıl Ortalarında İstanbul'un İasesi İçin Lüzumlu Hububatın Temini Meselesi," *İstanbul Üniversitesi İktisat Fakültesi Mecmuası* 11 (1949–1950): 397–416. The Venetian secretary in Istanbul in the 1630s, Angelo Alessandri, also calculated the city and its periphery at 800,000 inhabitants (in Pedani-Fabris, *Relazioni*, 672), as did the ambassador Pietro Civrano in 1682 (in Firpo, *Relazioni*, 1054).

in 1683, before reaching a peak of perhaps 130,000 inhabitants in the eighteenth century.[29] Meanwhile, Damascus, once thought to have declined, actually expanded in area by some 40 percent to 50 percent.[30] Cairo, which had about 150,000 to 200,000 inhabitants at the time of the Ottoman conquest in 1517, may have grown by half as much again by the late eighteenth century.[31] Taken together, the growth of these cities meant a major shift in Ottoman demography, leading the Venetian ambassador Pietro Civrano in 1682 to remark, "The population does not correspond to the size of the provinces; and there are more men who have withdrawn into the cities than inhabit the countryside."[32]

As Civrano's comment suggests, what makes this shift so remarkable is not just the rate of urban growth but the fact that it took place at a time when overall population was falling (see Chapter 8). Presented with such a paradox, some historians have been inclined to doubt the whole phenomenon of either urban expansion or rural contraction. Nevertheless, there are strong parallels for this development in southern Italy, for example, which also suffered climatic and political disasters in this period. In the Papal States, the city of Rome grew abruptly from about 80,000 to 100,000 during the 1590s, swelling to about 120,000 by 1656. As with Istanbul, this growth in population did not reflect demographic or economic development in the realm so much as the attraction of urban provisioning and security at a time of crisis. Over the same period in the Kingdom of Naples, the disparity was even more drastic: After doubling over the course of the sixteenth century, the inhabitants of the kingdom peaked at around 540,000 households in 1595, before falling to around 500,000 over the following generation. The city of Naples itself, on the other hand, ballooned from about 210,000 people in a count of 1547 to some 300,000 or even 400,000 by the middle of the seventeenth century.[33] These examples confirm that the Ottoman case, though extreme, is neither incredible nor unique.

29 André Raymond, *Grandes villes arabes à l'époque ottomane* (Paris: Sindbad, 1985), 57. Cf. Marcus, *Middle East on the Eve of Modernity*, appendix on population. Elsewhere Raymond gives an estimate of 40 percent growth from the sixteenth to the seventeenth century: See André Raymond, "The Population of Aleppo in the Sixteenth and Seventeenth Centuries According to Ottoman Census Documents," *International Journal of Turkish Studies* 16 (1984): 447–60.

30 Raymond, *Grandes villes arabes*, 55.

31 André Raymond, *Cairo* (Cambridge, MA: Harvard University Press, 2000), chapter 11.

32 Firpo, *Relazioni*, 1054.

33 Peter Burke, "Southern Italy in the 1590s: Hard Times or Crisis?" in *The European Crisis of the 1590s*, ed. P. Clark (London: Allen and Unwin, 1985).

Meanwhile, the sad condition of Ottoman refugees from the famine and violence of the Celali years excited both pity and alarm. Ottavio Bon, Venetian ambassador in Constantinople from 1604 to 1608, sent back ever more dramatic descriptions of the thousands, then tens of thousands of new arrivals to the capital and its suburbs. Starting in the summer of 1605 he warned, "The rebels are found throughout all the provinces of Asia and they bring such trouble to various parts that many are abandoning the country, some coming here, others at the borders into Persia, and others have withdrawn into the fortified cities to save themselves from their hands, and so the countryside and the villages are being depopulated and remain little cultivated."[34] By September, Üsküdar was crowded with over ten thousand refugees who had "filled the caravanserais and all the streets . . . and in such a state of misery, especially the great number of children, that it is amazing . . . "[35] By late 1606, as intensifying strife and starvation struck Anatolia, the refugee situation went from bad to worse:

> The inhabitants can no longer sustain themselves. They have abandoned their own homes, and with their children and what little they can take, they have retreated to Üsküdar and here to Constantinople. They excite such compassion in those who see them that it is a thing of wonder. Then they try to give away or to sell their own children, and they perish for want of necessities . . . [36]

Sensing the threat posed by uncontrolled migration, Sultan Ahmed I in 1610 and Sultan Murad IV in 1635 issued orders to expel the refugees. Only those holding residence for ten, or in some cases twenty years, were allowed to stay, and others were to be sent back to their villages.[37] Although the main concern was Constantinople, similar commands were issued to towns and cities in the provinces.[38] Deportation orders descended into frightening scenes of flight and chaos, as we find in the eyewitness account of an Armenian chronicler, Grigor. According to his descriptions, the first expulsion order came at the behest of the recently victorious general Kuyucu Murad:

34 *A.S.V. Dispacci-Costantinopoli* 61 (2 July 1605).

35 *A.S.V. Dispacci-Costantinopoli* 62 (10 Sept. 1605).

36 *A.S.V. Dispacci-Costantinopoli* 63 (15 Oct. 1606).

37 See Faroqhi, *Towns and Townsmen*, 283–6 and Mantran, *Istanbul*, 50.

38 Uluçay, *XVII. Asırda Saruhan'da Eşkiyalık ve Halk Hareketleri*, 158, quotes one such order from the Manisa court records.

> "From whatever nation you may be, those of you who have come from Anatolia should get your affairs in order in three months. I am expelling all of you and sending you back to your homes. You have been warned – when the time comes, do not complain that you are not ready."

The migrants – mostly refugees from the Celali Rebellion – tried to buy time instead, "in the hope that a solution would come from man or God." Enforcement grew more violent until the sultan apparently had men going house to house to search out hiding refugees, where they beat them and threw them out on the street.

Yet by the next expulsion order in 1635, it is clear the situation had only gotten worse. According to the chronicler Grigor, Murad IV had received complaints from the region of Sivas that:

> "Although our population is few and our country is in ruins, the tax demands show no sign of stopping. Most of our people have gone to Istanbul and its periphery and settled there. Now those few of us who remain cannot support the tax demands. Either order them to come back here, or let us go join them."

Infuriated, the sultan supposedly ordered the death penalty for urban migrants who refused to leave. However, officials balked at enforcing his command – not least because many of the original supposed fugitives were by now old men.[39]

Throughout the eighteenth century, sultans continued to issue inspection and expulsion orders for Istanbul and Bursa, but evidently in vain.[40] Military defeats drove out new war refugees,[41] and famine and banditry continued to push peasants into towns and cities in search of food and safety.[42] By the 1700s, it would appear from court records that many of the migrant communities had established their own neighborhoods, especially on the periphery of Istanbul, and that some had opened

39 Hrand Andreasyan, "Celâlilerden Kaçan Anadolu Halkının Geri Gönderilmesi," in *İsmail Hakkı Uzunçarşılı'ya Armağan* (Ankara: TTK, 1976). Similar, if less dramatic, descriptions can also be found in the Venetian dispatches from Constantinople, e.g., *filze* 66 (5 Feb. 1609), 68 (17 Oct. 1609), and 75 (17 May 1613).

40 For more on the eighteenth-century migrant problem, see Fariba Zarinebaf, *Crime and Punishment in Istanbul, 1700–1800* (Berkeley: University of California Press, 2010), chapter 2.

41 M. Aktepe, "XVIII. Asrın İlk Yarısında İstanbul'un Nüfus Mes'elesine Dâir Bâzı Vesikalar," *Tarih Dergisi* 9 (1958): 1–30 and Rukiye Bulut, "XVIII. Yüzyılda İstanbul Nüfusunun Artmaması İçin Alınan Tedbirler," *Belgelerle Türk Tarihi Dergisi* 1 (1967): 30–2.

42 See, e.g., Halaçoğlu, *XVIII. Yüzyılda Osmanlı İmparatorluğu'nun İskân Siyaseti*, 78.

grocers or other small business.[43] What began as a refugee movement became a permanent shift in the balance of population between urban and rural areas.

The Crisis in Ottoman Cities

The sudden influx of migrants came at an already difficult time for Ottoman towns and cities. Even as flight and famine emptied villages in the Balkans, Anatolia, and Syria, many of the empire's urban areas were in turmoil. The political disturbances of the 1600s undermined the authority of appointed officials. Ottoman trade and industry suffered, and tax revenues fell. Urban population growth and rural agricultural decline added to problems of provisioning. Housing fell short, infrastructure decayed, and sanitation deteriorated. Natural disasters including fires, earthquakes, and epidemics exacerbated the situation.

The crisis in urban administration appeared with the weakening of central authority in the provinces. It is true that much recent scholarship has vindicated the effectiveness of Ottoman urban administration against the accusations of chaos and mismanagement found in earlier accounts of the Islamic city:[44] The narrow winding streets and bustling *suqs* that bewildered Western observers often had a logic and an order of their own.[45] Nevertheless, municipal governments in the Ottoman world lacked the executive power and strong corporate and representative institutions that had arisen in European cities over the previous centuries. In practical terms, the urban *kadıs* and *muhtesibs* (market inspectors) working together with powerful guilds and wealthy households operated the day-to-day administration. However, given the rapid turnover and weak power base of imperial appointees, the whole apparatus relied as much on the resourcefulness and cooperation of local powers as on any

43 Suraiya Faroqhi, "Migration into Eighteenth-Century "Greater Istanbul" As Reflected in the Kadi Registers of Eyüp," *Turcica* 30 (1998): 163–83.

44 See Ira Lapidus, *Muslim Cities in the Later Middle Ages* (Cambridge, MA: Harvard University Press, 1967); Janet Abu-Lughod, "The Islamic City – Historic Myth, Islamic Essence, and Contemporary Relevance," *International Journal of Middle East Studies* 19 (1987): 155–76; and André Raymond, "Islamic City, Arab City: Orientalist Myths and Recent Views," *British Journal of Middle Eastern Studies* 21 (1994): 3–18.

45 For instance, Richard Bulliet, *The Camel and the Wheel* (New York: Columbia University Press, 1990) has argued that the greater efficiency of transportation by camel eliminated the need for wide straight streets to accommodate wheeled traffic.

formal structure of authority.[46] In Damascus alone, the Ottomans had to appoint forty-five new governors over the course of the seventeenth century;[47] and during the 1700s, Aleppo saw about a hundred new governors come and go in the space of as many years.[48] By that time the urban Janissary garrisons – once a source of security and imperial authority – had become centers of rioting and disorder.

Meanwhile, many urban economies were in turmoil. The rapid inflation that began in the 1590s, along with the prevailing insecurity and its threat to the caravan trade, pushed Ottoman commerce and industry into sharp recession during the early seventeenth century. At the same time, imperial fiscal problems and confusion in the Ottoman monetary system created tremendous instability in the marketplace.[49] Although there are still no comprehensive studies of Ottoman economic performance in these years, anecdotal evidence leaves a strong impression of crisis. Bursa, specialized in the production of luxury silk, epitomized the worst of this predicament. There, as in many other major cities, records of tax farm incomes have allowed historians to quantify levels of activity in certain commercial sectors.[50] In general, these incomes experienced a sharp fall from their peak in 1580 down to 1601, before plummeting another 75 percent in real terms in the following decade. Meanwhile, inflation and disruption to supplies roughly tripled the cost of Bursa silk production, destroying its competitive edge with manufacturers in Europe.[51] In the next century, tax farm incomes recovered roughly two-thirds of their sixteenth-century values; however, as previously noted, population roughly doubled in the same period, so in per capita terms the city's economy still declined.

For smaller cities, some of our best evidence comes from the accounts of pious foundations, which typically earned their incomes through a mix of rural and urban rents. To take one example, the renowned *zaviye* (dervish lodge) of Celaleddin Rumi in Konya, a major urban proprietor, suffered "violent fluctuations" of revenues in the 1590s, and then a

46 See Raymond, *Grandes villes arabes*, 227, and Marcus, *Middle East on the Eve of Modernity*, chapter 3.

47 Raymond, *Grandes villes arabes*, 26.

48 Marcus, *Middle East on the Eve of Modernity*, 80–1.

49 See Pamuk, *Monetary History*, chapter 8.

50 See Özer, *XVI. Yüzyılın Sonlarında Bursa*, chapter 4.

51 Murat Çızakça, "Price History and the Bursa Silk Industry: A Study in Ottoman Industrial Decline, 1550–1650," *The Journal of Economic History* 40 (1980): 533–50.

virtual "collapse" by the 1640s.[52] Meanwhile, other foundations in the city suffered heavy losses as the central covered market fell into ruins; and holdings in Ankara, too, lost half or more of their real value.[53] Other Anatolian *vakıfs* reported significant losses as a direct consequence of Little Ice Age weather and associated natural disasters.[54]

Consequently, municipal revenues and services contracted, leaving towns and cities even less able to cope with the influx of refugees. Many, if not most, of the migrants arrived without property or employment, forming a new mass of urban poor, aggravating chronic problems of crime and public health.[55] It would seem from court records of the early 1600s that the migrants tended to hire themselves out as servants, unskilled builders, or peddlers, or else work as bodyguards and irregular soldiers.[56] In Bursa, some were so desperate for work that they even volunteered to man the imperial galleys – traditionally a harsh punishment for criminals.[57] Real wages throughout the empire, down 30 percent to 40 percent from pre-crisis levels, remained stagnant until the mid-1700s;[58] and data from probate inventories (discussed below) have left an impression of gaping inequalities in urban wealth and living standards.[59] Throughout this period, Istanbul and other major cities witnessed the emergence of a growing and permanent underclass of orphans, prostitutes, beggars, day-laborers, and criminals.[60]

52 Suraiya Faroqhi, "Agricultural Crisis and the Art of Flute-Playing: The Worldly Affairs of the Mevlevî Dervishes (1595–1652)," *Turcica* 22 (1988): 43–70.

53 Suraiya Faroqhi, "A Great Foundation in Some Difficulties; or Some Evidence on Economic Contraction in the Ottoman Empire of the Mid-Seventeenth Century," *Revue d'histoire maghrebine* 47–48 (1987): 109–21.

54 See K. Orbay, "Financial Consequences of Natural Disasters in Seventeenth-Century Anatolia: A Case Study of the Waqf of Bayezid II," *International Journal of Turkish Studies* 15 (2009): 63–82.

55 See, e.g., Refik, *Hicrî On Birinci Asırda İstanbul Hayatı*, document 44, and Ahmet Refik, *Hicrî On İkinci Asırda İstanbul Hayatı (1100–1200)* (Istanbul: Devlet Matbaası, 1930), document 241.

56 Faroqhi, *Towns and Townsmen*, 278–82.

57 Gerber, *Economy and Society in an Ottoman City*, 24–6. Early Ottoman *mühimme defters*, by contrast, make frequent orders for more convicts to man the galleys – almost to the point where it seems the sultan wanted local officials to invent crimes to gather more men for the ships. On the recruiting of oarsmen in the sixteenth century, see Imber, "Navy of Süleyman the Magnificent."

58 Özmücür, "Real Wages."

59 C. Establet et al., "La mesure de l'inégalité dans la société ottomane: Utilisation de l'indice de Gini pour le Caire et Damas vers 1700," *Journal of the Economic and Social History of the Orient* 37 (1994): 177–82.

60 Zarinebaf, *Crime and Punishment in Istanbul*, chapter 2.

As the empire faced fiscal crisis, spending on public works declined as well, taking away another major source of employment. After the completion of the famous Blue Mosque in 1616, which had evidently employed a large number of refugees,[61] the sixteenth-century construction boom in Istanbul ground to a halt, throwing thousands out of work.[62] As the major urban foundations faced collapsing revenues, they also cut back severely on services. The *zaviye* of Celaleddin Rumi, for instance, sharply reduced its employment and charitable works and eventually closed its soup kitchen. By the eighteenth century some major imarets found that their charitable resources fell short of rising demand.[63]

Rural to urban migration also fueled ongoing problems of urban provisioning, especially in the capital. Not only were there now more urban mouths to feed, but there were also fewer rural hands to feed them. The imbalance meant that the provisioning troubles of the late sixteenth century endured, even as mortality and flight eased the population pressure of the Ottoman countryside. For instance, a 1635 imperial order expelling refugees claimed that "now that the *reaya* have left their lands and fled to other provinces since the Celali invasion, the *timar*-holders have cheated or delayed on their harvests… "[64] Meanwhile, urban meat consumption suffered a "drastic drop" even as sheep numbers recovered.[65] Throughout the seventeenth century, officials continued to blame a new influx of refugees for spreading famine and disease; as late as 1734, we find an imperial order condemning ongoing flight to the capital for "a shortage of agriculture" (*kıllet-i ziraat*).[66]

Fixed prices for imperial purchases continued to part ways with real market values. As the Venetian ambassador Cristoforo Valier described it: "The governing of provisions is such that one cannot sell anything except at a price limited to half what it seems worth to those with the cargo, nor can it be stocked nor purchased for resale," and consequently the situation in the capital alternated between cheap abundance and total

61 Andreasyan, "Celâlilerden Kaçan Anadolu Halkının Geri Gönderilmesi."

62 Mantran, *Istanbul*, 44.

63 See Peri, "Waqf and Ottoman Welfare Policy" and Singer, "Serving up Charity." An imperial order of the time (MD 85/217) also mentions the closing of a Bursa hospital complex.

64 Quoted in Uluçay, *XVII. Asırda Saruhan'da Eşkiyalık ve Halk Haraketleri*, 159.

65 Faruk Tabak, "The Ottoman Countryside in the Age of the Autumn of the Mediterranean c.1560–1870" (PhD diss., SUNY Binghamton, 2000), 396.

66 See Bulut, "XVIII. Yüzyılda İstanbul Nüfusunun Artmaması İçin Alınan Tedbirler" and Aktepe, "XVIII. Asrın İlk Yarısında İstanbul'un Nüfus Mes'elesine Dâir Bâzı Vesikalar" for examples.

privation from week to week.[67] However, the situation in Istanbul was likely better than that of provincial cities, which could face real famine during natural disasters.[68] Damascus, for example, faced significant drought and shortages in 1608, 1652, 1670–1, 1679, 1691–2, 1708–9, and 1719–20.[69]

Frequent earthquakes and fires presented further challenges. Given the fractured geology of the Eastern Mediterranean, at least some part of Ottoman lands suffered a significant tremor nearly every year.[70] The seventeenth century may not have been a particularly bad time for seismic activity, but the rapid growth of cities left the empire especially vulnerable to earthquakes. Not a few caused serious destruction and significant loss of life: In Anatolia in 1668, for instance, the death toll supposedly reached well into the thousands or even tens of thousands.[71] Other tremors were notable for their destruction of monuments and infrastructure, including the quake of 1766, which ruined the mosque of Mehmed the Conqueror and caused considerable damage to the capital's major buildings and its water supply.[72] Worst of all were earthquakes that set off conflagrations, such as the great fire of İzmir in 1688, which destroyed much of the city and left over 5,000 dead.[73]

The mostly wooden cities of Anatolia and the Balkans[74] burned down with alarming frequency over the seventeenth and eighteenth centuries. Even before the crisis, narrow streets and cramped architecture had created a dangerous environment for fires. With the flood of refugees and the breakdown of fire prevention and control over the late 1500s and

67 Firpo, *Relazioni*, 629.

68 McGowan, "Age of the Ayans," 651–2.

69 J. Pascual and C. Establet, *Familles et fortunes à Damas* (Damascus: Institut français de Damas, 1994), 18, and Yaron Ayalon, "Famines, Earthquakes, Plagues: Natural Disasters in the Ottoman Syria in the Writings of Visitors," *Osmanlı Araştırmaları* 32 (2008): 223–47.

70 See N. Ambraseys and C. Finkel, *The Seismicity of Turkey and Adjacent Areas: A Historical Review, 1500–1800* (Istanbul: M. S. Eren, 1995) for a comprehensive account of seismic activity in Ottoman times. Additional documents on earthquakes may be found in Mustafa Cezar, "Osmanlı Devrinde İstanbul Yapılarında Tahribat Yapan Yangınlar ve Tabii Afetler," in *Türk San'atı Tarihi*, vol. 1 (Istanbul: Berksoy Matbaası, 1963) and Orhan Kılıç, "Mühimme Defterlerine Göre XVI. Yüzyılın İkinci Yarısında Osmanlı Devleti'nde Meydana Gelen Depremler," *Osmanlı* 5 (1999): 671–7.

71 Ambraseys and Finkel, *Seismicity*, 77–84.

72 Ibid., 136–40.

73 *Zübde-i Vekayiât*, 300, and Ambraseys and Finkel, *Seismicity*, 90–3.

74 Cities in the Arab world, by contrast, were mostly brick and stone and consequently did not suffer such serious fires – see Raymond, *Grandes villes arabes*, 153–4.

early 1600s, conflagrations multiplied in frequency and severity,[75] especially during times of drought.[76] Ambassador Contarini claimed in 1612 that apart from the major monuments "you see nothing in these cities but a confused mass of poorly planned wooden tenements;"[77] and his successor Ruzzini noted a century later how "the wood and other perishable materials that form the houses," along with the large population and general lack of precaution, exposed the capital to a constant cycle of conflagrations and epidemics.[78] The chronicles of the seventeenth century recorded a major fire in Istanbul – one large enough to destroy a market or an entire neighborhood – about once every five to six years.[79] It would probably be no exaggeration to say that the equivalent of the entire city was burned down and rebuilt at one time or another during the 1600s. Despite a new fire brigade and new building codes under Ahmed III (r. 1703–1730), the situation in Istanbul barely improved in the eighteenth century, with significant conflagrations in 1717, 1720–21, 1756, 1770, 1782, and 1784.[80] The rapidly expanding port of İzmir may have been even more fire-prone than the imperial capital; some two thirds of the city burned to the ground, along with most of its food stocks, in another conflagration of 1742.[81]

Between these natural disasters and the wear and tear of time, urban infrastructure decayed. Throughout the 1600s, most housing in Anatolia remained poor and in short supply.[82] For example, over half of the homes sold in Ankara in the eighteenth century still contained only a single room for an entire family.[83] In the Arab world, where urban

75 E.g., Refik, *Hicrî On Birinci Asırda İstanbul Hayatı*, document 34. The Janissaries, who had once served as an effective fire-fighting force (e.g., MD 6/171), had lost all discipline during the crisis, sometimes engaging in looting instead (e.g., *Tarih-i Selânikî*, 640, 739–40).

76 The connection between drought and urban fires is evident, for instance, in the major Istanbul fire of 1660. See the description in *Tarih-i Gılmanî*, 94–100.

77 Firpo, *Relazioni*, 501.

78 Pedani-Fabris, *Relazioni*, 775–6.

79 For catalogues of seventeenth-century fires, see Cezar, "Osmanlı Devrinde İstanbul Yapılarında Tahribat Yapan Yangınlar" and Hrand Andreasyan, "Eremya Çelebi'nin Yangınlar Tarihi," *İstanbul Üniversitesi Edebiyat Fakültesi Tarih Dergisi* 27 (1973): 59–84. The various Ottoman chronicles consulted for the present study contain at least thirty-nine references to twenty-two different major fires in Constantinople and its suburbs from the 1560s to 1710s.

80 Zarinebaf, *Crime and Punishment in Istanbul*, 53–6.

81 Elena Frangakis, *The Commerce of Smyrna in the 18th Century* (Athens: Center for Asia Minor Studies, 1992), 55–6.

82 Faroqhi, *Men of Modest Substance.*

83 Taş, *XVIII. Yüzyılda Ankara*, 212.

population densities were highest, the problem may have been even worse.[84] Meanwhile, streets and sewers fell apart through years of neglect and even sabotage. As early as the 1590s, we find an imperial order complaining that the pavement throughout Istanbul had been broken up that and sewage was spilling over the streets and walkways.[85] Fifty years later, another order recorded how the giant sewage line under the main public square, the At Meydanı, had lost its water flow, leaving a nauseating back-up of human waste.[86]

Even more distressing was the decay of city water supplies. The Ottomans had once placed a strong emphasis on water as a public good, above all in the capital, maintaining and augmenting the supply through pious foundations and public works. The system had witnessed its most spectacular growth under chief architect Mimar Sinan in the mid-1500s, adding some 46 kilometers of waterways along five major and many smaller canals. By the late sixteenth century, the supply used fifteen major aqueducts running 120 kilometers altogether, managed by a guild of professional hydrological engineers, filling as many as a thousand fountains in Istanbul.[87]

From the 1590s onward, water supplies in Constantinople faced repeated breakdowns and shortages. The problems started as early as the first signs of drought in 1591, when illegal diversion of the pipes threatened to disrupt an already overstretched system.[88] Throughout the seventeenth century, new migrants on the edge of the city aggravated these shortages by carving out illegal access to waterways.[89] Moreover, the empire's fiscal crisis left the city unable to keep up with the pace of maintenance and repairs, much less expand the system to match its growing population.[90] By the early eighteenth century, even where the

[84] See Raymond, *Grandes villes arabes*, 56, and Mantran, *Istanbul*, 39–41, for estimates of population densities in Ottoman cities.

[85] Refik, *Hicrî On Birinci Asırda İstanbul Hayatı*, document 25.

[86] MD 90/163.

[87] Kazım Çeçen, *İstanbul'da Osmanlı Devrindeki Su Tesisleri* (Istanbul: İstanbul Teknik Üniversitesi, 1984) and Abdullah Martal, "XVI. Yüzyılda Osmanlı İmparatorluğunda Su-Yolculuk," *Belleten* 52 (1988): 1585–652.

[88] MD 68/86.

[89] E.g., Refik, *Hicrî On Birinci Asırda İstanbul Hayatı*, document 95.

[90] Robert Mantran, "Réflexions sur les problèmes de l'eau à Istanbul du XVIe au XVIIIe siècle," in *IIIrd Congress on the Economic and Social History of Turkey, Princeton 24–26 August 1983*, ed. H. Lowry and R. Hattox (Istanbul: Isis, 1990). The problem shows up repeatedly in imperial orders as well: See, e.g., MD 89/66, MD 89/127, and MD 89/249.

waterways remained perfectly functional, it seems rising demands and droughts brought recurring shortages.[91]

In the provinces, the situation was often worse. Anatolian and Balkan towns reported similar breakdowns in their waterways in the wake of the violence; and these poor provincial centers would have struggled to find money and resources for repairs.[92] Moreover, Anatolia may have been fortunate by comparison with the expanding urban centers of the Arab provinces. While certain Arab cities, such as Tunis and Algiers, received their water from public Ottoman aqueducts, others like Cairo and Damascus still depended on private water-carriers funded by pious foundations.[93] In some cases, the Little Ice Age crisis only aggravated longstanding water supply problems.[94] As the long dry months of summer led to chronic shortages, competition over water could erupt into violent conflict.[95] During droughts, the quality and safety of the water could rapidly deteriorate and threaten public health.[96] For instance, the court records of Aleppo record cases of pipes stuffed with old rags or even manure to maintain water pressure at fountains.[97]

Closely linked to the problem of water came a crisis in urban sanitation. Even Western travelers accustomed to the notorious filth of early modern Europe were sometimes shocked by the conditions in Ottoman towns and cities.[98] In spite of the relative cleanliness of the people themselves, thanks to public baths, the crowded streets and alleys often stank with refuse.[99] Overcrowding and poor housing no doubt contributed to

91 E.g., Refik, *Hicrî On İkinci Asırda İstanbul Hayatı*, document 106.

92 See, e.g., Bildirici, *Tarihi Su Yapıları*, 282; MD 82/257; and MD 89/127. Recently published Bursa court records also contain a number of reports of broken down and neglected urban waterworks: See Nurhan Abacı, ed. *The Ottoman Judges and Their Registers: The Bursa Court Register B-90/295 (AH 1081/AD 1670–71)* (Cambridge, MA: Harvard, Dept. of Near Eastern Languages and Studies, 2007), documents 122, 424, and 601.

93 Raymond, *Grandes villes arabes*, 158–63.

94 See Singer, *Palestinian Peasants and Ottoman Officials*, 101–4: In times of drought, Jerusalem's wells and fountains could dry up and peasants would break into the water pipes.

95 Marcus, *Middle East on the Eve of Modernity*, 299–301.

96 Better-documented cases from early modern Europe tend to support the idea that drought contributed to the spread of fecal bacterial infections. See Post, *Food Shortage, Climatic Variability, and Epidemic Disease*, 276–7.

97 Marcus, *Middle East on the Eve of Modernity*, 263.

98 See Üçel-Aybet, *Avrupalı Seyyahların Gözünden Osmanlı Dünyası*, chapter 4, for examples.

99 Quite possibly, the problem proved worse in Muslim world because, unlike in early modern Europe, there were no urban hogs to eat trash. The seriousness of this issue was recently revealed in modern Cairo following the Egyptian government's culling of pigs after the outbreak of swine flu in 2009.

the problem. Particularly in the Arab world, where urban population densities were highest, sanitation was often sporadic and haphazard, and human and animal waste was piled up onto the roads.[100] In the troubled times of the seventeenth century, it appears that once comprehensive street cleaning ordinances of the classical age[101] fell into disuse, and even basic regulations on slaughtering animals inside city walls were widely ignored.[102] The situation was not equally bad everywhere: In Aleppo, for instance, there are signs that some trash was still collected and sold for fuel, and that the market inspector (*muhtesib*) continued to regulate the quality and safety of wares.[103] However, throughout the empire as a whole, especially for the hundreds of thousands in and around the capital, an already unhealthy environment had become still more crowded and dangerous.

Urban Disease and the Demographic Drain

These breakdowns in sanitation led to frequent contagions, high death rates, and ultimately serious population loss that dragged down the demographic recovery of the empire. Although research on Ottoman disease and mortality remains at any early stage, there is sufficient evidence to show that Ottoman cities suffered a significant excess of burials over births. Not only major epidemics but also constant endemic diseases took their toll on urban populations. Comparison with better-documented cases from early modern Europe would strongly suggest that Ottoman city-dwellers, and especially the millions of rural-to-urban migrants, would have been especially vulnerable.

Deadly epidemics, especially bubonic plague, have gathered the most attention from both contemporary observers and modern historians. European travelers were at turns fascinated and horrified by the frequent outbreaks of contagion they witnessed in Ottoman cities, which as we saw in Chapter 3, lacked adequate systems for quarantine. Our best analysis of epidemic outbreaks in these years comes from the study of European consular reports in the work of Daniel Panzac.[104] Although

[100] Raymond, *Grandes villes arabes*, 148–51.

[101] See Akgündüz, *İslam ve Osmanlı Çevre Hukuku*, 161–7.

[102] Eşref Eşrefoğlu, "İstanbul'un Tarihi Et Meselesi," *Belgelerle Türk Tarihi Dergisi* 55 (1972): 13–14. For more examples, see MD 82/84 and Refik, *Hicrî On Birinci Asırda İstanbul Hayatı*, document 87.

[103] Marcus, *Middle East on the Eve of Modernity*, chapter 7.

[104] Panzac, *Population et santé dans l'Empire ottoman* (Istanbul: Isis, 1996) and *La peste dans l'Empire ottoman*.

Panzac was probably mistaken in identifying most of these epidemics as bubonic plague, his error does not alter the basic picture of contagion and mortality in these years.[105] Whatever diagnosis we give for these epidemics, their effects were undoubtedly devastating.

By Panzac's reckoning, major infections ran a sort of relay race among Ottoman urban centers, keeping them in constant circulation. Most cities would have been struck by a serious infection such as plague on average once every forty years, losing about 30 percent of their population each time.[106] Meanwhile, Istanbul served as a unique center for epidemics, suffering from some serious infection described as "plague" at least once every other year.[107] In the most serious outbreaks, as in the early 1620s, early 1660s, and late 1770s, the death tolls in the city could approach those of the Plague of Justinian or the Black Death. In the first instance, Sir Thomas Roe, reported some 200,000 deaths in the capital;[108] and according to the Ottoman writer Evliya Çelebi, Sultan Murad IV took a count of all the deaths during the worst of the plague and found that some 70,000 had perished in a week.[109] According to one estimate, the epidemic of 1778–87 killed some 150,000 to 200,000 people in Istanbul alone before spreading to the Balkans and later into Asia.[110] Adding up over time, the recurrence of these epidemics must have cost the empire millions of lost subjects.[111]

105 Panzac, *La peste dans l'Empire ottoman*, 194. In fact, his observations on this point actually make more sense for diseases like typhus and dysentery, spread by primarily by humans, than they would for vector diseases like flea-borne bubonic plague.

106 Ibid., 362.

107 Ibid., chapter 9. The implication would be that Istanbul, as a giant population center, would have created a distinct disease pool, wherein once epidemic diseases had become endemic – a theory developed in William McNeill, *Plagues and People* (New York: Doubleday, 1977).

108 *Negotiations of Sir Thomas Roe*, 419–20, 427, and 430.

109 *Seyahatname*, vol. 1, 187.

110 Panzac, *La peste dans l'Empire ottoman*, chapter 3.

111 Panzac has argued that the prevalence of plague alone would have been enough to keep the empire's population stagnant. By his reckoning, a population growing at 0.5% each year would take forty-five years to recover from a disastrous outbreak which might kill off 20% of the empire's people (ibid., 378–80). However, Panzac's estimate of a 20% population loss appears somewhat high. A look at European population figures of the time suggests that bubonic plague outbreaks usually produced two- to four-fold increases in mortality, up to six-fold in more extreme cases. In rural parishes, however, such catastrophic mortality was rare, even in plague years, when a doubling of mortality was more typical – still about 8%, given the high death rates of the time (Biraben, *Les hommes et la peste*, 194–6, 227–30). Moreover, birth rates in infected populations tended to rebound somewhat in the wake of sudden calamities like plague (ibid., chapter 4). In Aleppo, for instance, one survey finds as many as 4.8 children per couple in the

However, deaths by epidemic diseases may have paled in comparison to losses from ordinary endemic infections. Judging from nineteenth-century figures, the historical demographer Justin McCarthy has concluded that "epidemics . . . were an occasional disaster to the population, but they were no match for the toll taken by endemic diseases," and he has emphasized the higher mortality of infections in major cities.[112] Likewise, the earliest comprehensive mortality statistics in the region, for early nineteenth-century Cairo and Alexandria, reveal that gastrointestinal infections led all other causes of death at 34.9 percent and 37.4 percent, respectively, followed by pulmonary infections at 24.1 percent and 28.3 percent. Among infant deaths, the former figure rose to well over half.[113]

Our best observations on disease from the seventeenth and eighteenth centuries confirm these later impressions. In particular, we have the comprehensive descriptions of the English naturalist Alex Russell, M.D., who resided in Aleppo during the 1740s and 1750s and made note of every serious illness in the city.[114] Although Russell observed one outbreak of bubonic plague, which he described in great detail, most of his account is taken up with a myriad of other common infections. Depending on the season, everything from fevers to smallpox to dysentery struck the city; and not a year went by without substantial losses. Other travelers passing through Egypt also took particular note of the gruesome parasitic diseases which infected so much of the population along the Nile.[115]

Perhaps the strongest evidence for high death rates comes from the registration of probate inventories in series known as *tereke defters.* While usually studied for their value in social and economic history, these registers also list deaths by month, allowing historians to reconstruct seasonal

wake of an epidemic in the mid-eighteenth century, far above the average for Ottoman cities in normal times (Establet, *Familles et fortunes à Damas*, 53, and Marcus, *Middle East on the Eve of Modernity*, 200–1). Therefore, such epidmics should have been enough to seriously diminish, but not entirely flatten, a (hypothetical) natural growth rate of 0.5%.

[112] Justin McCarthy, "Factors in the Analysis of the Population of Anatolia, 1800–1878," *Asian and African Studies* 21 (1987): 33–63, at 39.

[113] Panzac, *La peste dans l'Empire ottoman*, 370–1. Note the error on table 42 – the text makes it apparent that the numbers for "maladies gastro-intestinales" have been switched with those for "maladies infectieuses."

[114] Alex Russell, *The Natural History of Aleppo, Containing a Description of the City, and the Principal Natural Productions in Its Neighbourhood Together with an Account of the Climate, Inhabitants, and Diseases, Particularly of the Plague*, second ed. (London: 1794).

[115] E.g., *Polonyalı Simeon'un Seyahatnamesi*, 110, and Constantin-François Volney, *Travels through Egypt and Syria, in the Years 1783, 1784 & 1785* (New York: 1798), chapter 18.

mortality.[116] While far from comprehensive, the data demonstrate a clear annual pattern: Mortality rose a little in winter, dropped in the spring, and then soared in late summer, before returning to normal in the autumn. This seasonality points strongly to the role of ordinary gastrointestinal infections and perhaps malaria in urban mortality, exacerbated by the heat and poor summer water supply as previously described.[117] The picture is also confirmed by the occasional instances of early summer and late autumn mortality peaks, which might be traced to bubonic plague or famine, respectively.[118]

Terekes and other court records also reveal something about the important question of infant mortality. We do not have actual records of child deaths, but we do have records indicating family size in certain rural and urban areas, and these figures reveal a striking pattern. For instance, a survey of some 2,705 cases involving families in the Konya court records of the early eighteenth century has given an average of 3.24 children for rural households but only 2.24 children for urban households.[119] Similarly, another author has found that while rural households in different parts of Anatolia ranged about 5.5 to 6.5 members, their urban counterparts managed only 4 to 5.5 members.[120] Although we lack comprehensive statistics, court records from a number of cities in the seventeenth and eighteenth centuries usually give figures averaging just two children per woman.[121] While birth control might have played some role in this

[116] For studies of *tereke defters* with monthly or seasonal data, see Ali Aktan, "Kayseri Kadı Sicillerindeki Tereke Kayıtları Üzerinde Bazı Değermelendirmeler (1738–1749)," in *II. Kayseri ve Yöresi Tarihi Sempozyum Bildirileri* (Kayseri: Erçiyes Üniversitesi, 1998); Ömer Lütfi Barkan, "Edirne Askeri Kassamı'na Âit Tereke Defterleri," *Belgeler* 3 (1966): 1–479; Establet and Pascual, *Familles et fortunes à Damas*; Hüseyin Özdeğer, *1463–1640 Yılları Bursa Şehir Tereke Defterleri* (Istanbul: Bayrak, 1988); and Said Öztürk, *Askeri Kassama Ait Onyedinci Asır İstanbul Tereke Defterleri* (Istanbul: Osmanlı Araştırmaları Vakfı, 1995).

[117] The pattern strongly resembles one independently derived from a study of gravestones in classical Rome, pointing to largely the same leading causes of death. See Walter Scheidel, "Roman Age Structure: Evidence and Models," *The Journal of Roman Studies* 91 (2001): 1–26, at 17.

[118] See especially Establet and Pascual, *Familles et fortunes à Damas*, chapter 2.

[119] Hayri Erten, *Konya Şer'iyye Sicilleri Işığında Ailenin Sosyo-Ekonomik ve Kültürel Yapısı (XVIII. Yüzyıl İlk Yarısı)* (Ankara: Kültür Bakanlığı Yayınları, 2001), 98. Note that all the numbers given here only concern married couples appearing in court, and not the considerable population of bachelors we would also find in cities.

[120] Duben, "Turkish Families."

[121] E.g., Taş, *XVIII. Yüzyılda Ankara*, 225; Ömer Düzbakar, "XVII. Yüzyıl Sonlarında Bursa'da Ekonomik ve Sosyal Hayat" (PhD diss., Ankara Üniversitesi, 2003), 169–71; and Muşmal, "XVII. Yüzyılın İlk Yarısında Konya," 73–4. There are some exceptions

rural–urban disparity, it seems unlikely.[122] In general, the same court records suggest that wealthy families tended to have more children and that urban populations were wealthier than rural. Most of the difference probably stemmed from child disease and mortality in larger population centers.

Furthermore, many of these endemics in cities would have been epidemic to rural migrants. In other words, these were illnesses that native urban populations caught as children, when they were more likely to recover and grow up with immunity. Those coming in from the countryside without immunities would be much more likely to catch them and die as adults. These would have included not only familiar childhood ailments such as measles and chickenpox, but also a variety of water-borne diseases (of the sort that can still infect foreigners today), and worst of all smallpox – often the greatest killer among recent arrivals to early modern cities in Europe.[123]

The chronic poverty, poor housing, and lax sanitation previously described would have heightened the risk of infection, especially among poor migrants. Analyses of mortality in early modern Europe in times of severe weather, drought, and famine bear out this conclusion. In most such cases, the leading causes of death were diseases like typhus that thrived amid the unhealthy conditions of refugees in cities, and to a lesser extent illnesses that preyed on the malnourished.[124] Comments in Venetian dispatches also suggest many so-called "plagues" in Istanbul

worth explaining here. The first, already mentioned, is the high birth rate in Aleppo as it recovered from an outbreak of bubonic plague. The second is Damascus, where rates of polygamy were much higher, meaning that although household size may have been larger, actual births per woman were probably not: See Establet, *Familles et fortunes à Damas*, 56–7 *et passim*. The Kayseri *terekes* also give almost three children per woman, but do not include cases of deaths without heirs (i.e., men and women without any children) and, to judge by the numbers of "*hacis*" and "*seyyids*," disproportionately registered wealthy individuals.

[122] Basim Musallam, *Sex and Society in Islam: Birth Control before the Nineteenth Century* (New York: Cambridge University Press, 1983) has made the case for widespread birth control in middle-class Muslim households in the centuries following the Black Death. While a definite possibility, there is still too little evidence to say whether these practices had any significant effect on the urban versus rural birth rate.

[123] See, e.g., Patrick Galloway, "Annual Variations in Deaths by Age, Deaths by Cause, Prices, and Weather in London 1670 to 1830," *Population Studies* 39 (1985): 487–505.

[124] This conclusion is best illustrated by the comparative study of the 1740–42 pan-European mortality crisis in Post, *Food Shortage, Climatic Variability, and Epidemic Disease*. For more statistical correlations among social and climate factors and mortality, see Andrew Appleby, "Nutrition and Disease: The Case of London," *Journal of Interdisciplinary History* 6 (1975): 1–22 and Appleby, "Epidemics and Famine in the Little Ice Age."

were actually opportunistic infections. In March of 1601, for example, a Venetian ambassador observed that "the plague, according to the custom in these parts, has hitherto appeared rather among the lower ranks, who live disorderly and careless lives, than in the other condition of people."[125]

Taking all of these factors into account, we can postulate a significant excess of burials over births in Ottoman towns and cities, even allowing for some undercounting of infants. Starting with the figures on family size, we find that even adult married couples had barely enough children to reproduce themselves. Moreover, many of these were not "couples" at all: Just over one in five women were actually in polygamous households,[126] and taking that figure into account, the urban net reproduction rate was probably less than one. Added to that, much of the urban population must have consisted of young migrants who suffered from elevated death rates and poor economic (and thus marriage) prospects. Finally, this ordinarily high mortality was punctuated every generation or so by natural disasters like plague, which could wipe out a good proportion of urban populations. Although there is plenty of room to question any of the individual numbers or details, it is hard to escape the overall conclusion that Ottoman cities created a serious demographic drain.

Furthermore, anecdotal evidence confirms that the lure of the cities – their relatively steady provisions and protection from bandits – guaranteed that whatever the calamities of urban life, more immigrants would always come in to fill the void left by high mortality. In the two decades following the disastrous plague of 1674 in Bursa, for example, population fell more sharply in the surrounding villages than within the city itself.[127] While more people probably caught the plague in the crowded urban area than in the surrounding countryside, villagers must have rushed in to fill the gap left by urban deaths. In the case of Aleppo, an unusual tax on non-Muslim migrants also reveals that as late as 1695 nearly a quarter of all (adult male) Christians in the city were migrants from outside

125 *A.S.V. Dispacci-Costantinopoli* 53 (3 May 1601).

126 Ottomanists have generally been at pains to emphasize the low rate of polygamy in the empire – typically less than 10%. However, this apparently small number understates the proportion of women involved, since each polygamous household contained at least two wives, and sometimes three or four. While these families typically recorded more children, each wife actually had on average fewer offspring than women in monogamous marriages, thus creating a net drain on population.

127 Gerber, *Economy and Society in an Ottoman City*, 15–20.

the region, mostly from Anatolia,[128] which suggests that something like 1 percent of the district population had to be replaced by newcomers every year.

Comparisons with contemporary Europe only emphasize the severity of this urban graveyard effect in Ottoman lands. In a classic study of London's role in early modern England, the historian E. A. Wrigley offered some perspective on the role a great metropolis could play in a nation's demography. Given the English capital's slight preponderance of deaths over births, he reasoned that London alone absorbed some 12,000 births from the rest of England each year, or the natural increase of some 2.5 million people in the countryside – nearly half the English population outside of London itself.[129] Although Wrigley's calculations were only rough estimates, later more detailed examinations have arrived at similar conclusions. Family reconstitution studies demonstrate a level of only six or seven births for every ten deaths right up until the late eighteenth century. Put another way, London's population of around 600,000 must have been responsible for about 400,000 excess deaths from 1700 to 1750.[130]

To put such figures in an Ottoman perspective, we need to bear in mind that London did not reach the size of Istanbul until the middle decades of the eighteenth century. Furthermore, London was the lone metropolis of England until the Industrial Revolution, whereas Istanbul shared that distinction with the great cities of the Arab world and to a lesser extent with cities such as Bursa and İzmir. While London held about one tenth of the English population in the early eighteenth century – considered extreme at the time – the proportion of all town and city dwellers in the Ottoman Empire may have reached 15 percent – a figure far in excess of most other large early modern countries, such as France or for that matter China.[131] If conditions in the larger Ottoman towns

128 Bruce Masters, "Patterns of Migration to Ottoman Aleppo in the 17th and 18th Centuries," *International Journal of Turkish Studies* 4 (1987): 75–89.

129 E. A. Wrigley, "A Simple Model of London's Importance in Changing English Society and Economy 1650–1750," *Past and Present* 37 (1967): 44–70.

130 John Landers, "London's Mortality in the 'Long Eighteenth Century': A Family Reconstitution Study," in *Living and Dying in London*, ed. W. Bynum and R. Porter (London: Wellcome Institute, 1991).

131 See Roger Owen, *The Middle East in the World Economy* (New York: I. B. Tauris, 1993), 24–5, and Wagstaff, *Evolution of Middle Eastern Landscapes*, 200, for estimates. For a comparative look at early modern urbanization, see Paul Bairoch, *Cities and Economic Development* (Chicago: University of Chicago Press, 1988) and Maddison, *Contours of the World Economy*, 40–3.

and cities were no worse than those of London, then their mortality rates could have wiped out over half of an otherwise respectable rural population recovery of 0.5 percent per annum.[132]

However, such a comparison actually understates the case, since mortality in Ottoman cities was almost certainly higher than that in Britain. We have seen in this chapter how urban living standards suffered in the first years of crisis and never fully recovered. The density, poverty, poor housing and water supply, and deficient sanitation of many of these cities all contributed to death rates that must have exceeded even those in contemporary Northern Europe. These ordinary death rates were topped off by periodic outbreaks of plague and other epidemics, at a time when European quarantine systems succeeded in containing those threats. In such circumstances, urban mortality may have been high enough to wipe out most of the natural increase in the countryside even once the worst of the Little Ice Age crisis had already passed. That would be a pessimistic estimate to be sure, but by no means unreasonable.

Conclusion

The people of the Ottoman countryside continued to flock to towns and cities year after year, driven less by the promise of a better life than by the search for food and security in an age of violence and uncertainty. They arrived to find economic turmoil, deteriorating housing and infrastructure, and a host of endemic and epidemic diseases. As with the invasion of nomads, this flight to the cities represented one more crucial shift in Ottoman ecology that would alter the region for centuries to come. This time the movement was more subtle; yet its impact weighed on the empire year after year, producing a demographic drain that proved equally profound. By the nineteenth century, probably millions of Ottomans had in effect died of rural-to-urban migration, seriously delaying the recovery of the region's population and agriculture.

[132] For comparisons of mortality and migration into cities in other Mediterranean countries, see De Vries, *European Urbanization*, chapter 10.

11

PROVISIONING AND COMMERCE

Over the course of the seventeenth and eighteenth centuries, Ottoman agriculture gradually shifted from subsistence and provisioning to commerce and export. Rural disorder and diminishing imperial authority in the provinces unraveled aspects of the old provisioning systems. The abandonment of the *timar* system and relentless fiscal demands drove a transformation of imperial finance and landholding, encouraging the commercialization of farming. Meanwhile, the empire's growing military vulnerabilities encouraged the search for allies and trading partners, binding the empire more tightly to the European state system and prompting more concessions to foreign merchants. By the end of the eighteenth century, Ottoman lands were being drawn into a Europe-centered world economy.

Underlying these economic changes was a broader shift in land use in the Eastern Mediterranean. Over the seventeenth and eighteenth centuries, Ottoman agriculture diversified out of lowland grain monocultures and moved into the uplands, and the Columbian Exchange brought new cash crops and new modes of subsistence. At the same time, alterations in climate and settlement patterns may have produced environmental changes, including erosion, siltation, and malaria, accelerating the move away from the plains.

This transformation of the empire's ecology remained incomplete even by the dawn of the nineteenth century. Nevertheless, the gradual abandonment of imperial autarchy and the opening to Western markets had profound consequences for the Ottomans, for better and for worse. The expansion of commerce and the spread of cash crops and pasture in place of subsistence farming financed a modest revival of the Ottoman economy and treasury, but at the same time hastened the eclipse of imperial power. The empire could no longer marshal all the resources of a vast territory into state-directed efforts of provisioning, settlement, or war as in centuries past. Nor could the state still effectively regulate prices and production in a consumer-oriented provisionist system. Instead, the empire slowly embarked on that path of exporting commodities and importing European manufactures common to what would become the Third World. The labor and resources once directed to feed and equip an empire were slowly but inexorably diverted away to support the booming populations and industry of rising Western powers.

From Provisioning to Commerce

While basic systems of civil and military provisioning persisted, the direct imperial management of key resources typical of the classical age gradually ceded to decentralization, privatization, and commercialization. If conditions had been more favorable, then the seventeenth-century demographic decline might have actually revived Ottoman provisionism by taking pressure off land and resources, much as population loss had led to improvements in the standard of living in Western Europe in the wake of the Black Death.[1] However, the same natural and human disturbances that upset the empire's population and agriculture created crises in Ottoman budgets and resource management as well; and so, during the eighteenth century "the largely self-contained imperial system disintegrated."[2]

The first problem arose from the disorderly way in which lands had been abandoned and communications disrupted during the worst of the Celali violence and Little Ice Age famines. As demonstrated in previous chapters, persistent unrest and nomadic incursions hindered the recovery of agriculture in the provinces and thus the chance to acquire a greater surplus for provisioning. Ottoman documents suggest that the prevalent disorder of the 1600s also upset the usual supply chains and scattered once available labor to extract key resources, creating a chain reaction of shortages. The depopulation of Keşan (near Edirne), for example, was cited in a single year for both a want of horses for the imperial message service[3] and for a grain shortage in the nearby island

[1] See Borsch, *Black Death in Egypt and England*, for data on England and a comparison with Mamluk Egypt.

[2] Daniel Goffman, *Izmir and the Levantine World* (Seattle: University of Washington Press, 1990), 55.

[3] MD 90/118.

of Bozcaada (Tenedos).[4] Another imperial order of the 1630s observed how the disorders in Karaman had interrupted the supply of saltpeter, which in turn endangered gunpowder manufacture.[5] Likewise, in the early 1600s, forest protection and timber provisioning were severely disrupted, and Ottoman naval construction recovered only partway and with considerable difficulty during the Cretan War.[6] The loss of control over the Black Sea, as Cossack pirates raided ports and shipping and then later as Russia pushed into the Crimea, also dealt a serious blow to imperial management of resources.[7]

Taxation and administration in the countryside gradually devolved to local notables. By the mid-eigheenth century, rulers more or less adapted to the new decentered political order forged in conflict over the 1600s; and the weakening of centralized authority cleared the way for provincial dynasties to seize power, often with the help of small private armies. By the late 1700s, these *ayans* or *derebeys,* as they were known, had established nearly autonomous rule in much of Anatolia and the Balkans.[8] At the same time, Mamluk factions fought for control of the Egyptian countryside; the wealthy al-Da'ud clan claimed dominion over much of Iraq; and the puritanical Wahabi sect stirred up rebellion in the Arabian Desert. In theory, the *ayans* recognized Ottoman sovereignty, and in practice they often cooperated with the designs of the central state, even furnishing some of their mercenary soldiers for wars of the eighteenth century. Nevertheless, the virtual independence of many local rulers seriously diminished the imperial government's capacity to direct the flow of settlement and resources in the manner of the fifteenth and sixteenth centuries. Military provisioning in particular suffered from the venality and intransigence of local *ayans* called on for supplies.[9] By the late 1700s,

4 MD 90/464.

5 MD 84/79.

6 For observations of Ottoman difficulties with naval provisioning and construction in the early seventeenth century, see *Negotiations of Sir Thomas Roe,* 22–3, 37–9 *et passim,* and Pedani-Fabris, *Relazioni,* 533–4. Bostan, *Osmanlı Bahriye Teşkilâtı,* gives an exhaustive treatment of the mid- to late seventeenth-century naval effort.

7 Ostapchuck, "Human Landscape of the Ottoman Black Sea."

8 For the original analysis of the rise of the *ayans,* see Mustafa Akdağ, "Genel Çizgilerle XVII. Yüzyıl Türkiye Tarihi," *Tarih Araştırmaları Dergisi* 4 (1966): 201–47, and İnalcık, "Military and Fiscal Transformation." For a more recent case study, see Nuri Çevikel, "The Rise of the Ottoman Ayans: A Case Study of the Province of Cyprus during the Eighteenth Century," *International Journal of Turkish Studies* 15 (2009): 83–94.

9 See Virginia Aksan, "Feeding the Ottoman Troops on the Danube, 1768–1774," *War and Society* 13 (1995): 1–14, and *Ottoman Wars 1700–1870: An Empire Besieged* (New York: Longman, 2007), 147–51 *et passim.*

the sultans were less autocrats than powerful negotiators in an evolving compromise of rule.[10]

Along with this shift in political authority came an equally profound transformation of Ottoman landholding and taxation. Throughout the early to mid-1600s, as described in Chapter 8, the imperial government multiplied the number of short-term tax farms as an expedient to raise cash. By late in the century, absentee tax farmers, taking no interest in long-term productivity, used the system to fleece the peasantry in one district after another. By 1695, the resulting crisis in Ottoman agriculture prompted the imperial government to introduce an entirely new system, as described here by the contemporary chronicler Sarı Mehmed Paşa:

> In the well-protected domains in the regions of Damascus, Aleppo, Diyarbakır, Mardin, Adana, Malatya, Ayntab, Tokat, and other regions, most of the villages were under the control of some leading men of state (*ricâl-i devlet*) and the *ayans* of the provinces, including the tax farms of the governors, agents, and chiefs. However, those men did not reside there. And since control over every [tax farm] passed to a new person every year, and since no one observed the poverty of the *reaya* or gave them timely help with seeds and other necessary implements, they were forced out of necessity to borrow money from usurers. Not only were their profits from agriculture and gardening not enough to meet the interest on the loans, but the men in power would also oppress them and take their entire harvest... Therefore, most were scattered and wretched and even those who remained were suffering; and this created considerable losses for the imperial treasury. From then on, these sorts of villages and territories were sold at auction... to be assigned as a sort of *malikâne* ("estate") property on condition that it could not be passed to another during the lifetime of the possessor. Henceforth, they could not be broken up or transferred.[11]

In this new system, known simply as *malikâne*, the state raised money mainly through auctions of lifetime tax farms, in effect selling off significant parts of the empire. Although *malikânes* fell short of freehold, and although the *reaya* on these new estates maintained certain rights of usufruct, the process came very close to privatizing the land. By the late eighteenth century, *malikânes* contributed a major part of

[10] See Dina Khoury, "The Ottoman Centre versus Provincial Power-Holders: An Analysis of the Historiography," in *The Cambridge History of Turkey*, vol. 3, ed. S. Faroqhi (New York: Cambridge University Press, 2007) and Şükrü Hanioğlu, *A Brief History of the Late Ottoman Empire* (Princeton, NJ: Princeton University Press, 2008), chapter 1.

[11] *Zübde-i Vekayiât*, 512–13.

imperial revenue and entirely eclipsed the old *tımar* system in parts of the empire.[12]

At the same time, powerful families and corrupt officials in the provinces started seizing land illegally, establishing private estates known as *çiftliks*. This process, which began during the Celali Rebellion and the Great Flight,[13] accelerated during the depopulation and disorders of the seventeenth century, especially in the Balkans. In recent decades, Ottomanists have generated a considerable volume of research and debate on *çiftliks*.[14] While originally analyzed in Marxist terms as part of Eastern Europe's "second serfdom,"[15] it would now appear that they were more modest affairs, by no means in the same category as the vast grain fields of Polish or Russian landlords. Most encompassed around 25 ha to 50 ha, used a mix of sharecropping and wage labor, and focused on commercial production.[16]

The rise of *malikâne* and *çiftlik* estates over the eighteenth century hastened the decline of the old agrarian order based on prebendal landlords and peasant autonomy. In its place arose a powerful new class of provincial landholders who profited from new opportunities in cash crop production for burgeoning urban and foreign markets. Many of these new *malikâne* and *çiftlik* holders remained absentee rentiers. But on the whole, the eighteenth century witnessed a "general, long-term shift from the classical, socially disinterested military service elite to a more engaged, locally rooted civilian notable (*ayan*) class of provincial office-holders."[17] Thanks in part to this development, the Ottoman revenues revived dramatically in the early to mid-eighteenth century, and the imperial government used its fiscal breathing space to reestablish a sound coinage. In effect, willingly or not, the imperial government

[12] For descriptions of the system and its impact, see Mehmed Genç, "Osmanlı Maliyesinde Malikâne Sistemi," in *Osmanlı İmparatorluğunda Devlet ve Ekonomi* (Istanbul: Ötüken, 2003) and Ariel Salzmann, "Measures of Empire: Tax Farmers and the Ottoman *Ancien Régime* 1695–1807" (PhD diss., Columbia University, 1995).

[13] E.g., MD 78/4012 and MD 83/11.

[14] See Ç. Keyder and F. Tabak, eds., *Landholding and Commercial Agriculture in the Middle East* (Binghamton: SUNY Press, 1991) for an overview.

[15] E.g., Stoianovich, "Land Tenure and Related Sectors of the Balkan Economy."

[16] Bruce McGowan, *Economic Life in Ottoman Europe* (New York: Cambridge University Press, 1981), 76–7 *et passim*. McGowan's conclusions are supported by research on late *tahrirs*: See Stefan Pareva, "Rural Agrarian Structure in the Edirne Region during the Second Half of the Seventeenth Century," *Études Balkaniques* 3 (2000): 83–123 and Zarinebaf, *Historical Geography of Ottoman Greece*, chapter 1.

[17] Winter, *Shiites of Lebanon*, 108. See also Khoury, *State and Provincial Society*, which follows one such family in Mosul.

compromised on its direct control of land and resources to achieve a more stable and profitable agrarian system. While many traces of "provisionism" remained, by the late eighteenth century the empire had significantly liberalized agriculture and commerce, marking a shift of imperial policy from "welfare to wealth."[18]

The Ottoman Empire and the World Economy

During the same period, Ottoman lands opened to more foreign trade, drawing the empire into the expanding circuit of European commerce. As shown in previous chapters, the sixteenth-century empire could dictate its terms of trade with Christian powers, and its policies tended in the direction of tighter restrictions, especially when it came to commodities vital for provisioning. Concessions to foreign nations were offered from a position of strength, and were usually intended as an aid to the Ottomans' wartime allies. The principal trading partners remained the merchant city-states of Italy and the Adriatic; and for almost a century after the European discovery of America, the rising world of Atlantic trade remained fairly distant on the economic horizon.

For the Ottomans, as for other Mediterranean powers, the arrival of Northern European merchants at the close of the sixteenth century transformed local commerce. French, English, and Dutch traders arrived in turn on the shores of the empire; and over the later decades of the sixteenth century, each secured certain circumscribed rights of access to Ottoman markets in charters known as "capitulations."[19] At first, these new trading partners had little impact on the wider economy, agriculture, or flow of resources in Ottoman lands. However, as the empire sought new allies in its long war with the Habsburgs during the Celali crisis, it opened the terms of these charters. France, for instance, received its first trading privileges as early as 1569, but no permission to buy grain until 1597. The country gained a still more generous set of capitulations in 1604, including rights to leather, wax, and cotton.[20] As other Western powers negotiated for, in effect, "most favored nation" status, such market access spread to Dutch merchants and to the English Levant Company, founded in 1581.[21]

[18] Ağır, "From Welfare to Wealth," especially chapter 4.

[19] See Etem Eldhem, "Capitulations and Western Trade," in *The Cambridge History of Turkey*, vol. 3, ed. Suraiya Faroqhi (New York: Cambridge University Press, 2006).

[20] McGowan, *Economic Life in Ottoman Europe*, 35–6.

[21] See Frangakis, *Commerce of Smyrna*, chapter 4.

At the same time, changes in Ottoman taxation favored foreign commerce over domestic industry. During the seventeenth century, the imperial government cut duties on English and Dutch traders by half, to 3 percent, to give them an advantage over the enemy Spanish and Portuguese. Perversely, the discount also gave them an advantage over local Muslim traders, who still paid the formerly preferential 4 percent tariff. Throughout the century, this same privilege spread to other European nations, such as France, in the familiar "most favored nation" pattern. Meanwhile, internal customs duties (the rates paid for moving goods from one part of the empire to another) and other taxes on local producers actually went up in order to raise revenue.[22] From 1589 to 1626, the revenue from western Anatolian external customs nearly doubled from 3,603,334 to 6,469,140 *akçes*.[23]

Over the course of the seventeenth and eighteenth centuries as the imperial government relaxed its control over exports, new mercantile communities moved to profit from the pent-up demand for Ottoman goods. İzmir, in particular, grew from a modest port into a booming hub for foreign commerce. By the late seventeenth century, many of the city's 80,000 to 90,000 inhabitants belonged to thriving communities of Greek, Jewish, Armenian, and European traders, each operating supply networks for goods like cotton and tobacco from the west Anatolian hinterland.[24] In the Balkans, a new class of Orthodox Christian merchants organized extensive networks of maritime and overland trade in agricultural products, as export restrictions fell into disuse and customs officials proved easy to bribe. According to Traian Stoianovich, Macedonia and Thessaly exported some "40% of their grain and over half their cotton and tobacco production" by the late eighteenth century. Meanwhile, Serbia became a major provider of pigs and pork and Hungary a major source of cattle to Habsburg lands and beyond.[25] Likewise, the overseas commerce of Egypt and the Levant took off around

22 Mehmet Genç, "Osmanlı Devletinde İç Gümrük Rejimi," in *Osmanlı İmparatorluğunda Devlet ve Ekonomi* (Istanbul: Ötüken, 2003). For a microcosm of these policies and their impact on Ottoman trade and domestic industry, see Bruce Masters, *The Origins of Western Economic Dominance in the Middle East* (New York: New York University Press, 1988).

23 Goffman, *Izmir and the Levantine World*, 57.

24 On the rise of Izmir, see Frangakis, *Commerce of Smyrna* and Goffman, *Izmir and the Levantine World.*

25 Stoianovich, "Conquering Balkan Orthodox Merchant," 260. See also Traian Stoianovich, "Land Tenure and Related Sectors of the Balkan Economy, 1600–1800," *Journal of Economic History* (1953): 398–411.

1700, particularly exports of coffee, silk, wool, and cotton to France.[26] Overall, exports of raw fibers more than tripled by the 1780s, at which point the Ottomans may have sent as much cotton to Europe as they had produced in the entire empire before the crisis.[27] Internal trade still exceeded foreign commerce, which is hardly surprising for such a vast and hitherto self-sufficient empire. However, by the late eighteenth century, that gap was closing.[28]

Research into Ottoman tax records provides some remarkable insights into the new role of exports in the eighteenth-century Ottoman economy. Taken together, the value of tax farms in all sectors of manufacture and commerce rose by an average of 90 percent from the crisis of the late 1600s to the 1770s; and far from collapsing in the face of European competition, the value of domestic textile production nearly doubled. However, most economic growth depended on rising cash crop exports, especially cotton, while most internal trade and industry apparently stagnated.[29] The results more or less appear to bear out French traveler C.-F. Volney's observations as he traveled through Egypt in the 1780s, that "the consumption of the country consists almost entirely of articles of luxury completely finished, and the produce given in return is principally in raw materials."[30]

[26] Daniel Panzac, "International and Domestic Maritime Trade in the Ottoman Empire during the 18th Century," *International Journal of Middle East Studies* 24 (1992): 189–206.

[27] With regard to wool, French figures indicate a rise in İzmir's exports from only half a million pounds around 1700 to a peak of 3,823,835 pounds in 1783 (Frangakis, *Commerce of Smyrna*, 328–9), while the total value of all animal fiber exports to France roughly tripled from around 1.5 million *livres* in 1701–2 to about 4.5 million *livres* by 1786–87 (McGowan, *Economic Life in Ottoman Europe*, 40). Meanwhile, Turkish cotton exports climbed from only 667,279 pounds in 1725 up to 2,190,027 pounds in 1785 then doubled again during the Napoleonic wars: See Orhan Kurmuş, "The Cotton Famine and Its Effects on the Ottoman Empire," in *The Ottoman Empire and the World Economy*, ed. Huri İslamoğlu (Cambridge: Cambridge University Press, 1987). To put some perspective on the figure, the entire annual cotton production of the Çukurova, perhaps the richest cotton-producing area in the empire outside of Egypt, had reached only 1.5 million pounds during the 1570s: See Suraiya Faroqhi, "Notes on the Production of Cotton and Cotton Cloth in 16th and 17th Century Anatolia," in ibid.

[28] For estimates, see Panzac, "International and Domestic Maritime Trade." Wagstaff, *Evolution of Middle Eastern Landscapes*, 203–4, suggests a wider but still rapidly narrowing difference in the late 1700s.

[29] Mehmet Genç, "18. Yüzyıla Ait Osmanlı Malî Verilerinin İktisadi Faaliyetin Göstergesi Olarak Kullanılabilirliği Üzerinde Bir Çalışma," in *Osmanlı İmparatorluğunda Devlet ve Ekonomi* (Istanbul: Ötüken, 2003).

[30] Volney, *Travels*, 132.

There is certainly some truth to some Ottomanists' claim that the empire was "peripheralized" in the expanding capitalist world economy.[31] However, the arguments of world-systems theory need some qualification. First, the empire's integration into European commerce was more consequence than cause of its domestic economic troubles. Moreover, the empire enjoyed a diverse array of exports, in contrast to the plantation monocultures or single extractive industries of most "peripheral" regions.[32] Finally, as we will explore in the following sections, changes in Ottoman agriculture and commerce were not solely economic developments but also part of a broader transformation in Ottoman land use and perhaps even the landscape itself.[33]

The Transformation of Ottoman Land Use

Changes in Ottoman trade and agriculture had an environmental as well as an economic and political context. As described in the recent work of Faruk Tabak,[34] developments in Ottoman land use fit into a broader pattern of Mediterranean change, which began with the crisis of the late sixteenth century. All across the basin, as population pressure subsided, the "tyranny of wheat" in the plains gave way to a more diversified agriculture in the hills. Meanwhile, the decline of the once lucrative

[31] World-systems theory has exercised a major influence in Ottoman historiography in recent decades, perhaps more than in any other region of world history. Wallerstein's original corpus, *The Modern World-System*, 3 vols. (New York: Academic Press, 1974–89), devotes considerable space to Ottoman lands; and the unofficial journal of world-systems theory, *Review*, has frequently incorporated the work of Ottomanists at SUNY. See, for example, K. Boratav et al., "Ottoman Wages and the World Economy, 1839–1913," *Review* 8 (1985): 379–406; Murat Çızakça, "Incorporation of the Middle East into the European World-Economy," *Review* 8 (1985): 353–77; İslamoğlu, *Ottoman Empire and the World-Economy*; Reşat Kasaba, *The Ottoman Empire and the World Economy* (Albany: SUNY Press, 1988); and Çağlar Keyder, "Large-Scale Commercial Agriculture in the Ottoman Empire?" in *Landholding and Commercial Agriculture in the Middle East*, ed. Ç. Keyder and F. Tabak (Binghamton: SUNY Press, 1991).

[32] Şevket Pamuk, "The Ottoman Empire in Comparative Perspective," *Review* 11 (1988): 127–49.

[33] Recently, some world-systems historians have begun to incorporate environmental history perspectives and vice versa, producing a still new but potentially useful field of inquiry. See Jason Moore, "Nature and the Transition from Feudalism to Capitalism," *Review* 26 (2003); A. Hornborg et al., eds., *Rethinking Environmental History: World-System History and Global Environmental Change* (Lanham, MD: Alta Mira Press, 2007); and A. Hornborg and C. Crumley, eds., *The World System and the Earth System: Global Socioenvironmental Change and Sustainability since the Neolithic* (Walnut Creek, CA: Left Coast Press, 2007).

[34] Tabak, *Waning of the Mediterranean*.

Mediterranean spice trade and sugar plantations shifted investment into new cash crops.

The timely arrival of new plants from the Columbian Exchange helped the process along. Although the first mention of tobacco, corn, potatoes, tomatoes, and other New World plants in the Mediterranean dates back to the early 1500s, these crops did not play a significant role in European or Ottoman diet until at least the following century.[35] The use of some American plants and animals may have spread in a roundabout way from the Portuguese through India and across the Arabian Sea, or alternatively through North Africa, then Turkey, the Balkans, and finally Italy and France.[36] This circuitous path may explain the anomalous fact that American corn acquired the name *granoturco* ("Turkish grain") in Italian but *mısır* ("Egypt") in Turkish; and likewise how a domesticated bird of the Americas acquired the name "turkey" in English but *hindi* ("Indian") in the language of Turkey itself.[37]

Thanks to its addictive properties, tobacco was the first seed of the Columbian Exchange to take root in Ottoman lands, despite fierce imperial opposition. Its spread may be dated, rather appropriately, with the diffusion of coffee and coffee shops across the empire in the late sixteenth century.[38] By the early 1600s, we find the first imperial complaints that the weed had supplanted vegetables in peasant gardens and had distracted valuable labor and resources from growing food.[39] Ahmed I tried to ban tobacco as early as 1609, and over the following decades, especially in times of religious revival and puritanical zeal, smoking was denounced for starting fires[40] and for leading to all sorts of moral

35 Traian Stoianovich, "Le maïs dans les Balkans," *Annales* (1966): 1026–40 and Jean-Jacques Hemandiquer, "Les débuts du maïs en Méditerranée (premier aperçu)," in *Histoire économique du monde méditerranéen: Melanges en honneur de Fernand Braudel* (Toulouse: Privat, 1972).

36 Jean Andrews, "Diffusion of Mesoamerican Food Complex to Southeastern Europe," *Geographical Review* 83 (1993): 194–204.

37 One theory has it that the name dates from an emergency import of maize from the Balkans into Italy during a famine in the peninsula in 1590–91: See Hermandiquer, "Les débuts du mais." However, another author argues that anything foreign in Italy in the sixteenth century tended to get labeled "Turkish" regardless of actual provenance: See Paolo Preto, *Venezia e i Turchi* (Florence: G. C. Sansoni, 1975), 119.

38 Ralph Hattox, *Coffee and Coffeehouses* (Seattle: University of Washington Press, 1985). The celebrated Ottoman scholar Kâtip Çelebi also wrote an essay on coffee, claiming it was introduced in 1601 and discussing the various prohibitions and debates it inspired (*Balance of Truth*, 50–8).

39 MD 82/343. See also Goffman, *Izmir and the Levantine World*, 74.

40 MD 85/380. See also *Tarih-i Gılmanî*, 13–14, and *Târîh-i Naîmâ*, 1219–22.

vices.[41] In one infamous (but apparently factual) episode, Sultan Murad IV traveled the streets of the capital incognito, catching smokers red-handed and rounding them up for execution.[42] Tobacco was legalized only in 1646 and was taxed starting in the 1690s. By the early eighteenth century, smoking was widespread, and Anatolia became not only a major consumer but also a major exporter, as tobacco became a valuable cash crop.

Maize, however, brought the most profound changes to Ottoman lands. Whereas potatoes, tomatoes, and peppers remained little more than Ottoman culinary accessories before the nineteenth century,[43] maize offered a compelling alternative to grain as a basic subsistence crop. For farmers willing to adjust to the new plant, it could better tolerate the frequent years of drought, it yielded far more per seed and per acre, and it responded more readily to irrigation. Its stalks and cobs served as fuel and fodder, and it could grow in the same fields alongside gourds and beans.[44] Moreover, maize fit perfectly into the changing patterns of land use across Ottoman territory and throughout the Mediterranean. It was an ideal crop to provide basic nourishment for agricultural workers and sharecroppers, especially in small garden plots and at higher elevations, freeing land and labor for cash crops, fodder, and pasture. Apparently, the state and the army were less inclined to tax or requisition maize than wheat or barley.[45] Without maize, the rise of *çiftliks* and their other Mediterranean equivalents might well have proved ecologically unmanageable.[46]

Nevertheless, maize and other New World crops spread gradually and unevenly throughout the empire. The Nile valley and the Levant probably took to the new plants first, as implied in Turkish designation of corn as "Egyptian." However, we have few indications that maize or other American foodstuffs constituted basic staples in most of the Arab

41 The antismoking crusade appears to have roots in both religious opposition to "innovation" (*bid'at*) and also unease about the way new luxuries and social mingling in coffee shops blurred distinctions of class and rank. See Ayşe Saraçgil, "Generi voluttuari e ragion di stato: Politiche repressive del consumo di vino, caffé e tobacco nell'Impero ottomano nei seccoli XVI e XVII," *Turcica* 28 (1996): 163–93.

42 *Târîh-i Naîmâ*, 1393–4.

43 Tülay Artan, "Aspects of the Ottoman Elite's Food Consumption: Looking for 'Staples,' 'Luxuries' and 'Delicacies' in a Changing Century," in *Consumption Studies in the History of the Ottoman Empire*, ed. D. Quataert (Binghamton: SUNY Press, 2000).

44 McNeill, *Mountains of the Mediterranean*, 87–92.

45 Stoianovich, "Le maïs dans les Balkans."

46 See Tabak, *Waning of the Mediterranean*, chapters 4 and 5.

world. In Syria, corn apparently served as a cheap alternative in times of dearth.[47] Among Turks as well, maize appears to have supplemented rather than supplanted the old grains. In Anatolia, corn was generally considered famine food.[48] In the Balkans, by contrast, maize became the main source of calories for a large part of the peasantry; and this adaptation may account for the region's demographic revival in the eighteenth century compared with other parts of the Ottoman Empire.[49] By the mid-nineteenth century, corn production in Bosnia reached twice that of wheat.[50]

Changes in the Land?

Throughout the seventeenth and eighteenth centuries, these changes in land use may have accelerated in a positive feedback loop with changes in the land itself. In his recent research, Faruk Tabak also argued that the onset of Little Ice Age weather patterns at a time of demographic retreat would have led to accelerated soil erosion, siltation, and the spread of malaria in the plains. In response, the peasantry would have moved their fields farther into the hills and mountains, leading to more clearing and plowing along slopes, and yet more erosion. Meanwhile, the once extensive grain fields of the lowlands would have reverted to seasonal pasture. Thus physical changes in the landscape as well as changing ecological and economic circumstances would have driven diversification of land use.[51]

The theory is striking and quite plausible, but unfortunately the evidence remains ambiguous. First, such an interpretation of environmental change assumes that Little Ice Age climate in Ottoman lands was wetter, rather than drier – a common error, as we saw in Chapter 5. However,

[47] Brigitte Marino, "L'approvisionnement en céréales des villes de la Syrie ottomane (XVIe–XVIIIe siècles)," in *Nourir les cités de méditerranée – Antiquité-temps moderns*, ed. B. Marin and C. Virlouet (Paris: Maisonneuve, 2003).

[48] Tabak, "Ottoman Countryside in the Age of the Autumn of the Mediterranean," 372.

[49] Stoianovich, "Le maïs dans les Balkans."

[50] Justin McCarthy, "Ottoman Bosnia, 1800 to 1878," in *The Muslims of Bosnia-Herzegovina*, ed. M. Pinson (Cambridge, MA: Harvard University Press, 1994), 63.

[51] These ideas, which were originally formulated in the author's 2000 dissertation, are elaborated in part II of his recent book. Many of the original concepts come of out of the work of John McNeill (*Mountains of the Mediterranean*, 86–7 *et passim*). The idea of a retreat from malarial plains in the seventeenth and eighteenth centuries has also figured in Balkan historiography: See Mark Mazower, *The Balkans: A Short History* (New York: Modern Library, 2002), 27 *et passim*.

this mistake is by no means fatal to the theory. After all, Near Eastern precipitation in the seventeenth and eighteenth centuries was not significantly lower than normal, only more erratic. (In the climatologists' jargon, it demonstrated higher interannual variability.) The period witnessed a number of years with intense rainfall and flooding, sometimes following serious droughts. It is not hard to imagine a scenario wherein dry abandoned fields and terraces were washed away in sudden heavy downpours. The Little Ice Age, therefore, did not have to be uniformly wet to carry away soil and create malarial swamps.

Nevertheless, such suppositions lead us to another problem with the theory, which is the uncertain nature and timing of Mediterranean soil erosion and deposition. Originally analyzed in terms of alternating wet and dry periods, these processes now appear far more complex. Agricultural practices, geological properties, and sudden catastrophic episodes all play a part in the current analysis of Mediterranean sediments, alongside the once dominant role of climate shifts.[52] Once again, the new evidence from the environmental sciences does not necessarily invalidate Tabak's theory. It is possible that the abandonment of farms along with deforestation in the hills could have exposed Ottoman lands to sudden erosion. Archaeological evidence from Greece tends to support this theory as well: In that country, erosion and alluviation have historically followed the sudden expansion and contraction of agriculture, and moreover, some significant Greek alluvial deposits may date to around the seventeenth century.[53] Unfortunately, in other parts of the Ottoman world, including Anatolia, the archaeological record remains far less certain. While empirical evidence may implicate human land use for soil

[52] The original climatic theory of Mediterranean erosion and deposition comes from the pioneering work of Claudio Vita-Finzi, *The Mediterranean Valleys* (London: Cambridge University Press, 1969). For recent developments in the field, see John Bintliff, "Time, Process and Catastrophism in the Study of Mediterranean Alluvial History: A Review," *World Archaeology* 33 (2002): 417–35; Grove and Rackham, *Nature of Mediterranean Europe*, chapter 16; and Karl Butzer, "Environmental History in the Mediterranean World: Cross-Disciplinary Investigation of Cause-and-Effect for Degradation and Soil Erosion," *Journal of Archaeological Science* 32 (2005): 1773–1800. For experimental data on Mediterranean erosion, see results of the ongoing MEDALUS project,whose first studies are published in N. Geeson et al., eds., *Mediterranean Desertification: A Mosaic of Processes and Responses* (Chichester: Wiley, 2002).

[53] T. Van Andel et al., "Land Use and Soil Erosion in Prehistoric and Historical Greece," *Journal of Field Archaeology* 17 (1990): 379–96 and Laurent Lespez, "Geomorphic Responses to Long-Term Land Use Changes in Eastern Macedonia (Greece)," *Catena* 51 (2003): 181–208.

loss in general,[54] the archaeological and historical record can rarely trace specific instances of erosion and alluviation to particular years or events in historical times.[55]

The evidence on deforestation remains similarly mixed. On the one hand, Ottoman evidence gives some definite indications of excessive logging and burning during the seventeenth and eighteenth centuries. It appears that the system of protected imperial forests broke down in the early years of crisis, leading to the destruction of old-growth trees. During the 1630s and 1640s, sultans issued a number of orders that deplored widespread burning, grazing, logging, and charcoal making in major timber preserves of the Balkans and Anatolia and reassigned soldiers as *kurucus*.[56] Furthermore, ongoing wars of the seventeenth and eighteenth centuries increased demand for wood, especially large ship timbers like galley oars. By the 1640s, according to the description of Ambassador Contarini, "where just a few years before they cut close to the sea, now they have to go three or four days inland."[57] During the later years of the Cretan War, even the once inexhaustible forests of the Kocaeli region began to give out, forcing the state to seek large ship timbers farther along the Black Sea coast. Meanwhile, the official price of a mainmast reached some 5,000 *akçes*, and the real market value of such giant timber may have reached several times more – provided it could be found at all.[58] Moreover, war stoked so much demand for charcoal to smelt iron that at one point in the early 1700s the *kadı* of Samakov (Bulgaria) petitioned Istanbul to forbid the construction of new furnaces, complaining they had already created a shortage of firewood.[59] Finally, the rise of large private landholdings – whether *çiftliks* or *malikânes* – undercut traditional

54 Among recent studies on Turkish soil erosion, see I. Çelik, "Land-Use Effects on Organic Matter and Physical Properties of Soil in a Southern Mediterranean Highland of Turkey," *Soil and Tillage Research* 83 (2005): 270–7 and F. Evrendilek et al., "Changes in Soil Organic Carbon and Other Physical Soil Properties along Adjacent Mediterranean Forest, Grassland, and Cropland Ecosystems in Turkey," *Journal of Arid Environments* 59 (2004): 743–52.

55 See P. Boehm and D. Gerold, "Historische und aktuelle Bodenerosion in Anatolien," *Geographische Rundschau* 47 (1995): 720–5.

56 E.g., MD 85/269, MD 85/295, MD 85/639, and MD 90/58.

57 Firpo, *Relazioni*, 806–7.

58 Bostan, *Osmanlı Bahriye Teşkilâtı*, 106–19.

59 Genç, "18. Yüzyılda Osmanlı Ekonomisi ve Savaş." By some estimates, it would have taken about 12 ha of coppiced woodland to smelt a single ton of iron in the preindustrial Mediterranean (Horden and Purcell, *Corrupting Sea*, 184). Concening the demands of war on forest resources in general, see McNeill, "Woods and Warfare in World History."

peasant access to forest resources and encouraged more commercial exploitation of timber.[60]

On the other hand, we find little evidence for the sort of widespread clearance that might have led to serious erosion and alluviation.[61] Some protected hardwood groves may have been destroyed, but overall, forest cover probably expanded as agriculture contracted. The first scientific surveys of Ottoman forests in the nineteenth century still found considerable supplies of lumber for commercial use.[62] Moreover, despite the historical prejudice against pastoralists for destroying forests and soil,[63] recent empirical studies indicate that plowing generates far more erosion than grazing.[64] Therefore, the nomadic invasions of the period probably did not lead to any serious rise in land degradation either. Although studies of pollen and charcoal samples confirm that some regions suffered deforestation in Ottoman times, they cannot specifically link changes in vegetation with particular climatic and historical events.[65]

The evidence on malaria and settlement patterns remains ambiguous. Malaria received plenty of attention from both Ottoman and Western observers in these centuries, and no doubt, infectious mosquitoes plagued many valleys and coastal plains.[66] In the nineteenth century, invading armies and immigrant refugees continued to face deadly outbreaks of malaria in Anatolia, the Balkans, and Syria.[67] Yet there is no strong evidence that the illness was in any way new to the region or linked to developments of the Little Ice Age crisis. The Hungarian plains, for instance, had been notorious for malaria outbreaks since the sixteenth century.[68] Detailed studies on Greek settlement and land use

[60] Dursun, "Forest and the State," 42 *et passim.*

[61] McNeill, *Mountains of the Mediterranean,* chapter 3, draws a similar conclusion for the Taurus Moutains, in contrast to the serious erosion found in some other montane Mediterranean regions.

[62] Louis Bricogne, "Les forets de l'Empire ottoman," *Revue des eaux et forets* 16 (1877): 273–89 and 321–35.

[63] See Planhol, "Les nomades, la steppe, et la foret en Anatolie."

[64] Çelik, "Land-Use Effects on Organic Matter" and Evrendilek et al., "Changes in Soil Organic Carbon."

[65] E.g., G. Wilcox, "A History of Deforestation as Indicated by Charcoal Analysis of Four Sites in Eastern Anatolia," *Anatolian Studies* 24 (1974): 117–33 and Sytze Bottema, "A Pollen Diagram from the Syrian Anti-Lebanon," *Paleorient* 3 (1975–77): 259–68.

[66] See, e.g., Panzac, *La peste dans l'Empire ottoman,* 55, and Mazower, *Balkans,* chapter 1.

[67] L. Bruce-Chwatt and J. Zulueta, *The Rise and Fall of Malaria in Europe* (New York: Oxford University Press, 1980), 21–31; Norman Lewis, "Malaria, Irrigation, and Soil Erosion in Central Syria," *Geographical Review* 39 (1949): 278–90; and Tunçdilek, *Türkiye İskân Coğrafyası,* 23–4.

[68] Sugar, *Southeastern Europe,* 108.

have revealed a movement from the plains to the hills in the 1700s, but the shift might reflect a retreat to safety rather than an escape from malaria,[69] a pattern that could hold for parts of Anatolia as well.[70] After all, such flight to the hills had been a feature of crisis in Mediterranean lands since ancient times, and malaria was likely just one contributing factor.[71] Tabak's theory remains intriguing, but any decisive statement on the role of erosion, alluviation, and malaria in transforming Ottoman land use in the seventeenth and eighteenth centuries will have to await further historical and archaeological evidence.

Conclusion: The Opening of Ottoman Lands

In the wake of the Little Ice Age crisis, the Ottoman Empire gradually diversified its agriculture and opened to Western commerce. Slowly but inexorably, Ottoman lands responded to the blandishments of the world economy and succumbed to their comparative advantage as an exporter of commodities in return for manufactured imports. The transformation proved as much ecological as economic, as Ottoman land use underwent a fundamental change in response to new markets, new crops, and new demographic and environmental realties.

The opening of Ottoman lands spelled the end of the top-down imperial management of provisions and settlement that had secured the empire's power in centuries past, without yet supplying anything as effective in its place. As explained in Part I, Ottoman territory had never been the most wealthy or populous, but still the Ottoman Empire had once been capable of managing its subjects and resources to support the largest city and conduct the most formidable army in Europe, if not the world. By the late eighteenth century, that capacity had clearly diminished. Nor had the imperial government really hit upon a workable new system for sustained, consistent mobilization of its military in the manner of rising

69 M. Wagstaff and E. Frangakis, "The Port of Patras in the Second Ottoman Period: Economy, Demography, and Settlements c.1700–1830," *Revue du monde musulman et de la Méditeranée* 66 (1992): 79–94; E. Frangakis and M. Wagstaff, "Settlement Pattern Change in the Morea, 1700–1830," *Byzantine and Modern Greek Studies* 11 (1987): 163–92; E. Frangakis and M. Wagstaff, "The Height Zonation of Population in the Morea c.1830," *Annual of the British School at Athens* 87 (1992): 439–46; and Machiel Kiel, "The Rise and Decline of Turkish Boeotia, 15th–19th Century," in *Recent Developments in the History and Archaeology of Central Greece*, ed. J. Bintliff (Oxford: Oxbow, 1997).

70 Hütteroth, *Laendliche Siedlungen*, chapter 9.

71 McNeill, *Mountains of the Mediterranean*, 75–6.

bureaucratic and absolutist European states.[72] To borrow from Charles Tilly's analysis,[73] the empire had once been a "coercion-intensive" state par excellence – one relying on the direct imperial management of military resources – whose capacity for warfare had far outclassed its "capital-intensive" rivals like Venice. However, during the Little Ice Age crisis the imperial government's resources and extractive capabilities diminished. In the meantime, it failed to make a successful transition to the "capitalized coercion" of Western European nation-states, who soon emerged as the leading military powers of the eighteenth century, combining centralized bureaucratic power with consensual taxation of the rising commercial classes to fund their wars.[74]

While it is interesting to consider the Ottoman Empire's eighteenth-century transformation in similar terms of political negotiation,[75] it would be inappropriate to blur the distinctions. Rulers of states like Britain compromised with rising commercial classes in order to expand their base of taxation so they could compete with foreign rivals, and in the process they adopted fiscal and economic policies more favorable to revenue and growth. By contrast, the Ottoman imperial center negotiated with capital and provincial factions mainly so it could preserve enough political consensus to keep the state intact during the protracted turmoil of the Little Ice Age, without necessarily promoting fiscal or economic institutions favorable to the domestic economy.[76] It was no small accomplishment that the Ottoman dynasty persevered when so many others fell during the "general crisis." However, the result of this bargaining was ultimately less, not more, sustained military power. Likewise, the expansion of private landholdings and market-oriented agriculture in the eighteenth century represented not so much a synergy of state and commercial interests and power, but rather a way of reconciling developments already beyond the state's control, driven by ecological changes and foreign economic pressures. From the perspective of Ottoman power, the gains from privatization and bargaining with provincial elites could not make up for the loss of central control over resources and settlement.

72 For comparative analyses, see Agoston, "Habsburgs and Ottomans" and Aksan, "Locating Ottomans."

73 Charles Tilly, *Coercion, Capital, and European States AD 990–1992* (Cambridge, MA: Blackwell, 1992).

74 See, e.g., John Brewer, *The Sinews of Power: War, Money and the English State, 1688–1783* (Cambridge, MA: Harvard University Press, 1990).

75 E.g., Salzmann, "Measures of Empire."

76 For more on this comparison, see E. Balla and N. Johnson, "Fiscal Crisis and Institutional Change in the Ottoman Empire and France," *Journal of Economic History* 69 (2009): 809–45 and Fritschy, "State Formation and Urbanization Trajectories."

Ecologically, the change meant a loss of food and natural resources for domestic consumption, further holding back the region's demographic recovery.

Conclusion to Part III: The Ottoman Transformation in Ecological Perspective

During the Little Ice Age crisis, Ottoman lands witnessed three major shifts in human ecology: First, much of the semiarid region switched from farming to pastoralism. Second, population movements from rural to high-mortality urban areas accelerated, even as overall population shrank. Third, farming in much of the empire diversified away from subsistence grain monocultures into a varied, commercialized, and often export-oriented agriculture. While not necessarily signs of decline, these developments did significantly slow the revival of Ottoman population. Moreover, these transformations ensured the empire's slow recovery following the crisis took a different form from its rapid growth in the fifteenth and sixteenth centuries.

Adopting this environmental perspective, we can now analyze Ottoman developments in this period through short- and long-term feedback loops. Synthesizing the evidence in this study, we can see how over a period of months or years the disasters of the Little Ice Age would have had a synergistic nature, with problems of flight, famine, and unrest driving a downward spiral of mortality (Figure 11.1). Examined over a period of decades or generations, we can imagine the change in demographic momentum as a shift from a virtuous circle of security and settlement to a vicious cycle of insecurity and flight (Figures 11.2 and 11.3). Throughout the long crisis and its aftermath, therefore, the Ottoman Empire revealed some of the same environmental vulnerabilities as its ancient and medieval predecessors in the Near East. Agriculture remained highly sensitive to climatic fluctuations, as did the delicate balance between the desert and sown. The region continued to feel the ravages of epidemic diseases more than perhaps any other part of the world, exacerbated by unusually high rates of urbanization.

These developments stand in contrast to ecological trends in most of the early modern world, which one environmental historian has characterized as an "unending frontier" of new resources.[77] In China, the destructive transition from the Ming to the Qing may have wiped out a

77 Richards, *Unending Frontier.* The book includes a chapter on nearly every part of the world except the Near East.

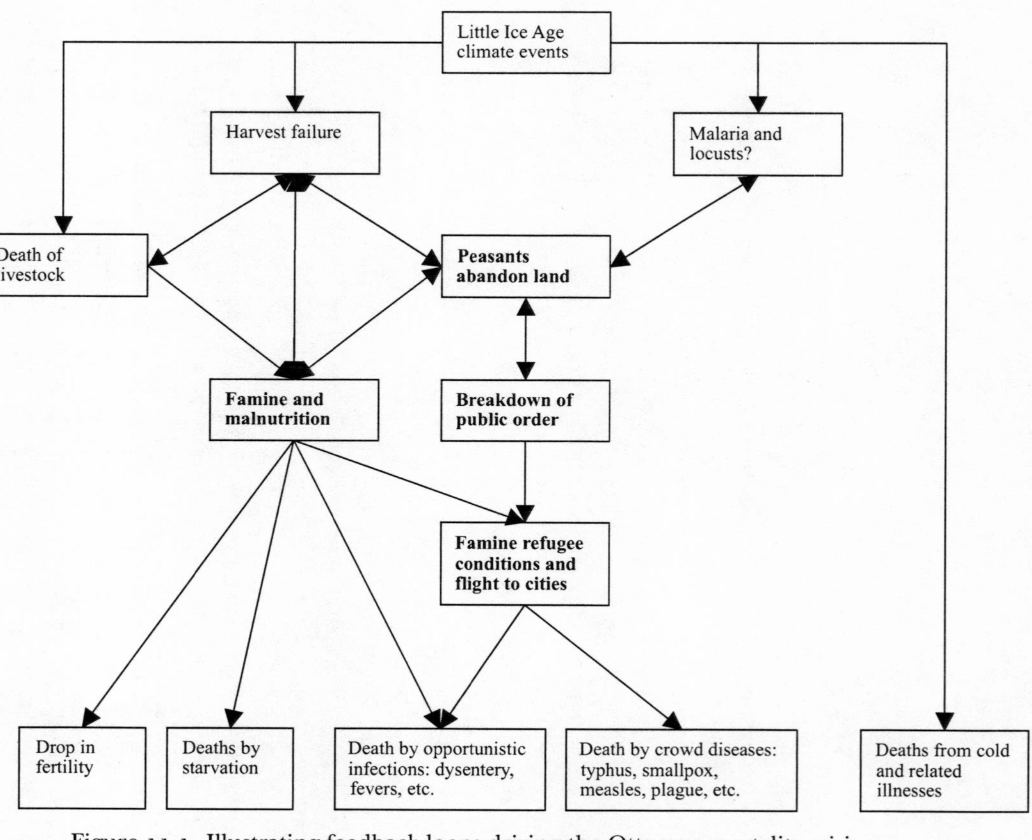

Figure 11.1. Illustrating feedback loops driving the Ottoman mortality crisis.

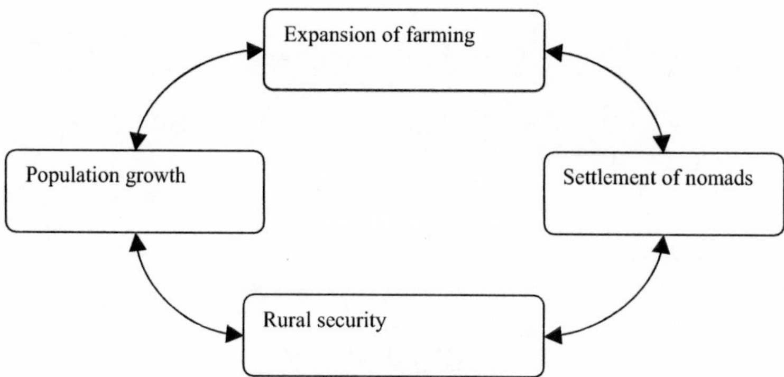

Figure 11.2. Illustrating the virtuous cycle of growth in the sixteenth century.

third of the population, but it represented only a temporary setback in a long-term trend of agricultural intensification, frontier expansion, and demographic growth.[78] Although's Russia's "Time of Troubles" resembled the Celali Rebellion with its scenes of violence, flight, and famine, it barely slowed the empire's ecological momentum, as it conquered the vast Eurasian steppe, and its population multiplied several times over in the following two centuries.[79] In the Ottoman Empire, by contrast, there had never really been a frontier of settlement, but rather an evolving balance of agriculture and pastoralism and of resource and population movements between the countryside and urban areas.

Therefore, the slow pace of Ottoman recovery stands out even more from a global perspective. By the mid-nineteenth century, at which point Ottoman lands had only just attained levels of the 1580s, populations across Europe and Asia had doubled and in some cases redoubled: Continental Europe grew by around 135 percent, and English population rose roughly fourfold.[80] Even Germany, devastated by the Thirty Years War, had more than recovered its population by the mid-eighteenth century and more than doubled its numbers by the mid-nineteenth.[81] Whereas once the number of the Ottoman Empire's subjects had placed it in the class of major world empires, by 1850 it probably held fewer people

78 See, e.g., Perdue, *Exhausting the Earth* and Roberts, *Rice Tigers Silt and Silk.*

79 From perhaps 11 million to 60 million, but earlier figures are rather imprecise. See John Landers, *The Field and the Forge* (New York: Oxford University Press, 2003), 25.

80 Massimo Livi-Bacci, *A Concise History of World Population*, 4th ed. (Malden, MA: Blackwell, 2006), 26 and 66.

81 On Germany's postwar demographic recovery, see Wilson, *Thirty Years War*, 795.

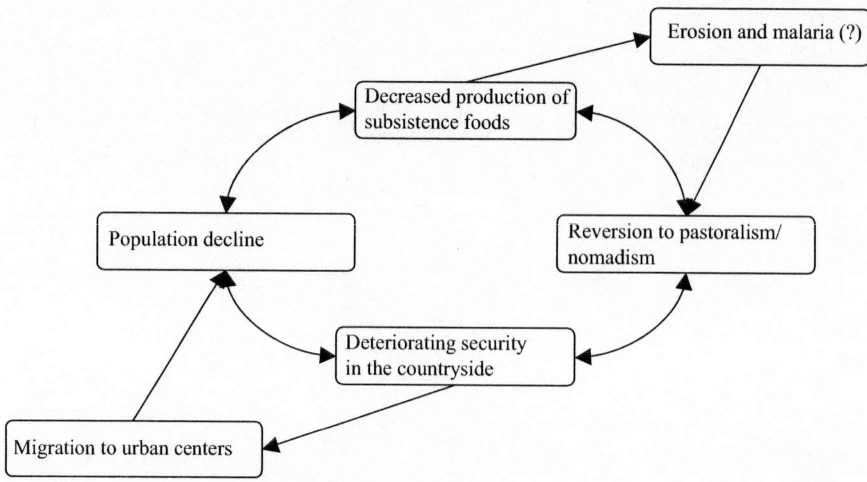

Figure 11.3. Illustrating the vicious cycle of contraction in the seventeenth and eighteenth centuries.

than France or Japan and could no longer even compare with countries such as China, now more than ten times its size. Significant in themselves, these comparisons underscore the powerful role of ecological factors in shaping the fate of the empire by the early 1800s, as confrontations with Europe drove another far-reaching transformation in Ottoman lands.

Only in the mid- to late nineteenth century with the imposition of centralizing, modernizing reforms did the picture start to change again.[82] Aggressive military measures began to restore authority in the provinces, and new methods of sanitation and quarantine cut the death rate. By the 1860s, population in the region was rapidly on the rise once more, eventually to multiply tenfold by the twenty-first century. Demographic growth and an influx of refugees brought agriculture and settlement back into the semiarid plains, as the state tried to brush aside nomadic tribes as an embarrassing anachronism.[83] Meanwhile, new railways and steamships opened the interior to trade and extraction, as parts of the empire started

[82] For overviews of nineteenth-century Ottoman history and after, see Erik Zürcher, *Turkey: A Modern History* (London: I. B. Tauris, 1993); Donald Quataert, *The Ottoman Empire, 1700–1922* (New York: Cambridge University Press, 2005); and Hanioğlu, *Brief History of the Late Ottoman Empire*.

[83] See Kasaba, *Moveable Empire*, chapter 4, and Selim Deringil, "'They Live in a State of Nomadism and Savagery': The Late Ottoman Empire and the Post-Colonial Debate," *Comparative Studies in Society and History* 45 (2003): 311–42.

to industrialize. These changes would not save the Ottoman Empire from dissolution and dismemberment in the First World War, but they would continue to shape the region as it entered the era of nation-states in the twentieth century and beyond. Such developments, however, take us beyond the Little Ice Age crisis and its aftermath and to another chapter of Ottoman environmental history, which has yet to be written.

CONCLUSION

This book has offered a new interpretation of Ottoman history from the sixteenth to the eighteenth centuries. It has argued that in order to understand the empire's successes, crises, and transformations, historians must take into account the ecological conditions of the early modern Near East and the profound impacts and repercussions of the Little Ice Age. In Part I, this study made the case for an expansive "imperial ecology" that underlay the empire's rapid expansion in the classical age but which became increasingly vulnerable to war and natural disaster as population pressure set in over the late 1500s. Part II examined the impact of Little Ice Age climatic fluctuations from the late sixteenth through the early eighteenth centuries, demonstrating the strong links between extreme climate events and the outbreak of the Celali Rebellion and the recurring disorders of the 1600s. Finally, Part III made the case that transformations in human ecology – particularly the spread of nomadic pastoralism, migration to urban areas, and a shift to new crops for commerce and exports – slowed the demographic recovery of Ottoman lands, leaving the empire relatively depopulated by the mid-nineteenth century.

As outlined in the introduction, these findings have significant implications for both Ottoman and world history. First, recognizing the impact of the Little Ice Age forces us to rethink the current debate over Ottoman "decline." It is no longer tenable to blame the empire's troubles of the 1600s simply on the decay of old institutions or the challenges of a rising Europe. Nor, on the other hand, can we minimize the depth of Ottoman crises in these years as just the birth pangs of a new phase of empire. The reality for the vast majority of Ottomans in the long seventeenth century was one of repeated drought, freezing winters, harvest failures, violence, starvation, and disease in which a sizeable portion of the empire perished. In a world now facing global warming, the significance of climate change on human affairs should be readily apparent; and it is all the more remarkable that it would be overlooked among historians studying a time and place when perhaps eight in ten people survived from year to year dependent on a stable climate for the next season's harvest.

Second, analyzing the Ottoman crisis offers further insights into the wider "general crisis" of which it formed an important part. The early onset and enduring impact of the "general crisis" in Ottoman lands illustrates the important role of environmental conditions in determining the severity and duration of crisis in different regions. The Ottoman experience highlights how some parts of the world were more vulnerable than others to the extremes of the Little Ice Age and faced more difficulty reestablishing pre-crisis patterns of growth. Moreover, the Ottoman case emphasizes the nature of the seventeenth-century global crisis as a major turning point in world history. The event catalyzed a global shift in power as some countries recovered more quickly than others demographically, politically, and economically.

Third, this book helps advance a new paradigm of Near East environmental history. Rather than stability or decline, the region has witnessed recurring ecological crises and protracted recoveries. The vulnerabilities of agriculture in irrigated systems and marginal semiarid lands, the sudden shifts between settled cultivation and nomadic pastoralism, the high rates of urbanization, and epidemic outbreaks all played a key role in the Ottoman crisis, just as in crises of centuries and millennia past. Therefore, the Ottoman example may hopefully serve as a useful comparison for historians and archaeologists analyzing similar events in ancient and medieval times.

Fourth, this book has tried to demonstrate how a thorough interdisciplinary investigation can analyze the role of climate in history without either minimizing its impacts or simplifying its effects. In this book, we can see how environmental factors, human agency, and historical accident all played their part in the transformation of a major world empire. As further evidence surfaces, both climatic and historical, parts of the story will no doubt become clearer still, shedding more light on the particular workings of climate in Ottoman and world history.

Finally, it is hard to study the Ottoman case without reflecting on its significance for countries facing climate change today. The Ottoman Empire of the late sixteenth century certainly encountered a difficult situation, and in retrospect some of its mistakes are obvious. The region was naturally vulnerable to climatic shocks, but the heavy demands of the imperial capital and imperial warfare left it more vulnerable still. Ottoman agriculture was already sensitive to the impact of freezing weather and drought, but at the same time population pressure and settlement expansion had left the peasantry with little margin of safety. Farmers and pastoral nomads had traded places along the margins of desert and sown for millennia, but Ottoman sultans in successive generations also failed to devise more effective measures to turn back the tide in favor of secure and settled cultivation.

However, sometimes the empire just suffered excruciating bad luck: a historical factor all too often overlooked, but one that must always play a role in the chaotic drama of climate events. The worst episodes of the Little Ice Age often struck at the most sensitive moments of the Ottomans' most critical wars. The predictable loss of crops in the Great Drought of the 1590s was followed by a less foreseeable but equally disastrous plague among cattle and sheep. An Anatolian peasantry which had accepted its lot for generations suddenly broke out in a violent uprising – although not without provocation.

Therefore, we may judge the Ottomans for their handling of the crisis, but it might be unfair to judge them too harshly. All told, the empire and its subjects had been dealt a difficult hand. They might have played their cards more skillfully, but it also appears in retrospect that the deck had been stacked against them. The Ottomans could have hedged their bets more carefully as well, but they had no way of knowing what cards they would draw next.

Here the contrasts with the present age of global warming are unmistakable. Even with the benefit of modern climate science, it is hard to see how most of the world today would be better prepared for such catastrophic climate events than were the hapless victims of the Little Ice Age. Of course, there will probably not be another Celali Rebellion in the future – but then again, not even the Ottomans themselves could have foreseen the disasters that befell their empire four centuries ago. Their errors and unpreparedness appear obvious to us only with the benefit of hindsight. Today, at least, we have their example and others from history to help us prepare, and some faint idea of what climate might come in the years ahead.

BIBLIOGRAPHY

I. Primary Sources

Unpublished Documents

Başbakanlık Arşivi (Istanbul)

Mühimme Defters (MD): 1–90, and *Zeyli* 1–9 (also using published defters as listed below)
Maliyyeden Müdevver (MAD): Avarızhane Defterleri
Ali Emri Tasnifi: III. Mehmed and I. Ahmed

Archivio di Stato (Venice)

Senato – Dispacci – Bailo, Costantinopoli: 28–55 (including "*Registre*" copies of missing and damaged *filze*) and 65
Provveditori alle Biave: 4–6

Published Documents and Documents Transcribed as Dissertations

6 *Numaralı Mühimme Defteri (972/1564–1565)*. 3 vols. Ankara: T. C. Başbakanlık, Devlet Arşivleri Genel Müdürlüğü, 1995.

Abacı, Nurhan. *The Ottoman Judges and Their Registers: The Bursa Court Register B-90/295 (AH 1081/AD 1670–71)*. Cambridge, MA: Harvard, Dept. of Near Eastern Languages and Studies, 2007.

Akkan, Meltem. "60/2 Numaralı Kayseri Şeriye Sicili (H.1065/M.1655)." PhD diss., Erçiyes Üniversitesi, 2003.

Aköz, Alâadin. "Şeriye Sicillerine Göre XVI. Yüzyıl Sonunda ile XVII. Yüzyıl Başlarında Karaman." PhD diss., Selçuk Üniversitesi, 1987.

Barozzi, N. and G. Berchet, eds. *Le relazioni degli stati Europei lette al senato dagli ambasciatori veneziani nel secolo decimosettimo, vol. V – Turchia*. Venice: P. Naratovich, 1856.

Binark, İsmet. *3 Numaralı Mühimme Defteri, 966–968/1558–1560*. 2 vols. Ankara: T. C. Başbakanlık Devlet Arşivleri Genel Müdürlüğü, 1993.

———. *12 Numaralı Mühimme Defteri, 978–979/1570–1572*. 3 vols. Ankara: T. C. Başbakanlık Devlet Arşivleri Genel Müdürlüğü, 1996.

Binark, İ. and G. Necati. *5 Numaralı Mühimme Defteri (973 / 1565–1566).* 2 vols. Ankara: T. C. Başbakanlık Devlet Arşivleri Genel Müdürlüğü, 1994.

Bostancı, H. Muharrem. "19 Numaralı Mühimme Defteri." PhD diss., İstanbul Üniversitesi, 2002.

Bursa, Fatih. "Manisa'nın 14 Numaralı H.1002 Tarihli Şeriyye Sicil Defteri." PhD diss., Niğde Üniversitesi, 2002.

Çapar, Ahmet. "61/1 Numaralı Kayseri Şeriye Sicili (H.1061/M.1650) Transkripsiyonu ve Değerlendirilmesi." PhD diss., Erçiyes Üniversitesi, 2002.

Deveci, Sefure. "55/2 Numaralı Kayseri Şer'iyye Sicili (H.1055/M.1645) Transkripsiyon ve Değerlendirme." PhD diss., Erçiyes Üniversitesi, 2002.

Dujcev, Ivan. *Avvisi di Ragusa: Documenti sull'Impero turco nel sec. XVII e sulla guerra di Candia.* Rome: Pont. Inst. Orienatlium Studiorum, 1935.

Firpo, Luigi, ed. *Relazioni di ambasciatori veneti al senato XIII: Costantinopoli.* Turin: Bottega d'Erasmo, 1984.

Gök, Eren. "89 Numaralı Mühimme Defteri." PhD diss., Marmara Üniversitesi, 2003.

Gültepe, Necati. "H.1106–7 Tarihli Mühimme Defterine Göre Devlet Kararları (MD 107)." PhD diss., İstanbul Üniversitesi, 1992.

Günay, Musa. "55 Numaralı Mühimme Defteri." PhD diss., Ondokuz Mayıs Üniversitesi, 1996.

Heyd, Uriel. *Ottoman Documents on Palestine, 1552–1615; a Study of the Firman according to the Mühimme Defteri.* Oxford: Clarendon Press, 1960.

Kandıra, Durmuş. "84 Numaralı Mühimme Defteri." PhD diss., İstanbul Üniversitesi, 1995.

Kutluk, Halil. *Tükiye Ormancılığı ile İlgili Tarihi Vesikalar 893–1339 (1487–1923).* Istanbul: Tarım Bakanlığı, 1948.

———. *The Negotiations of Sir Thomas Roe, in his Embassy to the Ottoman Porte, from the year 1621 to 1628, inclusive.* London: Society for the Encouragement of Learning, 1740.

Orhonlu, Cengiz. *Osmanlı Tarihine âit Belgeler: Telhisler (1597–1607).* Istanbul: Edebiyat Fakültesi Basımevi, 1970.

———. *Osmanlı Ormancılığı ile İlgili Belgeler.* 3 vols. Ankara: Türk Cumhurriyeti Orman Bakanlığı, 1999.

Öz, Mehmet. *Canık Sancağı Avârız Defteri (1642).* Ankara: Atatürk Kültür Dil ve Tarih Yüksek Kurumu Yayınları, 2008.

Öz, M. and F. Acun. *Karahisar-ı Şarkî Sancağı Mufassal Avârız Defteri (1642–43 Tarihli).* Ankara: Atatürk Kültür Dil ve Tarih Yüksek Kurumu Yayınları, 2008.

Pedani-Fabris, Maria, ed. *Relazioni di Ambasciatori Veneti al Senato XIV: Costantinopoli Relazioni Inedite (1512–1789).* Turin: Bottega d'Erasmo, 1996.

Refik, Ahmet. *Hicrî On İkinci Asırda İstanbul Hayatı (1100–1200).* Istanbul: Devlet Matbaası, 1930.

———. *Hicrî On Birinci Asırda İstanbul Hayatı (1000–1100).* Istanbul: Devlet Matbaası, 1931.

———. *Onaltıncı Asırda İstanbul Hayatı.* Istanbul: Devlet Matbaası, 1935.

———. *Anadolu'da Türk Aşiretleri (966–1200).* 2nd ed. Istanbul: Enderun Kitabevi, 1989.

Sahillioğlu, H. and E. İhsanoğlu. *Topkapı Sarayı Arşivi H.951–952 Tarihli ve E-12321 Numaralı Mühimme Defteri.* Istanbul: IRCICA, 2002.

Şahin, Mehmet. "Kuyucu Murad Paşa'nın Celâlî Seferi Mühimmesi (1607)." Yüksek Lisans Tezi, İstanbul Üniversitesi, 2002.

Salignac, Jean de Gontaut Biron, baron de. *Ambassade en Turquie de Jean de Gontaut Biron, baron de Salignac, 1605 à 1610.* 3 vols. Paris: H. Champion, 1888–89.

Sarınay, Yusuf. *82 Numaralı Mühimme Defteri, 1026–1027/1617–1618: Özet, Transkripsiyon, İndeks ve Tıpkıbasım.* Ankara: T. C. Başbakanlık Devlet Arşivleri Genel Müdürlüğü, 2000.

———. *83 Numaralı Mühimme Defteri, 1036–1037/1626–1628: Özet, Transkripsiyon, İndeks ve Tıpkıbasım.* Ankara: T. C. Başbakanlık Devlet Arşivleri Genel Müdürlüğü, 2001.

———. *85 Numaralı Mühimme Defteri, 1040–1041 (1042)/1630–1631 (1632): Özet, Transkripsiyon, İndeks.* Ankara: T. C. Başbakanlık Devlet Arşivleri Genel Müdürlüğü, 2002.

Sener Murat et al. *7 Numaralı Mühimme Defteri, 975–976/1567–1569: Tıpkıbasım.* Ankara: T. C. Başbakanlık Devlet Arşivleri Genel Müdürlüğü, 1997.

Tulum, M. and A. Nezihi. *Mühimme Defteri 90.* Istanbul: Türk Dünyası Araştırmaları Vakfı, 1993.

Ülker, Hikmet. *Sultan'ın Emir Defteri: 51 Numaralı Mühimme Defteri.* Istanbul: Tarih ve Tabiat Vakfı, 2003.

Ünal, Mehmet Ali. *Mühimme Defteri 44.* İzmir: Akademi Kitabevi, 1995.

Yıldırım, Osman. *85 Numaralı Mühimme Defteri, 1040–1041 (1042)/1630–1631 (1632).* Ankara: T. C. Başbakanlık Devlet Arşivleri Genel Müdürlüğü, 2002.

Yıldız, Murat. "92 Numaralı ve 1657–8 Tarihli Mühimme Defteri." PhD diss., Fırat Üniversitesi, 2005.

Chronicles and Travelogues

Abdurrahman Abdi Paşa. *Vekayi'nâme.* Edited by Fahri Çetin Derin. PhD diss., Istanbul University, 1993.

Al-Damurdashi. *Al-Damurdashi's Chronicle of Egypt 1688–1755.* Translated by D. Crecelius and 'Abd al-Wahhab Bakr. Leiden: Brill, 1991.

———. *Anonim Osmanlı Tarihi (1099–1116/1688–1704).* Edited by Adülkadir Özcan. Ankara: Türk Tarihi Kurumu Basımevi, 2000.

Arak'el of Tabriz. *The History of Vardapet Arak'el of Tabriz.* Translated by George Bournoutian. Costa Mesa, CA: Mazda Publishers, 2005.

Atsız, Bugra. *Das Osmanische Reich um die Mitte des 17. Jahrhunderts nach den Chroniken des Vecihi (1637–1660) und des Mehmed Halifa (1633–1660).* Munich: Rudolf Trofenik, 1977. (contains a complete reproduction of each chronicle)

Biddulph, William. *The Travels of Certaine Englishmen into Africa, Asia, Troy, Bythinia, Thracia, and to the Blacke Sea.* London, 1609.

Blount, Henry. *A Voyage into the Levant.* London, 1638.

Bostanzade Yahya Efendi, "Vak'a-ı Sultan Osman Han." Published in modern Turkish as Orhan Gökyay, "II. Osman'ın Şehadeti" in *Atsız Armağanı,* 187–256. Istanbul: Ötüken Yayınevi, 1976.

Covel, John. "Extracts from the Diaries of John Covel, 1670–1679." In *Early Voyages and Travels in the Levant,* edited by J. Bent. New York: Ben Franklin, 1972.

de Bruyn, Cornelis. *A Voyage to the Levant: Or, Travels in the Principal Parts of Asia Minor, the Islands of Scio, Rhodes, Cyprus, & C.* London, 1702.

Defterdar Sarı Mehmed Paşa. *Zübde-i Vekayiât.* Edited by Abdülkadir Özcan. Ankara: Türk Tarihi Kurumu Basımevi, 1995.

Evliya Çelebi. *Seyahatname.* Edited by Y. Dağlı et al. 8 vols. Istanbul: Yapı Kredi Yayınları, 2001–2005.

———. *The Famine in Asia Minor: Its History Compiled from the Pages of the Levant Herald* [1875]. Istanbul: Isis Press, 1989.

Forster, E., ed. *The Turkish Letters of Ogier Ghiselin de Busbecq.* Oxford: Clarendon Press, 1927.

Gelibolu Mustafa Âlî. *Künhü'l-Ahbâr.* Edited by Faris Çerçi. 3 vols. Kayseri: Erçiyes Üniversitesi, 2000.

Grelot, Guillaume-Joseph. *A Late Voyage to Constantinople.* London, 1683.

Hasan Bey-zâde Ahmed Paşa. *Hasan Bey-Zâde Târîhi.* Edited by Şevki Nezihi. Ankara, Türk Tarih Kurumu Basımevi, 2004.

Hüseyin Tuği, "Vak'a-i Sultan Osman Han." [published in two versions: Fahir İz, "XVII. Yüzyılda Halk Dili ile Yazılmış bir Tarih Kitabı: Hüseyin Tuği 'Vak'a-i Sultan Osman Han.'" *Türk Dili Araştırmaları Yıllığı Belleten* (1967): 119–55 and Mithat Sertoğlu, "Tuği Tarihi." *Belleten* **11** (1947): 489–514].

Ibn-Battuta. *Travels in Asia and Africa.* Edited by H.A.R. Gibb. New Delhi: Manohar Publishers, 2006.

İbrahim Peçevi. *Peçevî Tarihi.* Edited by Murat Uraz. Istanbul: Neşriyat, 1968.

İsazade. *İsazade Tarihi.* Edited by Ziya Yılmazer. Istanbul: Fetih Cemiyeti, 1996.

Kâtip Çelebi. *Fezleke-yi Kâtip Çelebi (= Fezleket-üt-Tevarih).* 2 vols. Istanbul: Ceride-i Havadis Matbaası, 1870.

———. *The Balance of Truth.* Translated by G. L. Lewis. London: Allen and Unwin, 1957.

———. *Kâtip Çelebi'den Seçmeler.* Edited by Orhan Gökyay. Istanbul: M.E.B., 1968.

Knolles, Richard. *The Turkish History from the Original of That Nation, to the Growth of the Ottoman Empire [etc.] with a Continuation to the Present Year MDCLXXXVII whereunto is added the Present State of the Ottoman Empire by Sir Paul Rycaut, late Consul of Smyrna.* 6th ed. 3 vols. London, 1687.

Mehmed Halife. *Târih-i Gılmanî.* Edited by Kâmil Su. Ankara: Kültür Bakanlığı, 1986.

Mustafa Sâfi. *Zübdetü't-Tevarih.* Edited by İbrahim Çuhadar. Ankara: Türk Tarih Kurumu, 2003.

Naima Mustafa Efendi. *Târîh-i Naîmâ.* Istanbul: Danışman Yayınevi, 1967.

Polonyalı Simeon. *Polonyalı Simeon'un Seyahatnamesi* [1608–1619]. Translated by Hrand Andreasyan. Istanbul: Baha Matbaası, 1964.

Roe, Sir Thomas. *A True and Faithfull Relation, presented to His Majestie and the Prince, of what hath lately happened in Constantinople, concerning the death of Sultan Osman and the setting up of Mustafa his Uncle.* London: B. Downes, 1622.

Russell, Alexander. *The Natural History of Aleppo, Containing a Description of the City, and the Principal Natural Productions in Its Neighbourhood Together with an Account of the Climate, Inhabitants, and Diseases, Particularly of the Plague.* 2nd ed. London, 1794.

Selânikî Mustafa Efendi. *Tarih-i Selânikî.* Edited by Mehmet İpşirli. Ankara: Türk Tarih Kurumu, 1999.

———. Silahdar Fındıklı Mehmed Ağa. *Silahdar Tarihi.* Istanbul: Devlet Matbaası, 1928.

———. Solakzade Mehmed Hemdemî Çelebi. *Solakzâde Tarihi.* Edited by Vahid Çabuk. Ankara: Kültür Bakanlığı, 1989.

———. "*The Strangling and Death of the Great Turke and His Two Sonnes.*" London: I. Dawson, 1622.

———. Topçular Kâtibi 'Abdülkâdir Efendi. *Topçular Kâtibi 'Abdülkâdir Efendi Tarihi.* Edited by Ziya Yılmazer. Ankara: Türk Tarih Kurumu, 2003.

Volney, Constantin-François. *Travels through Egypt and Syria, in the Years 1783, 1784 & 1785.* New York: J. Tiebout, 1798.

Zak'aria of Agulis. *The Journal of Zakaria of Agulis.* Translated by George Bournoutian. Costa Mesa, CA: Mazda, 2003.

Zak'aria of K'anak'er. *The Chronicle of Deacon Zak'aria of K'anak'er.* Translated by George Bournoutian. Costa Mesa, CA: Mazda, 2004.

II. Secondary Sources

Abdulla, Muhammad. "Climatic Fluctuations and Natural Disasters in Arabia between Mid-17th and Early 20th Centuries." *GeoJournal* **37** (1995): 176–80.

Abou-el-Haj, Rifat. *The 1703 Rebellion and the Structure of Ottoman Politics.* Leiden: Brill, 1984.

———. *The Formation of the Modern State: The Ottoman Empire 16th–18th Century.* Albany: SUNY Press, 1991.

Abu-Lughod, Janet. "The Islamic City – Historic Myth, Islamic Essence, and Contemporary Relevance." *International Journal of Middle East Studies* **19** (1987): 155–76.

Adams, J., M. Mann, and C. Amman. "Proxy Evidence for an El Niño-Like Response to Volcanic Forcing." *Nature* **426** (2003): 274–8.

Adams, Robert. *Land behind Baghdad: A History of Settlement on the Diyala Plains.* Chicago: University of Chicago Press, 1965.

Adas, Michael. "From Avoidance to Confrontation: Peasant Protest in Precolonial and Colonial Southeast Asia." *Comparative Studies in Society and History* **23** (1981): 217–47.

Afyoncu, Erhan. "Türkiye'de Tahrir Defterlerine Dayalı Olarak Hazırlanmış Çalışmalar Hakkında Bazı Görüşler." *Türkiye Araştırmaları Literatür Dergisi* **1** (2003): 267–86.

Ağır, Seven. "From Welfare to Wealth: Ottoman and Castilian Grain Trade Policies in a Time of Change." PhD diss., Princeton University, 2009.

Agoston, Gabor. "Habsburgs and Ottomans: Defense, Military Change, and Shifts in Power." *Turkish Studies Association Bulletin* **22** (1998): 126–41.

______. "A Flexible Empire: Authority and Its Limits on the Ottoman Frontiers." *International Journal of Turkish Studies* **9** (2003): 15–31.

______. *Guns for the Sultan: Military Power and the Weapons Industry in the Ottoman Empire.* New York: Cambridge University Press, 2005.

Ak, Mustafa. "Osmanlı Coğrafya Çalışmaları." *Türkiye Araştırmaları Literatür Dergisi* **2** (2004): 163–211.

Akdağ, Mustafa. "Celâlî Fetreti." *Ankara Üniversitesi Dil ve Coğrafya Fakültesi Dergisi* **16** (1958): 53–107.

______. *Celâlî İsyanları.* Ankara: Ankara Üniversitesi Basımevi, 1963.

______. "Celâli İsyanlarından Büyük Kaçgunluk." *Tarih Araştırmaları Dergisi* **2** (1964): 1–49.

______. "Genel Çizgilerle XVII. Yüzyıl Türkiye Tarihi." *Tarih Araştırmaları Dergisi* **4** (1966): 201–47.

______. "Kara-Yazıcı." In *İslam Ansiklopedisi,* edited by M. Houtsma. Istanbul: Maarif Matbaası, 1940–88.

______. *Türkiye'nin İktisadi ve İçtimai Tarihi.* Ankara: Türk Tarih Kurumu Basımevi, 1971.

______. *Türk Halkının Dirlik ve Düzenlik Kavgası.* Ankara: Bilgi Yayınevi, 1975.

Akgündüz, Ahmed. *İslam ve Osmanlı Çevre Hukuku.* Istanbul: Osmanlı Araştırmaları Vakfı, 2009.

Akkemik, Ü. and A. Aras. "Reconstruction (1689–1994) of April–August Precipitation in the Southern Part of Central Turkey." *International Journal of Climatology* **25** (2005): 537–48.

Akkemik, Ü. et al. "Anadolu'nun Son 350 Yılında Yaşanan Önemli Kurak ve Yağışlı Yıllar." *Türkiye Kuvarterner Sempozyumu* **5** (2005): 129–35.

______. "A Preliminary Reconstruction (AD 1635–2003) of Spring Precipitation Using Oak Tree Rings in the Western Black Sea Region of Turkey." *International Journal of Biometeorology* **49** (2005): 297–302.

______. "Tree-Ring Reconstructions of Precipitation and Streamflow for Northwestern Turkey." *International Journal of Climatology* **28** (2008): 173–83.

Aköz, Alâadin. "XVI. yy. Sonunda Karaman." *Osmanlı Araştırmaları* **9** (1989): 331–45.

Aksan, Virginia. *An Ottoman Statesman in War and Peace.* Leiden: Brill, 1995.

______. "Feeding the Ottoman Troops on the Danube, 1768–1774." *War and Society* **13** (1995): 1–14.

______. "Locating the Ottomans among Early Modern Empires." *Journal of Early Modern History* **3** (1999): 103–35.

______. *Ottoman Wars 1700–1870: An Empire Besieged.* New York: Pearson, 2007.

Aktan, Ali. "Kayseri Kadı Sicillerindeki Tereke Kayıtları Üzerinde Bazı Değerlendirmeler (1738–1749)." In *II. Kayseri ve Yöresi Tarih Sempozyumu Bildirileri,* 47–68. Kayseri: Erçiyes Üniversitesi, 1998.

Aktepe, M. Münir. "XVIII. Asrın İlk Yarısında İstanbul'un Nüfus Mes'elesine Dâir Bâzı Vesikalar." *Tarih Dergisi* **9** (1958): 1–30.

______. *Patrona İsyanı.* Istanbul: Edebiyat Fakültesi Basımevi, 1958.

Albion, Robert. *Forests and Sea Power: The Timber Problem of the Royal Navy 1652–1862*. Cambridge, MA: Harvard University Press, 1926.

Allman, James. "The Demographic Transition in the Middle East and North Africa." *International Journal of Middle East Studies* **12** (1980): 277–301.

Ambraseys, N. and C. Finkel. *The Seismicity of Turkey and Adjacent Areas: A Historical Review, 1500–1800*. Istanbul: M. S. Eren, 1995.

Anderson, Perry. *Lineages of the Absolutist State*. London: N.L.B., 1974.

Andreasyan, Hrand. "Bir Ermeni Kaynağına Göre Celâlî İsyanları." *İstanbul Üniversitesi Edebiyat Fakültesi Tarih Dergisi* **13** (1963): 27–42.

______. "Abaza Mehmed Paşa." *Tarih Dergisi* **13** (1967): 131–42.

______. "Eremya Çelebi'nin Yangınlar Tarihi." *İstanbul Üniversitesi Edebiyat Fakültesi Tarih Dergisi* **27** (1973): 59–84.

______. "Celâlilerden Kaçan Anadolu Halkının Geri Gönderilmesi" In *İsmail Hakkı Uzunçarşılı'ya Armağan*, 45–53. Ankara: Türk Tarih Kurumu, 1976.

Andrews, Jean. "Diffusion of the Mesoamerican Food Complex to Southeastern Europe." *Geographical Review* **83** (1993): 194–204.

Angel, J. Lawrence. "Ecology and Population in the Eastern Mediterranean." *World Archaeology* **4** (1972): 88–105.

Appleby, Andrew. "Nutrition and Disease: The Case of London." *Journal of Interdisciplinary History* **6** (1975): 1–22.

______. *Famine in Tudor and Stuart England*. Stanford, CA: Stanford University Press, 1978.

______. "Epidemics and Famine in the Little Ice Age." In *Climate and History*, edited by R. Rotberg and T. Rabb, 65–83. Princeton, NJ: Princeton University Press, 1981.

Appuhn, Karl. "Inventing Nature: Forests, Forestry, and State Power in Renaissance Venice." *The Journal of Modern History* **72** (2000): 861–89.

Arbel, Benjamin. "Sauterelles et mentalités: le cas de la Chypre vénitienne." *Annales* **44** (1989): 1057–74.

Arslan, Hüseyin. *Osmanlı'da Nüfus Hareketleri (XVI. Yüzyıl): Yönetim, Nüfus, Göçler, İskânlar, Sürgünler*. Istanbul: Kaknüs, 2001.

Artan, Tülay. "Aspects of the Ottoman Elite's Food Consumption: Looking for 'Staples,' 'Luxuries' and 'Delicacies' in a Changing Century." In *Consumption Studies in the History of the Ottoman Empire*, edited by D. Quataert, 107–200. Binghamton: SUNY Press, 2000.

Ashtor, Eliyahu. "The Economic Decline of the Middle East during the Later Middle Ages: An Outline." *Asian and African Studies* **15** (1981): 253–86.

Aston, T. H., ed. *Crisis in Europe, 1560–1660*. Garden City, NY: Anchor Books, 1967.

Ataman, Bekir Kemal. "Ottoman Demographic History (14th–17th Centuries): Some Considerations." *Journal of the Economic and Social History of the Orient* **35** (1992): 187–98.

Atwell, William. "Some Observations on the 'Seventeenth-Century Crisis' in China and Japan." *The Journal of Asian Studies* **45** (1986): 223–44.

______. "A Seventeenth-Century 'General Crisis' in East Asia?" *Modern Asian Studies* **24** (1990): 661–82.

———. "Volcanism and Short-Term Climatic Change in East Asian and World History, c. 1200–1699." *Journal of World History* **12** (2001): 29–99.

Ayalon, Yaron. "Famines, Earthquakes, Plagues: Natural Disasters in Ottoman Syria in the Writings of Visitors." *Osmanlı Araştırmaları* **32** (2008): 223–47.

Aydın, Sabahattin. "Modern Tıp Penceresinden Osmanlı Tıp Anlayışına Bakış." In *Osmanlılarda Sağlık*, edited by C. Yılmaz and N. Yılmaz. Istanbul: Biofarma, 2006.

Aymard, Maurice. *Venise, Raguse, et la commerce de blé pendant la seconde moitié du XVIe siècle.* Paris: SEVPEN, 1966.

Baer, Marc. "The Great Fire of 1660 and the Islamization of Christian and Jewish Space in Istanbul." *International Journal of Middle East Studies* **36** (2004): 159–81.

Bairoch, Paul. *Cities and Economic Development: From the Dawn of History to the Present.* Chicago: University of Chicago Press, 1988.

Balta, E. "The Bread in Greek Lands during the Ottoman Rule." *Tarih Araştırmaları Dergisi* **16** (1994): 199–226.

Bang, Frederik. "The Role of Disease in the Ecology of Famine." In *Famine: Its Causes, Effects and Management*, edited by John Robson, 61–75. New York: Gordon and Breach, 1981.

Barkan, Ömer Lütfi. "XV ve XVI. Asırlarda Osmanlı İmparatorluğunda Toprak İşçiliğinin Organizasyonu Şekilleri: Kulluklar ve Ortakçı Kullar." *İktisat Fakültesi Mecmuası* **1** (1939–40): 29–74.

———. "Türkiye'de İmparatorluk Devirlerinin Nüfus ve Arazi Tahrirleri ve Hâkana Mahsus İstatik Defterleri (I)." *İktisat Fakültesi Mecmuası* **2** (1940): 20–59.

———. "Türkiye'de İmparatorluk Devirlerinin Nüfus ve Arazi Tahrirleri ve Hâkana Mahsus İstatik Defterleri (II)." *İktisat Fakültesi Mecmuası* **2** (1941): 214–47.

———. "Bir İskân ve Kolonizasyon Metodu Olarak Sürgünler." *İktisat Fakültesi Mecmuası* **11–15** (1949–1954).

———. "'Tarihî Demografi' Araştırmaları ve Osmanlı Tarihi." *Türkiyat Mecmuası* **10** (1953): 1–26.

———. "H. 933–934 (M.1527–1528) Malî Yılına Ait Bir Bütçe Örneği." *İktisat Fakültesi Mecmuası* **15** (1953–1954): 278–329.

———. "La "Méditeranée" de Fernand Braudel: Vue d'Istamboul." *Annales* (1954): 189–200.

———. "Essai sur les données statistiques de régistres de recensement dans l'Empire ottoman aux XVe et XVIe siècles." *Journal of the Economic and Social History of the Orient* **1** (1958): 9–36.

———. "Edirne Askeri Kassamı'na Âit Tereke Defterleri." *Belgeler* **3** (1966): 1–479.

———. "Research on the Ottoman Fiscal Surveys." In *Studies in the Social and Economic History of the Middle East*, edited by M. Cook, 163–71. London: Oxford University Press, 1970.

———. "The Price Revolution of the Sixteenth Century: A Turning Point in the Economic History of the Near East." *International Journal of Middle East Studies* **6** (1975): 3–28.

———. *Türkiye'de Toprak Meselesi.* Istanbul: Gözlem Yayınları, 1980.

Barkey, Karen. *Bandits and Bureaucrats: The Ottoman Route to State Centralization.* Ithaca, NY: Cornell University Press, 1994.

———. *Empire of Difference: The Ottomans in Comparative Perspective.* New York: Cambridge University Press, 2008.

Bar-Matthews, M., A. Ayalon, and A. Kaufman. "Middle to Late Holocene (6,500 Yr. Period) Paleoclimate in the Eastern Mediterranean Region from Stable Isotopic Composition of Speleothems from Soreq Cave, Israel." In *Water, Environment and Society in Times of Climatic Change,* edited by A. Issar and N. Brown, 203–14. Dordrecht: Kluwer Academic Publishing, 1998.

Barth, Frederik. *Nomads of South Persia.* New York: Humanities Press, 1964.

Bechman, Roland. *Trees and Man: The Forest in the Middle Ages.* New York: Paragon House, 1990.

Becker, Peter. "Zur Theorie und Praxis von Regierung und Verwaltung in Zeiten der Krise." In *Kulturelle Konsequenzen der "Kleinen Eiszeit,"* edited by W. Behringer et al., 347–67. Göttingen: Vandenhoeck & Ruprecht, 2005.

Behar, Cem. *Osmanlı İmparatorluğu'nun ve Türkiye'nin Nüfusu 1500–1927.* Ankara: T. C. Başbakanlık Devlet İstatik Enstitüsü, 1996.

Behringer, Wolfgang. *A Cultural History of Climate.* Cambridge, UK: Polity, 2010.

Behringer, W. et al., eds. *Kulturelle Konsequenzen der "Kleinen Eiszeit."* Göttingen: Vandenhoeck and Ruprecht, 2005.

Beldiceanu, N. and I. Beldiceanu-Steinherr. "Recherches sur la province de Qaraman au XVIe siècle, étude et actes." *Journal of the Economic and Social History of the Orient* **11** (1968): 1–129.

———. "Riziculture dans l'Empire ottoman (XIVe–XVe siècles)." *Turcica* **10** (1978): 9–28.

Beldiceanu-Steinherr, Irene. "Un transfuge qaramanide auprès de la Porte ottomane: Reflexions sur quelques institutions." *Journal of the Economic and Social History of the Orient* **16** (1973): 155–67.

Beldiceanu-Steinherr, I. and J.-L. Bacqué-Grammont. "A propos de quelques causes de malaises sociaux en Anatolie central." *Archivum Ottomanicum* **7** (1982): 71–116.

Berkeş, Niyazi. *The Development of Secularism in Turkey.* Montreal: McGill University Press, 1964.

Bildirici, Mehmet. *Tarihi Su Yapıları: Konya, Karaman, Niğde, Aksaray, Yalvaç, Side, Mut, Silifke.* Ankara: T. C. Bayındırlık ve İskân Bakanlığı, 1994.

Bintliff, John. "Time, Process and Catastrophism in the Study of Mediterranean Alluvial History: A Review." *World Archaeology* **33** (2002): 417–35.

Biraben, Jean-Noel. *Les hommes et la peste en France et dans les pays européens et méditerranéens.* Paris: Mouton, 1975.

Boehm, P. and D. Gerold. "Historische und aktuelle Bodenerosion in Anatolien." *Geographische Rundschau* **47** (1995): 720–5.

Boomgaard, Peter. "Crisis Mortality in Seventeenth Century Indonesia." In *Asian Population History,* edited by T. Liu, 191–220. New York: Oxford University Press, 2001.

Boratav, K. et al. "Ottoman Wages and the World Economy, 1839–1913." *Review* **8** (1985): 379–406.

Börekçi, Günhan. "A Contribution to the Military Revolution Debate: The Janissaries' Use of Volley Fire during the Long Ottoman-Habsburg War of 1593–1606 and the Problem of Origins." *Acta Orientalia* **59** (2006): 407–38.

———. "Factions and Favorites at the Courts of Sultan Ahmed I (r. 1603–17) and His Immediate Predecessors." PhD diss., Ohio State University, 2010.

Borsch, Stuart. "Environment and Population: The Collapse of Large Irrigation Systems Reconsidered." *The Journal of Interdisciplinary History* **46** (2004): 451–68.

———. *The Black Death in Egypt and England.* Austin: University of Texas Press, 2005.

Boserup, Ester. *The Conditions of Agricultural Growth: The Economics of Agrarian Change under Population Pressure.* London: Allen and Unwin, 1965.

Bostan, İdris. *Osmanlı Bahriye Teşkilâtı: XVII. Yüzyılda Tersâne-i Âmire.* Ankara: Türk Tarih Kurumu, 1992.

———. "Osmanlı Bahriyesinde Sağlık Hizmetleri." In *Osmanlılarda Sağlık*, edited by C. Yılmaz and N. Yılmaz. Istanbul: Biofarma, 2006.

Bottema, S. et al., eds. *Man's Role in the Shaping of the Eastern Mediterranean Landscape.* Rotterdam: A. A. Balkema, 1990.

Bottema, Sytze. "A Pollen Diagram from the Syrian Anti-Lebanon." *Paleorient* **3** (1975/7): 259–68.

Braudel, Fernand. *The Mediterranean and the Mediterranean World in the Age of Philip II.* New York: Harper and Row, 1972.

———. *The Structures of Everyday Life.* New York: Harper and Row, 1981.

Brázdil, R. et al. "Historical Climatology in Europe – the State of the Art." *Climatic Change* **70** (2005): 363–430.

———. "European Climatology of the Past 500 Years: New Challenges for Historical Climatology." *Climatic Change* **101** (2010): 7–40.

Brewer, John. *The Sinews of Power: War, Money and the English State, 1688–1783.* Cambridge, MA: Harvard University Press, 1990.

Bricogne, Louis. "Les forets de l'Empire ottoman." *Revue des eaux et forets* **16** (1877): 273–89 and 321–35.

Briffa, K. et al. "European Tree Rings and Climate in the Sixteenth Century." *Climatic Change* **43** (1999): 151–68.

———. "Influence of Volcanic Eruptions on Northern Hemisphere Summer Temperature over the Past 600 Years." *Nature* **393** (1999): 450–5.

Broecker, Wallace. "Was a Change in Thermohaline Circulation Responsible for the Little Ice Age?" *Bulletin of the National Academy of Sciences* **97** (2000): 1339–42.

Brooks, George. *Landlords and Strangers: Ecology, Society, and Trade in Western Africa, 1000–1630.* Boulder, CO: Westview Press, 1993.

Brooks, Nick. "Cultural Responses to Aridity in the Middle Holocene and Increased Social Complexity." *Quaternary International* **151** (2006): 29–49.

Brown, Neville. *History and Climate Change: A Eurocentric Perspective.* London: Routledge, 2001.

Bruce-Chwatt, L. and J. Zulueta. *The Rise and Fall of Malaria in Europe.* New York: Oxford University Press, 1980.

Brumfield, Allaire. "Agriculture and Rural Settlement in Ottoman Crete, 1669–1898." In *A Historical Archaeology of the Ottoman Empire*, edited by U. Baram and L. Carroll, 37–78. New York: Springer, 2000.

Bulliet, Richard. *The Camel and the Wheel.* New York: Columbia University Press, 1990.

———. *Islam: The View from the Edge.* New York: Columbia University Press, 1994.

———. *Cotton, Climate, and Camels in Early Islamic Iran: A Moment in World History.* New York: Columbia University Press, 2009.

Bulmuş, Birsen. "The Plague in the Ottoman Empire, 1300–1838." PhD diss., Georgetown University, 2008.

Bulut, Rukiye. "XVIII. Yüzyılda İstanbul Nüfusunun Artmaması İçin Alınan Tedbirler." *Belgelerle Türk Tarihi Dergisi* **1** (1967): 30–2.

Burke, Edmund. "The Transformation of the Middle Eastern Environment 1500 B.C.E.–2000 C.E." In *The Environment and World History*, edited by E. Burke and K. Pommeranz, 81–117. Berkeley: University of California Press, 2009.

Burke, Peter. "Southern Italy in the 1590s: Hard Times or Crisis?" In *The European Crisis of the 1590s: Essays in Comparative History*, edited by P. Clark, 177–90. London: Allen and Unwin, 1985.

Butzer, Karl. "Environmental History in the Mediterranean World: Cross-Disciplinary Investigation of Cause-and-Effect for Degradation and Soil Erosion." *Journal of Archaeological Science* **32** (2005): 1773–800.

Cahen, Claude. *Pre-Ottoman Turkey.* London: Sidgwick and Jackson, 1968.

Çakır, Baki. "Geleneksel Dönem (Tanzimat Öncesi) Osmanlı Bütçe Gelirleri," in *Osmalı Maliyesi Kurumlar ve Bütçeler.* Edited by M. Genç and E. Özvar, 167–96. Istanbul: Osmanlı Bankası Arşiv ve Araştırma Merkezi, 2006.

Camuffo, D. and S. Enzi. "Chronology of 'Dry Fogs' in Italy, 1374–1891." *Theoretical and Applied Climatology* **50** (1994): 31–3.

———. "The Climate of Italy from 1675–1715," in *Climatic Trends and Anomalies in Europe 1675–1715.* Edited by B. Frenzel et al., 243–54. Stuttgart: Fischer, 1994.

———. "Locust Invasions and Climatic Factors from the Middle Ages to 1800." *Theoretical and Applied Climatology* **43** (1991): 43–73.

Camuffo, Dario "Freezing of the Venetian Lagoon since the 9th Century AD in Comparison to the Climate of Western Europe and England." *Climatic Change* **10** (1987): 43–66.

Carmichael, Ann. "Infection, Hidden Hunger, and History." In *Hunger and History: The Impact of Changing Consumption Patterns on Society*, edited by R. Rottberg and T. Rabb, 51–66. Cambridge: Cambridge University Press, 1983.

Cartwright, Frederick. *Disease in History.* New York: Crowell, 1972.

Casale, Giancarlo. *The Ottoman Age of Exploration.* New York: Cambridge University Press, 2010.

Cavalli-Sforza, Luigi. *Genes, Peoples, and Languages.* Berkeley: University of California Press, 2000.

Caviedes, César N. *El Niño: Storming through the Ages.* Gainesville: University Press of Florida, 2001.

Çeçen, Kazım. *İstanbul'da Osmanlı Devrindeki Su Tesisleri.* Istanbul: İstanbul Teknik Üniversitesi, 1984.

Çelik, I. "Land-Use Effects on Organic Matter and Physical Properties of Soil in a Southern Mediterranean Highland of Turkey." *Soil and Tillage Research* **83** (2005): 270–7.

Çevikel, Nuri. "The Rise of the Ottoman Ayans: A Case Study of the Province of Cyprus during the Eighteenth Century." *International Journal of Turkish Studies* **15** (2009): 83–94.

Cezar, Mustafa. "Osmanlı Devrinde İstanbul Yapılarında Tahribat Yapan Yangınlar ve Tabii Afetler." In *Türk San'atı Tarihi,* vol. 1, 326–414. Istanbul: Berksoy Matbaası, 1963.

______. *Osmanlı Tarihinde Levendler.* Istanbul: Çelikcilt Matbaası, 1965.

Christensen, Peter. *The Decline of Iranshahr: Irrigation and Environments in the History of the Middle East, 500 B.C. to A.D. 1500.* Copenhagen: Museum Tusculanum, 1993.

Cipolla, Carlo. *Guns, Sails, and Empires: Technological Innovation and the Early Phases of European Expansion, 1400–1700.* New York: Minerva, 1965.

Çızakça, Murat. "Price History and the Bursa Silk Industry: A Study in Ottoman Industrial Decline, 1550–1650." *The Journal of Economic History* **40** (1980): 533–50.

______. "Ottomans and the Mediterranean: An Analysis of the Ottoman Shipbuilding Industry as Reflected by the Arsenal Registers of Istanbul 1529–1650." In *Le Genti del Mare Mediterraneo,* edited by R. Ragosta, 773–89. Naples: Lucio Pironti, 1981.

______. "Incorporation of the Middle East into the European World-Economy." *Review* **8** (1985): 353–77.

Cohn, Samuel. "The Black Death: End of a Paradigm." *American Historical Review* (2002): 703–38.

Congourdeau, Marie-Helene. "La société byzantine face aux grandes pandémies." In *Maladie et société à Byzance,* edited by E. Patlagean, 21–42. Spoleto: Centro di studi sull'alto Medioevo, 1993.

Congourdeau, M.-H. and M. Melhaoui. "La perception de la peste en pays chrètien byzantin et musulman." *Revue des études byzantines* **59** (2000): 95–124.

Conrad, Lawrence. "The Plague in the Early Medieval Near East." PhD diss., Princeton University, 1981.

______. "Ta'un and Waba Conceptions of Plague and Pestilence in Early Islam." *Journal of the Economic and Social History of the Orient* **25** (1982): 268–307.

______. "Epidemic Disease in Formal and Popular Thought in Early Islamic Society." In *Epidemics and Ideas: Essays on the Historical Perception of Pestilence,* edited by T. Ranger and P. Slack, 77–99. New York: Cambridge University Press, 1992.

Cook, Michael. *Population Pressure in Rural Anatolia, 1450–1600.* London: Oxford University Press, 1972.

Crosby, Alfred. *Ecological Imperialism: The Biological Expansion of Europe, 900–1900.* New York: Cambridge University Press, 1986.

Crowley, Thomas. "Causes of Climate Change over the Past 1000 Years." *Science* **289** (2000): 270–7.

Cullen, H. and P. DeMenocal. "North Atlantic Influence on Tigris-Euphrates Streamflow." *International Journal of Climatology* **20** (2000): 853–63.

Cullen, H. et al. "Impact of the North Atlantic Oscillation on Middle Eastern Climate and Streamflow." *Climatic Change* **55** (2002): 315–38.

Cunningham, A. and O. Grell. *The Four Horsemen of the Apocalypse: Religion, War, Famine, and Death in Reformation Europe.* New York: Cambridge University Press, 2000.

Cvetkova, Bistra A. "Le service des celep et le ravitaillement en bétail dans l'Empire ottoman (XVe–XVIIIe s.)." *Études historiques* **3** (1966): 145–72.

Dalfes, H., G. Kukla, and H. Weiss, eds. *Third Millennium B.C. Climate Change and Old World Collapse.* Berlin: Springer, 1997.

Darling, Linda. *Revenue-Raising and Legitimacy: Tax Collection and Finance Administration in the Ottoman Empire (1560–1660).* Leiden: Brill, 1996.

______. "Political Change and Political Discourse in the Early Modern Mediterranean World." *Journal of Interdisciplinary History* **38** (2008): 505–31.

D'Arrigo, R. and H. Cullen. "A 350-Year (AD 1628–1980) Reconstruction of Turkish Precipitation." *Dendrochronologia* **19** (2001): 853–63.

David, Geza. "The Age of Unmarried Male Children in the *Tahrir Defters* (Notes on the Coefficient)." *Acta Orientalia Hungarica* **31** (1977): 347–57.

______. "Demographische Veranderungen in Ungarn zur Zeit der Türkenherrschaft." *Acta Historica* **39** (1988): 79–87.

______. "Data on the Continuity and Migration of the Population in 16th Century in Ottoman Hungary." *Acta Orientalia Hungarica* **45** (1991): 219–52.

______. "16.–17. Yüzyıllarda Macaristan'ın Demografik Durumu." *Belleten* **59** (1995): 341–52.

Davis, Diana. *Resurrecting the Granary of Rome: Environmental History and French Colonial Expansion in North Africa.* Athens: Ohio University Press, 2007.

Decker, Michael. "Plants and Progress: Rethinking the Islamic Agricultural Revolution." *Journal of World History* **20** (2009): 187–206.

de Groot, A. and J. Rogers. "Laranda," in *Encyclopedia of Islam Online.* http://www.brillonline.nl/.

DeMenocal, Peter. "Cultural Responses to Climate Change during the Late Holocene." *Science* **292** (2001): 667–73.

Demirci, Süleyman. "Demography and History: The Value of the *Avârızhâne* Registers for Demographic Research: A Case Study of the Ottoman Sub-Provinces of Konya, Kayseri, Sivas and Bozok, 1620s–1700." Paper presented at the 19th Middle East History and Theory Conference, University of Chicago, 2004.

______. "*Avârız* and *Nüzul* Levies in the Ottoman Empire: A Case Study of the Province of Karaman, 1620s–1700." *Belleten* **70** (2007): 561–88.

______. *The Functioning of Ottoman Avâriz Taxation: An Aspect of the Relationship between Center and Periphery.* Istanbul: Isis, 2009.

Demirel, Ömer. "1700–30 Tarihlerinde Ankara'da Ailenin Niceliksel Yapısı." *Belleten* **54** (1990): 945–61.

Demirel, Ö. et al. "Osmanlılarda Ailenin Demografik Yapısı." In *Sosyo-Kultürel Değişme Sürecinde Türk Ailesi.* Ankara: T. C. Başbakanlık Aile Kurumu, 1993.

Deringil, Selim. "'They Live in a State of Nomadism and Savagery': The Late Ottoman Empire and the Post-Colonial Debate." *Comparative Studies in Society and History* **45** (2003): 311–42.

De Silva, S. and G. Zielinski. "Global Influence of the AD 1600 Eruption of Huaynaputina, Peru." *Nature* **393** (1998): 455–8.

de Vries, Jan. *The Dutch Rural Economy in the Golden Age 1500–1700.* New Haven, CT: Yale University Press, 1974.

______. *The Economy of Europe in an Age of Crisis, 1600–1750.* New York: Cambridge University Press, 1976.

______. "Measuring the Impact of Climate on History: The Search for Appropriate Methodologies." *Journal of Interdisciplinary History* **10** (1980): 599–630.

______. *European Urbanization, 1500–1800.* Cambridge, MA: Harvard University Press, 1984.

de Vries, J. and A. van der Woude. *The First Modern Economy.* New York: Cambridge University Press, 1997.

Dewald, Jonathan. "Crisis, Chronology, and the Shape of European Social History." *The American Historical Review* **113** (2008): 1031–52.

Diamond, Jared. *Guns, Germs, and Steel: The Fates of Human Societies.* New York: Norton, 1999.

______. *Collapse: How Societies Choose to Fail or Succeed.* New York: Norton, 2005.

Dols, Michael. *The Black Death in the Middle East.* Princeton, NJ: Princeton University Press, 1977.

______. "The Second Plague Pandemic and Its Recurrences in the Middle East." *Journal of the Economic and Social History of the Orient* **22** (1979): 162–89.

Drnda, Hatidza Car. "Pljevlja'd (Taşluca) Nüfusun Yapısı – 15. Yüzyılın İkinci Yarısı ve 16. Yüzyıl." *Belleten* **74** (2010): 113–26.

Duben, Alan. "Turkish Families and Households in Historical Perspective." *Journal of Family History* **10** (1985): 75–97.

Duben, A. and C. Behar. *Istanbul Households: Marriage, Family and Fertility 1880–1940.* New York: Cambridge University Press, 1991.

Dunning, Chester. "Does Jack Goldstone's Model of Early Modern State Crises Apply to Russia?" *Comparative Studies in Society and History* **39** (1997): 572–92.

______. *Russia's First Civil War: The Time of Troubles and the Founding of the Romanov Dynasty.* College Park, PA: Penn State University Press, 2001.

Dupâquier, Jacques. "Subsistence Crises in France 1650–1725." In *Famine, Disease and the Social Order in Early Modern Society,* edited by J. Walker and R. Schofield, 189–99. Cambridge: Cambridge University Press, 1989.

Dursun, Selçuk. "Forest and the State: History of Forestry and Forest Administration in the Ottoman Empire." PhD diss., Sabancı University, 2007.

Düzbakar, Ömer. "XVII. Yüzyıl Sonlarında Bursa'da Ekonomik ve Sosyal Hayat." PhD diss., Ankara Üniversitesi, 2003.

Eaton, Richard. *The Rise of Islam and the Bengal Frontier.* Berkeley: University of California Press, 1993.

Eddy, John. "Solar History and Human Affairs." *Human Ecology* **22** (1994): 23–36.

Eldem, Etem. "Capitulations and Western Trade." In *The Cambridge History of Turkey*, vol. 3, edited by S. Faroqhi, 283–335. New York: Cambridge University Press, 2006.

Elvin, Mark. *The Pattern of the Chinese Past.* Stanford, CA: Stanford University Press, 1973.

______. "The Environmental Legacy of Imperial China." *China Quarterly* **156** (1999): 733–56.

______. *The Retreat of the Elephants: An Environmental History of China.* New Haven, CT: Yale University Press, 2004.

Emile-Geay, Julien. "Volcanoes and ENSO over the Past Millennium." *Journal of Climate* **21** (2008): 3134–49.

Endfield, Georgina. *Climate and Society in Colonial Mexico.* London: Blackwell, 2008.

Engin, İsmail. "Tahtacılar: Kimdir ve Kökenleri Nereden Gelir?" *Toplumsal Tarih* **4–5** (1995–1996).

Erder, Leila. "The Measurement of Pre-Industrial Population Changes: The Ottoman Empire from the 15th to the 17th Century." *Middle East Studies* **11** (1975): 284–301.

Erder, L. and S. Faroqhi. "Population Rise and Fall in Anatolia 1550–1620." *Middle East Studies* **15** (1979): 322–45.

Erdoğru, Akıf. "Karaman Vilayeti Kanunnameleri." *Ankara Üniversitesi Osmanlı Tarihi Araştırma ve Uygulama Merkezi Dergisi* **4** (1993): 467–516.

______. "Some Observations on the Urban Population of Karaman Province in the Reign of Murad III with Regard to the Mufassal Defters." In *Histoire économique et sociale de l'Empire ottoman et de la Turquie,* edited by D. Panzac, 341–7. Paris: Peeters, 1995.

Erdur, Oğuz. "Reappropriating the 'Green': Islamist Environmentalism." *New Perspectives on Turkey* **17** (1997): 151–66.

Ergun, Pervin. *Türk Kültüründe Ağaç Kültü.* Ankara: Atatürk Kültür Merkezi Bakanlığı, 2004.

Erinç, S. and N. Tunçdilek. "The Agricultural Regions of Turkey." *Geographical Review* **42** (1952): 179–203.

Erler, Mehmet. *Osmanlı Develti'nde Kuraklık ve Kıtlık Olayları (1800–1880).* Istanbul: Libra, 2010.

Erten, Hayri. *Konya Şer'iyye Sicilleri Işığında Ailenin Sosyo-Ekonomik ve Kültürel Yapısı (XVIII. Yüzyıl İlk Yarısı).* Ankara: Kültür Bakanlığı Yayınları, 2001.

Eşrefoğlu, Eşref. "İstanbul'un Tarihi Et Meselesi." *Belgelerle Türk Tarihi Dergisi* **55** (1972): 13–14.

Establet, C. and J. Pascual. *Familles et fortunes à Damas.* Damascus: Institut français de Damas, 1994.

Establet, C. et al. "La mesure de l'inégalité dans la société ottomane: Utilisation de l'indice de Gini pour le Caire et Damas vers 1700." *Journal of the Economic and Social History of the Orient* **37** (1994): 177–82.

Etkes, Haggay. "The Impact of Short Term Climate Fluctuations on Rural Population in the Desert Frontier Nahiye of Gaza (ca. 1519–1557)." Paper presented at the National Bureau of Economic Research conference "Climate Change: Past and Present," June 30, 2008.

Evrendilek, F. et al. "Changes in Soil Organic Carbon and Other Physical Soil Properties along Adjacent Mediterranean Forest, Grassland, and Cropland Ecosystems in Turkey." *Journal of Arid Environments* **59** (2004): 743–52.

Eyice, Semavi. *Karadağ ve Karaman Çevresinde Arkeolojik İncelemeler.* Istanbul: İstanbul Üniversitesi, 1971.

Fagan, Brian. *Floods, Famines and Emperors.* New York: Basic Books, 1999.

______. *The Little Ice Age.* New York: Basic Books, 2000.

Fang, Jin-Qi and Guo Liu. "Relationship between Climatic Change and the Nomadic Southward Migrations in Eastern Asia during Historical Times." *Climatic Change* **22** (1992): 151–69.

Faroqhi, Suraiya. "The Tekke of Haci Bektaş: Social Position and Economic Activities." *International Journal of Middle East Studies* **7** (1976): 183–208.

______. "Anadolu İskânı ile Terkedilmiş Köyler Sorunu." In *Türkiye'de Toplumsal Bilim Araştırmalarında Yaklaşımlar ve Yöntemler Semineri,* edited by S. Karabağ and Y. Yeşilçay, 293–302. Ankara: Orta Doğu Teknik Üniversitesi, 1977.

______. "Rural Society in Anatolia and the Balkans during the Sixteenth Century, I." *Turcica* **9** (1977): 161–95.

______. "Rural Society in Anatolia and the Balkans during the Sixteenth Century, II." *Turcica* **11** (1979): 103–53.

______. "Sixteenth Century Periodic Markets in Various Anatolian "Sancaks": İçel, Hamid, Karahisar-ı Sahib, Kütahya, Aydin, and Menteşe." *Journal of the Economic and Social History of the Orient* **22** (1979): 32–80.

______. "Taxation and Urban Activities in Sixteenth-Century Anatolia." *International Journal of Turkish Studies* **1** (1980): 19–53.

______. "Camels, Wagons, and the Ottoman State in the Sixteenth and Seventeenth Centuries." *International Journal of Middle East Studies* **14** (1982): 523–39.

______. "Urban Development in Ottoman Anatolia (XVI.–XVII. Centuries)." *ODTÜ Mimarlık Fakültesi Dergisi* **7** (1982): 35–51.

______. "The Peasants of Saideli in the Late Sixteenth Century." *Archivum Ottomanicum* **8** (1984): 215–50.

______. *Towns and Townsmen of Ottoman Anatolia.* New York: Cambridge University Press, 1984.

______. "Town Officials, *Timar*-Holders, and Taxation: The Late Sixteenth-Century Crisis as Seen from Çorum." *Turcica* **18** (1986): 53–82.

______. "Agriculture and Rural Life in the Ottoman Empire (ca. 1500–1878)." *New Perspectives on Turkey* **1** (1987): 3–34.

______. "A Great Foundation in Some Difficulties; or Some Evidence on Economic Contraction in the Ottoman Empire of the Mid-Seventeenth Century." *Revue d'histoire maghrebine* **47–48** (1987): 109–21.

______. *Men of Modest Substance: House Owners and House Property in Seventeenth-Century Ankara and Kayseri.* New York: Cambridge University Press, 1987.

______. "Political Tensions in the Anatolian Countryside around 1600: An Attempt at Interpretation." In *Türkische Miszellen,* edited by J. Bacqué-Grammont et al., 117–30. Istanbul: Editions Divit, 1987.

———. "Notes on the Production of Cotton and Cotton Cloth in Sixteenth- and Seventeenth-Century Anatolia." In *The Ottoman Empire and the World Economy*, edited by Huri İslamoğlu, 262–70. Cambridge: Cambridge University Press, 1987.

———. "Agricultural Crisis and the Art of Flute-Playing: The Worldly Affairs of the Mevlevî Dervishes (1595–1652)." *Turcica* **22** (1988): 43–70.

———. "Towns, Agriculture and the State in Sixteenth-Century Ottoman Anatolia." *Journal of the Economic and Social History of the Orient* **33** (1990): 125–56.

———. "Political Activity among Ottoman Taxpayers and the Problem of Sultanic Legitimation." *Journal of the Economic and Social History of the Orient* **35** (1992): 1–39.

———. "Labor Recruitment and Control in the Ottoman Empire (Sixteenth and Seventeenth Centuries)." In *Manufacturing in the Ottoman Empire and Turkey*, edited by D. Quataert, 13–58. Binghamton: SUNY Press, 1994.

———. "Crisis and Change, 1590–1699." In *An Economic and Social History of the Ottoman Empire*, vol. 2, edited by H. İnalcık and D. Quataert, 411–636. New York: Cambridge University Press, 1994.

———. "Seeking Wisdom in China: An Attempt to Make Sense of the Celali Rebellions." In *Zafarname: Memorial Volume of Felix Tauer*, edited by R. Vesely and E. Gombar, 101–24. Prague: Enigma, 1996.

———. "Migration into Eighteenth-Century 'Greater Istanbul' as Reflected in the Kadi Registers of Eyüp." *Turcica* **30** (1998): 163–83.

———. "A Natural Disaster as an Indicator of Agricultural Change." In *Natural Disasters in the Ottoman Empire*, edited by E. Zachariadou, 251–63. Heraklion: Crete University Press, 1999.

———. "Ottoman Peasants and Rural Life: The Historiography of the 20th Century." *Archivum Ottomanicum* **18** (2000): 153–82.

———. *The Ottoman Empire and the World around It.* Leiden: Brill, 2004.

———. *The Ottoman Empire: A Short History.* Translated by Shelley Frisch. Princeton: Markus Wiener, 2009.

Felis, T. et al. "A Coral Oxygen Isotope Record from the Red Sea Documenting NAO, ENSO, and North Pacific Teleconnections on Middle East Climate Variability since the Year 1750." *Paleoceanography* **15** (2000): 679–94.

Fernandes, Leonor. "The City of Cairo and Its Food Supplies during the Mamluk Period." In *Nourir les cités de Méditerranée – Antiquité-temps moderns*, edited by B. Marin and C. Virlouvet, 519–38. Paris: Maisonneuve, 2003.

Findley, Carter. *Bureaucratic Reform in the Ottoman Empire.* Princeton, NJ: Princeton University Press, 1980.

———. *Ottoman Civil Officialdom.* Princeton, NJ: Princeton University Press, 1989.

Finkel, Caroline. *The Administration of Warfare: The Ottoman Military Campaigns in Hungary 1593–1606.* Vienna: VWGÖ, 1988.

———. *Osman's Dream: The History of the Ottoman Empire 1300–1923.* New York: Basic Books, 2005.

Finlay, Roger. "Natural Decrease in Early Modern Cities." *Past and Present* **92** (1981): 169–74.

Fırat, Fehim. "Türkiye'de Orman ve Erozyon Problemleri." *İstanbul Üniversitesi Orman Fakültesi Dergisi* **14** (1964): 1–27.

Fischer, David Hackett. *The Great Wave: Price Revolutions and the Rhythm of History.* New York: Oxford University Press, 1996.

Fleet, Kate. "Ottoman Grain Exports from Western Anatolia at the End of the Fourteenth Century." *Journal of the Economic and Social History of the Orient* **40** (1997): 283–94.

Fleischer, Cornell. *Bureaucrat and Intellectual in the Ottoman Empire: The Historian Mustafa Âli (1541–1600).* Princeton, NJ: Princeton University Press, 1986.

Fleming, James. *Historical Perspectives on Climate Change.* New York: Oxford University Press, 1998.

Flynn, D. and A. Giraldez. "Silver and Ottoman Monetary History in Global Perspective." *Journal of European Economic History* **31** (2002): 9–43.

———. "Path Dependence, Time Lags and the Birth of Globalization." *European Review of Economic History* **8** (2003): 81–108.

Fodor, Pal. "The Grand Vizieral *Telhis*: A Study in the Ottoman Central Administration 1566–1656." *Archivum Ottomanicum* **15** (1997): 137–88.

Frangakis, Elena. *The Commerce of Smyrna in the Eighteenth Century (1700–1820).* Athens: Center for Asia Minor Studies, 1992.

Frangakis, E. and M. Wagstaff. "Settlement Pattern Change in the Morea, 1700–1830." *Byzantine and Modern Greek Studies* **11** (1987): 163–92.

———. "The Height Zonation of Population in the Morea c. 1830." *Annual of the British School at Athens* **87** (1992): 439–46.

Free, M. and A. Robock. "Global Warming in the Context of the Little Ice Age." *Journal of Geophysical Research* **104** (1999): 19057–70.

Fritschy, Wantje. "State Formation and Urbanization Trajectories: State Finance in the Ottoman Empire before 1800, as Seen from a Dutch Perspective." *Journal of Global History* **4** (2009): 405–28.

Gadgil, M. and R. Guha. *This Fissured Land: An Ecological History of India.* New Delhi: Oxford University Press, 1992.

Galley, Chris. "A Model of Early Modern Urban Demography." *The Economic History Review* **48** (1995): 448–69.

Galloway, Patrick. "Annual Variations in Deaths by Age, Deaths by Cause, Prices, and Weather in London 1670 to 1830." *Population Studies* **39** (1985): 487–505.

———. "Basic Patterns in Annual Variations in Fertility, Nuptiality, Mortality, and Prices in Pre-Industrial Europe." *Population Studies* **42** (1988): 275–302.

García-Herrera, R. et al. "Description and General Background to Ships' Logbooks as a Source of Climatic Data." *Climatic Change* **73** (2005): 13–36.

Geertz, Clifford. *Agricultural Involution.* Berkeley: University of California Press, 1963.

Geeson, N. et al., eds. *Mediterranean Desertification: A Mosaic of Processes and Responses.* Chichester: Wiley, 2002.

Genç, Mehmet. *Osmanlı İmparatorluğunda Devlet ve Ekonomi.* Istanbul: Ötüken, 2000.

Gerber, Haim. *The Social Origins of the Modern Middle East.* London: Mansell, 1987.

———. *Economy and Society in an Ottoman City: Bursa 1600–1700.* Jerusalem: Hebrew University, 1988.

Gergis, J. and A. Fowler. "A History of ENSO Events since A.D. 1525: Implications for Future Climate Change." *Climatic Change* **92** (2009): 343–87.

Glacken, C. J. *Traces on the Rhodian Shore: Nature and Culture in Western Thought from Ancient Times to the End of the Eighteenth Century.* Berkeley: University of California Press, 1967.

Glaser, Rüdiger. *Klimageschichte Mitteleuropas.* Darmstadt: Primus Verlag, 2001.

Goffman, Daniel. *İzmir and the Levantine World.* Seattle: University of Washington Press, 1990.

Gökmen, Ertan. "Batı Anadolu'da Çekirge Felâketi (1850–1915)." *Belleten* **74** (2010): 127–80.

Goldstone, Jack. *Revolution and Rebellion in the Early Modern World.* Berkeley: University of California Press, 1991.

Gordan, Stewart. "War, Military, and the Environment: Central India, 1560–1820." In *Natural Enemy, Natural Ally: Toward an Environmental History of War,* edited by R. Tucker and E. Russell, 42–64. Eugene: University of Oregon Press, 2004.

Göyünç, Nejat. "'Hâne' Deyimi Hakkında." *İstanbul Üniversitesi Edebiyat Fakültesi Tarih Dergisi* **32** (1979): 331–48.

Göyünç, N. and W. Hütteroth. *Land an der Grenze: Osmanische Verwaltung im heutigen türkisch-syrisch-irakischen Grenzgebiet im 16. Jahrhundert.* Istanbul: EREN, 1997.

Grant, Jonathan. "Rethinking Ottoman 'Decline': Military Technology Diffusion in the Ottoman Empire, Fifteenth to Eighteenth Centuries." *Journal of World History* **10** (1999): 179–201.

Greene, Molly. "Beyond the Northern Invasion: The Mediterranean in the Seventeenth Century." *Past and Present* **174** (2002): 42–71.

Greenwood, Anthony. "Istanbul's Meat Provisioning: A Study of the Celep-Keşan System." PhD diss., University of Chicago, 1988.

Griggs, C. et al. "A Regional High-Frequency Reconstruction of May–June Precipitation in the North Aegean from Oak Tree Rings, A.D. 1089–1989." *International Journal of Climatology* **27** (2007): 1075–89.

Griswold, William. *The Great Anatolian Rebellion, 1591–1611.* Berlin: K. Schwarz, 1983.

———. "Climatic Change: A Possible Factor in the Social Unrest of Seventeenth Century Anatolia." In *Humanist and Scholar: Essays in Honor of Andreas Tietze,* edited by H. Lowry and D. Quataert, 37–58. Istanbul: Isis, 1993.

———. "Djalali," in *Encyclopedia of Islam Online,* http://www.brillonline.nl/.

Grotzfeld, H. "Klimageschichte des Vorderen Orients 800–1800 AD nach arabischen Quellen." *Würzburger Geographische Arbeiten* **80** (1991): 21–43.

Grove, A. and O. Rackham. *The Nature of Mediterranean Europe.* New Haven, CT: Yale University Press, 2001.

Grove, Jean. *Little Ice Ages: Ancient and Modern.* London: Routledge, 2004.

Grove, J. and A. Conterio. "Climate in the Eastern and Central Mediterranean, 1675 to 1715." In *Climatic Trends and Anomalies in Europe 1675–1715,* edited by B. Frenzel et al., 275–86. Stuttgart: Fischer, 1994.

———. "The Climate of Crete in the Sixteenth and Seventeenth Centuries." *Climatic Change* **30** (1995): 223–47.

Grove, J. and A. Grove. "Little Ice Age Climates in the Eastern Mediterranean." In *European Climate Reconstructed from Documentary Data: Methods and Results,* edited by B. Frenzel, 45–50. Stuttgart: Fischer, 1992.

Grove, Richard. *Green Imperialism: Colonial Expansion, Tropical Island Edens, and the Origins of Environmentalism 1600–1800.* New York: Cambridge University Press, 1995.

Grove, R. and J. Chappell. "El Niño Chronology and the History of Global Crises during the Little Ice Age." In *El Niño: History and Crisis,* edited by R. Grove and J. Chappell, 5–34. Cambridge: White Horse Press, 2000.

Güçer, Lütfi. "XVIII. Yüzıl Ortalarında İstanbul'un İasesi İçin Lüzumlu Hububatın Temini Meselesi." *İstanbul Üniversitesi İktisat Fakültesi Mecmuası* **11** (1949–1950): 397–416.

———. "XVI. Yüzyıl Sonlarında Osmanlı İmparatorluğu Dahilinde Hububat Ticaretinin Tâbi Olduğu Kayıtlar." *İstanbul Üniversitesi İktisat Fakültesi Dergisi* **12** (1951): 79–98.

———. "XV.–XVII. Asırlarda Osmanlı İmparatorluğunda Tuz İnhisarı ve Tuzlaların İşletme Nizamı." *İstanbul Üniversitesi İktisat Fakültesi Mecmuası* **23** (1962–1963): 81–143.

———. *Osmanlı İmparatorluğunda Hububat Meselesi ve Hububattan Alınan Vergiler.* Istanbul: İstanbul Üniversitesi, 1964.

Gülalp, Haldun. "Universalism versus Particularism: Ottoman Historiography and The 'Grand Narrative.'" *New Perspectives on Turkey* **13** (1995): 151–69.

Gümüşçü, Osman. *Tarihî Coğrafya Açısından Bir Araştırma: XVI. Yüzyıl Larende (Karaman) Kazasında Yerleşme ve Nüfus.* Ankara: Türk Tarih Kurumu, 2001.

———. "Internal Migrations in Sixteenth Century Anatolia." *Journal of Historical Geography* **30** (2004): 231–48.

Gunn, Joel, ed. *The Years without a Summer: Tracing A.D. 536 and Its Aftermath.* Oxford: Archaeopress, 2000.

Güran, Tevfik. "The State Role in the Grain Supply of Istanbul: The Grain Administration, 1793–1839." *International Journal of Turkish Studies* **3** (1984): 27–41.

Habib, Irfan. *The Agrarian System of Mughal India.* 2nd ed. New Delhi: Oxford University Press, 1999.

Halaçoğlu, Yusuf. *XVIII. Yüzyılda Osmanlı İmparatorluğu'nun İskân Siyaseti ve Aşiretlerin Yerleştirilmesi.* Ankara: Türk Tarih Kurumu, 1988.

Hammer-Purgstall, Joseph von. *Histoire de l'Empire ottoman,* vols. 7–13. Translated by J.-J. Hellert. Paris, 1838–39.

Hanioğlu, Şükrü. *A Brief History of the Late Ottoman Empire.* Princeton, NJ: Princeton University Press, 2008.

Hassan, Fekri. "Historical Nile Floods and Their Implications for Climatic Change." *Science* **212** (1981): 1142–5.

———. "Environmental Perception and Human Responses in History and Prehistory." In *The Way the Wind Blows: Climate, History, and Human Action,* edited by R. McIntosh et al., 121–40. New York: Columbia University Press, 2000.

Hathaway, Jane. *A Tale of Two Factions: Myth, Memory, and Identity in Ottoman Egypt and Yemen.* Albany: SUNY Press, 2003.

Hattox, Ralph. *Coffee and Coffeehouses.* Seattle: University of Washington Press, 1985.

Hays, J. N. *The Burdens of Disease: Epidemics and Human Response in Western History.* New Brunswick, NJ: Rutgers University Press, 1998.

Hemandiquer, Jean-Jacques. "Les débuts du maïs en Méditerranée (premier aperçu)." In *Histoire économique du monde méditerranéen: Mélanges en honneur de Fernand Braudel,* 227–34. Toulouse: Privat, 1972.

Heyd, Uriel. *Ottoman Documents on Palestine, 1552–1615: A Study of the Firman according to the Mühimme Defteri.* Oxford: Clarendon Press, 1960.

Hinz, Walther. *Islamische Masse und Gewichte.* Leiden: Brill, 1955.

Hodgson, Marshall. *The Venture of Islam, III: The Gunpowder Empires and Modern Times.* Chicago: University of Chicago Press, 1974.

Hole, Frank. "Agricultural Sustainability in the Semi-Arid Near East." *Climate of the Past* 3 (2007): 193–203.

Horden, P. and N. Purcell. *The Corrupting Sea: A Study of Mediterranean History.* Oxford: Blackwell, 2000.

Hornborg, A. and C. Crumley, eds. *The World System and the Earth System: Global Socioenvironmental Change and Sustainability since the Neolithic.* Walnut Creek, CA: Left Coast Press, 2007.

Hornborg, A. et al., eds. *Rethinking Environmental History: World-System History and Global Environmental Change.* Lanham, MD: Altamira Press, 2007.

Horowitz, Richard. "International Law and State Transformation in China, Siam, and the Ottoman Empire during the Nineteenth Century." *Journal of World History* **15** (2004): 445–86.

Howard, David. "Ottoman Historiography and the Literature of 'Decline' in the Sixteenth and Seventeenth Centuries." *Journal of Asian History* **22** (1988): 52–76.

Hughes, J. Donald. *Ecology in Ancient Civilizations.* Albuquerque: University of New Mexico Press, 1975.

______. *An Environmental History of the World: Humankind's Changing Role in the Community of Life.* London: Routledge, 2002.

______. *The Mediterranean: An Environmental History.* Santa Barbara, CA: ABC-CLIO, 2005.

Huntington, Elsworth. *The Pulse of Asia: A Journey in Central Asia Illustrating the Geographical Basis of History.* Boston: Houghton Mifflin, 1907.

Hütteroth, Wolf-Dieter. *Ländliche Siedlungen im südlichen Inneranatolien in den letzen vierhundert Jahren.* Göttingen: Universität Göttingen, 1968.

______. "The Influence of Social Structure on Land Division in Inner Anatolia." In *Turkey: Geographic and Social Perspectives,* edited by P. Benedict et al., 19–47. Leiden: Brill, 1974.

______. "Settlement Desertion in the Gezira between the 16th and 19th Century." In *The Syrian Land in the 18th and 19th Century,* edited by Thomas Philipp, 285–97. Stuttgart: Franz Steiner, 1992.

______. "Between Dicle and Firat: Turkey, Northeastern Syria and Northwestern Iraq in the 16th Century." In *VIIIth International Congress on the Economic and Social History of Turkey (1998),* edited by Nurhan Abacı, 15–24. Morrisville, NC: Lulu Press, 2006.

———. "Ecology of the Ottoman Lands." In *The Cambridge History of Turkey, 3: The Later Ottoman Empire 1603–1839*, edited by S. Faroqhi, 18–43. New York: Cambridge University Press, 2007.

Hütteroth, W. and K. Abdulfattah. *Historical Geography of Palestine, Transjordan and Southern Syria.* Erlangen: Fränkische Geographische Ges., 1977.

Imber, Colin. "The Navy of Süleyman the Magnificent." *Archivum Ottomanicum* **6** (1980): 211–82.

———. "The Reconstruction of the Ottoman Fleet after the Battle of Lepanto." In *Studies in Ottoman History and Law*, 85–102. Istanbul: Isis, 1996.

———. "The Status of Orchards and Fruit-Trees in Ottoman Law." In *Studies in Ottoman History and Law*, 207–16. Istanbul: Isis Press, 1996.

———. *The Ottoman Empire, 1350–1650: The Structure of Power.* New York: Palgrave Macmillan, 2002.

———. "İbrahim Peçevi on War: A Note on the European Military Revolution." In *Frontiers of Ottoman Studies: State, Province, and the West*, vol. 2, edited by C. Imber, K. Kiyotaki, and R. Murphey, 7–22. London: I. B. Tauris, 2005.

İnalcık, Halil. "Ottoman Methods of Conquest." *Studia Islamica* **2** (1954): 103–29.

———. "Adâletnâmeler." *Belgeler* **2** (1965): 49–145.

———. "The Ottoman Decline and Its Effects upon the *Reaya.*" In *Aspects of the Balkans: Continuity and Change*, edited by H. Birnbaum and S. Vyronis, 341–54. The Hague: Mouton, 1972.

———. *The Ottoman Empire: The Classical Age, 1300–1600.* London: Weidenfeld and Nicolson, 1973.

———. "The Socio-Political Effects of the Diffusion of Firearms in the Middle East." In *War, Technology and Society in the Middle East*, edited by V. Parry and M. Yapp, 195–217. New York: Oxford University Press, 1975.

———. "Impact of the *Annales* School on Ottoman Studies and New Findings." *Review* **1** (1978): 69–96.

———. "The Question of the Closing of the Black Sea under the Ottomans." *Archeion Pontou* **35** (1979): 74–110.

———. "Military and Fiscal Transformation in the Ottoman Empire, 1600–1700." *Archivum Ottomanicum* **6** (1980): 283–337.

———. "Rice Cultivation and the *Çeltükçi-Re'âyâ* System in the Ottoman Empire." *Turcica* **14** (1982): 69–141.

———. "Şikâyet Hakkı: *'Arz-ı Hâl* ve *'Arz-ı Mahzar'lar.*" *Osmanlı Araştırmaları* **7–8** (1988): 33–54.

İnalcık, H. and D. Quataert, eds. *An Economic and Social History of the Ottoman Empire*, 2 vols. New York: Cambridge University Press, 1995.

İslamoğlu, Huri. "M.A. Cook's *Population Pressure in Rural Anatolia 1450–1600*: A Critique of the Present Paradigm in Ottoman History." *Review of Middle East Studies* **3** (1978): 120–35.

———. "Die Osmanische Landwirtschaft im Anatolien des 16. Jahrhunderts: Stagnation oder regionale Entwicklung?" *Jahrbuch zur Geschichte und Gesellschaft des Vorderen und Mittlern Orients* (1985–1986): 165–212.

———. "State and Peasants in the Ottoman Empire: A Study of Peasant Economy in North-Central Anatolia during the Sixteenth Century." In *The Ottoman*

Empire and the World-Economy, edited by Huri İslamoğlu, 101–34. Cambridge: Cambridge University Press, 1987.

———. "Les paysans, le marché et l'état en Anatolie au XVIe siècle." *Annales* (1988): 1025–43.

———. *State and Peasant in the Ottoman Empire.* Leiden: Brill, 1994.

İslamoğlu, H. and S. Faroqhi. "Crop Patterns and Agricultural Production Trends in Sixteenth-Century Anatolia." *Review* **2** (1979): 401–36.

Israel, Jonathan. "Mexico and the 'General Crisis' of the Seventeenth Century." *Past and Present* **63** (1974): 33–57.

Issar, A. and M. Zohar. *Climate Change – Environment and Civilization in the Middle East.* Berlin: Springer, 2004.

Issawi, Charles. *The Economic History of Turkey, 1800–1914.* Chicago: University of Chicago Press, 1980.

———. *The Fertile Crescent 1800–1914: A Documentary Economic History.* New York: Oxford University Press, 1988.

Izzi Dien, M. *The Environmental Dimensions of Islam.* Cambridge: Lutterworth Press, 2000.

Jacobeit, J. et al. "European Surface Pressure Patterns for Months with Outstanding Climate Anomalies during the Sixteenth Century." *Climatic Change* **43** (1999): 201–21.

Jennings, Ronald. "Urban Population in Anatolia in the Sixteenth Century: A Study of Kayseri, Karaman, Amasya, Trabzon, and Erzurum." *International Journal of Middle East Studies* **7** (1976): 21–57.

———. "Zimmis in Early 17th Century Ottoman Judicial Records: The Sharia Court of Anatolia in Kayseri." *Journal of the Economic and Social History of the Orient* **21** (1978): 225–93.

———. "Limitations of the Judicial Powers of the Kadi in 17th Century Ottoman Kayseri." *Studia Islamica* **50** (1979): 151–84.

———. "Firearms, Bandits, and Gun Control: Some Evidence on Ottoman Policy toward Firearms in the Possession of *Reaya*, from the Judicial Records of Kayseri, 1600–27." *Archivum Ottomanicum* **6** (1980): 339–80.

———. The Population, Society, and Economy of the Region of Erçiyes Dağı in the 16th Century." In *Contributions á l'histoire économique et sociale de l'Empire ottoman*, edited by J. Bacqué-Grammont and P. Dumont, 149–250. Louvain: Peeters, 1983.

———. "The Population, Taxation, and Wealth in the Cities and Villages of Cyprus according to the Detailed Population Survey (*Defter-i Mufassal*) of 1572." In *Raiyyet Rüsûmu: Essays Presented to Halil Inalcik*, edited by Carolyn Gross, 175–89. Cambridge, MA: Harvard University Press, 1986.

———. "The Society and Economy of Maçuka in the Ottoman Judicial Registers of Trabzon, 1560–1640." In *Continuity and Change in Late Byzantine and Early Ottoman Society*, edited by A. Bryer and H. Lowry, 129–54. Birmingham: University of Birmingham, 1986.

———. "The Locust Problem in Cyprus." *Bulletin of the School of Oriental and African Studies* **51** (1988): 279–313.

———. "Village Agriculture in Cyprus." In *5. Milletlerarası Türkiye Sosyal ve İktisat Tarihi Kongresi*, 469–76. Ankara: Türk Tarih Kurumu, 1989.

———. "Plague in Trabzon and Reactions to It according to Local Judicial Registers." In *Humanist and Scholar: Essays in Honor ofAndreas Tietze*, edited by H. Lowry and D. Quataert, 27–36. Istanbul: Isis, 1993.

Jones, M. et al. "Eastern Mediterranean-Indian-African Summer Climate Connections through the Past 2000 Years." *Geophysical Research Abstracts* **6** (2004): 00418.

Jones, P. D. "High-Resolution Palaeoclimatology of the Last Millennium: A Review of Current Status and Future Prospects." *The Holocene* **19** (2009): 3–49.

Kadıoğlu, Mikdat. *Bildiğiniz Havaların Sonu: Küresel İklim Değişimi ve Türkiye.* Istanbul: Güncel Yayınları, 2001.

Kafadar, Cemal. "When Coins Turned into Drops of Dew and Bankers into Robbers of Shadows: The Boundaries of the Ottoman Economic Imagination." PhD diss., McGill University, 1988.

———. "Les troubles monétaires de la fin du XVIe siècle et la prise de conscience ottomane du déclin." *Annales* **46** (1991): 381–400.

———. *Between Two Worlds: The Construction of the Ottoman State.* Berkeley: University of California Press, 1995.

———. "The Question of Ottoman Decline." *Harvard Middle East and Islamic Review* **4** (1997–98): 30–75.

———. "Janissaries and Other Riffraff of Ottoman Istanbul: Rebels without a Cause?" In *Identity and Identity Formation in the Ottoman World*, edited by B. Tezcan and K. Barbir, 113–34. Madison: University of Wisconsin Press, 2007.

Karabörk, M. and E. Kahya. "The Teleconnections between Extreme Phases of the Southern Oscillation and Precipitation Patterns over Turkey." *International Journal of Climatology* **23** (2003): 1607–25.

Karaca, M. et al. "Cyclone Track Variability over Turkey in Association with Regional Climate." *International Journal of Climatology* **20** (2000): 1225– 36.

Karaduman, Gönur. "Kayseri in the End of the 16th Century in Light of the Court Records, 988–1002/1580–1592." PhD diss., Boğaziçi Üniversitesi, 1995.

Karpat, Kemal. *Ottoman Population 1830–1914.* Madison: University of Wisconsin Press, 1985.

———. "The Ottoman Family: Documents Pertaining to Its Size." *International Journal of Turkish Studies* **4** (1987): 137–45.

Karpat, Kemal, ed. *The Ottoman Empire and Its Place in World History.* Leiden: Brill, 1974.

Kasaba, Reşat. *The Ottoman Empire and the World Economy.* Albany: SUNY Press, 1988.

———. *A Moveable Empire: Ottoman Nomads, Migrants, and Refugees.* Seattle: University of Washington Press, 2009.

Keyder, Çağlar. "Small Peasant Ownership in Turkey: Historical Formation and Present Structure." *Review* **7** (1983): 53–107.

———. "Large-Scale Commercial Agriculture in the Ottoman Empire?" In *Landholding and Commercial Agriculture in the Middle East*, edited by Ç. Keyder and F. Tabak, 1–13. Binghamton: SUNY Press, 1991.

Keys, David. *Catastrophe: An Investigation into the Origins of the Modern World.* New York: Ballantine, 2000.

Khalid, F. and J. O'Brien, eds. *Islam and Ecology*. New York: Cassell, 1992.

Khazanov, Anatoly. *Nomads and the Outside World*. Madison: University of Wisconsin Press, 1994.

Khoury, Dina. *State and Provincial Society in the Ottoman Empire*. New York: Cambridge University Press, 1997.

______. "The Ottoman Centre versus Provincial Power-Holders: An Analysis of the Historiography." In *The Cambridge History of Turkey, 3: The Later Ottoman Empire 1603–1839*, edited by S. Faroqhi, 135–56. New York: Cambridge University Press, 2007.

Kiel, Machiel. "Tatar Pazarcık: A Turkish Town in the Heart of Bulgaria, Some Brief Remarks on Its Demographic Development 1485–1874." In *X. Türk Tarih Kongresi*, 2567–81. Ankara: Türk Tarih Kurumu, 1986.

______. "The Rise and Decline of Turkish Boeotia, 15th–19th Century." In *Recent Developments in the History and Archaeology of Central Greece*, edited by J. Bintliff, 315–58. Oxford: Archaeopress, 1997.

______. "The Ottoman Imperial Registers: Central Greece and Northern Bulgaria in the 15th–19th Century, the Demographic Development of Two Areas Compared." In *Reconstructing Past Population Trends in Mediterranean Europe (3000BC–1800AD)*, edited by J. Bintliff and K. Sbonias, 195–218. Oxford: Oxbow, 1999.

______. "Ottoman Sources for the Demographic History and the Process of Islamisation of Bosnia-Hercegovina and Bulgaria in the Fifteenth-Seventeenth Centuries." *International Journal of Turkish Studies* **10** (2004): 93–119.

Kılıç, Orhan. "Mühimme Defterlerine Göre XVI. Yüzyılın İkinci Yarısında Osmanlı Devleti'nde Meydana Gelen Depremler." *Osmanlı* **5** (1999): 671–7.

______. "1585 Yılında Tebriz Serferi'ne Çıkan Osmanlı Ordusunun İkmal ve İaşesi." *Askeri Tarih Bülteni* **46** (1999): 109–36.

______. "Mühimme Defterlerine Göre 16. Yüzyılın İkinci Yarısında Osmanlı Devleti'nde Doğal Afetler." In *Pax Ottomanica, Studies in Memoriam Prof. Dr. Nejat Göyünç*, 793–820. Haarlem: SOTA, 2001.

______. "Osmanlı Devleti'nde Meydana Gelen Kıtlıklar." *Türkler* **10** (2002): 718–30.

______. *Genel Hatlarıyla Dünya'da ve Osmanlı Devleti'nde Salgın Hastalıklar*. Elazığ: Fırat Üniversitesi Basımevi, 2004.

Klein, Cippora. "Fluctuations of the Level of the Dead Sea and Climatic Fluctuations in Erez Israel during Historical Times." PhD diss., Hebrew University of Jerusalem, 1986.

Koç, Yunus. "XVI. Yüzyılın İkinci Yarısında Köylerin Parçalanması Sorunu: Bursa Kazası Ölçeğinde Bir Araştırma," in *XIII. Türk Tarih Kongresi*, 1961–69. Ankara: Türk Tarih Kurumu, 2002.

______. "The Structure of the Population of the Ottoman Empire." In *The Great Ottoman-Turkish Civilization*, vol. 2, edited by Kemal Çiçek, 531–48. Ankara: Yeni Türkiye, 2000.

______. "Osmanlı'da Kent İskânı ve Demografisi (XV.–XVIII. Yüzyıllar)." *Türkiye Araştırmaları Literatür Dergisi* **6** (2005): 161–210.

Kolodziejczyk, Dariusz. "The Defter-i Mufassal of Kamaniçe from ca. 1681: An Example of Late Ottoman Tahrir, Reliability, Function, Principles of Publication." *Osmanlı Araştırmaları* **13** (1993): 91–8.

Konyalı, İ. H. *Karaman Tarihi.* Istanbul: Baha Matbaası, 1967.

Köprülü, M. Fuad. *The Origins of the Ottoman Empire.* Translated by Gary Leiser. Binghamton: SUNY Press, 1992.

Krader, Lawrence. "The Ecology of Nomadic Pastoralism." *International Social Science Journal* **11** (1959): 499–510.

Kunniholm, Peter. "Archaeological Evidence and Non-Evidence for Climate Change." *Philosophical Transactions of the Royal Society of London* **330** (1990): 645–55.

Kunt, I. Metin. *The Sultan's Servants: The Transformation of Ottoman Provincial Government, 1550–1650.* New York: Columbia University Press, 1983.

Kurmuş, Orhan. "The Cotton Famine and Its Effects on the Ottoman Empire." In *The Ottoman Empire and the World-Economy,* edited by Huri İslamoğlu, 160–9. Cambridge: Cambridge University Press, 1987.

Kutiel, H. et al. "Circulation and Extreme Rainfall Conditions in the Eastern Mediterranean during the Last Century." *International Journal of Climatology* **16** (1996): 73–92.

Laiou-Thomodakis, Angeliki. *Peasant Society in the Late Byzantine Empire.* Princeton, NJ: Princeton University Press, 1977.

Lamb, H. H. *Climate, History, and the Modern World.* 2nd ed. London: Routledge, 1995.

______. "Volcanic Dust in the Atmosphere; with a Chronology and Assessment of Its Meteorological Significance." *Philosophical Transactions of the Royal Society of London (Series A. Mathematical and Physical Sciences)* **266** (1970): 425–533.

Landers, John. "London's Mortality in the 'Long Eighteenth Century': A Family Reconstitution Study." In *Living and Dying in London,* edited by W. Bynum and R. Porter, 1–28. London: Wellcome Institute, 1991.

______. *The Field and the Forge: Population, Production and Power in the Pre-Industrial West.* New York: Oxford University Press, 2003.

Lapidus, Ira. *Muslim Cities in the Later Middle Ages.* Cambridge, MA: Harvard University Press, 1967.

Le Roy Ladurie, Emmanuel. *Times of Feast, Times of Famine.* Garden City, NY: Doubleday, 1971.

______. "L'Aménorrhée de famine (XVIIe–XXe siècles)." *Annales* **24** (1969): 1589–601.

______. *The Peasants of Languedoc.* Translated by John Day. Urbana: University of Illinois Press, 1976.

______. *Carnival in Romans.* Translated by Mary Feeny. New York: G. Braziller, 1979.

______. *Histoire humaine et comparée du climat, I: Canicules et glaciers.* Paris: Fayard, 2004.

Lespez, Laurent. "Geomorphic Responses to Long-Term Land Use Changes in Eastern Macedonia (Greece)." *Catena* **51** (2003): 181–208.

Lewis, Bernard. "Some Reflections on the Decline of the Ottoman Empire." *Studia Islamica* **9** (1958): 111–27.

———. *The Emergence of Modern Turkey.* New York: Oxford University Press, 1968.

Lewis, Norman. "Malaria, Irrigation, and Soil Erosion in Central Syria." *Geographical Review* **39** (1949): 278–90.

———. *Nomads and Settlers in Syria and Jordan, 1800–1980.* New York: Cambridge University Press, 1987.

Linden, Eugene. *The Winds of Change: Climate, Weather, and the Destruction of Civilizations.* New York: Simon and Schuster, 2006.

Lindner, Rudi. *Nomads and Ottomans in Medieval Anatolia.* Bloomington: Indiana University Press, 1983.

———. "What Was a Nomadic Tribe?" *Comparative Studies in Society and History* **24** (1982): 689–711.

Liu, Ts'ui-Jung et al., eds. *Asian Population History.* New York: Oxford University Press, 2001.

Livi-Bacci, Massimo. *Population and Nutrition: An Essay on European Demographic History.* New York: Cambridge University Press, 1991.

———. *A Concise History of World Population.* 4th ed. Malden, MA: Blackwell, 2006.

Lombard, Maurice. "Le bois dans la Méditeranée musulmane (VIIe–XIe siècles)." *Annales* (1959): 234–55.

Lowry, Heath. *The Nature of the Early Ottoman State.* Binghamton: SUNY Press, 2003.

———. "Pushing the Stone Uphill: The Impact of Bubonic Plague on Ottoman Urban Society in the Fifteenth and Sixteenth Centuries." *Osmanlı Araştırmaları* **23** (2003): 93–132.

Luterbacher, J. and E. Xoplaki. "500-Year Winter Temperature and Precipitation Variability over the Mediterranean Area and Its Connection to the Large-Scale Atmospheric Circulation." In *Mediterranean Climate: Variability and Trends,* edited by Hans-Jürgen Bölle, 133–54. Berlin: Springer, 2002.

Luterbacher, J. et al. "The Late Maunder Minimum – a Key Period for Studying Decadal Climate Change in Europe." *Climatic Change* **49** (2001): 441–62.

———. "European Seasonal and Annual Temperature Variability, Trends, and Extremes since 1500." *Science* **303** (2004): 1499–503.

———. "Mediterranean Climate Variability over the Last Centuries: A Review." In *The Mediterranean Climate: An Overview of the Main Characteristics and Issues,* edited by P. Lionello et al., 27–148. Amsterdam: Elsevier, 2006.

———. "Circulation Dynamics and Its Influence on European and Mediterranean January–April Climate over the Past Half Millennium: Results and Insights from Instrumental Data, Documentary Evidence and Coupled Climate Models." *Climatic Change* **101** (2010): 201–34.

Macfarlane, Alan. *The Savage Wars of Peace: England, Japan and the Malthusian Trap.* Oxford: Blackwell, 1997.

Macit, Yunus. "Osmanlı Türklerinde Çevre Bilinci." *Türkler* **10** (2002): 589–97.

Maddison, Angus. *Contours of the World Economy, 1–2030 AD.* New York: Oxford University Press, 2007.

Maeda, Hirotake. "The Forced Migrations and Reorganization of the Regional Order in the Caucasus by Safavid Iran: Preconditions and Developments

Described by Fazli Khuzani." Paper presented at "Reconstruction and Interaction of Slavic Eurasia and Its Neighboring Worlds," Slavic Research Center, Hokkaido University, Sapporo, 2004.

Magee, Gary. "Disease Management in Pre-Industrial Europe: A Reconsideration of the Efficacy of the Local Responses to Epidemics." *Journal of European Economic History* **26** (1997): 605–26.

Makovsky, Alan. "Sixteenth-Century Agricultural Production in the Liwa of Jerusalem: Insights from the *Tapu Defters* and an Attempt at Quantification." *Archivum Ottomanicum* **9** (1984): 91–127.

Mann, Michael. "Large-Scale Climate Variability and Connections with the Middle East in Past Centuries." *Climatic Change* **55** (2002): 287–314.

Mantran, Robert. *Istanbul dans la seconde moitié du XVIIe siècle.* Paris: Maisonneuve, 1962.

———. "Réflexions sur les problèmes de l'eau à Istanbul du XVIe au XVIIIe siècle." In *IIIrd Congress on the Economic and Social History of Turkey, Princeton 24–26 August 1983*, edited by H. Lowry and R. Hattox, 107–13. Istanbul: Isis, 1990.

———. *Histoire d'Istanbul.* Paris: Fayard, 1996.

Marcus, Abraham. *The Middle East on the Eve of Modernity: Aleppo in the 18th Century.* New York: Columbia University Press, 1989.

Marino, Brigitte. "L'Approvisionnement en céréales des villes de la Syrie ottomane (XVIe–XVIIIe siècles)." In *Nourir les cités de Méditerranée – Antiquité-temps moderns*, edited by B. Marin and C. Virlouvet, 491–517. Paris: Maisonneuve, 2003.

Marino, John. *Pastoral Economics in the Kingdom of Naples.* Baltimore: Johns Hopkins University Press, 1988.

Markgraf, V. and H. Diaz. "The Past ENSO Record: A Synthesis." In *El Niño and the Southern Oscillation: Multiscale Variability and Global and Regional Impacts*, edited by H. Diaz and V. Markgraf, 465–88. Cambridge: Cambridge University Press, 2000.

Marks, Robert. *Rice Tigers Silt and Silk: Environment and Economy in Late Imperial South China.* New York: Cambridge University Press, 1998.

Marmé, Michael. "Locating Linkages or Painting Bull's-Eyes around Bullet Holes? An East Asian Perspective on the Seventeenth-Century Crisis." *The American Historical Review* **113** (2008): 1080–9.

Marsh, George Perkins. *Man and Nature* [1864]. Seattle: University of Washington Press, 2000.

Martal, Abdullah. "XVI. Yüzyılda Osmanlı İmparatorluğunda Su-Yolculuk." *Belleten* **52** (1988): 1585–652.

Mass, C. and D. Portman. "Major Volcanic Eruptions and Climate: A Critical Evaluation." *Journal of Climate* **2** (1989): 566–93.

Masters, Bruce. "Patterns of Migration to Ottoman Aleppo in the 17th and 18th Centuries." *International Journal of Turkish Studies* **4** (1987): 75–89.

———. *The Origins of Western Economic Dominance in the Middle East: Mercantilism and the Islamic Economy in Aleppo, 1600–1750.* New York: New York University Press, 1988.

May, Jacques. *The Ecology of Malnutrition in the Far and Near East.* New York: Hafner, 1963.

Mazower, Mark. *The Balkans: A Short History.* New York: Modern Library, 2002.

———. *Salonica, City of Ghosts: Christians, Muslims, and Jews, 1430–1950.* London: HarperCollins, 2004.

McCann, James. "Climate and Causation in African History." *International Journal of African Historical Studies* **32** (1991): 261–80.

McCarthy, Justin. "Factors in the Analysis of the Population of Anatolia, 1800–1878." *Asian and African Studies* **21** (1987): 33–63.

———. "Ottoman Bosnia, 1800 to 1878." In *The Muslims of Bosnia-Herzegovina,* edited by M. Pinson, 54–83. Cambridge, MA: Harvard University Press, 1994.

———. *The Ottoman Peoples and the End of Empire.* New York: Bloomsbury, 2001.

McGowan, Bruce. "Food Supply and Taxation on the Middle Danube (1568–1579)." *Archivum Ottomanicum* **1** (1969): 139–96.

———. *Economic Life in Ottoman Europe: Taxation, Trade, and the Struggle for Land.* New York: Cambridge University Press, 1981.

———. "The Age of the Ayans, 1699–1812." In *An Economic and Social History of the Ottoman Empire,* vol. 2, edited by H. İnalcık and D. Quataert, 637–758. New York: Cambridge University Press, 1994.

McKeown, Thomas. "Food, Infection, and Population." In *Hunger and History: The Impact of Changing Consumption Patterns on Society,* edited by R. Rottberg and T. Rabb, 29–50. Cambridge: Cambridge University Press, 1983.

McNeill, J. R. *The Mountains of the Mediterranean World.* New York: Cambridge University Press, 1992.

———. "China's Environmental History in World Perspective." In *Sediments of Time: Environment and Society in Chinese History,* edited by M. Elvin and Liu Ts'ui-jung, 31–52. New York: Cambridge University Press, 1998.

———. "Woods and Warfare in World History." *Environmental History* **9** (2004): 388–410.

McNeill, William. *Europe's Steppe Frontier.* Chicago: University of Chicago Press, 1964.

———. *Plagues and Peoples.* New York: Doubleday, 1977.

Mikhail, Alan. "The Nature of Ottoman Egypt: Irrigation, Environment, and Bureaucracy in the Long Eighteenth Century." PhD diss., University of California Berkeley, 2008.

———. "The Nature of Plague in Late Eighteenth-Century Egypt." *Bulletin of the History of Medicine* **82** (2008): 249–75.

Miskimin, Harry. *The Economy of Later Renaissance Europe.* New York: Cambridge University Press, 1977.

Montgomery, David. *Dirt: The Erosion of Civilizations.* Berkeley: University of California Press, 2007.

Murphey, Rhoads. "Reflections on Ottoman Tribal Policy as Recorded in the Eighteenth-Century Law Court Records of Aleppo," in *IX. Türk Tarih Kongresi,* 945–53. Ankara: Türk Tarih Kurumu, 1981.

———. "The Ottoman Centuries in Iraq: Legacy or Aftermath? A Survey Study of Mesopotamian Hydrology and Ottoman Irrigation Projects." *Journal of Turkish Studies* **11** (1987): 17–29.

———. "Provisioning Istanbul: The State and Subsistence in the Early Modern Middle East." *Food and Foodways* **2** (1988): 217–63.

———. "Ottoman Medicine and Transculturalism from the Sixteenth through the Eighteenth Century." *Bulletin of the History of Medicine* **66** (1992): 376–403.

———. *Ottoman Warfare 1500–1700.* New Brunswick, NJ: Rutgers University Press, 1999.

———. "Population Movements and Labor Mobility in Balkan Contexts: A Glance at Post-1600 Ottoman Social Realities." In *Southeast Europe in History: The Past, the Present and the Problems of Balkanology*, 87–96. Ankara: Ankara Üniversitesi, 1999.

———. "Evolving versus Static Elements in Ottoman Geographical Writing between 1598 and 1729: Perceptions, Perspectives and Real-Life Experience of 'the Northern Lands' (*Taraf Al-Shimali*) over 130 Years." *International Journal of Turkish Studies* **10** (2004): 73–82.

Murrin, John. "Things Fearful to Name: Bestiality in Early America." In *The Human/Animal Boundary: Historical Perspectives*, edited by A. Creager and W. Jordan, 115–56. Rochester, NY: University of Rochester Press, 2002.

Musallam, Basim. *Sex and Society in Islam: Birth Control before the Nineteenth Century.* New York: Cambridge University Press, 1983.

Muşmal, Hüseyin. "XVII. Yüzyılın İlk Yarısında Konya'da Sosyal ve Ekonomik Hayat (1640–50)." PhD diss., Selçuk Üniversitesi, 2000.

Neumann, J. "Climatic Changes in Europe and the Near East in the Second Millennium BC." *Climatic Change* **23** (1993): 231–45.

Neumann, J. and S. Parpola. "Climatic Change and the Eleventh-Tenth-Century Eclipse of Assyria and Babylonia." *Journal of Near Eastern Studies* **46** (1987): 161–82.

Newfield, Tim. "A Cattle Panzootic in Early Fourteenth-Century Europe." *Agricultural History Review* **57** (2009): 155–90.

Noordegraf, Leo. "Dearth, Famine, and Social Policy in the Dutch Republic at the End of the Sixteenth Century." In *The European Crisis of the 1590s: Essays in Comparative History*, edited by P. Clark, 67–83. London: Allen and Unwin, 1985.

Ó Gráda, Cormac. *Famine: A Short History.* Princeton, NJ: Princeton University Press, 2009.

Oğuzoğlu, Yusuf. "17. Yüzyılda Konya Şehrindeki İdari ve Sosyal Yapılar." In *Konya*, edited by F. Halıcı, 97–108. Ankara: Konya Kültür ve Turizm Derneği Yayını, 1984.

Okawara, Tomoki. "Size and Structure of Damascus Households in the Late Ottoman Period as Compared with Istanbul Households." In *Family History in the Middle East*, edited by Beshara Doumani, 51–76. Binghamton: SUNY Press, 2003.

Orbay, Kayhan. "Financial Consequences of Natural Disasters in Seventeenth-Century Anatolia: A Case Study of the Waqf of Bayezid II." *International Journal of Turkish Studies* **15** (2009): 63–82.

Orhonlu, Cengiz. *Osmanlı İmparatorluğunda Aşiretleri İskân Teşebbüsü, 1691–1696.* Istanbul: İstanbul Üniversitesi, 1963.

______. *Osmanlı İmparatorluğunda Derbend Teşkilâtı.* Istanbul: İstanbul Üniversitesi, 1967.

Orland, I. et al. "Climate Deterioration in the Eastern Mediterranean as Revealed by Ion Microprobe Analysis of a Speleothem That Grew from 2.2 to 0.9 kya Soreq Cave, Israel." *Quaternary Research* **71** (2009): 27–35.

O'Rourke, K. and J. Williamson. "When Did Globalization Begin?" *European Review of Economic History* **6** (2002): 23–50.

Ostapchuk, Victor. "The Human Landscape of the Ottoman Black Sea in the Face of Cossack Naval Raids." *Oriente Moderno* **20** (2001): 23–95.

Owen, Roger. *The Middle East in the World Economy.* New York: I.B. Tauris, 1993.

Öz, Mehmet. "XVII. Yüzyıl Ortasına Doğru Canik Sancağı." In *Prof. Dr. Bayram Kodaman'a Armağan,* edited by Mehmet Ali Ünal, 193–206. Samsun: n.p., 1993.

______. "Tahrir Defterlerine Göre Vezirköprü Yöresinde İskân ve Nüfus (1485–1576)." *Belleten* **57** (1993): 509–31.

______. "XVI. Yüzyıl Anadolusu'nda Köylülerin Vergi Yükü ve Geçim Durumu Hakkında Bir Araştırma." *Osmanlı Araştırmaları* **17** (1997): 77–90.

______. "XVI. Yüzyılda Anadolu'da Tarımda Verimlilik Problemi." In *XIII. Türk Tarih Kongresi,* 1643–51. Ankara: Türk Tarih Kurumu, 1999.

______. "Tahrir Defterlerindeki Sayısal Veriler." In *Osmanlı Devleti'nde Bilgi ve İstatik,* edited by H. İnalcık and Ş. Pamuk, 18–27. Ankara: T. C. Başbakanlık Devlet İstatistik Enstitüsü, 2000.

______. "Agriculture in the Ottoman Classical Period." In *The Great Ottoman-Turkish Civilization,* vol. 2, edited by Kemal Çiçek, 32–40. Ankara: Yeni Türkiye, 2000.

______. "Population Fall in Seventeenth Century Anatolia: Some Findings for the Districts of Canik and Bozok." *Archivum Ottomanicum* **22** (2004): 159–71.

Özcan, Abdülkadir. "Osmanlı Ordusunda Sağlık Hizmetlerine Bir Bakış." In *Osmanlılarda Sağlık,* edited by C. Yılmaz and N. Yılmaz, 99–110. Istanbul: Biofarma, 2006.

Özdeğer, Hüseyin. *1463–1640 Yılları Bursa Şehir Tereke Defterleri.* Istanbul: Bayrak, 1988.

Özel, Oktay. "17. Yüzyıl Osmanlı Demografi ve İskan Tarihi Için Önemli Bir Kaynak: 'Mufassal' *Avârız Defterleri.*" In *XII. Türk Tarih Kongresi,* 735–43. Ankara: Türk Tarih Kurumu, 1994.

______. "Avarız ve Cizye Defterleri." In *Osmanlı Devleti'nde Bilgi ve İstatik,* edited by H. İnalcık and Ş. Pamuk, 35–50. Ankara: T. C. Başbakanlık Devlet İstatistik Enstitüsuü, 2000.

______. "Population Changes in Ottoman Anatolia During the 16th and 17th Centuries: The 'Demographic Crisis' Reconsidered." *International Journal of Middle East Studies* **36** (2004): 183–205.

______. "Nüfus Baskısından Krize: 16.–17. Yüzyıllarda Anadolu'nun Demografi Tarihine Bir Bakış." In *VIIIth International Conference on the Economic and Social History of Turkey,* edited by Nurhan Abacı, 219–28. Morrisville, NC: Lulu Press, 2006.

Özer, Ergenç. *XVI. Yüzyılın Sonlarında Bursa.* Ankara: Türk Tarih Kurumu, 2006.

Özkan, B. and H. Akçaöz. "Impacts of Climate Factors on Yields for Selected Crops in Southern Turkey." *Mitigation and Adaptation Strategies for Global Change* **7** (2002): 367–80.

Özkaya, Yücel. "Osmanlı İmparatorluğunda XVIII. Göç Sorunu." *Tarih Araştırmaları Dergisi* **14** (1982): 171–203.

Özmücür, S. and Ş. Pamuk. "Real Wages and Standards of Living in the Ottoman Empire, 1489–1914," *The Journal of Economic History* **62** (2002): 293–321.

Öztürk, Mustafa. "Osmanlı Dönemi Fiyat Politikası ve Fiyatların Tahlili." *Belleten* **55** (1991): 87–100.

Öztürk, Said. *Askeri Kassama Ait Onyedinci Asır İstanbul Tereke Defterleri.* Istanbul: Osmanlı Araştırmaları Vakfı, 1995.

Özvar, Erol. "Osmanlı Devletinin Bütçe Harcamaları (1509–1788)." In *Osmanlı Maliyesi Kurumlar ve Bütçeler,* edited by M. Genç and E. Özvar, 197–238. Istanbul: Osmanlı Bankası Arşiv ve Araştırma Merkezi, 2006.

Özveren, Eyüp. "The Black Sea and the Grain Provisioning of Istanbul in the *Longue Durée.*" In *Nourir les cités de Méditerranée – Antiquité-temps moderns,* edited by B. Marin and C. Virlouvet, 223–50. Paris: Maisonneuve, 2003.

Pamuk, Orhan. *Beyaz Kale.* Istanbul: Can Yayınları, 1985.

Pamuk, Şevket. "The Ottoman Empire in Comparative Perspective." *Review* **11** (1988): 127–49.

______. "Ottoman Interventionism in Economic and Monetary Affairs." *Revue d'histoire maghrebine* **25** (1998): 361–7.

______. "Osmanlı Ekonomisinde Devlet Müdahaleciliğine Yeniden Bakış." *Toplum ve Bilim* **83** (1999/2000): 133–45.

______. *A Monetary History of the Ottoman Empire.* New York: Cambridge University Press, 2000.

______. "Osmanlı Kentlerinde Tüketici Fiyatları ve Üçretlere İlişkin Veriler." In *Osmanlı Devleti'nde Bilgi ve İstatik,* edited by H. İnalcık and Ş. Pamuk, 51–9. Ankara: T. C. Başbakanlık Devlet İstatistik Enstitüsü, 2000.

______. "The Price Revolution in the Ottoman Empire Reconsidered." *International Journal of Middle East Studies* **33** (2001): 69–89.

______. "Prices in the Ottoman Empire." *International Journal of Middle East Studies* **36** (2004): 451–68.

Panzac, Daniel. "La population de l'Empire ottoman et ses marges du XVe au XIXe siècle: Bibliographie (1941–1980) et bilan provisoire." *Revue de l'Occident musulman et de la Méditeranée* **31** (1981): 119–35.

______. *La Peste dans l'Empire ottoman, 1700–1850.* Paris: Peeters, 1985.

______. "International and Domestic Maritime Trade in the Ottoman Empire during the 18th Century." *International Journal of Middle East Studies* **24** (1992): 189–206.

______. "Mourir à Alep au XVIIIe siècle," in *Population et santé dans l'Empire ottoman,* 1–17. Istanbul: Isis, 1996.

______. "Alexandrie: Peste et croissance urbaine (XVIIe–XIXe siècles)." In *Population et santé dans l'Empire ottoman,* 45–55. Istanbul: Isis, 1996.

______. "Politique sanitaire et fixation des frontieres: l'exemple ottoman (XVIIe–XIXe siècles)." *Turcica* **31** (1999): 87–108.

Pareva, Stefka. "Agrarian Land and Harvest in Southwest Peloponnese in the Early 18th Century." *Etudes Balkaniques* (2003): 83–123.

Parker, Geoffrey. *The Military Revolution: Military Innovation and the Rise of the West, 1500–1800.* New York: Cambridge University Press, 1996.

———. "Crisis and Catastrophe: The Global Crisis of the Seventeenth Century Reconsidered." *The American Historical Review* **113** (2008): 1053–79.

———. *The World Crisis: Thirty Years of War, Famine, Plague, Regicide, and Radicalism, 1635–1665.* (Forthcoming)

Parker, G. and L. Smith. *The General Crisis of the Seventeenth Century.* 2nd ed. London: Routledge, 1997.

Parmenter, R. et al. "Incidence of Plague Associated with Increased Winter–Spring Precipitation in New Mexico." *American Journal of Tropical Medicine and Hygiene* **61** (1999): 814–21.

Parry, V. J. "Materials of War in the Ottoman Empire." In *Studies in the Economic History of the Middle East,* edited by M. Cook, 219–29. London: Oxford University Press, 1970.

Pascual, Jean-Paul. *Damas à la fin du XVIe siècle.* Damascus: Institut français de Damas, 1983.

Peirce, Leslie. *The Imperial Harem: Women and Sovereignty in the Ottoman Empire.* New York: Oxford University Press, 1993.

Perdue, Peter. *Exhausting the Earth: State and Peasant in Hunan, 1500–1850 A.D.* Cambridge, MA: Harvard University Press, 1987.

———. *China Marches West: The Qing Conquest of Central Asia.* Cambridge, MA: Harvard University Press, 2005.

Perdue, P. and H. İslamoğlu, eds. *Shared Histories of Modernity: China, India, and the Ottoman Empire.* London: Routledge, 2009.

Peri, Oded. "Waqf and Ottoman Welfare Policy: The Poor Kitchen of Hasseki Sultan in Eighteenth-Century Jerusalem." *Journal of the Economic and Social History of the Orient* **35** (1992): 167–86.

Perry, John. "Forced Migration in Iran during the Seventeenth and Eighteenth Centuries." *Iranian Studies* **8** (1975): 199–215.

Pfister, Christian. "The Little Ice Age: Thermal and Wetness Indices for Central Europe." *Journal of Interdisciplinary History* **10** (1980): 665–96.

———. "Spatial Patterns of Climatic Change in Europe A.D. 1675 to 1715." In *Climatic Trends and Anomalies in Europe 1675–1715,* edited by B. Frenzel et al., 287–316. Stuttgart: Fischer, 1994.

———. "Documentary Evidence on Climate in Sixteenth Century Europe." *Climatic Change* **43** (1999): 55–110.

———. *Wetternachhersage: 500 Jahre Klimavariationen und Natur Katastrophen (1496–1995).* Bern: Paul Haupt, 1999.

Pfister, C. and R. Brázdil. "Climatic Variability in Sixteenth Century Europe and Its Social Dimensions: A Synthesis." *Climatic Change* **43** (1999): 5–53.

Piterberg, Gabriel. *An Ottoman Tragedy: History and Historiography at Play.* Berkeley: University of California Press, 2003.

Planhol, Xavier de. *De la plaine pamphylienne aux lacs pisidiens: Nomadisme et vie paysanne.* Paris: Maisonneuve, 1958.

———. "Les nomades, la steppe, et la forêt en Anatolie." *Geographische Zeitschrift* **52** (1965): 101–16.

———. *Les fondements geographiques de l'histoire de l'Islam.* Paris: Flammarion, 1968.

Pomeranz, Kenneth. *The Great Divergence: China, Europe, and the Making of the Modern World Economy.* Princeton, NJ: Princeton University Press, 2000.

Ponting, Clive. *A Green History of the World.* London: Penguin, 1991.

Popper, William. *The Cairo Nilometer.* Berkeley: University of California Press, 1951.

Post, John. *Food Shortage, Climatic Variability, and Epidemic Disease in Preindustrial Europe.* Ithaca, NY: Cornell University Press, 1985.

Preto, Paolo. *Venezia e i Turchi.* Florence: Sansoni, 1975.

Pryor, John. *Geography, Technology, and War: Studies in the Maritime History of the Mediterranean.* New York: Cambridge University Press, 1988.

Pyne, Stephen. *Vestal Fire: An Environmental History, Told through Fire, of Europe and Europe's Encounter with the World.* Seattle: University of Washington Press, 1997.

Quinn, William. "A Study of Southern Oscillation-Related Climatic Activity for AD 622–1900 Incorporating Nile River Flood Data." In *El Niño: Historical and Paleoclimate Aspects of the Southern Oscillation,* edited by H. Diaz and V. Markgraf, 119–50. Cambridge: Cambridge University Press, 1992.

Quinn, W. et al. "El Niño Occurrences over the Past Four and a Half Centuries." *Journal of Geophysical Research* **92** (1987): 14449–63.

Rabb, T. and R. Rotberg, eds. *Climate and History.* Princeton, NJ: Princeton University Press, 1981.

Rácz, Lajos. "The Climate of Hungary during the Maunder Minimum (1675–1715)." In *Climatic Trends and Anomalies in Europe,* edited by B. Frenzel et al., 95–107. Stuttgart: Fischer, 1994.

———. "Variations of Climate in Hungary (1540–1779)." In *European Climate Reconstructed from Documentary Data: Methods and Results,* edited by B. Frenzel, 125–36. Stuttgart: Fischer, 1992.

———. *Climate History of Hungary since 16th Century: Past, Present and Future.* Pécs: Centre for Regional Studies of the Hungarian Academy of Sciences, 1999.

———. "The Price of Survival: Transformations in Environmental Conditions and Subsistence Systems in Hungary in the Age of Ottoman Occupation." *Hungarian Studies* **24** (2010): 21–39.

Raymond, André. "Les grandes épidémies de peste au Caire aux XVIIe et XVIIIe siècles." *Bulletin d'études orientales* **25** (1973): 203–10.

———. "The Population of Aleppo in the Sixteenth and Seventeenth Centuries according to Ottoman Census Documents." *International Journal of Turkish Studies* **16** (1984): 447–60.

———. *Grandes villes arabes à l'époque ottomane.* Paris: Sindbad, 1985.

———. "Islamic City, Arab City: Orientalist Myths and Recent Views." *British Journal of Middle Eastern Studies* **21** (1994): 3–18.

———. *Cairo.* Cambridge, MA: Harvard University Press, 2000.

Reddaway, J. and G. Bigg. "Climatic Change over the Mediterranean and Links to the More General Atmospheric Circulation." *International Journal of Climatology* **16** (1996): 651–61.

Reid, Anthony. "The Seventeenth Century Crisis in Southeast Asia." *Modern Asian Studies* **24** (1990): 639–59.

———. "Southeast Asian Population History and the Colonial Impact." In *Asian Population History*, edited by T. Liu et al., 45–62. New York: Oxford University Press, 2001.

Repapis, C. et al. "A Note on the Frequency of Occurence of Severe Winters as Evidenced in Monastery and Historical Records from Greece during the Period 1200–1900 A.D." *Theoretical and Applied Climatology* **39** (1988): 213–17.

Richards, John. "The Seventeenth-Century Crisis in South Asia." *Modern Asian Studies* **24** (1990): 625–38.

———. *Mughal India*. Cambridge: Cambridge University Press, 1993.

———. *The Unending Frontier: An Environmental History of the Early Modern World*. Berkeley: University of California Press, 2003.

Rind, D. "The Sun's Role in Climate Variations." *Science* **296** (2002): 673–8.

Roberts, Neill. *The Holocene: An Environmental History*. Oxford: Blackwell, 1998.

Roberts, N. and H. Wright. "Vegetational, Lake-Level, and Climatic History of the Near East and Southwest Asia." In *Global Climates since the Last Glacial Maximum*, edited by H. Wright et al., 194–220. Minneapolis: University of Minnesota Press, 1993.

Robock, A. and Jianping Mao. "The Volcanic Signal in Surface Temperature Observations." *Journal of Climate* **8** (1995): 1086–103.

Romano, Ruggiero. *Conyunturas opuestas: Las crisis del siglo XVII en Europa e Hispanoamérica*. Mexico City: El Colegio de México, 1993.

Rosen, Arlene. *Civilizing Climate: Social Responses to Climate Change in the Ancient Near East*. Lanham, MD: Altamira, 2007.

Roux, Jean-Paul. *Les traditions des nomades de la Turquie méridionale*. Paris: Maisonneuve, 1970.

Ruben, Walter. *Kırşehir: Eine altertümliche Kleinstadt Inneranatoliens*. Würzburg: Ergon, 2003.

Sadji, Dana. "Decline and Its Discontents." In *Ottoman Tulips, Ottoman Coffee: Leisure and Lifestyle in the Eighteenth Century*, edited by Dana Sajdi, 1–40. London: I.B. Tauris, 2007.

Sahillioğlu, Halil. "Années *Sıvış* et crises monétaires dans l'Empire ottoman." *Annales* **24** (1969): 1070–91.

Sallares, Robert. *The Ecology of the Ancient Greek World*. Ithaca, NY: Cornell University Press, 1991.

Salzmann, Ariel. "Measures of Empire: Tax Farmers and the Ottoman *Ancien Régime 1695–1807*." PhD diss., Columbia University, 1995.

———. "Privatizing the Empire: Pashas and Gentry during the Ottoman Eighteenth Century." In *The Great Ottoman-Turkish Civilization*, vol. 2, edited by Kemal Çiçek, 132–9. Ankara: Yeni Türkiye, 2000.

Saraçgil, Ayşe. "Generi voluttuari e ragion di stato: Politiche repressive del consumo di vino, caffé e tobacco nell'Impero Ottomano nei secoli XVI e XVII." *Turcica* **28** (1996): 163–93.

Sasmazer, Lynne. "Provisioning Istanbul: Bread Production, Power, and Political Ideology in the Ottoman Empire." PhD diss., Indiana University, 2000.

Schamiloglu, Uli. "The Rise of the Ottoman Empire: The Black Death in Medieval Anatolia and Its Impact on Turkish Civilization." In *Views from the Edge: Essays in Honor of Richard Bulliet,* edited by N. Yavari et al., 255–79. New York: Columbia University Press, 2004.

Schimmelman, A. et al. "A Large California Flood and Correlative Climatic Factors 400 Years Ago." *Quaternary Research* **49** (1998): 51–61.

Scott, James. *Seeing Like a State: How Certain Schemes to Improve the Human Condition Have Failed.* New Haven, CT: Yale University Press, 1998.

Selçuk, Ali. *Tahtacılar.* Istanbul: Yeditepe, 2004.

Semple, E. C. *The Geography of the Ancient Mediterranean: Its Relation to Ancient History.* New York: H. Holt, 1931.

Sen, Amartya. *Poverty and Famines: An Essay on Entitlement and Deprivation.* Oxford: Clarendon Press, 1981.

Setton, Kenneth. *Venice, Austria, and the Turks in the Sixteenth Century.* Philadelphia: American Philosophical Society, 1991.

Shakow, Aaron. "Marks of Contagion: Bubonic Plague in the Early-Modern Mediterranean, 1720–1762." PhD diss., Harvard University, 2009.

Shanahan, T. et al. "Atlantic Forcing of Persistent Drought in West Africa." *Science* **324** (2009): 377–80.

Shank, J. B. "Crisis: A Useful Category of Post-Social Scientific Historical Analysis?" *The American Historical Review* **113** (2008): 1090–9.

Sharlin, Allan. "Natural Decrease in Early Modern Cities: A Reconsideration." *Past and Present* **79** (1978): 126–38.

Shaw, B. D. "Climate, Environment, and History: The Case of Roman North Africa." In *Climate and History: Studies in Past Climates and their Impact on Man,* edited by T. Wigley et al., 379–403. New York: Cambridge University Press, 1981.

Shaw, Stanford. *Between Old and New: The Ottoman Empire under Selim III, 1789–1807.* Cambridge, MA: Harvard University Press, 1971.

Shefer-Mossensohn, Miri. *Ottoman Medicine: Healing and Medical Institutions, 1500–1700.* Binghamton: SUNY Press, 2009.

Shindell, Drew. "Volcanic and Solar Forcing of Climate Change during the Preindustrial Era." *Journal of Climate* **16** (2003): 4094–107.

Shindell, D. et al. "Dynamic Winter Climate Response to Large Tropical Volcanic Eruptions since 1600." *Journal of Geophysical Research* **109** (2004): D05104.

Shmuelevitz, Aryeh. "MS Pococke No. 31 as a Source for the Events in Istanbul in the Years 1622–1624." *International Journal of Turkish Studies* **3** (1985–86): 107–21.

Simons, Bruno. "Le blé dans les rapports vénéto-ottomans au XVIe siècle." In *Contributions à l'histoire économique et sociale de l'Empire ottoman,* edited by J. Bacqué-Grammont and P. Dumont, 267–86. Louvain: Peeters, 1983.

Singer, Amy. "Peasant Migration: Law and Practice in Early Ottoman Palestine." *New Perspectives on Turkey* **8** (1992): 49–65.

———. *Palestinian Peasants and Ottoman Officials.* New York: Cambridge University Press, 1994.

———. "Ottoman Palestine (1516–1800): Health, Disease, and Historical Sources." In *Health and Disease in the Holy Land*, edited by M. Wasserman and S. Kottek, 189–206. Lewiston, NY: Edwin Mellen Press, 1996.

———. "Serving up Charity: The Ottoman Public Kitchen." *Journal of Interdisciplinary History* **35** (2005): 481–500.

Singh, Chetan. "Forests, Pastoralists, and Agrarian Society in Mughal India." In *Nature, Culture, and Imperialism: Essays on the Environmental History of Asia*, edited by D. Arnold and R. Guha, 21–48. Delhi: Oxford University Press, 1995.

Sivignon, Michel. *Les pasteurs du Pinde septentrional*. Lyon: Centre d'études et de recherches sur la géographie de l'Europe, 1968.

Slack, Paul. "The Disappearance of Plague: An Alternate View." *The Economic History Review* **34** (1981): 469–76.

———. "The Response to Plague in Early Modern England: Public Policies and Their Consequences." In *Famine, Disease and the Social Order in Early Modern Society*, edited by J. Walker and R. Schofield, 167–88. Cambridge: Cambridge University Press, 1989.

Slicher van Bath, B. H. *Agrarian History of Western Europe*. London: E. Arnold, 1963.

Smil, Vaclav. *Enriching the Earth: Fritz Haber, Carl Bosch, and the Transformation of World Food Production*. Boston: MIT Press, 2001.

Soysal, Mustafa. *Die Siedlungs- und Landschaftsentwicklung der Çukurova*. Erlangen: Fränkische Geographische Gesellschaft, 1976.

Spooner, Brian. "Desert and Sown: A New Look at an Old Relationship." In *Studies in Eighteenth Century Islamic History*, edited by T. Naff and R. Owen, 236–49. Carbondale: Southern Illinois University Press, 1977.

Stathakopoulos, Dionysios. "Reconstructing the Climate of the Byzantine World: State of the Problem and Case Studies." In *People and Nature in Historical Perspective*, edited by J. Laszlovsky and P. Szabó, 247–61. Budapest: Central European University, 2003.

Stevens, Carol. *Russia's Wars of Emergence*. New York: Pearson Longman, 2007.

Stirling, Paul. *Turkish Village*. New York: Wiley, 1965.

Stoianovich, Traian. "Land Tenure and Related Sectors of the Balkan Economy, 1600–1800." *The Journal of Economic History* (1953): 398–411.

———. "The Conquering Balkan Orthodox Merchant." *The Journal of Economic History* **20** (1960): 234–313.

———. "Le maïs dans les Balkans." *Annales* (1966): 1026–40.

Stothers, Richard. "Volcanic Dry Fogs, Climate Cooling, and Plague Pandemics in Europe and the Middle East." *Climatic Change* **42** (1999): 713–23.

Stoye, John. *The Siege of Vienna*. New York: Pegasus, 2000.

Subrahmanyam, Sanjay. "Du Tage au Gange au XVIe siècle: Une conjoncture millénariste à l'échelle eurasiatique." *Annales* (2001): 51–84.

Sugar, Peter. *Southeastern Europe under Ottoman Rule, 1354–1804*. Seattle: University of Washington Press, 1977.

———. "Major Changes in the Life of the Slav Peasantry under Ottoman Rule." *International Journal of Middle East Studies* **9** (1978): 297–305.

Sümer, Faruk. "Karaman-Oghullari (Karamanids)," in *Encyclopedia of Islam Online.* http://www.brillonline.nl/.

Svanidzé, Mihail. "L'Économie rurale dans le *vilâyet* d'Akhaltzıkhé (Çıldır) d'après le 'registre détaillé' de 1595." In *Contributions à l'histoire économique et sociale de l'Empire ottoman,* edited by J. Bacqué-Grammont and P. Dumont, 251–66. Leuven: Peeters, 1983.

Tabak, Faruk. "The Ottoman Countryside in the Age of the Autumn of the Mediterranean c. 1560–1870." PhD diss., SUNY Binghamton, 2000.

———. *The Waning of the Mediterranean, 1550–1870.* Baltimore: Johns Hopkins University Press, 2008.

Tabak, F. and Ç. Keyder, eds. *Landholding and Commercial Agriculture in the Middle East.* Binghamton: SUNY Press, 1991.

Taş, Hülya. *XVIII. Yüzyılda Ankara.* Ankara: Türk Tarih Kurumu, 2006.

Taylor, Carl. "Synergy among Mass Infections, Famines, and Poverty." In *Hunger and History: The Impact of Changing Consumption Patterns on Society,* edited by R. Rottberg and T. Rabb, 285–304. Cambridge: Cambridge University Press, 1983.

Tekeli, İlhan. "Osmanlı İmparatorluğu'ndan Günümüze Nüfusun Zorunlu Yer Değiştirmesi ve İskân Sorunu." *Toplum ve Bilim* **50** (1990): 49–71.

Telelis, Ioannis. "Medieval Warm Period and the Beginning of the Little Ice Age in the Eastern Mediterranean: An Approach of Physicial and Anthropogenic Evidence." In *Byzanz als Raum: zu Methoden und Inhalten der historische Geographie des östlichen Mittelmeerraumes,* edited by Klaus Belk, 223–43. Vienna: Österreichischen Akademie der Wissenschaften, 2000.

———. "Climatic Fluctuations in the Eastern Mediterranean and the Middle East AD 300–1500 from Byzantine Documentary and Proxy Physical Paleoclimatic Evidence – A Comparison." *Jahrbuch der Österreichischen Byzantinistik* **58** (2008): 167–207.

Telelis, I. and E. Chrysos. "The Byzantine Sources as Documentary Evidence for the Reconstruction of Historical Climate." In *European Climate Reconstructed from Documentary Data: Methods and Results,* edited by B. Frenzel, 17–31. Stuttgart: Fischer, 1992.

Tezcan, Baki. "Searching for Osman: A Reassessment of the Deposition of the Ottoman Sultan Osman II (1618–1622)." PhD diss., Princeton University, 2001.

———. "The 1622 Military Rebellion in Istanbul: A Historiographical Journey." In *Mutiny and Rebellion in the Ottoman Empire,* edited by Jane Hathaway, 25–45. Madison: University of Wisconsin Press, 2003.

———. "Khotin 1621, of How the Poles Changed the Course of Ottoman History." *Acta Orientalia* **62** (2009): 185–98.

———. "The Ottoman Monetary Crisis of 1585 Revisited." *Journal of the Economic and Social History of the Orient* **52** (2009): 460–504.

———. "The Second Empire: The Transformation of the Ottoman Polity in the Early Modern Era." *Comparative Studies of South Asia Africa and the Middle East* **29** (2009): 556–83.

———. "The History of a "Primary Source": The Making of Tughi's Chronicle on the Regicide of Osman II." *Journal of the School of Oriental and African Studies* **72** (2009): 41–62.

———. *The Second Ottoman Empire: Political and Social Transformation in the Early Modern World.* New York: Cambridge University Press, 2010.

Theilman, J. and F. Cate. "A Plague of Plagues: The Problem of Plague Diagnosis in Medieval England." *Journal of Interdisciplinary History* **37** (2007): 371–93.

Thirgood, J. V. *Man and the Mediterranean Forest: A History of Resource Depletion.* New York: Academic Press, 1981.

———. "The Barbary Forests and Forest Lands, Environmental Destruction and the Vicissitudes of History." *Journal of World Forest Management* **2** (1986): 137–84.

Thomas, Keith. *Man and the Natural World.* New York: Oxford University Press, 1983.

Thomson, Ann. "Perceptions des populations du Moyen-Orient." In *Orient et lumieres,* edited by A. Moalla, 41–7. Grenoble: Université de Grenoble, 1987.

Tilly, Charles. *Coercion, Capital, and European States AD 990–1992.* Cambridge, MA: Blackwell, 1992.

Todorova, Maria. "Was There a Demographic Crisis in the Ottoman Empire in the Seventeenth Century?" *Etudes Balkaniques* **2** (1988): 55–63.

———. *Balkan Family Structure and the European Pattern: Demographic Developments in Ottoman Bulgaria.* Washington, DC: American University Press, 1993.

Totman, Conrad. *The Green Archipelago: Forestry in Preindustrial Japan.* Berkeley: University of California Press, 1989.

———. *Early Modern Japan.* Berkeley: University of California Press, 1993.

———. *A History of Japan.* Oxford: Blackwell, 2000.

Touchan, R. and M. Hughes. "Dendrochronology in Jordan." *Journal of Arid Environments* **42** (1999): 291–303.

Touchan, R. et al. "A 396-Year Reconstruction of Precipitation in Southern Jordan." *Journal of the American Water Resources Association* **35** (1999): 49–59.

———. "Preliminary Reconstructions of Spring Precipitation in Southwestern Turkey from Tree-Ring Width." *International Journal of Climatology* **23** (2003): 157–71.

———. "Reconstructions of Spring/Summer Precipitation for the Eastern Mediterranean from Tree Ring Widths and Its Connection to Large-Scale Atmospheric Circulation." *Climate Dynamics* **25** (2005): 75–98.

———. "Standardized Precipitation Index Reconstructed from Turkish Tree-Ring Widths." *Climatic Change* **72** (2005): 339–53.

Trouet, V. et al. "Persistent Positive North Atlantic Oscillation Mode Dominated the Medieval Climatic Anomaly." *Science* **324** (2009): 78–80.

Tuan, Yi-Fu. "Discrepancies between Environmental Attitude and Behaviour: Examples from Europe and China." *Canadian Geographer* **12** (1968): 176–91.

Tuchscherer, Michel. "Approvisionnement des villes saintes d'Arabie en blé d'Egypte d'après des documents ottomans des années 1670." *Anatolia Moderna* **5** (1994): 79–99.

Tunçdilek, Necdet. *Türkiye İskân Coğrafyası.* Istanbul: İstanbul Üniversitesi, 1967.

Türkeş, M. and E. Erlat. "Climatological Responses of Winter Precipitation for the Eastern Mediterranean in Turkey to Variability of the North Atlantic Oscillation during the Period 1930–2001." *Theoretical and Applied Climatology* **81** (2005): 45–69.

Üçel-Aybet, Gülgün. *Avrupalı Seyyahların Gözünden Osmanlı Dünyası ve İnsanları (1530–1699).* Istanbul: İletişim, 2003.

Ülgener, Sabri. *Darlık Buhranları ve İslam İktisat Siyaseti.* Ankara: Mayaş, 1984.

Uluçay, M. Ç. *XVII. Asırda Saruhan'da Eşkiyalık ve Halk Haraketleri.* Istanbul: Resimli Ay Matbaası, 1944.

Ursinus, Michael. "Natural Disasters and Tevzi: Local Tax Systems of the Post-Classical Era in Response to Flooding, Hail, and Thunder." In *Natural Disasters in the Ottoman Empire,* edited by E. Zachariadou, 265–72. Heraklion: Crete University Press, 1999.

Utterström, Gustaf. "Climatic Fluctuations and Population Problems in Early Modern History." *The Scandinavian Economic History Review* **3** (1955): 3–47.

Uzun, Ahmet. "Osmanlı Devleti'nde Şehir Ekonomisi ve İaşe." *Türkiye Araştırmaları Literatür Dergisi* **3** (2005): 211–35.

Uzunçarşılı, İsmail. *Osmanlı Devleti'nin Merkez ve Bahriye Teşkılatı.* Ankara: Türk Tarih Kurumu, 1988.

Van Andel, T. et al. "Land Use and Soil Erosion in Prehistoric and Historical Greece." *Journal of Field Archaeology* **17** (1990): 379–96.

van Creveld, Martin. *Supplying War: Logistics from Wallenstein to Patton.* New York: Cambridge University Press, 2004.

van Zeist, W. and H. Woldring. "A Postglacial Pollen Diagram from Lake Van in Eastern Anatolia." *Review of Paleobotany and Palynology* **26** (1978): 249–76.

Varlık, Nukhet. "Disease and Empire: A History of Plague Epidemics in the Early Modern Ottoman Empire (1453–1600)." PhD diss., University of Chicago, 2008.

Vatin, N. and G. Veinstein. *Le sérail ébranlé: Essai sur les morts, dépositions et avènements des sultans ottomans (XIVe–XIXe siècle).* Paris: Fayard, 2003.

Veinstein, Gilles. "Some Views on Provisioning in the Hungarian Campaigns of Suleyman the Magnificent." In *Osmanistische Studien zur Wirtschafts- und Sozialgeschichte in Memoriam Vančo Boškov,* edited by H. Majer, 177–85. Wiesbaden: O. Harrassowitz, 1986.

———. "Un achat français de blé dans l'Empire ottoman au mileu du XVIe siècle." In *L'Empire ottoman, la République de Turquie et la France,* edited by H. Batu and J. Bacqué-Grammont, 15–36. Istanbul: Isis, 1986.

———. "Sur les sauterelles à Chypre, en Thrace et en Macédonie à l'époque ottomane." In *Armağan: Festschrift für Andreas Tietze,* edited by I. Baldauf, 211–26. Prague: Enigma, 1994.

———. "La grande sécheresse de 1560 au nord de la Mer Noire: Perceptions et réactions des autorités ottomanes." In *Natural Disasters in the Ottoman Empire,* edited by E. Zachariadou, 273–81. Heraklion: Crete University Press, 1999.

Venzke, Margaret. "The Question of Declining Cereals Production in the 16th Century: A Sounding on the Problem-Solving Capacity of the Ottoman Cadastres." *Journal of Turkish Studies* **8** (1984): 251–64.

______. "Rice Cultivation in the Plain of Antioch in the 16th Century." *Archivum Ottomanicum* **12** (1992): 175–276.

______. "The Ottoman Tahrir Defterleri and Agricultural Productivity." *Osmanlı Araştırmaları* **17** (1997): 1–61.

Virlouvet, C. and O. Yıldırım. "Les annones de Rome et de Constantinople-Istanbul." In *Nourir les cités de Méditerranée – Antiquité-temps modernes*, edited by B. Marin and C. Virlouvet, 37–44. Paris: Maisonneuve, 2003.

Vita-Finzi, Claudio. *The Mediterranean Valleys: Geological Changes in Historical Times.* London: Cambridge University Press, 1969.

von Glahn, Richard. "Myth and Reality of China's Seventeenth-Century Monetary Crisis" *The Journal of Economic History* **56** (1996): 429–54.

Vural, Y. et al. "The Frozen Bosphorus and Its Paleoclimatic Implications Based on a Summary of the Historical Data." In *The Black Sea Flood Question: Changes in Coastline, Climate, and Human Settlement*, edited by V. Yanko-Hombach et al., 633–50. Dordrecht: Springer, 2007.

Wagstaff, J. M. *The Evolution of Middle Eastern Landscapes: An Outline to A.D. 1840.* London: Croom Helm, 1985.

Wagstaff, M. and E. Frangakis. "The Port of Patras in the Second Ottoman Period: Economy, Demography, and Settlements c. 1700–1830." *Revue du monde musulman et de la Méditeranée* **66** (1992): 79–94.

Wahbia, A. and T. Sinclair. "Simulation Analysis of Relative Yield Advantage of Barley and Wheat in an Eastern Mediterranean Climate." *Field Crops Research* **91** (2005): 287–96.

Wainwright, J. and J. Thornes. *Environmental Issues in the Mediterranean.* London: Routledge, 2004.

Wakeman, Frederic. "China and the Seventeenth-Century Crisis." *Late Imperial China* **7** (1986): 1–26.

Walker, Brett. *The Conquest of Ainu Lands.* Berkeley: University of California Press, 2001.

Wallerstein, Immanuel. *The Modern World-System.* 3 vols. New York: Academic Press, 1974–89.

Walter, J. and R. Schofield, eds. *Famine, Disease and the Social Order in Early Modern Society.* Cambridge: Cambridge University Press, 1989.

______. "Famine, Disease and Crisis in Early Modern Society." In *Famine, Disease and the Social Order in Early Modern Society*, edited by J. Walter and R. Schofield, 1–74. Cambridge: Cambridge University Press, 1989.

Wanner, Heinz. "Die Kleine Eiszeit – mögliche Gründe für ihre Enstehung." In *Nachhaltige Geschichte: Festschrift für Christian Pfister*, edited by Andre Kirchhofer, 91–108. Zurich: Chronos, 2009.

Watson, Andrew. *Agricultural Innovation in the Early Islamic World: The Diffusion of Crops and Farming Techniques, 700–1100.* New York: Cambridge University Press, 1983.

Watts, Sheldon. *Epidemics and History: Disease, Power, and Imperialism.* New Haven, CT: Yale University Press, 1997.

Webb, James. *Desert Frontier: Ecological and Economic Change along the Western Sahel 1600–1850.* Madison: University of Wisconsin Press, 1995.

Weir, David. "Markets and Mortality in France 1600–1789." In *Famine, Disease and the Social Order in Early Modern Society,* edited by J. Walker and R. Schofield, 201–34. Cambridge: Cambridge University Press, 1989.

Weiss, Barry. "The Decline of Late Bronze Age Civilization as a Possible Response to Climatic Change." *Climatic Change* **4** (1982): 173–98.

Weiss, Harvey. "Beyond the Younger Dryas: Collapse as Adaptation to Abrupt Climate Change in Ancient West Asia and the Ancient Eastern Mediterranean." In *Environmental Disasters and the Archaeology of Human Response,* edited by G. Bawdon and R. Reycraft, 75–98. Albuquerque, NM: Maxwell Museum of Anthropology, 2000.

Whetton, P. and I. Rutherford. "Historical ENSO Teleconnections in the Eastern Hemisphere." *Climatic Change* **28** (1994): 221–53.

White, Lynn. *Medieval Technology and Social Change.* Oxford: Clarendon, 1962.

White, Sam. "Rethinking Disease in Ottoman History." *International Journal of Middle East Studies* **42** (2010): 549–67.

Wick, L. et al. "Evidence of Late Glacial and Holocene Climatic Change and Human Impact in Eastern Anatolia: High-Resolution Pollen, Charcoal, Isotopic and Geochemical Records from the Laminated Sediments of Lake Van, Turkey." *The Holocene* **13** (2003): 665–75.

Wilcox, G. "A History of Deforestation as Indicated by Charcoal Analysis of Four Sites in Eastern Anatolia." *Anatolian Studies* **24** (1974): 117–33.

Wilkinson, Tony. "Demographic Trends from Archaeological Survey: Case Studies from the Levant and Near East." In *Reconstructing Past Population Trends in Mediterranean Europe (3000 B.C.–1800 A.D.),* edited by J. Bintliff and K. Sbonias, 45–64. Oxford: Oxbow, 1999.

Williams, Michael. *Deforesting the Earth: From Prehistory to Global Crisis.* Chicago: University of Chicago Press, 2003.

Wilson, Peter. *The Thirty Years War: Europe's Tragedy.* Cambridge, MA: Harvard University Press, 2009.

Winter, Stephan. "Osmanische Sozialdisziplinierung am Bespeil der Nomadenstämme Nordsyriens im 17.–18. Jahrhundert." *Periplus* **13** (2003): 51–70.

______. "The Province of Raqqa under Ottoman Rule, 1535–1800." Paper presented at the Great Lakes Ottoman Workshop, Toronto, 2006.

______. *The Shiites of Lebanon under Ottoman Rule, 1516–1788.* New York: Cambridge University Press, 2010.

Wittek, Paul. "Le rôle des tribus turques dans l'Empire ottoman." In *Mélanges Georges Smets,* 665–76. Brussels: E′ditions de la Revue encyclopédique, 1952.

Wrigley, E. A. "A Simple Model of London's Importance in Changing English Society and Economy 1650–1750." *Past and Present* **37** (1967): 44–70.

______. "Some Reflections on Corn Yield and Prices in Pre-Industrial Economies." In *Famine, Disease and the Social Order in Early Modern Society,* edited by J. Walter and R. Schofield, 235–78. Cambridge: Cambridge University Press, 1989.

Xoplaki, E. et al. "Variability of Climate in Meridional Balkans during the Periods 1675–1715 and 1780–1830 and Its Impact on Human Life." *Climatic Change* **48** (2001): 581–615.

———. "Wet Season Mediterranean Precipitation Variability: Influence of Large-Scale Dynamics and Trends." *Climate Dynamics* **23** (2004): 63–78.

Yılmaz, C. and N. Yılmaz. "Osmanlı Hastahane Yönetmelikleri: Vakfiyelerde Osmanlı Dârüşşifâları." In *Osmanlılarda Sağlık*, edited by C. Yılmaz and N. Yılmaz, 42–64. Istanbul: Biofarma, 2006.

———. "Evliya Çelebi'nin Seyahatnâmesi'ne Göre Osmanlılarda Sağlık Hayatı." In *Osmanlılarda Sağlık*, edited by N. Yılmaz and C. Yılmaz. Istanbul: Biofarma, 2006.

Yılmaz, C. and N. Yılmaz, eds. *Osmanlılarda Sağlık.* 2 vols. Istanbul: Biofarma, 2006.

Yusoff, K. "Ottoman Egypt in the 17th Century according to the Unique Manuscript *Zubdah Ikhtisar Tarikh al-Mahrusah.*" In *International Congress on Learning and Education in the Ottoman World, Istanbul, 12–15 April 1999*, edited by Ali Çaksu, 347–56. Istanbul: IRCICA, 2001.

Zachariadou, Elizabeth, ed. *Natural Disasters in the Ottoman Empire.* Heraklion: Crete University Press, 1999.

Zarinebaf, Fariba. *Crime and Punishment in Istanbul, 1700–1800.* Berkeley: University of California Press, 2010.

Zarinebaf, F., J. Bennet, and J. Davis. *A Historical and Economic Geography of Ottoman Greece: The Southwestern Morea in the 18th Century.* Athens: American School of Classical Studies, 2005.

Ze'evi, Dror. *An Ottoman Century: The District of Jerusalem in the 1600s.* Binghamton: SUNY Press, 1996.

Zilfi, Madeline. "The Kadızadelis: Discordant Revivalism in Seventeenth-Century Istanbul." *Journal of Near Eastern Studies* **45** (1986): 251–69.

Zinsser, Hans. *Rats, Lice and History.* New York: Black Dog and Leventhal, 1935.

Ziv, B. et al. "The Factors Governing the Summer Regime of the Eastern Mediterranean." *International Journal of Climatology* **24** (2004): 1859–71.

Zürcher, Erik. *Turkey: A Modern History.* London: I.B. Tauris, 1993.

INDEX

Other Books in the Series (continued from page iii)